"This is truly a unique and outstanding book that covers subtopics and microscopic details about primary and secondary psychoses across the life cycle that are not found in previous books about the subject. It is generously referenced and contains an unprecedented compilation and description of 120 rating scales relevant to assessing every aspect of psychosis before and after treatment. I highly recommend it to all psychiatrists and mental health professionals as a must-have reference text." —**Henry A. Nasrallah**, *MD, The Sydney W. Souers Professor and Chairman, Department of Neurology and Psychiatry, Saint Louis University School of Medicine*

"If we are to make any advances in finding the biological basis of psychosis and developing possible cures, we need a much better understanding of psychotic experiences so that they can be properly characterized and identified. This book provides the most wide-ranging and up-to-date account of psychosis currently available and is essential reading for anyone who wants to understand these devastating disorders." —**Chris Frith**, *FRS, FBA, Emeritus Professor of Neuropsychology, Wellcome Department of Imaging Neuroscience at University College London*

"In *The Assessment of Psychosis*, Drs. Flavie Waters and Massoud Stephane have collected an excellent compendium of papers about the nature of psychotic experience, how it manifests in various populations and how these symptoms are assessed. This is an interesting and useful book for people interested in psychosis research or working with populations where psychotic symptoms are common." —**John H. Krystal**, *MD, Robert L. McNeil, Jr. Professor of Translational Research and Chair of Psychiatry, Yale University School of Medicine*

"I regard this publication as much more than just the assessment of psychosis. It is a fundamental reappraisal of the concept, its history and its biology. There are many innovations to this multidisciplinary, multi-faceted text. These include the ambitious attempt to embrace the whole syndrome of psychosis from its earliest development and precursors to its manifestation in the context of underlying brain disease. The book will educate, intrigue and inspire clinicians, students, would-be experts, sufferers and champions of this perhaps most compelling psychiatric condition of all." —**Anthony David,** *MD, Professor, Section of Cognitive Neuropsychiatry, Institute of Psychiatry, King's College London*

THE ASSESSMENT OF PSYCHOSIS

This book reviews the descriptive features of psychotic symptoms in various medical conditions (psychiatric, early psychosis, general medical, neurological and dementia), non-medical settings (individuals without the need for care or at high risk for psychosis) and age groups (children and adolescents, adults, older adults). Similarly, the perspectives of many disciplines are provided (history, psychiatry, psychology, psychopathology, neurology, phenomenological philosophy) so that readers may become familiar with different approaches that are used to define, evaluate and categorize psychosis, at times independently of clinical diagnosis. This book is a resource book for those requiring an understanding of clinical and conceptual issues associated with psychosis, with chapters written by academics and clinicians who are leaders in their respective fields. The book also provides a guide regarding the methods of assessment for psychosis and its symptoms, with 120 rating scales, which are described and evaluated. *The Assessment of Psychosis* will be particularly useful to the clinical and research community, but also to readers interested in individual differences and human psychopathology.

Flavie Waters, PhD, is a leading cognitive neuroscientist who has made important contributions to the understanding of psychotic symptoms. She is the founder and scientific chair of the International Consortium on Hallucination Research and is the author of numerous scientific articles that have been highly cited. A common theme in her research is to combine different branches of knowledge that can come together in a boldly ambitious effort to better understand psychosis and pursue new interventions approaches.

Massoud Stephane, MD, is an influential psychiatrist and neuroscientist whose expertise spans neurology, psychiatry and in vivo brain imaging. A lot of his research is based on the patient experience as a starting point, and he made significant contributions to the understanding of hallucinatory experiences and cognitive and linguistic disturbances in schizophrenia. He is well published and highly cited in these domains.

THE ASSESSMENT OF PSYCHOSIS

A Reference Book and Rating Scales for Research and Practice

Edited by
Flavie Waters and
Massoud Stephane

Routledge
Taylor & Francis Group
NEW YORK AND LONDON

First published 2015
by Routledge
605 Third Avenue, New York, NY 10017

and by Routledge
2 Park Square, Milton Park, Abingdon, Oxon OX14 4RN

Routledge is an imprint of the Taylor & Francis Group, an informa business

Library of Congress Cataloging-in-Publication Data
The assessment of psychosis : a reference book and rating scales for research and practice / [edited by] Flavie Waters, Massoud Stephane.
p. ; cm.
Includes bibliographical references and index.
I. Waters, Flavie, editor. II. Stephane, Massoud, editor.
[DNLM: 1. Psychotic Disorders. 2. Psychiatric Status Rating Scales. WM 200]
RC467
616.89—dc23
2014023394

ISBN: 978-0-415-70932-3 (hbk)
ISBN: 978-0-415-70933-0 (pbk)
ISBN: 978-1-315-88560-5 (ebk)

Typeset in Bembo
by Apex CoVantage, LLC

To Adrien, Luke and Oliver

CONTENTS

CONTRIBUTORS

Osvaldo P. Almeida, MD, WA Centre for Health & Ageing, The University of Western Australia, Perth, Australia

Vaughan Bell, PhD, Institute of Psychiatry, Psychology and Neuroscience, King's College London, UK

Peter Bosanac, MD, St. Vincent's Mental Health Service, Fitzroy, Victoria; University of Melbourne, Australia

Arnaud Cachia, PhD, Center of Psychiatry & Neurosciences Paris; University Paris Descartes, Sorbonne-Paris-Cité, France

David J. Castle, MD, St. Vincent's Mental Health Service, Fitzroy, Victoria, Australia

Michael H. Connors, PhD, ARC Centre of Excellence in Cognition and Its Disorders, and Department of Cognitive Science, Macquarie University, Sydney, New South Wales, Australia

Andrew Ford, MD, WA Centre for Health & Ageing, The University of Western Australia, Perth, Australia

Mads Gram Henriksen, PhD, Center for Subjectivity Research and Psychiatric Center Hvidovre, University of Copenhagen, Denmark

Keira James, PhD, North Metropolitan Health Service Mental Health; McCusker Alzheimer's Research Foundation, Perth, Australia

Lennart Jansson, MD, Hvidovre Mental Health Center, University of Copenhagen, Denmark

Renaud Jardri, MD, University Medical Centre of Lille, France & Group for Neural Theory, Ecole Normale Supérieure, Paris, France

Ian Kelleher, MD, Royal College of Surgeons in Ireland, Beaumont Hospital, Dublin, Ireland

Robyn Langdon, PhD, ARC Centre of Excellence in Cognition and its Disorders, and Department of Cognitive Science, Macquarie University, Sydney, New South Wales, Australia

Frank Larøi, PhD, Department of Psychology: Cognition and Behaviour, University of Liège, Belgium

Simon McCarthy Jones, PhD, Department of Cognitive Science, Macquarie University, Sydney, Australia

Jaime Pahissa, MD, Centro Universitario CEMIC, Buenos Aires, Argentina

Josef Parnas, MD, DrMedSci, Center for Subjectivity Research and Psychiatric Center Hvidovre, University of Copenhagen, Denmark

Emmanuelle Peters, PhD, Department of Psychology, Institute of Psychiatry, Psychology and Neuroscience, King's College London, UK

Marion Plaze, MD, PhD, Center of Psychiatry & Neurosciences Paris, Sainte-Anne Hospital, SHU, Paris, France

Adrian Preda, MD, Department of Psychiatry and Human Behavior, School of Medicine, University of California, Irvine, USA

Andrea Raballo, MD, Department of Mental Health and Pathological Addiction, Reggio Emilia, Italy

Mujeeb Uddin Shad, MD, MSCS, Oregon Health & Science University, Portland, Oregon, USA

Iris E. Sommer, MD, PhD, Rudolf Magnus Institute of Neuroscience, Department of Psychiatry, University Medical Center Utrecht, Utrecht, the Netherlands

Sergio Starkstein, MD, School of Psychiatry and Clinical Neurosciences, The University of Western Australia; Fremantle Hospital, Australia

Massoud Stephane, MD, Department of Psychiatry, Oregon Health & Science University, Portland, Oregon, USA

Rabindra Tambyraja, MD, Department of Child and Adolescent Psychiatry, University of Minnesota, USA

Theo G. M. van Erp, PhD, University of California, Irvine, USA

Nicoletta M. van Veelen, MD, PhD, Rudolf Magnus Institute of Neuroscience, Department of Psychiatry, University Medical Center Utrecht, Utrecht, the Netherlands

Flavie Waters, MSc, MPsych, PhD, School of Psychiatry and Clinical Neurosciences, The University of Western Australia; Clinical Research Centre, North Metropolitan Health Service Mental Health, Perth, Australia

FOREWORD

Psychosis: The Human Experience

The experience of psychotic phenomena is distinctively human. Hallucinations, delusions and disordered thought processes are relevant to many mental disorders and occur in persons without mental illness, but observations in non-human species are challenging to define and validate. Advancing knowledge on psychosis relies on human observation and experimentation. Conceptual clarity and assessment method are essential in addressing these personal experiences within a social, psychological and biological framework. Toward this end this book is a treasure.

Beliefs and sensory experiences that appear unrelated to reality and are not consensually validated need not be viewed as manifestations of a mental disorder or an impediment to function. Joan of Arc is history's most outstanding example. Psychotic-like experiences in the non-ill populations are examined in this text, as are these experiences when they may mark a pathway toward a full psychotic disorder. Psychotic-like experiences may be associated with impaired functioning even in non-ill persons, especially when negative symptoms and cognition impairments are also present in a non-clinical framework.

The prototype for psychosis as illness has been schizophrenia. Hallucinations, delusions and disordered thinking are core criteria in diagnostic systems, including DSM and ICD. However, with emphasis on Schneiderian symptoms of first-rank DSM-III shifted the concept of schizophrenia away from the avolitional/dissociative pathology important in Kraepelin's dementia praecox and fundamental in Bleuler's view, towards a reality distortion self or ego boundary disturbance. We have a 100 year history recognizing hallucinations and delusions as neither primary nor unique to schizophrenia, and first-rank symptoms have been deemphasized in DSM-5. Schizophrenia remains a diagnosis of exclusion where other causes of psychosis take precedent. What may be unique in schizophrenia is not detected in commonly used assessment methods but may be identified with phenomenology methods in relation to concepts of the self. This is richly explored in this book and suggests a foundation for defining some unique attributes of psychotic experience relevant to the schizophrenia spectrum. The phenomenology of thought disorder is also addressed in this book and holds promise for differentiation between current diagnostic categories.

While it has long been recognized that much psychopathology cuts across current diagnostic boundaries, investigative paradigms that take this into account have only recently become prominent. These paradigms range from domains of psychopathology creating dimensions at the symptom level to endophenotypes that attempt to capture neurobiology of psychopathology represented by heritable traits captured in physiology, imaging and cognition. The mapping of phenotypes relevant to psychotic illnesses has greatly facilitated acquisition of knowledge on brain mechanisms and causal pathways in animal models of several disorders associated with psychosis. But the mapped phenotypes have uncertain relevance for psychosis per se. At the present time, the National Institute of Mental Health has given priority to research based on five behavioral constructs with known neural circuits: positive valence, negative valence, fear, cognition and social processes. The Research Domains Criteria provide an important paradigm for many aspects of psychopathology, but none for psychosis. In this context, the importance and timeliness of this book on psychosis receives emphasis. Advancing knowledge on these human phenomena is critically important, and psychosis remains a beacon for etiological and therapeutic discovery and sets the target for primary, secondary and tertiary prevention. This book is a most welcome contribution to the field addressing issues of fundamental importance to current understanding and the creation of new knowledge.

The contributors provide an informed and critical appraisal of current knowledge and understanding of psychotic experiences in humans. This book is for a broad audience, ranging from the interested layperson to professionals in philosophy and phenomenology, basic neuroscientists, epidemiologists and the clinical professionals concerned with brain dysfunction and the consequences of psychosis. It covers a wide range of psychotic experience in humans including different ages, different mental states and different population sources. The section on the assessment of psychotic symptoms is invaluable as a guide to 120 assessment methods. This book will be particularly helpful to the research and clinical community as a guide to concepts and assessment methods, but also as a reminder of the need for critical attention to human psychopathology.

William T. Carpenter, Jr.
Professor of Psychiatry and Pharmacology,
University of Maryland School of Medicine;
Former Director, Maryland Psychiatric Research Center;
Editor-in-Chief, *Schizophrenia Bulletin*

PREFACE

Despite remarkable advances in many aspects of the neuroscience of psychosis, this mental condition remains conceptually elusive, and its assessment and treatment, when treatment is needed, are highly challenging. This lack of tractable progress is due, at least in part, to the unique position of psychosis, the study of which cuts across many disciplines including medicine, psychology, sociology and philosophy. Depending on whether psychotic symptoms are related to schizophrenia, post-traumatic disorder, Parkinson's disease, systemic lupus erythematosus or eye disease, one might be treated by a psychiatrist, psychologist, psychogeriatrician, neurologist, rheumatologist or ophthalmologist. Similarly, depending on whether symptoms occur in healthy adults or in children, or in psychiatric settings, different advice will be proffered regarding how, and whether, to treat the condition. Together, knowledge gained about psychosis from research in any of the above disciplines can guide research on psychosis in other disciplines. There is therefore a need for clinicians and researchers concerned with psychosis to be familiar with the different perspectives and the different methods that may be used to define, evaluate or categorize symptoms in different settings, and at times independently of clinical diagnosis.

With psychosis of interest to so many disciplines, our specialization in psychiatry, neurology, psychopathology and psychology is a notable advantage as it brings a unique assortment of knowledge to this project. In undertaking this book, our aim was to provide a resource for those requiring an understanding of conceptual and clinical issues associated with psychosis phenomena and available assessment methods. Toward this end, we have asked the most prominent researchers in their field to write a chapter on their speciality area and provide an overview of assessment issues and methods. Contributors also provided short descriptions for the most frequently used rating scales in their area of research, which are presented in the last part of the book.

This is the first time that ratings scales for psychosis have been put together into one published volume. We sought to be as comprehensive as possible, but it is likely that we omitted some important scales. This field is rapidly expanding, and new scales are appearing all the time. The main rationale for the selection of scales was that they could assess the symptoms of psychosis in full or in part, and are commonly used in current clinical or research settings. It is hoped that our selection is appropriate, and that the book provides an accurate reflection of rating scales that are currently available.

We have divided the book into four parts. The first part provides accounts of psychosis from multiple perspectives relating to historical developments, disease, symptom, philosophy, phenomenology and neuroscience. The second part deals with the different populations presenting with psychotic features: healthy people who have psychotic-like symptoms but who are without the need for care, psychiatric populations, individuals who are at high risk for developing psychosis, persons with neurological and medical conditions, children, adolescents and aging adults.

The third part deals exclusively with individual symptoms of psychosis, or symptom grouping. Specifically, our focus is on hallucinations in different modalities, delusions (false beliefs), lack of insight, disorders of thought and language, self-disturbances and passivity symptoms. Our decision not to include psychomotor retardation and catatonic symptoms was driven by the paucity of literature and assessment methods.

The fourth part of the book presents a description of rating scales for assessing psychosis and psychotic symptoms. This section is aimed at providing a guide regarding the array of scales available. For each, a short description, sample questions as well as information regarding validity and reliability where available are provided. The full contact details of the corresponding author, and information regarding where to obtain the scales, are presented. Critical evaluation of the strengths and weaknesses of the most prominent scales are generally addressed in Parts 2 and 3. With interest, we note the recent development of psychosis assessment "apps" and hope to see more of these in the future.

We hope that you find this book useful.

Flavie Waters
Massoud Stephane

PART I
What Is Psychosis?

1

HISTORY OF CONCEPTS ABOUT PSYCHOSIS

What Was It, What Is It?

Simon McCarthy Jones

Psychosis: A Short History

The contemporary definition of *psychosis*, given in the International Classification of Diseases (ICD-10; World Health Organization [WHO], 1994) as "the presence of hallucinations, delusions, or a limited number of severe abnormalities of behaviour, such as gross excitement and overactivity, marked psychomotor retardation, and catatonic behaviour" (p. 10), is one only recently arrived at. For the majority of the approximately 170 years of its existence in medical discourse, psychosis referred to a much wider class of experiences. Indeed, the root of the word, which combines the noun "psyche" (meaning spirit/soul/mind) with the suffix "-osis," which associates its preceding noun with a pathological condition (Sommer, 2011), contains no indication it is likely to refer to the specific experiences we today associate it with. Furthermore, the original word *psykhosis,* as used in Ancient Greece, had no connotation of mental disorder, instead meaning animating, or giving soul or life to.

The term was originally introduced in part to replace words such as madness, insanity and lunacy (Davidson, 1954) as an "inoffensive synonym for insanity" (Sommer, 2011, p. 164), first appearing in a medical context in mid-19th century Germany. The term *neurosis* had been introduced in the second half of the 18th century by the Scottish physician William Cullen (1710–1790) as a term to cover "all diseases of the nervous system not accompanied by fever" (Cullen, as cited in Sommer, 2011, p. 162). Against this backdrop, psychosis was introduced to specifically refer to diseases of the brain and that resulted in mental disorder. The first use of the term appears to be in 1841 in Karl Friedrich Canstatt's (1807–1850) *Handbuch der Medicinischen*, where it was used synonymously with the term *psychic neurosis* to describe a psychic manifestation of a disease of the brain (Bürgy, 2008).

However, the person most often credited with introducing the term is the Austrian physician Baron Ernst Von Feuchtersleben (1806–1849). Feuchtersleben employed it in 1845 as a term to denote serious mental disorder (covering the four traditional categories of melancholia, mania, dementia and idiocy) and was keen to try and stress the interplay of the body and mind in creating psychosis (Beer, 1995, 1996a). At the time Feuchtersleben was faced by two extreme positions. People like Wilheim Griesinger (1817–1868) argued that "mental illnesses are diseases of the brain" (Griesinger, as cited in Beer, 1996a, p. 276), whereas others like Johann Heinroth (1773–1843), referred to as mentalists, argued that mental disorders were caused by psychological factors such as an excess of passion, or sin (Beer, 1996a). In contrast, Feuchtersleben queried if mental disorders were always due only to disorders of the brain (Beer, 1996a) and viewed the etiology of psychoses as lying in both a physical weakness of the brain and in a mental vulnerability (Bürgy, 2008). As such he conceptualized psychoses as having their roots in a "psychophysical reciprocal relation" which was "diseased in several directions" (Feuchtersleben, as cited in Beer, 1996a, p. 275).

Soon, others such as Carl Friedrich Flemming (1799–1880) were also employing the term psychosis. Flemming wrote the first textbook specifically on the psychoses (*The Pathology and Treatment of the Psychoses*), where he used the term psychoses to simply refer to mental disorders in general (Beer, 1996a). Psychosis was conceptualized by Flemming as being a psychological aspect of a neurosis (i.e., a physical disorder), and hence he also used the alternative term, *psychoneurosis* (Beer, 1996a). Flemming argued that "The brain is not merely the source of activity [physical and mental] but is the organic foundation of all expressions of the action of the soul" (Flemming, as cited in Beer, 1996a, p. 275). Despite their close link to neurological disorder, the introduction of the term psychoses meant mental pathology became increasingly viewed as a discrete entity (Bürgy, 2008).

Psychosis later came to be subdivided in different ways, including through organic-functional and exogenous-endogenous distinctions. Carl Fuerstner (1848–1906) introduced the term 'functional psychosis' because he did not view the psychoses as exclusively of organic aetiology (Beer, 1996b). After Fuerstner, Alois Alzheimer used the term 'real psychoses' as a synonym for organic psychosis, defining psychoses as "diseases of the cerebral cortex" (Beer, 1996b). Yet, there were those such as Franz Nissl (1860–1919) who thought the organic-functional distinction was worthless as, in his view, "In all psychoses of whatever type there are always positive cortical findings" (Nissl, as cited in Beer, 1996b, p. 240). Yet the term functional did not necessarily mean that there were no changes to the brain, rather that the mentals functions (will, thought, emotion) were altered in the absence of any detectable brain pathology (Beer, 1996b). Indeed, most late-nineteenth-century psychiatrists used the term functional to describe conditions which had no obvious anatomical changes, but were nevertheless thought to have molecular disturbances (Beer, 1996b). It was effectively due to the influence of Freud (1856–1939) that functional came to mean 'nonorganic' (Beer, 1996b).

In the 1890s the neurologist Paul Julius Moebius (author of such works as *On the Physiological Weakmindedness of Women*—clearly absurd—and *On the Hopelessness of Psychology*—let's not rush to judgment on this one) became frustrated with the functional-organic dichotomy (Lewis, 1971). He observed it was "now customary to distinguish between organic and functional nervous disorders, in the sense that in the former changes in the affected tissue are visible after death, but not in the latter. This differentiation is useless, because it is to a large extent dependent on the methods of investigation: the pathological findings are always being added to by advances in histology" (Moebius, 1893, as cited in Lewis, 1971, p.191). Moebius went on to introduce a new subdivision based on the aetiology of a mental disorder, which he termed "classification by causes" (Lewis, 1971). This was the distinction between exogenous and endogenous disorders. Moebius argued that exogenous diseases were those which there was a main cause (necessary for the disorder to arise) which impinged on the individual from without, e.g., alcohol, lead, toxins, etc. (Beer, 1996c). In contrast, endogenous diseases were those in which there could be a range of smaller secondary subsidiary causes which meant, in Moebius's reasoning, that "the chief [causal] factor must be in the individual himself, it must be a predisposition" (Lewis, 1971, p.191) or a "congenital debility" (Moebius, as cited in Beer, 1996c, p. 8). However, Moebius was vague in his definition of exogenous, and what exactly was meant by being "engendered from without" (Beer, 1995, p. 286). Karl Wernicke's (1848–1905) pupil, Karl Bonhoeffer (1868–1948) applied these terms to psychosis, coining the terms endogenous and exogenous psychosis (Beer, 1996a). He conceptualized endogenous psychosis as being caused by hereditary-degenerative factors, giving examples of manic-depressive insanity and hebephrenic and paranoid psychoses (Beer, 1996a). In contrast, exogenous psychoses were those in which a trigger event could be determined, and the model invoked to understand this was of the response of the brain to injury (Lewis, 1971). As Bonhoeffer could not find a direct mechanism linking factors such as trauma or alcohol with an ensuing mental disorder, he postulated intermediate products (formed in the body as a result of these events) that he designated as being responsible for exogenous psychoses such as delirium, Korsakoff's syndrome, epilepsy and hallucinatory conditions (Lewis, 1971).

Emil Kraepelin (1856–1926) initially classified disorders such as manic-depressive insanity, paranoia, involutional psychosis and degeneration psychoses as endogenous psychoses but did not include dementia praecox in this category (Beer, 1996a). He argued, regarding dementia praecox, that

> in consideration of the close relationship with the age of puberty, the presence of disturbances of menstruation, and the frequent appearance of the

> disease for the first time during pregnancy and puerperium, the further assumption is made that it is the result of auto-intoxication.
>
> *(Kraepelin, as cited in Beer, 1996c, p. 14)*

However, he later came to believe dementia praecox and manic-depressive insanity were the only two endogenous psychoses, and that in these, "heredity and predisposition play a significant, if not a decisive role" (Kraepelin, as cited in Beer 1996c, p. 15). He also began to use psychosis to refer to specific conditions and not to mental disorders in general, as he had done earlier (Beer, 1996a).

Other writers made further distinctions as to what characterized psychosis, with Karl Jaspers (1883–1969) and Kurt Schneider (1887–1967) being particularly influential. Jaspers used the criterion of insight, arguing that in "psychosis there is no lasting or complete insight. Where insight persists we do not speak of psychosis but personality disorder" (Jaspers, as cited in Beer, 1996a, p. 279). Jaspers also defined psychosis in clear contrast to neurosis and personality disorders. He argued that psychoses, in contrast to neuroses,

> are mental and affective illnesses . . . [and] are generally thought to open up a gulf between sickness and health. They spring from additional disease processes, whether these are hereditary disorders beginning at certain times of life or whether they are called into being by exogenous lesions.
>
> *(ibid.)*

However, he argued that the three major psychoses (epilepsy, schizophrenia and manic depression) were functional, due to a lack of evidence at the time of organic changes associated with them (Beer 1996b). His contemporary, Schneider, preferred the term *endogenous* (Beer, 1996b). By 1933, Schneider's psychiatric classification system drew a sharp line between understandable normal reactions to events and psychoses, which he only conceptualized there being two of—schizophrenia and manic depression. He argued that "one could conclude that schizophrenia is an organic-constitutional, perhaps a primary cerebral disorder . . . in which somatically speaking there are no transitions with normality" (Schneider, as cited in Beer, 1995, p. 319).

Systems such as Schneider's, which stressed that psychosis was a disease and that it was quite clear who was suffering from it and who was not (Beer, 1995), became important in the grotesque social/political context of the time. Given that the Nazis were asking psychiatrists which of their patients were *erbkrank* (congenitally mentally ill), a group that were then to be sterilized or murdered, people with a label of endogenous psychosis (which usually meant schizophrenia or manic-depressive insanity) were one group who came to be deemed *erbkrank* (Beer 1995, 1996a). As one of Kraepelin's pupils, Robert Gaupp (1870–1953), chillingly put it, "it is a great piece of good fortune (when it comes to diagnosis) that it is only a question of schizophrenia or manic-depressive insanity, that is—two hereditary diseases with the same eugenic significance" (Gaupp, as cited in Beer, 1996a, p. 279). This led to a number of psychiatrists trying to save their patients from being killed by giving them diagnoses of forms of neurosis, rather than schizophrenia (Lifton, 2000).

By 1968, the second edition of the *Diagnostic and Statistical Manual of Mental Disorders* (DSM-II, American Psychiatric Association [APA], 1968) continued to distinguish between "psychoses associated with organic brain syndromes" (e.g., alcoholic psychosis, psychosis associated with intracranial infection) and "psychoses not attributed to physical conditions listed previously" (e.g., schizophrenia, manic depression), with the latter group still referred to as "functional disorders" (p. 23). It defined psychosis through stating that "patients are described as psychotic when their mental functioning is sufficiently impaired to interfere grossly with their capacity to meet the ordinary demands of life. The impairment may result from a serious distortion in their capacity to recognize reality. Hallucinations and delusions, for example, may distort their perceptions" (p. 23). By the time of DSM-III (APA, 1980), although psychoses in organic mental disorders were still classified separately from schizophrenia, the term *functional* was not used, and the authors were clear to stress that this did

> not imply that nonorganic ('functional') mental disorders are somehow independent of brain processes. . . . Limitations in our knowledge, however, sometimes make it impossible to determine whether a given mental disorder in a given individual should be considered an organic mental disorder (because it is due to brain dysfunction of *known* organic etiology) or whether it should be diagnosed as other than an Organic Mental Disorder (because it is more adequately accounted for as a response to psychological or social factors . . . or because the presence of a specific organic factor has not been established [as in Schizophrenia]).
>
> *(p. 101)*

DSM-III also noted that DSM-II's definition of psychosis "did not conform to common usage, which generally limited use of the term to impairment in reality testing" (APA, 1980, p. 368). Instead, it offered its own definition of psychotic as

> a term indicating gross impairment in reality testing. It may be used to describe the behavior of an individual at a given time, or a mental disorder in which at some time during its course all individuals with the disorder have grossly impaired reality testing. . . . Direct evidence of psychotic behavior is the presence of either delusions or hallucinations without insight into their pathological nature.
>
> *(p. 367)*

The DSM-V (APA, 2013) defines the "primary symptoms of psychosis" (p. 89) as being delusions, hallucinations, disorganized thinking (speech), grossly disorganized or abnormal motor behaviour (including catatonia) and negative symptoms. However, in its definition of "psychotic features" (p. 827), it only lists delusions, hallucinations and formal thought disorder, highlighting that a set of positive symptoms are perhaps viewed as being at the heart of what the term *psychosis* is being used to describe. Notably, psychotic disorders are defined as including disorders such as schizophrenia as well as schizotypal personality disorder. This reflects the contemporary view of a continuum of psychotic experiences (van Os et al., 2009), which runs counter to the split historically made by people such as Jaspers and Schneider between personality disorders and psychosis. Notably, in the context of this present volume, DSM-IV provides an assessment measure, termed the "Clinician-Rated Dimensions of Psychosis Symptom Severity" (APA, 1994, p. 743), which assesses the aforementioned five domains, as well as impaired cognition, mania and depression, each on a 5-point scale. For example, the hallucination item uses the ratings (score) of 0 = *not present*, 1 = *equivocal* (severity or duration not sufficient to be considered psychosis), 2 = *present, but mild* (little pressure to act upon voices, not very bothered by voices), 3 = *present and moderate* (some pressure to respond to voices, or is somewhat bothered by voices) and 4 = *present and severe* (severe pressure to respond to voices, or is very bothered by voices).

The Lived Experience of Psychosis Today

Although formal definitions of psychosis have been given, what psychosis actually is for people who meet such criteria is much more than can be contained in a simple definition. To attempt to get a better idea of what the lived experience of psychosis is like, a meta-synthesis of qualitative studies of psychosis (specifically, those that employed interpretative phenomenological analysis) was performed by myself and colleagues (McCarthy-Jones et al., 2013) to examine what common themes emerged. This employed the findings of 97 individual studies, which included a total of 1,942 participants. The major themes and subthemes from this analysis are summarized below.

Consensual Reality and Self

The confusing, unshared perceptions (voices, visions) and/or paranoia, viewed as constitutive of psychosis today, tend to occur after initial prodromal changes, such as "a feeling of being uncomfortable and something just not being right" (Shea, 2010, p. 46). These experiences often lead to a feeling of being in a different reality (Dilks, Tasker & Wren, 2010), accompanied by feelings of confusion and fear (e.g., Robertson & Lyons, 2003), which can remain or even be amplified during admission to hospital (Laithwaite et al., 2007). In addition to consensual reality, the self can be lost in many senses, including losing the sense of having a coherent self (e.g., Geanellos, 2005), losing self-esteem (e.g., Rhodes et al., 2005) or losing one's self-identity as a result of labeling/stigma (e.g., Laliberte-Rudman et al., 2000) or unemployment (e.g., Mackrell & Lavender, 2004). Such stigma is often internalized, resulting in people judging "themselves as useless, incapable or insane" (Wagner & King, 2005, p. 143). People with psychosis also report being labeled as freaks (Chernomas et al., 2000) and being made to feel "like a different species" (Laliberte-Rudman et al., 2000, p. 140), which can lead to suicidal ideation (Skodlar et al., 2008). Self-identity and self-esteem can also be impacted by diagnosis, a "dehumanizing and devaluing transformation from being a person to being an illness . . . to being 'a schizophrenic'" (Dilks et al., 2010, p. 98), the negative effects of anti-psychotic medication such as weight gain and sexual dysfunction (e.g., Johnstone et al., 2009) and negative attitudes from clinicians (Bassett, Lloyd & Bassett, 2001; Rofail, Heelis & Gournay, 2009), with some people feeling treated "like a little child . . . like a spastic . . . like a nothing" (Humberstone, 2002, p. 370).

Yet, once the "fear and confusion of fragmentation" has passed (Geanellos, 2005, p. 12), a sense of a stable, understandable reality can be regained. Medication may help this process by increasing feelings of reality and enabling clear thinking (e.g., Jarosinski, 2008), as may peer-support groups (Hyde, 2001). As part of this process, confusing, senseless experiences may be transformed into understandable, meaningful experiences (e.g., Jarosinski, 2008), linked to a range of potential causes (e.g., Barker, Lavender & Marant, 2001). This sense of a coherent reality allows the regaining of a coherent self within this reality (e.g., Jarosinski, 2008). Yet, rebuilding the self is a delicate time (Shea et al. 2010), with a sense that the regained self and reality can be lost again, and of "not being confident with your own mind. Knowing that you can lose it, as it happened before" (McCann & Clark, 2004, p. 788). Once a sense of having a self is regained, a self-identity and a sense of self-esteem can be rebuilt on this foundation. Self-identity can be regained by asserting a unique individual identity (Humberstone, 2002) or work (Kennedy-Jones et al., 2005). In terms of regaining self-esteem, work appears to be particularly helpful (e.g., Dunn, Wewiorsky & Rogers, 2008), as is secure housing (Browne & Courtney, 2005a). Meaningful activity, having a task which goes beyond simply having a job (Wagner & King, 2005), is also of central importance.

Hope and Motivation

Hope is frequently lost. The loss of a viable future is a key reason for this (e.g., Knight, Wykes & Hayward, 2003), particularly if people lose their jobs (Perry, Terry & Shaw, 2007) or have their children taken away (Diaz-Caneja et al., 2004). Hallucinated voices can reinforce this hopelessness (Jarosinski, 2008), as can diagnosis (e.g., Judge et al., 2008), particularly when communicated in the form of "You've got schizophrenia, you will be ill for the rest of your life" (Schulze et al.,

2003, p. 304), as well as pessimistic attitudes from those in the mental health system towards re-employment (e.g., Chernomas et al. 2000) and recovery (Tooth et al., 2003). This loss of hope can often lead to a depressed, demotivated state (e.g., Bassett et al., 2001).

Regaining hope is hence crucial, as evidenced by statements such as "when . . . you're hearing voices . . . sometimes hope is the only thing you've got" (El-Mallakh, 2006, p. 61). Sources of hope include the support of family and friends (Wagner & King, 2005), medication (Usher, 2001), positive attitudes from clinicians and confidence about recovery (Green et al., 2008), being diagnosed (Dilks et al., 2010), the prospect of work or education (Usher, 2001), religion/spirituality (Humberstone, 2002), and understanding and/or meeting other people going through the same thing (Coffey et al., 2008). Patients hope for restoration of family relationships, close interpersonal relationships, employment, energy, health, spiritual fulfillment or just a 'normal' life (e.g., Chernomas et al., 2000). Maintaining hope is hard work (Tooth et al., 2003); "You just gotta fight. You can't give up" (Shea et al., 2010, p. 47).

Security in Body and World

The security of a reliable body may be lost, including altered sleeping patterns, eating patterns, and bodily pains (e.g., Koivisto, Janhonen & Vaisanen, 2002). Medication side-effects may impact the body, potentially increasing appetite and sleep (e.g., McCann & Clark, 2004), and causing physical pains, e.g., "like hell . . . like a screw being tightened in your brain" (Usher, 2001, p. 148). Loss of security in the world is also found, due to attacks from hallucinated voices (Boyd & Gumley, 2007), the negative effects of hospitalization (with some people using "imagery about imprisonment and torture"; Thornhill, Clare & May, 2004, p. 188), and the loss of financial security due to loss of employment (e.g., Gee et al., 2003) which can in turn adversely affect participant's housing situation (e.g., Browne & Courtney, 2005b) creating eviction fears and a loss of personal safety; "I got raped one night, no-one came, even though I screamed" (Warren & Bell, 2000, p. 198).

The body must therefore be re-secured. Sleep, aided by medication, for example, is helpful: "Medication is calming and I am a lot more relaxed. I have slept easier" (Rofail et al., 2009, p. 1491). Regaining a sense of peaceful safety in the world is also central to recovery, with secure housing being of great importance; "when you have a place of your own you are free to create a safe space" (Browne & Courtney, 2005b, p. 318), as well as a return to the security of work (Dilks et al., 2010). Yet stigma is a key barrier to returning to work (Bassett et al., 2001), as are psychotic experiences themselves (Gioia, 2006) and side-effects of medication (Kennedy-Jones et al., 2005). Many worry that the pressures of work might lead to relapse (Dilks et al., 2010), and are aware of the need to monitor the amount of stress work is placing on them (Kennedy-Jones et al., 2005).

Relationships

Psychotic experiences can lead to self-imposed isolation (Gee et al., 2003), due to withdrawal being used as a coping mechanism (Judge et al., 2008). However, isolation may also be due to the actions of others. For example, many people talk about the loss of relationships with friends/family who don't understand what they are going through (e.g., Chernomas et al., 2000). Stigma and discrimination can cause of the loss of many relationships (e.g., Gonzales-Torres et al., 2007), as can as medication through side-effects impairing social relationships (e.g., McCann & Clark, 2004). Psychosis can also form barriers to romantic relationships (e.g., Bassett et al., 2001) due to a lack of resources such as confidence, energy, and friends (Redmond, Larkin & Harrop, 2010) and housing (Warren & Bell, 2000). Psychosis also profoundly impacts on sexuality, due to problems including medication-related weight gain (Volman & Landeen, 2007) and medication-related sexual dysfunction (Chernomas et al., 2000). Sex for the purpose of reproduction is often discouraged; "You mention to the psychiatrist that you want to have a child and he says 'no, that's not possible, don't even think of it" (Gonzalez-Torres et al., 2007, p. 19), which many patients later regret (Chernomas et al., 2000). The parent-child relationship may also be negatively affected (e.g., Diaz-Caneja et al., 2004). The loss of such relationships causes great suffering (Wagner & King, 2005) and the ensuing loneliness can lead to suicide (Skodlar et al., 2008).

Reconnecting with people is an essential task but by no means always an easy one (Mauritz et al., 2009). This is due to factors such as the negative effects of medication, potentially having poor communication skills (Skodlar et al., 2008), the effects of stigma (Diaz-Caneja et al., 2004) as well as the need to potentially mend fences (Krupa, Woodside & Pocock, 2010). The aid to recovery of social relationships generally is frequently stressed (McCann & Clark, 2004). This can result in a lower probability of suicide (Skodlar et al., 2008), aid a return to work and in turn further aid social relations (Kennedy-Jones et al., 2005). The need to regain romantic relationships and to have a family is also important (Laliberte-Rudman et al., 2000) and can make people feel "normal" again (Redmond et al., 2010). Relationships with mental health professionals and hospital staff can also be instrumental to recovery (Nixon, Hagen & Peters, 2010). Being listened to, having continuity with a clinician during psychological therapies (McGowan, Lavender & Garety, 2005), and being "treated like a human being" (O'Toole et al., 2004, p. 321) by mental health professionals are cited as key to recovery.

Conclusions

The concept of psychosis has changed from an initial, broad term for mental disorders caused by physical changes to the brain to its narrower, more specific contemporary meaning. Many of the key issues historically debated surrounding psychosis still remain debated today, such as the existence of a continuum of psychotic experience stretching into the general population (David, 2010), the roles of psychological and neurological causation (Brendel, 2000), and the interplay between genetic and environmental factors (McCarthy-Jones et al., in press; van Os, Rutten & Poulton, 2008). Although the term is likely to accumulate (further) stigma and be replaced by another term in the future, the experiences that constitute it will remain a focus of research and a target for the development of more effective clinical interventions for those distressed by such experiences. Yet, those seeking to help, share in or develop an understanding of the lived experience of individuals with psychosis should be constantly aware of the broad impact of psychosis on all areas of life and its multifaceted nature. This implies that the assessment of psychosis must be more than just the assessment of the presence of experiences such as hallucinations and delusions; instead, it must be an assessment of how such experiences impair the basic human needs of people troubled by them.

Acknowledgement

This work was supported by a Macquarie University Research Fellowship.

References

American Psychiatric Association. (1968). *Diagnostic and statistical manual of mental disorders* (2nd ed.). Washington, DC: American Psychiatric Association.

American Psychiatric Association. (1980). *Diagnostic and statistical manual of mental disorders* (3rd ed.). Washington, DC: American Psychiatric Association.

American Psychiatric Association. (1994). *Diagnostic and statistical manual of mental disorders* (4th ed.). Washington, DC: American Psychiatric Association.

American Psychiatric Association. (2013). *Diagnostic and statistical manual of mental disorders* (5th ed.). Washington, DC: American Psychiatric Association.

Barker, S., Lavender, T., & Morant N. (2001). Client and family narratives on schizophrenia. *Journal of Mental Health, 10*(2), 199–212.

Bassett, J., Lloyd, C., & Bassett, H. (2001). Work issues for young people with psychosis: Barriers to employment. *British Journal of Occupational Therapy, 64*, 66–72.

Beer, M. D. (1995). The importance of the social and intellectual contexts in a discussion of the history of the concept of psychosis. *Psychological Medicine, 25*, 317–321.

Beer, M. D. (1996a). Psychosis: A history of the concept. *Comprehensive Psychiatry, 37*(4), 273–291.

Beer, M. D. (1996b). The dichotomies: Psychosis/neurosis and functional/organic: A historical perspective. *History of Psychiatry*, 7, 231–255.

Beer, M. D. (1996c). The endogenous psychoses: A conceptual history. *History of Psychiatry*, 7, 1–29.

Boyd, T., & Gumley, A. (2007). An experiential perspective on persecutory paranoia: A grounded theory construction. *Psychology and Psychotherapy: Theory, Research and Practice, 80*, 1–22.

Brendel, D. H. (2000). Philosophy of mind in the clinic: The relation between causal and meaningful explanation in psychiatry. *Harvard Review of Psychiatry, 8*(4), 184–191.

Browne, G., & Courtney, M. (2005a). Exploring the experience of people with schizophrenia who live in boarding houses or private homes: A grounded theory study. *Contemporary Nurse: A Journal for the Australian Nursing Profession, 18*, 233–246.

Browne, G., & Courtney, M. (2005b). Housing, social support and people with schizophrenia: A grounded theory study. *Issues in Mental Health Nursing, 26*, 311–326.

Bürgy, M. (2008). The concept of psychosis: Historical and phenomenological aspects. *Schizophrenia Bulletin, 34*(6), 1200–1210.

Chernomas, W. M., Clarke, D. E., & Chisholm F. A. (2000). Perspectives of women living with schizophrenia. *Psychiatric Services, 51*, 1517–1521.

Coffey, M., & Hewitt, J. (2008). You don't talk about the voices: Voice hearers and community mental health nurses talk about responding to voice hearing experiences. *Journal of Clinical Nursing, 17*, 1591–1600.

David, A. S. (2010). Why we need more debate on whether psychotic symptoms lie on a continuum with normality. *Psychological Medicine, 40*, 1935–1942.

Davidson, H. A. (1954). Psychiatry and euphemistic delusion. *American Journal of Psychiatry, 110*, 310–312.

Diaz-Caneja, A., & Johnson S. (2004). The views and experiences of severely mentally ill mothers—A qualitative study. *Social Psychiatry and Psychiatric Epidemiology, 39*, 472–482.

Dilks, S., Tasker, F., & Wren, B. (2010). Managing the impact of psychosis: A grounded theory exploration of recovery processes in psychosis. *British Journal of Clinical Psychology, 49*, 87–107.

Dunn, E. C., Wewiorski, N. J., & Rogers, E. S. (2008). The meaning and importance of employment to people in recovery from serious mental illness: Results of a qualitative study. *Psychiatric Rehabilitation Journal, 32*, 59–62.

El-Mallakh, P. (2006). Evolving self-care in individuals with schizophrenia and diabetes mellitus. *Archives of Psychiatric Nursing, 20*, 55–64.

Geanellos, R. (2005). Adversity as opportunity: Living with schizophrenia and developing a resilient self. *International Journal of Mental Health Nursing, 14*, 7–15.

Gee, L., Pearce, E., & Jackson M. (2003). Quality of life in schizophrenia: A grounded theory approach. *Health and Quality of Life Outcomes*, 1–11.

Gioia, D. (2006). Examining work delay in young adults with schizophrenia. *American Journal of Psychiatric Rehabilitation, 9*, 167–190.

Gonzalez-Torres, M. A., Oraa, R., Aristegui, M., Fernandez-Rivas, A., & Guimon, J. (2007). Stigma and discrimination towards people with schizophrenia and their family members: A qualitative study with focus groups. *Social Psychiatry and Psychiatric Epidemiology, 42*, 14–23.

Green, C. A., Polen, M. R., Janoff, S. L., Castleton, D. K., Wisdom, J. P., Vuckovic, N., et al. (2008). Understanding how clinician-patient relationships and relational continuity of care affect recovery from serious mental illness: STARS study results. *Psychiatric Rehabilitation Journal, 32*, 9–22.

Humberstone, V. (2002). The experiences of people with schizophrenia living in supported accommodation: A qualitative study using grounded theory methodology. *Australian and New Zealand Journal of Psychiatry, 36*, 367–372.

Hyde, P. (2001). Support groups for people who have experienced psychosis. *British Journal of Occupational Therapy, 64*, 169–174.

Jarosinski, J. M. (2008). Exploring the experience of hallucinations from a perspective of self: Surviving and persevering. *Journal of the American Psychiatric Nurses Association, 14*, 353–362.

Johnstone, R., Nicol, K., Donaghy, M., & Lawrie, S. (2009). Barriers to uptake of physical activity in community-based patients with schizophrenia. *Journal of Mental Health, 18*(6), 523–532.

Judge, A. M., Estroff, S. E., Perkins, D. O., & Penn, D. L. (2008). Recognizing and responding to early psychosis: A qualitative analysis of individual narratives. *Psychiatric Services, 59*, 96–99.

Kennedy-Jones, M., Cooper, J., & Fossey, E. (2005). Developing a worker role: Stories of four people with mental illness. *Australian Occupational Therapy Journal, 52*, 116–126.

Knight, M.T.D., Wykes, T., & Hayward P. (2003). People don't understand: An investigation of stigma in schizophrenia using interpretative phenomenological analysis (IPA). *Journal of Mental Health, 12*, 209–222.

Koivisto, K., Janhonen, S., & Vaisanen L. (2002). Applying a phenomenological method of analysis derived from Giorgi to a psychiatric nursing study. *Journal of Advanced Nursing, 39*, 258–265.

Krupa, T., Woodside, H., & Pocock, K. (2010). Activity and social participation in the period following a first episode of psychosis and implications for occupational therapy. *British Journal of Occupational Therapy, 73*, 13–20.

Laithwaite, H., & Gumley, A. (2007). Sense of self, adaptation and recovery in patients with psychosis in a forensic NHS setting. *Clinical Psychology and Psychotherapy, 14*, 302–316.

Laliberte-Rudman, D., Yu, B., Scott, E., & Pajouhandeh, P. (2000). Exploration of the perspectives of persons with schizophrenia regarding quality of life. *American Journal of Occupational Therapy, 54*, 137–147.

Lewis, A. (1971). "Endogenous" and "exogenous": A useful dichotomy? *Psychological Medicine, 1*, 191–196.

Lifton, R. J. (2000). *The Nazi doctors: Medical killing and the psychology of genocide*. New York, NY: Basic Books.

Mackrell, L., & Lavender, T. (2004). Peer relationships in adolescents experiencing a first episode of psychosis. *Journal of Mental Health, 13*, 467–479.

Mauritz, M., & van Meijel, B. (2009). Loss and grief in patients with schizophrenia: On living in another world. *Archives of Psychiatric Nursing, 23*, 251–260.

McCann, T. V., & Clark, E. (2004). Embodiment of severe and enduring mental illness: Finding meaning in schizophrenia. *Issues in Mental Health Nursing, 25*, 783–798.

McCarthy-Jones, S., Marriott, M., Knowles, R. E., Rowse, G., & Thompson, A. R. (2013). What is psychosis? A meta-synthesis of inductive qualitative studies exploring the experience of psychosis. *Psychosis, 5*, 1–16.

McCarthy-Jones, S., Green, M. J., Scott, R. J. Tooney, P. A., Cairns, M. J., et al. (in press). Preliminary evidence of an interaction between the FOXP2 gene and childhood emotional abuse predicting likelihood of auditory verbal hallucinations in schizophrenia. *Journal of Psychiatric Research*.

McGowan, J. F., Lavender, T., & Garety P. A. (2005). Factors in outcome of cognitive-behavioural therapy for psychosis: Users' and clinicians' views. *Psychology and Psychotherapy: Theory, Research and Practice, 78*, 513–529.

Nixon, G., Hagen, B., & Peters, T. (2010). Recovery from psychosis: A phenomenological inquiry. *International Journal of Mental Health and Addiction, 8*, 620–635.

O'Toole, M. S., Ohlsen, R. I., Taylor, T. M., Purvis, R., Walters, J., & Pilowsky L. S. (2004). Treating first episode psychosis—The service users' perspective: A focus group evaluation. *Journal of Psychiatric and Mental Health Nursing, 11*, 319–326.

Perry, B. M., Taylor, D., & Shaw, S. K. (2007). "You've got to have a positive state of mind": An interpretative phenomenological analysis of hope and first episode psychosis. *Journal of Mental Health, 16*, 781–793.

Redmond, C., Larkin, M., & Harrop, C. (2010). The personal meaning of romantic relationships for young people with psychosis. *Clinical Child Psychology and Psychiatry, 15*, 151–170.

Rhodes, J., Jakes, S., & Robinson J. (2005). A qualitative analysis of delusional content. *Journal of Mental Health, 14*, 383–398.

Robertson, E., & Lyons, A. (2003). Living with puerperal psychosis: A qualitative analysis. *Psychology and Psychotherapy: Theory, Research and Practice, 76*, 411–431.

Rofail, D., Heelis, R., & Gournay, K. (2009). Results of a thematic analysis to explore the experiences of patients with schizophrenia taking antipsychotic medication. *Clinical Therapeutics, 31*(Suppl. 1), 1488–1496.

Schulze, B., & Angermeyer M. C. (2003). Subjective experiences of stigma. A focus group study of schizophrenic patients, their relatives and mental health professionals. *Social Science and Medicine, 56*, 299–312.

Shea, J. M. (2010). Coming back normal: The process of self-recovery in those with schizophrenia. *Journal of the American Psychiatric Nurses Association, 16*, 43–51.

Skodlar, B., Tomori, M., & Parnas, J. (2008). Subjective experience and suicidal ideation in schizophrenia. *Comprehensive Psychiatry, 49*, 482–488.

Sommer, R. (2011). The etymology of psychosis. *American Journal of Orthopsychiatry, 81*(2), 162–166.

Thornhill, H., Clare, L., & May, R. (2004). Escape, enlightenment and endurance: Narratives of recovery from psychosis. *Anthropology and Medicine, 11*, 181–199.

Tooth, B., Kalyanasundaram, V., Glover, H., & Momenzadah S. (2003). Factors consumers identify as important to recovery from schizophrenia. *Australasian Psychiatry, 11*(Suppl. 1), S70–S77.

Usher, K. (2001). Taking neuroleptic medications as the treatment for schizophrenia: A phenomenological study. *Australian and New Zealand Journal of Mental Health Nursing, 10*, 145–155.

van Os, J., Linscott, R. J., Myin-Germeys, I., Delespaul, P., & Krabbendam, L. (2009). A systematic review and meta-analysis of the psychosis continuum: Evidence for a psychosis proneness–persistence–impairment model of psychotic disorder. *Psychological Medicine, 39*, 179–195.

van Os, J., Rutten, B. P. F., & Poulton, R. (2008). Gene-environment interactions in schizophrenia: Review of epidemiological findings and future directions. *Schizophrenia Bulletin, 36*, 1066–82.

Volman, L., & Landeen J. (2007). Uncovering the sexual self in people with schizophrenia. *Journal of Psychiatric and Mental Health Nursing, 14*, 411–417.

Wagner, L.C., & King, M. (2005). Existential needs of people with psychotic disorders in Parto Alegre, Brazil. *British Journal of Psychiatry, 186*, 141–145.
Warren, R., & Bell, P. (2000). An exploratory investigation into the housing preferences of consumers of mental health services. *Australian and New Zealand Journal of Mental Health Nursing, 9*, 195–202.
World Health Organization (1994). *The ICD-10 classification of mental and behavioural disorders: Clinical descriptions and diagnostic guidelines*. Geneva, Switzerland: World Health Organization.

2

PHILOSOPHICAL AND PHENOMENOLOGICAL PERSPECTIVES ON PSYCHOSIS

Josef Parnas

Introduction

Currently, we witness a certain disarray and turbulence in psychiatry's self-understanding, both as a science and as a profession (Hyman, 2010; Katschnig, 2010; Frances & Widiger, 2012). This turbulence has been triggered, or at least made audible, by the discussions surrounding the release of DSM-5 and the preparations for the ICD-11. On the one hand, we have seen a spectacular progress in neuroscience and molecular biology. On the other hand, the everyday, clinical psychiatry does not seem to have benefitted much from the scientific successes of the former disciplines.

It is in this particular context that philosophy and phenomenology demonstrate their relevance for psychiatry. We have argued elsewhere that an important source of the current stagnation in psychiatry is the vast oversimplification of the ontology (the nature of being) and epistemology of the "object of psychiatry" (symptoms, signs, syndromes, etc.), which has taken place in the wake of the "operational revolution" (Parnas, Sass & Zahavi, 2013; Nordgaard, Sass & Parnas, 2013; Parnas & Bovet, in press). "Operational" definitions *are not in fact operational* in any remotely significant epistemological or scientific sense. Rather, the DSM-III revolution resulted in a simplification of psychopathology to a lay level, phrasing its concepts in ordinary layman's terms, deprived of any overarching conceptual or phenomenological framework. Contemporary psychopathology involves a behaviorist, subjectivity-aversive stance that is insensitive to the qualitative diversity and heterogeneity of psychiatric phenomena as well as to their similarities in pattern. There are reasons, therefore, to believe that the lack of etiological and therapeutic progress, haunting psychiatry 30 years after its "operational" remake, is less related to the very existence of phenotype-based classifications or to a still insufficient resolution power of biotechnologies but is more importantly determined by an inadequate epistemology for addressing psychiatric phenotypes (Parnas & Bovet, in press).

Phenomenology, a study of consciousness and subjectivity, is, in my view, a necessary tool for arriving at any sensible taxonomy of the mental domain. In order to pursue a scientific-empirical project of explanatory reduction, we need a prior and serious study of the explanandum itself; that is, we need a mental taxonomy that is faithful to the phenomena of subjectivity. The science of the mind cannot progress if we only employ the distinctions that are dictated by the ideals of simplicity, apparent easiness of application and involve only a limited scholarly or clinical effort.

A need for a philosophical and phenomenological approach is also visible when it comes to studying the phenomena of psychosis. *Psychosis, psychotic* and its kin-related terms, such as *reality, rationality, reason, belief, truth, intersubjectivity, autonomy, responsibility* and so forth, are all primarily *non-empirical* concepts that cannot be examined in a straightforward, quantitative way without some prior, theoretical, philosophical reflection. Nor can these issues be studied without drawing careful and valid phenomenological distinctions. The purpose of this chapter is to expose some of these theoretical issues and try to connect them to the phenomenological nature of the forms of experience and belief that we designate as *psychotic.*

Phenomenology and Psychiatry

The term *phenomenology* signifies a "study of phenomena" or a "study of appearances." There are (at least) three uses of the term (Parnas & Zahavi, 2002; Parnas & Sass, 2008). In the Anglophone psychiatry, the term *phenomenology* refers to a common-sense description of symptoms and signs, performed from the third-person perspective (this kind of description is in Europe sometimes called "semiology"). In European psychiatry, the meaning of phenomenology has always been influenced by Karl Jaspers: Phenomenology is the study of subjective experience with the purpose of allowing the first person character of experience to come into view (Jaspers, 1913/1963). Note that the very expression "subjective experience" is a sort of tautology or pleonasm, because *all experience is necessarily subjective.*

The third use of the term (employed in this chapter), with affinities to Jaspers, understands phenomenology in its stronger, philosophical,[1] continental sense (Parnas & Zahavi, 2002; Parnas & Sass, 2008). It is a phenomenological investigation of experience ("symptoms"), expression ("signs") and existence. Philosophical phenomenological approach is mindful of common, but often implicit, ideological prejudices, convictions of "natural attitude,"—for example, premature objectivist- (strongly realist) or reductionist-assumptions—or of naïve tendencies to psychologize or normalize pathological phenomena. This suspension of explicit and implicit ontological dogmas and prejudices, called "phenomenological reduction" or "epoché," is a methodological device to reach out to "the things themselves." In other words, the goal of phenomenological investigation is to let the phenomena manifest themselves as they appear, undistorted by the psychiatrist's preconceptions. What is understood as phenomena is not only mental *contents* (e.g., a feeling of jealousy), their expressions or enactments, but also the *structures* (forms) of subjectivity (e.g., modes of intentionality, temporality, self-awareness, etc.).

The psyche does not consist of sharply separable, substantial intramental objects, exerting mechanical causality on each other. Rather, "it is (a) network of interdependent moments (i.e., non-independent parts[2]) . . . founded on intentional intertwining, motivation and mutual implication, *in a way that has no analogue in the physical*" (Husserl, 1977, p. 157; italics added). In other words, in the physical domain, part–whole relations are determined by efficient (often mechanical) causality, whereas in the mental realm, part–whole relations are those of implication, motivation, entailment and so forth. A rapidly emerging view in the philosophy of mind and neuroscience does not consider consciousness and cognition as being exclusively *confined to* the skull but rather as *extended*, that is, *constitutively including the physical and social Umwelt of the activity of the sentient organism.* On this view consciousness is "embodied, embedded, extended and enactive" (Clark, 2008, p. 1). Consciousness exhibits certain *structures*, crucially relevant for psychopathology, comprising intentionality (world-directedness), temporality, embodiment, self-awareness, and intersubjectivity (Parnas & Zahavi, 2002; Parnas & Sass, 2008). Theoretically speaking, a psychiatric symptom is not a well-demarcated thing-like object but rather a certain configuration, or Gestalt, that involves the flow of phenomenal consciousness with its intentional contents and forms (structures). The symptoms are certain wholes, or Gestalts, of interpenetrating experiences, beliefs, expressions and actions, all of them permeated by the patient's dispositions and by biographical (and not just biological) detail. The symptom individuates itself in the synchronic and diachronic contexts along all these dimensions, which combine into specific meaning-wholes. In short, a symptom/sign is not an entity "in itself"—easily or arbitrarily isolated out of the ongoing flow of consciousness, and described independently of its context. It follows that a study of subjectivity demands an adequately tailored epistemological framework. It is for this reason that Jaspers (1913/1963) emphasized the necessity of a comprehensive psychological-phenomenological framework for any psychopathological enterprise (a knowledge of "what people experience and how they experience it" [pp. 2–3; p 1, footnote 1]).

Defining Psychosis: Preliminaries

I will start with a conclusion that might assist the reader's way through the very heterogeneous composition of this chapter. This conclusion is simple: The concept of psychosis does not lend itself to any short, easy and unequivocal descriptive definition. The notion of psychosis is usually understood in two different, yet related, ways. The first kind of definition is *nosological*: Psychosis is a certain nosological entity, a *disease category* or a group of diseases. However, we have no robust extraclinical markers of psychiatric diagnoses, nor have we any immediate prospect for obtaining them. With the exception of certain organic conditions, all psychiatric diagnoses are based upon clinical descriptions of symptoms and signs. This leads us to the second, purely *descriptive* use of the term. A central task will be to try to answer the following question: *What is psychosis in a descriptive sense?* How can we define psychosis descriptively? It is not possible to address this question without a very short historical digression (see *Chapter 1* for the history of the term).

In the beginning of the 20th century, after having emancipated itself from the very inclusive 19th-century term *dementia, psychosis* came to designate a serious psychological disorder with hypothetical roots in a neurobiological disease "process," reflected in a "global personality change" (Jaspers, 1913/1963[3]; Schneider, 1950). Since that time, psychosis never came to be considered only on a purely descriptive-phenomenological level, disconnected from hypothetical, nosological-pathogenetic considerations. Rather, all definitions of psychosis were and are embedded in the extra-clinical (non-descriptive) references. These non-descriptive, nosological considerations have always been added to compensate for the insufficiency of a purely descriptive definition.

For example, classic psychoanalysis considered psychosis to be a regression to pre-oedipal developmental stages with the activation of the corresponding low-level "primitive" defence mechanisms (Fenichel, 1945). Contemporary psychoanalysis considers "psychosis" and "psychosis-proneness" as specific patterns of psychological organization (Kernberg, 1975). However, the notions of "regression" or "psychological organization" may (but need not to) be construed as referring to nosological constructs rather than to a directly observable, descriptive realm. The ICD-8 and ICD-9 grouped the psychoses into a triad according to their assumed etiologies: (a) endogenous/heritable (schizophrenia, manic-depressive illness), (b) organic/exogenous/toxic and (c) psychogenic (reactive) psychoses. The DSM-IV and DSM-5 do not use the term *psychosis* as a substantive but only employ the adjective *psychotic*.[4] In the DSM-IV (American Psychological Association [APA], 2000) and DSM-5 (APA, 2013), *psychotic* refers to the presence of certain symptoms and signs, that is, delusions, hallucinations, disorganized speech, certain catatonic features (in the DSM-5, also the negative symptoms). The DSM-5 uses the term *psychotic disorder* as a nosological category, comprising schizophrenia spectrum and psychotic, substance-use-related conditions. The definition of psychosis in the ICD-10 (World Health Organization [WHO], 1992) uses the same symptomatic indices as DSM-IV. The ICD-10 mentions, *in passim*, a general concept of psychosis, but the latter is only vaguely defined with a reference to a failure of "reality testing." In continuation with the nosological trend, it is today assumed that "psychotic disorders" are "brain disorders" (Insel et al., 2010; Cuthberg & Insel, 2010). In sum, psychosis has been and still is descriptively undefined or underdefined.

A Lay and Ethical Understanding of the Term "Psychosis": Some Implications

We have to begin by looking into a common-sense, lay understanding of the concept of psychosis. In psychiatry, where most of the disorders express themselves in the social-interpersonal space, lay understanding is often co-constitutive of the meaning of the descriptive terms. A layman refers to psychosis as "madness" (insanity, craziness, *folie, délire, Wahnsinn, Verrückheit*). Jaspers summarized the layman's view in the following way:

> For lay persons madness means senseless ravings, affectless confusion, delusion, incongruous affects, a 'crazy' personality, and [lay persons] think this all the more the more sensible and orientated the individual remains.
>
> *(Jaspers, 1963, pp. 577–578)*

The expression "affectless confusion" and the very last part of the sentence are significant: The more we take the person to be emotionally composed and unimpaired in her basic cognitive faculties, the more obviously his "craziness" articulates itself as "crazy." In other words, should, for example, an epileptic source of the "senseless raving" become apparent, the layman would be inclined to consider the person as being somatically ill rather than insane. It seems then that psychosis is a predicate that we ascribe to someone who has seriously transgressed the intersubjective bounds of rationality or the shared social perspective on the world. A common way to define this transgression is to equate it with the presence of delusion(s) (delusionality). This equation is unsatisfactory for several reasons that will be addressed below. Most importantly, delusion does not exhaust all characteristics of "madness" in layman's understanding, and it is but one of the "psychotic symptoms" specified in the current diagnostic systems (DSM-5 and ICD-10). Another way of addressing madness is to say that the patient has lost the ability to distinguish between what is real and what is imaginary, between the real and the irreal. However, a move from rationality to reality is spurious, because both concepts clearly overlap.

A part of a general, societal perspective on psychosis is the commonly accepted ethical and legal view on how to deal with the psychotic offenders. Such legal and ethical concerns permeate the notion of psychosis. This is to say that legal consequences *do not merely follow* from the concept of psychosis but are also *co-constitutive* of the very concept of psychosis. The very existence of a category called "psychosis" (madness) is co-constituted by ethical, social and political considerations.

Madness implies a loss or lack of personal *autonomy, responsibility* and therefore *accountability*. A crime, committed (in Europe) in a psychotic state is typically not sanctioned by the standard punitive measures because psychotic offenders cannot be considered to have acted as an autonomous, rational and free-willed individuals.

Reality, Sense of Reality, Reality Judgment and Reality Testing

Reality

The term *reality* is often opposed to the *world of psychosis*. Psychosis is therefore conceived of as standing outside the realm of the real, in some sort of imaginary world. The real is here typically understood from an ordinary, realist, "Newtonian" perspective, as that which exists (typically as middle-sized objects) independently of the acts of consciousness (e.g., fantasy or imagination), with an emphasis on the materiality of the world, its physical composition, laws of nature and objectivity, that is independence of human perspectives. Such definition is too restrictive, however, to do justice to human experience. For phenomenology, reality is a richer concept: It is a reality of a "lived world" (lifeworld), that is, a world imbued with meaning, conventions, relevance, affordances and objectivity, all (co)-constituted by our (inter)-subjectivity (sociality), with symbolic-communicative and cultural dimensions (Parnas & Sass, 2008). This shared lived world is not a spatial object or a *thing*, a huge container of all smaller, individual objects or things that find their natural place within its confines. Rather, the lifeworld is an encompassing *background* ("*das Umgreiffende*"; Jaspers, 1938), a *horizon*, which makes the manifestation of objects possible (Heidegger, 1953/1996). It needs to be added here that "lifeworld" is not a notion derived from some prior social-constructivist metaphysics. It is derived from phenomenological analyses of how reality manifests itself, how it is experienced and lived. This manifestation always includes social and symbolic elements (Bégout, 2005).

Sense of Reality

We should therefore not envisage our being in the world as a sort of dualist relation between two independent entities or things, a Cartesian ego (or brain) and the so-called external (transcendent) world. Human being is *Dasein* (being *there*); she is *always already* in the world (*in-der-Welt-Sein*). Subject and object are best considered as "*two abstract moments of a unique structure which is presence*" (Merleau-Ponty, 1945/2012, p. 492; italics added). Phenomenologically speaking, reality does not present itself first as a kind of raw, naked, external, physical reality, revealed to us by elementary sense data conveying its atomic features and only subsequently constructed and dressed with layers of meaning, assisted by concepts and reflection.

Rather, all grasp of reality, all cognition, happens from *within* our lived world, with its *prior* familiarity, everydayness and trustworthiness (Bégout, 2005).

Phenomenologically speaking, this is the most basic level of reality or the most basic mode of our being in the world, a level that Husserl (1982) called "*Urdoxa*" (primordial belief) and Merleau-Ponty (1945/2012), "perceptual faith" (*la foi perceptive*). We take the real for granted and our own presence in the midst of it is an unproblematical smooth given.

The belonging to the world is not a matter of having a belief-like intentional state with the content "the world exists"; rather, it involves (. . .) having a sense of reality, by which I mean a grasp of the distinction between "real," "present" and other *possibilities*, without which one could not encounter anything as "there" or, more generally, as "real." We generally "take for granted that others share *this same modal space* [i.e., ontological space, a space of what we consider as being possible] with us and that they are able to encounter things in the same way as we do" (Ratcliffe, 2012, pp. 479–480; italics and brackets added).

This original belonging to the world, *a sense of reality* is a sense of embodied (self)-presence in the midst of a shared world. The root of this sense is not primarily cognitive but affective in nature. "Felt reality" is not the product of a dispassionate disclosing of the world. As Husserl (1982) mentioned, our cognitive grasping of objects relies on a sense of being affected by, and belonging to, the world through inconspicuous affective-existential tonalities (Ratcliffe 2008), which make up the pre-reflective horizon of experience and frame our everyday commerce with objects, situations and other people. These "ontological feelings" (sense of presence) constitute the very matrix in which cognition and reflection take place (Damasio, 1999, 2003). Their overall structure is "touch-like" (Ratcliffe, 2008). Like in touch, a self-presence and experience of otherness are inextricably interwoven in the same unitary experiential structure. Similarly, already Jaspers (1913/1963) and Pierre Janet (1926) distinguished between the primary awareness of reality (sense of reality; *fonction du réel*), which is an immediate (directly given and implicit) certainty of reality and a reality created through a reflective "reality judgment" (*notion du réel*). "Conceptual reality carries conviction *only if a kind of presence is experienced*" (Jaspers, 1913/1963). The sense of reality is often disturbed in the schizophrenia spectrum disorders, and we will return to this issue below.

Reality Judgment

As Jaspers pointed out, we have also a possibility of a reflective judgment about reality (as when I am assessing how much money I can allow myself to spend on my family's vacation). Such explicit relation to reality is not a feeling or a pre-verbal experience but a cognitive, conceptual attitude. It contains reflection, changing of one's perspectives, and it involves judgments about the objects and states of affairs in the surrounding world and concerning oneself (e.g., the concept of "insight into illness"). Reality judgment partly depends on our rational and intellective capacities (e.g., IQ) but it is also dependent on the more primordial *sense* of reality (see below).

Reality Testing and Reality Monitoring

The sense of reality and unreflected presence in the intersubjective world is not based on a hypothetical "reality testing" (defined in cognitive science as an ability to distinguish imagination from perception) or "reality monitoring" (ability to distinguish external and internal stimuli). Both testing and monitoring considered on the phenomenal, experiential level (and not merely postulated as subpersonal neural processes), necessarily imply online comparisons of what we are experiencing with some representational models or criteria. If these functions really operated at the experiential level, we would find ourselves continuously comparing perceptions and fantasies with each other. But when I imagine myself sitting on the terrace of a Parisian café, my (self)-awareness of my imagining (my awareness of me, being engaged now in an act of imagining myself on the terrace of a Parisian café) *is precisely that which constitutes my experience as a case of imagining.* I need no reflective scrutiny or comparison with my current perceptions in order to "know" whether I am imagining or perceiving. In fact, even to say that "I know that I am perceiving or imagining" borders on incoherence, because we do not have any epistemic (or other) relation here at all. My self-awareness of imagining is a constitutive aspect of the very act of imagining. We are dealing here with a self-affection of intentionality of perception or imagination (Henry, 1973), or, to phrase it differently, we deal here with an intrinsic *reflexivity* (not *reflectivity*) of experience (Janzen, 2008).

It is possible, and perhaps likely, that the processes like reality testing and monitoring do actually take place on a subpersonal (neural) level, but this is not the case on the experiential level.

In summary, a modular process of "reality testing" does not articulate itself as a phenomenal experience or experientially accessible function. For this reason, "reality testing" should not be used as a psychiatric, phenomenological descriptor. To say that a patient suffers from deficient reality testing is just another way of saying that he is psychotic or close to being so. Instead, we should say that the patient's (reflective) reality judgment (critical, socially anchored reflection) is radically compromised, while keeping in mind that we are not referring to any modular, specific function.

Experience and Judgment

It is important to distinguish between experience and judgment, although this distinction is not categorical or absolute but may be best considered as a graded transition between two Gestaltic-prototypical opposites, the affective-pathic and the cognitive. The phenomenological notion of "experience," a translation of the German term *Erlebnis* (French *vecu*), refers to a pathic, passive *living through* a specific (self)-affection, for example, a sensation of pain, a mood, a feeling of joy, but also a qualitative, pathic ("what it is like") aspect of an act of thinking (i.e., there is a self-affecting, pathic dimension of cognition). A judgment, on the other hand, is a cognitive act, a belief, an assumption, a propositional attitude about certain states of affairs in the world. A judgment posits its object as being in a certain way, for example, as real, absent, likely and so forth (the so-called "thetic" component; Husserl, 1982). Experience may be associated with varying degrees of thetic positing: For example, in seeing a tree in front of us, we implicitly posit the tree as actually existing there, in front of us. Conversely, all judgments possess an experiential, affective dimension. There is a difference of "what it is like" to *believe* that something, to *doubt* that something, or to *hope* that something (Zahavi, 2005; vide supra on the self-affection of intentionality; Henry, 1973).

A distinction between experience and judgment plays an important role in the cognitive debate on the pathogenesis of delusion. Three approaches may be identified here: (1) "bottom-up" approach, claiming the primacy of experiential aberrations that subsequently lead to delusional explanatory attempts; (2) "top-down" approach, claiming a pathogenetic primacy of cognitive dysfunctions, especially metacognitive deficits; (3) mixed or hybrid models, where both factors (experiential and cognitive) operate jointly. The problem with this research and theoretical literature is twofold: First, it generally treats the delusion as a well-defined, homogenous symptom, without attending to its qualitative experiential differences, and, second, this discussion is typically fairly abstract, distant from any intimate familiarity with the realities of clinical psychiatry.

Rationality and Irrationality

The layman's view of psychosis (madness) tells us that the person's rationality, that is, her judgment, grasp, or understanding of reality, of the world, her self-understanding, reasoning and, very importantly, communicating with the other, is markedly dislocated from what is contextually and socially adequate, acceptable and therefore valid. Consider a patient who claims that his thoughts are controlled from invisible spaceships and he cannot be corrected in his claims. This patient appears to harbor beliefs that are outside the bounds of rationality in a certain radical way. Whether this radicality can be defined more precisely will be addressed below.

We therefore need to dwell briefly on the issue of rationality. Since Aristotle, a human being is considered as a *rational animal*; that is, humans are endowed with the capacity for reasoning, deliberation and are capable of a reflected decision. Non-human animals *are not irrational* but *a-rational*; they simply do not possess the capacity of reason as outlined above (a capacity for "higher mental functions" or "metacognition"). *Only humans can be irrational.*

The concept of rationality is a central theme of certain strands of analytic philosophy and it is also a topic increasingly investigated by cognitive neuroscience. Rationality is typically understood as a *reasoning capacity*, mainly dependent on serial, discursive-propositional steps of inferential logic. To consider another person as an ideally rational creature requires a fulfilment of the following conditions: (a) we understand the person's reasons for acting in a given way (action is consistent with its intent); (b) we ascribe to her a rationality of mental states, that is, her beliefs and desires comprise a consistent and coherent set or network; (c) her reasoning follows the rules of logic and probability calculus; (d) she tends to optimize her knowledge and possesses transparent preferences/inclinations. Such ideal rationality is, perhaps not surprisingly, not a very frequent finding of empirical population studies. Humans often reason heuristically and quickly, violate the rules of logic, ignore probability calculus, become easily biased by affective factors, and there are missing links in the coherence chain of their belief networks (Gigerenzer, 2007). In other words, there are different ways for rationality to operate. Moreover, *rationality is a normative concept* and a matter of degree (Stanovich, 2011).

Donald Davidson (1974), a prominent analytic philosopher, has coined the so-called principle of charity, which is a phenomenon highly relevant to psychiatry. Principle of charity is a default position in which we take rationality of our interlocutor for granted. It is an a priori ascription of rationality to another human being. Principle of charity may articulate itself psychologically as an implicit, automatic, *compensating* tendency to make one's interlocutor appear as being *more* rational than he *actually* is, for example, by smoothening out the bumps of his reasoning, filling up the gaps of his logic and normalizing the instances of his flagrant irrationality. The operations of the principle of charity may influence the diagnostic and other clinical tasks in psychiatry, when mental health professionals, for different reasons, normalize, psychologize or otherwise explain away the irrationality of their patients.[5]

In accordance with the common finding that humans reason both logically/reflectively and heuristically/speedily (Shafir & LeBoeuf, 2002), research in cognitive science distinguishes at least two types of rationality (a "dual process" view of rationality; Stanovich, 2011): Type 2 (also called "conscious," "off-line," "analytic," "explicit") and Type 1 (also called "automatic," "online," "heuristic," "tacit"). There is now a vast theoretical and empirical literature on this topic, which also includes research on social cognition (Theory of Mind [ToM]), neurocognitive abilities and IQ. Thus the "rationality performance" is positively correlated with the IQ in most, but not all, rationality measurements (Stanovich, 2011). The research on the issue of the *insight into illness* may also be included into the rationality research. This is an issue which is highly relevant for discussing the notion of psychosis. Psychodynamic theory considers poor insight as a defence mechanism, that is, a denial of being ill with the purpose of warding off, for example, depressive symptoms arising from awareness of having a chronic illness (Moore et al., 1999). In contrast, the cognitive account claims that poor insight is a "cognitive dysfunction" (Marková & Berrios, 1995), a "failure of metacognition" (David et al., 2012). Both accounts conceptualize the issue of insight in schizophrenia as a *problem of rational self-reflection*: Insight is just an instance of critical reflection on one's own psychological life. The *reflecting* self somehow notices a problem in the *reflected*, ongoing subjective life, which then may become rationally corrected. Both accounts implicitly assume that there is a clear separation between the self and the illness (between the reflecting self and the ongoing conscious life), an assumption that is highly questionable in the case of schizophrenia (Parnas & Henriksen, 2013; Henriksen & Parnas, 2014).

To sum up: In the neurocognitive studies, psychotic patients, especially those with schizophrenia, perform typically worse than their controls on many of the cognitive tests, although the differences often become washed out after controlling for differences in the IQ (e.g., Mirian et al., 2011). The magnitude, variance and consistency of these results are not sufficiently convincing to allow us to conclude that rationality, *as it is currently measured by the experimental tests of cognitive neurosciences*, is a major factor accounting for psychosis (Urfer-Parnas, Mortensen & Parnas, 2010). In other words, when talking about irrationality and psychosis, we need to turn to phenomenologically and ecologically more valid notions of rationality.

Common Sense as a Sense of Reality

Phenomenology is familiar with the two types of rationality: one, reflective, logical, and inferential, and the other, "practical rationality." But the notion of practical rationality is here different from, although somewhat overlapping, the notion of heuristic or tacit thinking of cognitive theory. Phenomenological analyses of practical rationality are derived from the analyses of *intentionality*, that is, consciousness' directedness to the world. Intentionality means that consciousness is always a consciousness of something. There are different types of intentionality: On the one hand, there is an active intentionality of perception, cognition, conation, signification, intentional feelings and so forth. This type of active intentionality may have different degrees of complexity, with different layers, where higher levels pre-suppose their foundation in the more elementary levels. For example, a cognitive judgement may be founded on the more elementary acts of perception.

The most basic, "passive" level of intentionality is the level of the so-called operative intentionality (*fungierende Intentionalität*; Husserl, 1982; Melreau-Ponty, 1945/2012), which is closely related to the basic *sense of presence*, described above as a *sense of reality*. The "reasoning" flowing from the sense of presence "is not a logic of the logicians but the logic of the world" (Tatossian, 1979, p. 12). It is a "common sense," understood here as *sensus communis*, of Antiquity. The ancient notion of *sensus communis* is useful and informative through its rich, polysemic nature: *Sensus communis* is a sixth sense, integrating our diverse perceptual modalities (intermodal integration); it is intersubjective, social sense, assuring our interpersonal understanding (social cognition), and finally, it is also related to our "inner sense" or "inner touch," that is, to the pre-reflective self-awareness. Thus common sense is not a specific-delimited and modular cognitive function but *a certain disposition towards the world* or a certain mode of being-in-the-world.

It may be further and more concretely described as a pre-reflective, pre-linguistic and pre-conceptual openness to affective salience, affordance, and proportion, a sense of adequacy and contextual relevance. It is an *attunement*, enabling us to negotiate our way in a world that is not pre-defined and static, but dynamic and constantly changing, moulded by the subject's own actions (Parnas & Bovet, 1991; Parnas, Bovet & Zahavi, 2002). "Common sense" is an *attitude* of being naturally and spontaneously immersed in the shared social world and at ease in it, and experiencing oneself, others, and the world naturally (unproblematically) through this attitude. The loss of common sense, which according to Blankenburg constitutes the core of schizophrenic autism, is dramatically described by one of his patients, Anne:

> What is it that I am missing? It is something so small, so strange, yet something so important. It is impossible to live without it. I find that I no longer have footing in the world. I have lost hold in regard to the simplest, everyday things. It seems that I lack the natural understanding for what is matter of course and obvious to others. . . .
>
> (. . .) Every person knows how to behave, to take a direction, or to think something specific . . . all these involve the rules that the person follows. . . . I am not able to recognize what these rules are. . . . I am missing the basics. (. . .) It is not knowledge, *it is prior to knowledge*. Every child knows these things.
>
> *(Blankenburg, 1971, p. 308; italics added; translation slightly modified)*

The notions of "common sense" and immediate "sense of reality" are, as mentioned, intimately interconnected. They imply a basic constitution of meaning-horizon, which articulates itself out of our embodied self-presence in a shared world. Both are pre-reflective, passive processes (involving "passive syntheses"; Husserl, 1982) that provide the foundation for the more explicit, active and thematic intentionalities, including a reflective judgment. It is likely that the psychodevelopmental notion of "basic trust" is closely related to phenomenology's "common sense" and "sense of reality."

Varieties of Irrationality

One possible way to classify irrationality for the description of psychosis is to divide it into two prototypical (and therefore overlapping) groups: (1) "propositional irrationality," which refers to all forms of psychosis that manifest themselves through the patient's verbal statements (sentences, propositions). The propositional irrationality includes all types of delusions, reporting of hallucinations or delusional explanations of abnormal experiences. (2) "Non-propositional" irrationality (or pragmatic-affective irrationality), in which psychosis primarily manifests itself through expression and behavior. All clinicians are familiar with cases of psychosis that manifests itself as a dislocation from intersubjectivity, revealing itself through affectivity, expressivity and action (e.g., catatonia, hebephrenic behavioral style). The reason for calling it as non-propositional irrationality is to indicate a significant distinction from delusionality, the latter being typically expressed in propositional statements ("I believe that . . .").

We will now have a look at two examples of non-propositional, expressive irrationality: catatonic posturing and catatonic stupor. Why do we take these phenomena as being indicative of the presence of psychosis? Typically, in such cases we do not have access to a self-report from the patient that could allow us to classify him as being delusional. Only in retrospect, the patient may, or may not, recall what went through his mind, and sometimes we learn something about, for example, his catastrophic or cosmic experiences and the associated, plainly delusional contents (e.g., that a single movement might have led to a world cataclysm). In the majority of cases we remain ignorant of the patient's experience and thought. What, then, in a confrontation with such patients, justifies the label of "psychosis"? First, there is a fundamental break of communication, and thus of intersubjectivity. Second, the patient's distorted expression is, from a phenomenological perspective, not an autonomous "external" feature but a manifestation of a certain Gestalt, jointly constituted by the patient's expression *and* inner world. What justifies the label of "psychosis" is the fact that in the catatonic expressivity we perceive an enacted understanding of the world that appears to be radically different from our own (i.e., we sense a radical dislocation from intersubjectivity).

Another variant of the "non-propositional irrationality" may manifest itself through strange action episodes, the so-called crazy actions (*Unsinnige Handlung*; Conrad, 1958; *dèlire en acte*; Minkowski, 1927), for example, sudden aimless trips, certain impulsive acts, often so trivial that they elude the clinician's attention. From a theoretical point of view, action is perhaps an even more significant manifestation of (ir)-rationality than what can be expressed through language (e.g., delusional statements). Conrad offers an example of a behavior that, in this particular case, turned out to be a forerunner of the onset of schizophrenia:

> H.K., 24, sergeant, was in a "dreadful" state of tension since the beginning of the attack on France [in 1940], in which he participated. An exceptional

> soldier, much appreciated by his superiors, full of ideals, but 'deeply' affected by several matters. . . . The dizziness of a victorious advance, punctuated with critical engagements with the enemy, was mixed up with feelings of disappointment in relation to his comrades, who could not resist the temptation of plundering; a behavior which he most deeply despised (. . .) When his troops' advance stopped in the vicinity of Paris, he took his service vehicle and, breaking the strict and explicit orders, drove with some privates under his command to Paris, in order to "draw their attention on the cultural values of the enemy." He was condemned to six weeks of prison. The psychosis broke out some months later.
>
> *(Conrad 1958, p. 35)*

Here, the gross transgression of the discipline, completely incongruent with the sergeant's former exemplary conduct, appeared in its motivation—"to approximate his soldiers to the culture of the enemy"—as completely "mad" in the eyes of his superiors[6] (Bovet & Parnas, 1993).

What is characteristic in the sergeant's acting is a peculiar dislocation from common sense, justifying the designation of "autistic activity" (Minkowski, 1927). It is not so much the problem of logic and theoretical rationality, but rather an expression of a loss of attunement to the tacit, pre-reflective, pre-conceptual, socially shared and contextually adequate "logic of the world" (common sense). His action reveals an understanding of the world that is seriously displaced from intersubjectivity (common sense). Taken in isolation, it would not suffice for the label of psychosis. Yet, this example is clinically very significant because, despite its apparent banality, it points to a lack of "common sense," a trait feature of the schizophrenia spectrum disorders, often preceding the onset of a fully articulated psychosis (Parnas et al., 2002; Parnas et al., 2011), and which, in a clinical situation, should awaken the psychiatrist's attention to a possibility of severe psychopathology.

Practical-affective irrationality may also manifest itself through a striking incongruence between the motivational/experiential content and the activity ensuing from that content:

> X, a patient diagnosed with schizotypal disorder, who later developed a frank schizophrenia, was tormented by a thought that he might have once killed a baby.[7] He spent his days walking through the city, searching inside the trash containers for a corpse of a baby. These ruminations were not clearly delusional. The patient himself considered them as "obsessions" and was very well aware that he never murdered anyone. His "obsessions" lacked a truly obsessive quality, because they did not evoke any immediate "internal resistance." However, he was unable to resist the urge to search in the city trash containers, despite the fact that he had no rational reason to expect finding a corpse exactly in those particular containers, since he had no specific idea of how or where he might have killed the baby.

In most cases of such "crazy actions," the patients' post hoc explanations are evasive, vague or strangely illogical—and only with difficulty can be "translated" into a propositional (delusional) belief format.

Another example of the "non-propositional irrationality" is a pervasive depressive condition with a profound sense of existential transformation, a sense of inability to reach out to the future, of "not being able to . . ." and pervasive guilt feelings. The guilt awareness is a very characteristic experience of the melancholic self-relation: the patient, in a certain sense, is a priori guilty. The verbally expressed, concrete remorse (e.g., "as a kid, I stole 2 dollars from my father . . .") is only a contingent thematization of the awareness of guilt.[8] Although all such features may not be quite translatable into a clearly articulated delusional format, they testify nonetheless (analogously to the catatonic expressivity) to a radically altered world- and self-understanding.

Still other "non-propositional" variants of irrationality comprise severe formal thought disorder (incoherence, neologisms), amnesia, disorientation, and global disorders of attention. They affect cognition, behavior, and communication (and hence rationality) to a degree where clinicians feel that the psychosis label is appropriate.

Delusion

Delusion is considered as a paradigmatic index of psychosis. It is today a very broad concept, referring to "false, erroneous beliefs," that is, thoughts and convictions, articulated as propositional statements (e.g., "I believe that the CIA contaminates the drinking water in order to make all males living here sexually impotent"). In its broad formulation, the delusion concept covers widely heterogeneous clinical variants from, say, a case of a demented elderly lady who hides her coffee from the house aid, because she is convinced that the aid would steal it, to a case of a schizophrenia patient who believes that others insert thoughts into his mind.

Defining psychosis through the presence of delusion (delusionality) does not solve the issue of the definition. The problem simply moves from defining irrationality of psychosis to defining the irrationality of delusion. Thus, the problem remains unsolvable because delusion, like psychosis, defies any simple definition. The common criteria (falsity, conviction, and incorrigibility) are usually ascribed to Jaspers. Yet, Jaspers (1913/1963) explicitly did not consider this triad *as defining* what delusion was (rather, he considered delusion as a non-reducible change of the structure of subjectivity). He imported his triad from the 19th-century psychiatry, and considered it as "external indicators" ("*aussere Merkmale*"), *suggesting* the presence of delusion but *not defining it*. The DSM-IV-TR goes somewhat further in its definition:

> A false personal belief based on incorrect inference about external reality and firmly sustained in spite of what almost everyone else believes and in spite of what constitutes incontrovertible proof or evidence to the contrary.
>
> *(p. 821)*

In fact, all components of this definition have been questioned (e.g., Sass, 1994; Bovet & Parnas, 1993; Spitzer, 1990; Parnas & Sass, 2008). A delusion need not to be (and sometimes is not) empirically false (e.g., delusions of jealousy may be empirically true); it may not be personal but involve other people or impersonal world affairs; it is not always about external reality (which is, as already mentioned, undefined), for it may involve body or mind as themes; it needs not to be, and frequently is not based on inferential reasoning (inference is, by the way, a pathogenetic rather than descriptive notion); nor does it need to be believed with full conviction to be clinically significant.[9] The "reality" of the DSM definition vacillates between the "objective," mind-independent (in-itself) realist version and a normative, consensual-social convention. These two kinds of reality need not to coincide. In the DSM-5, probably in response to the critique of previous DSM definitions, delusions are now defined, with impressive brevity, as "fixed beliefs that are not amenable to change in light of conflicting evidence." Apart from the likelihood that half of humanity harbors beliefs so defined, the definition is hardly useful for the training of psychiatrists or as a quick, disambiguating diagnostic reference aid.[10]

Although all delusional patients are psychotic, not all psychotic patients are delusional in the DSM/ICD sense of entertaining "false beliefs." It rarely happens that we assess, or even find it feasible or sensible to assess the empirical truth or falsity of a potentially delusional claim. Rather, as clinicians, we focus on the content's probability, plausibility, its way of presentation, other beliefs, experience and behavior. In the patient's claims and their presentation, we may sense that it is not merely a question of falsity/truth of a single claim that matters. Something more global may be at stake (e.g., something that transpires through the patient's way of arguing). This Gestalt-like whole comprises a fabric of branching, interconnected beliefs, attitudes and background assumptions, which ultimately inhere in the overall structure of subjectivity and existence. All these various contextual aspects, surrounding the focal propositional content, help the clinician to classify a given statement as an instance of delusion. Thus delusion is a certain characteristic prototype. This role of contextual aspects is illustrated by a modified example from Heinimaa (2002):

> The example takes place in Helsinki, Finland. A man seeks a psychiatric emergency and complains of anxiety and insomnia, because he knows that Russia is going to invade Finland tomorrow. It all happens at the heydays of Russian-Western relations. You, a young doctor on duty, would be liable to consider the statement as delusional (you would be more cautious in your judgment if all this happened few days after the 2008 Russian invasion of Georgia). However, if the patient turns out to be the chief of Finland's Intelligence Service, you would suspend your initial hunch and proceed with a very thorough psychiatric assessment. It turns out that the patient is

> justifying his conviction by a personal experience from the previous evening. Then, he attended a cocktail party at the Russian Embassy and there he got a very unpleasant feeling that the party had a kind of arranged, fabricated atmosphere. All people stared at him. Upon this information, you would suspect a psychotic condition preceded by a delusional mood. Finally, if the patient tells you that Russia has already invaded Finland three years ago but no one has yet noticed it, you would be liable (assuming that the patient is not sarcastic or joking) to think that the patient's "concept of invasion" (and its more encompassing framework) does not match yours, perhaps pointing to a degree of irrationality justifying the diagnosis of psychosis.

No simple definition of a propositional content is immune to the changing contexts and normative factors. It goes without saying that the difficulties confronting the definition of delusion weaken and destabilize the definitions of an entire group of psychosis-related phenomena such as self-reference, overvalued idea, paranoid ideation and magical thinking (see Jansson, *Chapter 4*).

Is Delusion a Belief?

In cognitive literature, the concept of belief is usually taken for granted, as referring to a propositional attitude in which we assume something to be true. Anthropological and linguistic research emphasizes, however, an intrinsic vagueness of the term *belief*, which appears to cover a wide variety of mental states (Needham, 1972). Thus, a more general (and perhaps more serious) problem that confronts the definition of delusion as a "false belief" is the question of whether delusion can be considered as an instance of belief or reality-assertion at all, à la "the CIA poisons the water in order to. . . ." As is well known, Jaspers and Schneider distinguished between the "true, or primary" delusions and "delusion-like ideas" (secondary delusions). It is the "delusion-like" ideas, rather than true delusions, that correspond to what the DSM and ICD manuals designate today as delusions, that is, false, erroneous judgments of some state of affairs.

Primary delusion involves a characteristic mode of experience—in which the content of any experience, for example, occurrent perception, thought, or recollection—articulates or reveals a delusional significance in a direct, unmediated ("*unmittelbar*") way. "*Unmittelbar*" (immediate) means not only temporally instantaneous, but entails also another sense, that is, "in a direct way," non-mediated by reflection or inference. The delusional meaning (e.g., of a percept) articulates itself in the perceived content like a revelation, formally similar to a strong esthetic or mystical experience (Henriksen & Parnas, 2014):

> A patient walking up the staircase to his psychiatrist's office, noticed through a window, a canvas with intense blue color, among some furniture stabled in

> the yard. Seeing the painting with its blue color, the patient became aware of being insane [an example of empirically true delusion].
>
> *(Blankenburg, 1965, p. 289; my addition in square brackets)*

This primary articulation of delusional meaning is not empathically understandable, partly because it is not mediated through the inferential reflective steps that the psychiatrist can simulate in his own mind. Primary delusion is not an inferential or empirical error, a mistaken view of reality. "To say simply that a delusion is a mistaken idea which is firmly held by the patient and which cannot be corrected gives only a superficial and incorrect answer to the problem," wrote Jaspers. It is primary in the (patho)-genetic rather than temporal sense. It points to a shattering of the basic forms of experience and hence a transformation of the patient's total awareness of reality (Jaspers 1913/1963; Schneider, 1946). What is changed is not an *opinion* about reality but the very structure of the global perspective on the world: the patient's existential-ontological framework, that is, his *sense of reality* (Bovet & Parnas, 1993; Parnas, 2004). Primary delusion cannot be considered as a knowledge statement about empirical matters in the public world (i.e., beliefs, such as "there is an Italian restaurant around the corner") but more as a quasi-metaphorical statement (Blondel, 1914; Spitzer, 1990; Parnas, 2004), expressing (pathic) *alterations in the structure of experience*, which affect the very *sense of reality*, that is, *the sense of embodied self-presence* to the shared world (i.e., the existential feelings; Ratcliffe, 2008). The ontological framework of experience is modified with the irruptions of altered articulations of space, time, causality and self-identity and so forth. For the patient, his delusional "evidence" stems primarily from a non-conceptual felt experience (an "egological experience," not unlike having a sensation of toothache); the latter being a touchstone of a private, unique and absolute (egological) sense of certitude (Müller-Suur, 1950, 1954). This certitude, even if thematically vague during the delusional mood (the nascent stages of delusion) is nonetheless overwhelming and unquestionable from the very start. *The sense of uncertainty of delusional mood is itself absolutely certain* (Müller-Suur, 1950). The certainty in schizophrenia articulates itself passively as a self-affection, self-illumination or sensation, whereas the "paranoiac" delusional certainty is "achieved," that is, it is hard earned and solidified through observation and reflection (Müller-Suur, 1950, 1954). Primary delusion cannot be challenged by a more fundamental dataset. The patients typically do not seek social validation, are indifferent to empirical proofs and only rarely act upon their delusions (Parnas, 2004). The sense of certainty (i.e., originary delusional experience) often persists, even after the patient is said to have remitted from a frankly delusional condition.

For the secondary/primary distinction of Jaspers, we have proposed other, more descriptive terms: "empirical" (secondary) vs. "autistic solipsistic" (primary) delusions[11] (Parnas, 2004). Empirical delusions display a propositional belief-structure; they concern our shared worldly framework and involve an incorrect judgment of reality, but the sense of reality remains mainly intact. These delusions typically deal with mundane affairs in which the patient is engaged and where he seeks the evidence to support his claims. An "empirical" delusional statement—such as "I know that I am persecuted by my boss"—is an epistemic statement with a structure similar to that of the statement "I know that Boston is the capital of Massachusetts."

"Autistic-solipsistic" (primary) delusions are of self-experiential origin (with an altered sense of reality) and reflect a fundamentally altered existential-ontological structure of subjectivity (Parnas, 2004). The cardinal point to realize here is that in the autistic-solipsistic delusions, reasoning processes *do not just follow from experience but are embedded in it.* They emerge from the chiasm of experience and judgement. The nature of reasoning processes (judgements) is not independent of the changes in the structure of experience. The sense of reality, which is necessarily *pre-supposed* in entertaining beliefs, may be changed or lost: "*With an altered sense of reality, patients cannot take things to be the case in the usual way, as the sense of 'is' and 'is not' has changed*" (Ratcliffe, 2008; italics added). We thus disagree with Jaspers on the issue of incomprehensibility of schizophrenia (Parnas & Sass, 2008). We may grasp (at least to a certain degree) the nature of the patient's experience upon adopting a phenomenological stance, in which we suspend our a priori, ordinary assumption (related to "principle of charity") of sharing with the patient the same "modal space" (*vide supra*). Through this kind of "radical empathy" (Ratcliffe, 2012), we attempt to make manifest what is most frequently overlooked, namely the altered *structures* of the patient's lived world, with other forms of spatiality, temporality and so forth. Thus, for the patient, his delusional evidence stems primarily from the unreflectively lived anomalous pathic experience, a source of a private (egological) conviction, which cannot be grasped within a "defective reality-testing" model (Sass, 1994). We may encounter here "a double book-keeping" (i.e., a peculiar co-existence of rationality and irrationality[12]). First-person accounts of such states suggest that the patient often feels a unique and superior access to another "true" reality, ahead of and more "sophisticated" than what is accepted as valid in the socially prevailing worldview (Saks, 2007; Parnas & Henriksen, 2013; Henriksen & Parnas, 2014).

Hallucination and Psychosis

Since Esquirol, hallucination has been defined as "perception without an object." This definition survived basically unchanged to become incorporated in the contemporary diagnostic systems, although in the DSM-5 it is defined as "perception-like" experience. The notion of hallucination was already problematized in mid-19th century at a debate of the Societé Médico-Psychologique in Paris. Three questions were discussed (Berrios, 2006): (1) Can hallucination be considered as a "normal" experience? (2) Is there a seamless continuum between sensation, image and hallucination? (3) Is the nature of hallucinations similar to that of dreams and ecstatic trance states?

In general, hallucination has been, and still is, considered mechanistically, as an abnormal signal from dysfunctional brain module(s) or neural network(s). Tamburini (1876) endorsed quite early this "signal view" of hallucination, considering it as a form of "*epilepsie sensorielle*" (quoted in Ey, 1973, p. 915). The nature of hallucination as *a species of perception* has been regularly questioned (Merleau-Ponty, 1945/2012; Ey, 1973).

Hallucinations are today claimed to occur in a substantial proportion of normal people and across a wide range of psychiatric (including non-psychotic) diagnoses (Larøi et al., 2012). These recent claims are, perhaps, mainly or in part, accounted for by methodological deficiencies (psychopathological oversimplification) of many recent studies (Stanghellini et al., 2012).

In relation to psychosis, our concern comprises two interrelated issues: First, does it make sense to consider hallucination as a unitary (homogenous) experiential phenomenon, and, second, does hallucination always signify a psychotic loss of rationality (and if so, in what way)?

It seems that the answer to both questions is negative. For example, in the visual hallucinations of a full-blown delirium tremens, the hallucinatory object is experientially given as a fully transcendent entity, characterized by "corporeality" (*Leibhaftigkeit*), and integrated in the patient's perceptual field. The patient therefore reacts as he would react to a perception. He is psychotic because his entire lived reality is altered. He has lost both a normal sense and judgment of reality. However, his hallucination remains a temporally circumscribed abnormal event, and is considered as such after recovery. Another type of organic hallucination is "eidolia," often with an intense and lively, transcendent pictorial character. However, the patient remains aware of its imaginary nature. "The pictures, however lively, remain mere images for the patient, pointing nowhere beyond themselves and without belonging to the perceived reality" (Ey, 1973, p. 334; my translation). The patient is not suffering from psychosis because "he is both aware of the perceived object and of its absence of reality" (Ey, 1973, p. 340; my translation). He remains in the intersubjective perceptual world, with intact sense and judgment of reality. Moreover, "the [morbid] experience is not a part of the historical continuity of his personality nor is it at the center of his lived situation" (Ey, 1973, p. 339; my translation).

In the auditory-verbal hallucinations (AVH) of schizophrenia, the patient is only rarely confronted with a hallucinatory object that appears as phenomenologically entirely transcendent ("external") or "objective." Nor is the experiencing of the hallucinatory object always best captured by the sensory, that is, acoustic-auditive terms. At the origin of AVH there is a progressive objectivation of the subject himself, who thereby becomes his own object. Hallucination arises from an original *pathic affection within the immanence of the patient's subjectivity*, articulated as *another presence* or a new alterity (e.g., the transition from a loss of the sense of "mineness" of thinking, through the stage of "audible thoughts," to auditory hallucinations, perhaps eventually externalized; Parnas & Sass, 2011). This sense of new alterity has typically no spatial or temporal structure characteristic of perceptual modality. There is an experience of an oppressing contiguity with the innermost sense of self: The affection happens abruptly, and its proximity bars any attempt of evasion to a protective distance. In short, hallucination is "lived as a radical, unique inversion of the subjective and the objective . . . which happens in the private intimacy of consciousness" (Ey, 1973, p. 69; my translation). As an essentially pathic event (Straus, 1935; Gennart, 2011), the original affection is undeniably real and true (as "egological" affection) from the first-person perspective. We, as psychiatrists, rephrase this experience into the third-person terms, calling it "hallucination." The patient often expresses the experience of "another presence" in the available sensory vocabulary even though his actual experience often lacks perceptual qualities (e.g., "soundless voices"; Bleuler, 1911/1950). Most often, the patient distinguishes his perceptions from hallucinations, and typically he does not expect the psychiatrist to be able to hear his "voices." Merleau-Ponty (1945/2012) said that what protects a normal man from hallucinations is an intact structure of the lived space. We can rephrase it by saying that a normal man is protected from hallucinations by his sense of reality or his (self)-presence, that is, by living pre-reflectively immersed in the shared perceptual world (in the shared modal space). Analogously to the origin of autistic-solipsistic (primary) delusions, auditory hallucinations in schizophrenia reflect a profound experiential alteration that may found another ontological framework and stance (e.g., a claim of a unique access to the deeper layers of reality). To the extent that the patient is able to keep his mundane and private frameworks adequately separated, he is in a successful position of "double book-keeping." When enacting or overwhelmed by his hallucinatory experience, the patient's sense and judgment of reality become sufficiently impaired as to qualify his condition as an instance of psychosis. In this perspective, hallucination and delusion, as well as passivity phenomena, appear to be much more closely related (Ey, 1973; Gennart, 2011) than what is commonly represented in the psychiatric literature. In the individual patient, these phenomena often substitute or complement each other.

Category and Dimension

All clinicians are familiar with "threshold cases," where it may seem arbitrary, or even impossible, to classify their patient in binary terms, either as psychotic or as non-psychotic. In the quantitative research, we find, as a rule, a dimensional trend in the distribution of empirical data,[13] and it seems that dimensional models of psychopathological data appear to be more reliable and more valid than the corresponding categorical, polythetic[14] approaches (Markon, Chmielewsky & Miller, 2011).

Many patients, especially those with schizophrenia spectrum disorders, display reality judgments or report anomalous experiences that we qualify as "subthreshold" or "psychosis-near" (Parnas, Bovet & Licht, 2005; Parnas & Sass, 2011; see Jansson, *Chapter 4*). It is important to note that an experience as such (in itself), no matter how unusual, can rarely by itself justify the label of "psychosis." Whatever affection I happen to live in my first-person perspective, it has undoubtedly a reality and truth status *as my experience*. The schizophrenia spectrum patients live a multitude of anomalous self-experiences (self-disorders), with varying degrees of felt concreteness (Parnas & Sass, 2011), yet often without any clear delusional interpretation that would involve a dislocation from the shared social framework. A thorough analysis of how different articulations of anomalous experience may relate to the concept of psychosis is beyond the scope of this chapter.

In general, as illustrated in the discussion of delusions and hallucinations, anomalous experience becomes an index of psychosis if it translates itself into judgments or behaviors that testify to a radically irrational self-understanding and understanding of the world.

Conclusions

Psychosis is a multidimensional notion designating a condition of being afflicted by a radical irrationality or a radical displacement from intersubjectivity (sociality), the latter broadly understood as a social matrix of the "we perspective." Such irrationality may manifest itself through propositional thought contents and their linguistic expressions (delusions), or it is implicit in the alterations of other anthropological dimensions, such as action, expression, affectivity and existential patterns (non-propositional irrationality).

The nature and degree of "radical irrationality" cannot be specified in advance, that is, without taking into account the contextual and normative factors. In other words, the concept of psychosis resists a simple, unequivocal definition, a difficulty that always stimulated compensatory attempts of invoking hypothetical causal mechanisms as a complement to insufficient description. I think that it is best to consider "psychosis" as a "family resemblance" construct with characteristic central prototypes and fluid boundaries. The concept of "psychotic symptoms" is not an unproblematic substitute for the notion of psychosis because psychotic symptoms are also complex, difficult to define, and their taxonomy requires careful phenomenological analyses.

The concept of psychosis, useful and perhaps indispensable from the clinical-descriptive, ethical and legal psychiatric perspectives, has, in my view, somewhat limited utility in etiological research. This is partly due to the problems of description and definition, but also because major mental disorders manifest themselves as spectra or quasi-continua, comprising psychotic and non-psychotic conditions. For example, the schizophrenia spectrum disorders (e.g., schizophrenia and schizotypal disorder) may share etiological mechanisms (Parnas et al., 2005) that, however, need not to reflect or coincide with the instances of "radical irrationality" (psychosis) *within* the spectrum. In other words, the etiological psychiatric research may benefit more from a phenomenological emphasis on the alterations of the basic structures of subjectivity (such as autism or self-disorders; Parnas, 2011; Henriksen & Parnas, 2012; Parnas & Gram Henriksen, Chapter 17) rather than on the developmentally compounded phenotypes, such as delusions, hallucinations or catatonia.

Notes

1 "Philosophical" or "continental" psychiatric phenomenlogy is of course influenced by the work of Edmund Husserl, Maurice Merleau-Ponty and Martin Heidegger. For a recent summary of this approach to psychiatry, see Parnas et al. (2013), and an excellent anthology by Broome et al. (2012).

2 Frequently proposed examples of "moments" (non-detachable parts) are color and extension. You cannot see a color without a surface and vice versa. They can only be detached in abstraction.

3 Jaspers' well-known claim that "un-understandability" implies "organic" causes is non sequitur. Claiming an organic background of un-understandability is not an analytic truth. Second, understandability is a matter of degree. Moreover, from a neuroscientific perspective, all mental phenomena are, in a sense, "organically" caused, that is, correlated with neurophysiological processes. The dichotomy between "organic" and "functional" disorders becomes increasingly blurred, and seems to be a function of technological sophistication. Biological research findings are being published on all studied psychiatric disorders.

4 This decision was taken during the construction of the DSM-III (Parnas & Bovet, in press).

5 It is quite common for relatives or close friends of the patient to explain away or psychologize away his instances of irrationality. In certain situations, for example, in certain therapeutic contexts, it may be beneficial to overlook or ignore some of pathological phenomena rather than to single them out as a problem that needs to be addressed. Some mental health professionals have a psychological difficulty with confronting madness and may be therefore excessively prone to "principle of charity."

6 What is a "crazy action" is evidently culture bound. In a contemporary Western army, the sergeant's act would not be considered as "mad."

7 Such ruminations appear sometimes to be linked to an inability to distinguish between different modes of intentionality—here, perhaps, between a remembered fantasy and a factual memory.

8 Such almost metaphysical guilt ideas may also be found in schizophrenia but are qualitatively different (for further considerations, see Bovet & Parnas, 1993; Cermolacce et al., 2003).

9 Clinically, this is a very difficult feature to assess, because patients often do not reveal their innermost convictions and often conceal their delusional ideation and/or entertain the attitude of "double book-keeping."

10 A dramatic example of the incapacity of the so-called "operational criteria" to resolve a diagnostic dispute is the case of Anders Breivik, a Norwegian mass-killer (Melle, 2013; Parnas, 2013).

11 The DSM-IV, DSM-5 and ICD-10 category of *bizarre* delusion is a *hybrid* of (1) the concept of delusion as a *false belief due to incorrect inference* (i.e., "secondary delusions") and (2) a particular delusional *content* that is considered "bizarre," and defined as "physically impossible," "totally implausible," "un-understandable" and so forth. This new category of "bizarre" delusion was probably introduced to reproduce in an "operational way" the concept of "primary delusion." However, this introduction did not contain any considerations on the nature of delusional experience and was only justified by a cursory reference to Kraepelin's remark that schizophrenic delusions often were "non-sensical" and to Jaspers' notion of "un-understandability" of primary or true delusions (Spitzer et al., 1993; for a critique, see Cermolacce et al., 2010).

12 An example, given by Bleuler (1911/1950) is of a university professor, who, after his discharge as having been "cured," dedicated a treatise to his mistress, signing it with "Lord of the Universe."

13 Dimensional transition does not rule out a more fundamental discontinuity and vice versa; that is, a categorical discontinuity does not preclude an underlying continuous transition.

14 Note that prototypical classifications have an in-built gradations of the diagnostic entities (Parnas & Bovet, in press).

References

American Psychiatric Association. (2000). *Diagnostic and statistical manual of mental disorders* (4th ed., text revision). Washington, DC: American Psychiatric Association.

American Psychiatric Association. (2013). *Diagnostic and statistical manual of mental disorders* (5th ed.). Washington, DC: American Psychiatric Association.

Bégout, B. (2005). *La découverte du quotidien*. Paris, France: Éditions Alia.

Berrios, G. (2006). *The history of mental symptoms*. Cambridge, UK: Cambridge University Press.

Blankenburg, W. (1965). Zur Differentialphänomenologie der Wahrnehmung. Eine Studie über abnormes Bedeutungserleben. *Nervenarzt, 36*, 285–298.

Blankenburg, W. (1971). *Der Verlust der natürlichen Selbstverständlichkeit. Ein Beitrag zur Psychopathologie symptomarmer Schizophrenien*. Stuttgart, Germany: Enke.

Bleuler, E. (1911/1950). Dementia Praecox oder Gruppe der Schizophrenien. In G. Aschaffenburg (Ed.), *Handbuch der Psychiatrie. Spezieller Teil, 4. Abteilung, 1. Häfte*. Leipzig: Deuticke. Trans. J. Zinkin and N. D. C. Lewis (1950), *Dementia praecox or the group of schizophrenias*. New York, NY: International University Press.

Blondel, C. (1914). *La conscience morbide. Essay de psychopathologie générale*. Paris, France: Felix Alcan.

Bovet, P., & Parnas, J. (1993). Schizophrenic delusions: A phenomenological approach. *Schizophrenia Bulletin, 19*, 579–597.

Broome, M. R., Harland, R., Owen, G. S., & Stringaris, A. (Eds.). (2012). *The Maudsley reader in phenomenological psychiatry*. Cambridge, UK: Cambridge University Press.

Cermolacce, M., Sass, L., & Parnas, J. (2010). What is bizarre in "bizarre delusions"? *Schizophrenia Bulletin, 36*, 667–697.

Clark, A. (2008). *Supersizing the mind: Embodiment, action, and cognitive extension.* Oxford, UK: Oxford University Press.

Conrad, K. (1958). *Die beginnende Schizophrenie. Versuch einer Gestaltanalyse des Wahns.* Stuttgart, Germany: Thieme.

Cuthbert, B. N., & Insel, T. R. (2010). Toward new approaches to psychotic disorders: The NIMH Research Domain Criteria project. *Schizophrenia Bulletin, 36,* 1061–1062.

Damasio, A. (1999). How the brain creates the mind. *Scientific American, 281,* 112–117.

Damasio, A. (2003). Feelings of emotion and the self. *Annals of the New York Academy of Sciences, 1001,* 253–261.

David, A. S., Bedford, N., Wiffen, B., & Gilleen, J. (2012). Failures of metacognition and lack of insight in neuropsychiatric disorders. *Philosophical Transactions of Royal Society, B367,* 1379–1390.

Davidson, D. (1974). *Inquiries into truth and interpretation.* Oxford, UK: Clarendon Press.

Ey, H. (1973). *Traité des hallucinations.* Tome I et II. Paris, France: Masson.

Fenichel, O. (1945). *The psychoanalytic theory of neurosis.* New York, NY: W. W. Norton.

Frances, A. J., & Widiger, T. (2012). Psychiatric diagnosis: Lessons from the DSM-IV past and cautions for the DSM-5 future. *Annual Review of Clinical Psychology, 8,* 109–130.

Gennart, M. (2011). *Corporéité et présence. Jalons pour une approche du corps dans la psychose.* Argenteuil, France: Le Cercle Hermeneutique.

Gigerenzer, G. (2007). *Gut feelings: The intelligence of the unconscious.* New York, NY: Viking Press.

Heidegger, M. (1953/1996). *Being and time.* Trans. J. Stambaugh. Albany, NY: State University of New York Press.

Heinimaa, M. (2002). Incomprehensibility: The role of the concept in DSM-IV definition of schizophrenic delusions. *Medicine, Health Care and Philosophy, 5,* 291–295.

Henriksen, M.G., & Parnas, J. (2012). Clinical manifestations of self-disorders and the gestalt of schizophrenia. *Schizophrenia Bulletin, 38*(4), 657–660.

Henriksen, M. G., & Parnas, J. (2014). Self-disorders and schizophrenia: A phenomenological reappraisal of poor insight and non-compliance. *Schizophrenia Bulletin,* 40, 542-547.

Henry, M. (1973). *The essence of manifestation.* Trans. G. Etzkorn. The Hague, Netherlands: Martinus Nijhoff.

Husserl, E. (1977). *Phenomenological psychology: Lectures from 1925.* Trans J. Scalon. The Hague, Netherlands: Martinus Nijhoff.

Husserl, E. (1982). *Ideas pertaining to a pure phenomenology and to a phenomenological philosophy: First book.* Trans. E. Kersten. The Hague, Netherlands: Kluwer.

Hyman, S. E. (2010). The diagnosis of mental disorders: The problem of reification. *Annual Review of Clinical Psychology, 6,* 155–179.

Insel, T. R, Cuthbert, B., Garvey, M., Heinssen, R., Kozak, M., Pine, D., et al. (2010). Research Domain Criteria (RDoC): Toward a new classification framework for research on mental disorders. *American Journal of Psychiatry, 167*(7), 748–151.

Janet, P. (1926). *De l'angoisse à l'extase.* Paris, France: Felix Alcan.

Janzen, G. (2008). *The reflexive nature of consciousness.* Philadelphia, PA: John Benjamins.

Jaspers, K. (1913/1963). *Allgemeine Psychopathologie: Ein Leitfaden für Studierende, Ärzte und Psychologen,* Berlin, Germany: Springer. Trans. J. Hoenig & M. W. Hamilton, *General psychopathology.* Chicago, IL: University of Chicago Press.

Jaspers, K. (1938). *Existenzphilosophie.* Berlin, Germany: de Gruyter.

Katschnig, H. (2010). Are psychiatrists an endangered species? Observations on internal and external challenges to the profession. *World Psychiatry, 9*, 21–28.

Kernberg, O. F. (1975). *Borderline conditions and pathological narcissism*. New York, NY: Jason Aroson.

Larøi, F., Sommer, I. E., Blom, J. D., Fernyhough, C., ffytche, D. H., Hugdahl, K., et al. (2012). The characteristic features of auditory verbal hallucinations in clinical and non-clinical groups: State-of-the-art overview and future directions. *Schizophrenia Bulletin, 38*, 724–733.

Markon, K. E., Chmielewski, M., & Miller, C. J. (2011). The reliability and validity of discrete and continuous measures of psychopathology: A quantitative review. *Psychological Review, 137*, 856–879.

Marková, I. S., & Berrios, G. E. (1995). Insight in clinical psychiatry revisited. *Comprehensive Psychiatry, 36*, 367–376.

Melle, I. (2013). The Breivik case and what psychiatrists can learn from it. *World Psychiatry, 12*, 16-21.

Merleau-Ponty, M. (1945/2012). *Phenomenology of perception*. Trans. D. A. Langes. London, UK: Routledge.

Minkowski, E. (1927). *La schizophrénie. Psychopathologie des schizoïdes et des schizophrenes*. Paris, France: Payot.

Mirian, D., Henrichs, W., & Vaz S. M. (2011). Exploring logical reasoning abilities in schizophrenia patients. *Schizophrenia Research, 127*, 178–180.

Moore, O., Cassidy, E., Carr, A., & Callaghan, E. O. (1999). Unawareness of illness and its relationship with depression and self-deception in schizophrenia. *European Psychiatry, 14*, 264–269.

Müller-Suur, H. (1950). Das Gewissheitsbewusstsein beim schizophrenen und beim paranoischen Wahnerleben. *Fortschritte der Neurologie Psychiatrie und ihrer Grenzgebiete, 18*, 44–51.

Müller-Suur, H. (1954). Die Wirksamkeit allgemeiner Sinnhorizonte im schizophrenen Wahnerleben. *Fortschritte der Neurologie Psychiatrie und ihrer Grenzgebiete, 22*, 38–44.

Needham, R. (1972). *Belief, language, and experience*. Chicago, IL: University of Chicago Press.

Nordgaard, J., Sass, L. A., & Parnas, J. (2013). The psychiatric interview: Validity, structure, and subjectivity. *European Archives of Psychiatry and Clinical Neuroscience, 263*(4), 3533–64.

Parnas, J. (2004). Belief and pathology of self-awareness: A phenomenological contribution to the classification of delusions. *Journal of Consciousness Studies, 11*, 148–161.

Parnas, J. (2011). A disappearing heritage: The clinical core of schizophrenia. *Schizophrenia Bulletin, 37*, 1121–1130.

Parnas, J. (2013). The Breivik case and "conditio psychiatrica." *World Psychiatry, 12*, 21–22.

Parnas, J., & Bovet, P. (1991). Autism in schizophrenia revisited. *Comprehensive Psychiatry, 32*, 7–21.

Parnas, J., & Bovet, P. (in press). Psychiatry made easy: Opeartion(al)ism and some of its consequences. In K. S. Kendler, & J. Parnas (Eds.), *Philosophical issues in psychiatry III: The nature and sources of historical change*. Oxford, UK: Oxford University Press.

Parnas, J., Bovet, P., & Licht, D. (2005). Cluster A personality disorders: A review (followed by peer commentaries). In M. Maj, H. Aksiskal, J. E. Mezzich, & A. Okasha (Eds.), *Personality disorders* (pp. 1–74). WPA Series: Evidence and Experience in Psychiatry. Chichester, UK: John Wiley & Sons.

Parnas, J., Bovet, P., & Zahavi, D. (2002). Schizophrenic autism: Clinical phenomenology and pathogenetic implications. *World Psychiatry, 1*, 131–136.

Parnas, J., & Henriksen, M. G. (2013). Subjectivity and schizophrenia: Another look at incomprehensibiliyu and tratment non-compliance. *Psychopathology, 46*, 320-329.

Parnas, J., Raballo, A., Handest, P., Jansson, L., Vollmer-Larsen, A., & Saebye, D. (2011). Self-experience in the early phases of schizophrenia: 5-year follow-up of the Copenhagen Prodromal Study. *World Psychiatry, 10*(3), 200–204.

Parnas, J., & Sass, L. A. (2008). Varieties of "phenomenology": On description, understanding, and explanation in psychiatry. In K. Kendler & J. Parnas (Eds.), *Philosophical issues in psychiatry: Explanation, phenomenology, and nosology* (pp. 239–277). Baltimore, MD: Johns Hopkins University Press.

Parnas, J., & Sass, L. A. (2011). The structure of self-consciousness in schizophrenia. In S. Gallagher (Ed.), *The Oxford handbook of the self* (pp. 521–546). Oxford, UK: Oxford University Press.

Parnas, J., Sass, L. A., & Zahavi, D. (2013). Rediscovering psychopathology: The epistemology and phenomenology of the psychiatric object. *Schizophrenia Bulletin, 39*, 270–277.

Parnas, J., & Zahavi, D. (2002). The role of phenomenology in psychiatric classification and diagnosis. In M. Maj, J. J. Gaebel, N. Lopez-Ibor, & N. Sartorius (Eds.), *Psychiatric diagnosis and classification* (pp. 137–162). Chichester, UK: John Wiley & Sons.

Ratcliffe, M. (2008). *Feelings of being: Phenomenology, psychiatry and the sense of reality*. Oxford, UK: Oxford University Press.

Ratcliffe, M. (2012). Phenomenology as a form of empathy. *Inquiry: An Interdisciplinary Journal of Philosophy, 55*(5), 473–495.

Saks, E. R. (2007). *The center cannot hold*. New York, NY: Hyperion.

Sass, L. (1994). *The paradoxes of delusion*. Ithaca, NY: Cornell University Press.

Schneider, K. (1946). *Klinische psychopathologie* (Clinical psychopathology). Trans. 1959. Stuttgart, Germany: Georg Thieme Verlag.

Schneider, K. (1950). *Klinische Psychopathologie*. (3. vermehrte Auflage der Beiträge zur Psychiatrie ed.) Stuttgart, Germany: Thieme. Trans. M. W. Hamilton & E. W. Anderson (1959). New York, NY: Grune & Stratton.

Shafir, E, & LeBoeuf, R. A. (2002). Rationality. *Annual Review of Psychology, 53*, 491–517.

Spitzer, M. (1990). On defining delusions. *Comprehensive Psychiatry, 31*, 377–397.

Spitzer, R., First, M., Kendler., K, & Stein, D. (1993). The reliability of three definitions of bizarre delusions. *American Journal of Psychiatry, 150*, 880–884.

Stanghellini, G., Langer, A. I., Lambrossini, A., & Cangas, A. J. (2012). Quality of hallucinatory experience: Difference between clinical and non-clinical samples. *World Psychiatry, 11*, 110–113.

Stanovich, K. E. (2011). *Rationality & the reflective mind*. Oxford, UK: Oxford University Press.

Straus, E. (1935). *Vom Sinn der Sinne. Ein Beitrag zur Grundlegung der Psychologie*. Berlin, Germany: Springer.

Tamburini, A. (1876). *Contribuzione alle fisiologie e patologie del linguaggio*. Reggio Emillia.

Tatossian, A. (1979). *Phénoménologie des psychoses*. Paris, France: Masson.

Urfer-Parnas, A., Mortensen, E.L., & Parnas, J. (2010). Core of schizophrenia: Estrangement, dementia, or neurocognitive disorder? *Psychopathology, 43*, 300–311.

World Health Organization (1992). *The ICD-10 classification of mental and behavioural disorders: Clinical descriptions and diagnostic guidelines*. Geneva, Switzerland: World Health Organization.

Zahavi, D. (2005). *Subjectivity and selfhood: Investigating the first-person perspective*. Cambridge, MA: MIT Press.

3

THE BRAIN

From Transition to First-Episode Psychosis

Renaud Jardri, Marion Plaze and Arnaud Cachia

Introduction

Psychotic symptoms (i.e., hallucinations, delusions, thought disorders) are found in a range of psychiatric and neurological conditions, including schizophrenia, schizoaffective disorders, affective disorders with psychotic features, delirium, personality disorder and substance withdrawal. The brain mechanisms of psychosis in these conditions can be difficult to evaluate since they occur sometimes as superimposed on existing abnormalities and comorbidities that characterize these disorders. A focus on first-episode psychosis (FEP) thus represents our best opportunity to observe brain mechanisms of overt psychosis, in the absence of confounds associated with treatment, longer illness duration or comorbidities.

FEP is a clinical entity that is defined as a complex array of non-specific symptoms encompassing severe delusional beliefs, frequent affective instabilities and depersonalization. FEP typically occurs during adolescence, but as previously stated, this disorder needs to be distinguished from schizophrenia, which is one of its possible evolutive forms (Insel, 2010; van Os & Kapur, 2009). Because of the considerable potential prognosis value, several studies have focused on the identification of biomarkers able to assist clinicians in diagnosing FEP and on determining when high-risk (HR) individuals might convert to psychosis (Fusar-Poli et al., 2013; Smieskova et al., 2010). Brain imaging constitutes an ideal method to reach such a goal because it is easy to implement and is frequently used at different stages of the disorder for therapeutic guidance (Linden, 2012). The growing progress in magnetic resonance imaging (MRI) technology has paved the way for the non-invasive exploration of neural structures and functions in humans.

Imaging explorations of the brain may first concern the gray matter compartment. Based on T1-weighted MRI, the local cortical volume using voxel-based morphometry (i.e., VBM; Ashburner, 2009), thickness (Fischl & Dale, 2000) or sulcation/gyrification (Mangin, Jouvent & Cachia, 2010) can be measured. The white-matter compartment can also be explored using VBM as well as diffusion MRI (dMRI), which provide microstructural measures of fractional anisotropy as well as parallel and transverse diffusivity (Pierpaoli & Basser, 1996). Indirect access to functional neuronal activity can be obtained using T2*-weighted MRI sequences, which rely on the ferromagnetic properties of hemoglobin when oxygenated or deoxygenated (e.g., blood oxygen level dependent signal, or BOLD; Logothetis et al., 2001). Finally, the molecular composition of a given voxel can be explored using MR spectroscopy. Whatever variable of interest, group analyses always require the normalization of individual brains into a common stereotactic space. The most common normalized spaces are the Talairach and the Montreal Neurological Institute (MNI) spaces.

The Neural Basis of First-Episode Psychosis

Brain imaging studies in FEP have classically involved samples of limited size because of the practical constraints associated with the recruitment, evaluation and scanning of FEP patients, (Radua et al., 2012), but small sample sizes have at times affected the reliability of the findings (Button et al., 2013). The recent development of meta-analytic tools for brain imaging data has enabled researchers to overcome such limitations. For example, a recent meta-analysis combined the findings from different MRI modalities and pooled together 43 studies comparing 965 individuals with FEP to 1,040 healthy controls (Radua et al., 2012). This multimodal meta-analysis explored the deviations in local cortical volume (VBM) and functional activation during cognitive tasks (BOLD fMRI) in FEP patients. The specific influence of age or antipsychotic medications was explored through meta-regression. Patients with FEP exhibited significant bilateral differences in cortical volume and BOLD levels in the insula, superior temporal gyri and the anterior cingulate cortex in its perigenual portion (ACC; see **Figure 3.1**).

The specific functions sustained by these brain areas are relatively complex, but the anterior insula and ACC have been demonstrated to be involved in the detection of perceptual or affective salience (Menon & Uddin, 2010), a process under dopaminergic control (Bromberg-Martin, Matsumoto & Hikosaka, 2010). ACC has regularly been found to be involved in participants with increased genetic risk for schizophrenia (Whalley et al., 2006) and during the transition to psychosis (Borgwardt et al., 2008), whereas aberrant salience has been proposed as a potential underlying mechanism for psychotic symptoms (Kapur, 2003; Speechley, Whitman & Woodward, 2010). In addition, the folding pattern of the ACC has been reported to be abnormal in FEP and HR individuals (Le Provost et al., 2003; Palaniyappan et al., 2013; Yucel et al., 2003). Because the folding pattern is determined in utero (between 10 and 15 weeks of fetal life for the ACC region) and does not change after birth (Cachia et al., 2013), the abnormal ACC folding

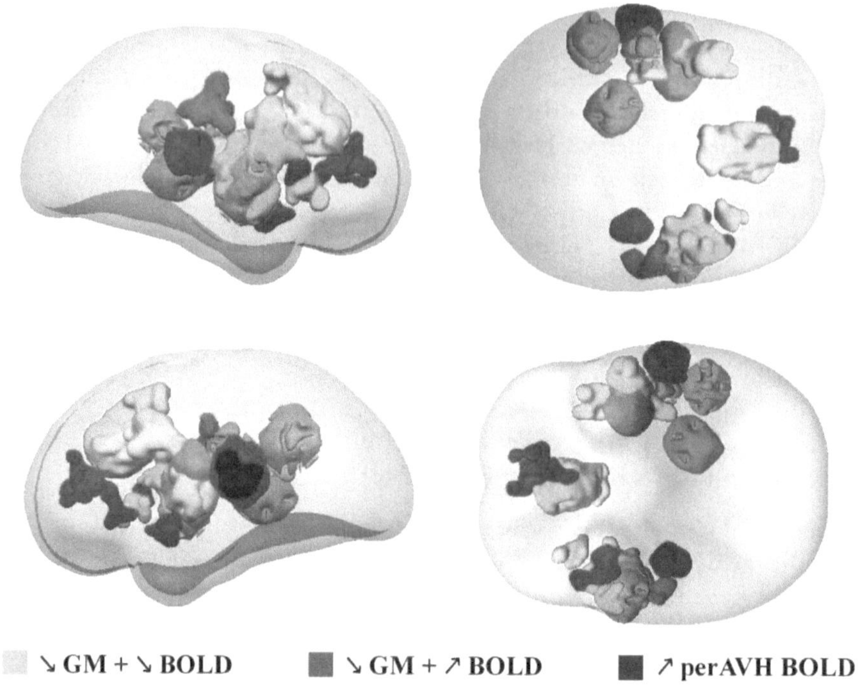

FIGURE 3.1 Structural and functional brain imaging of psychosis. Findings from the multimodal meta-analysis of first-episode psychosis by Radua et al. (2012). Brain areas exhibiting both reduced cortical thickness (GM) and decreased functional activation (BOLD) are colored light (anterior insula, dorsal anterior cingulate cortex). Brain areas exhibiting both reduced cortical thickness and increased functional activation (or reduced deactivation) are colored dark (posterior insula, ventral anterior cingulate cortex). Brain areas exhibiting overactivation during auditory-verbal hallucinations (perAVH) in patients with paranoid schizophrenia are in medium (anterior insula, Broca's convolution, hippocampal complex, superior temporal gyri, supramarginal gyri), according to the coordinate-based meta-analysis by Jardri, Pouchet, Pins & Thomas (2011).

pattern observed in FEP and HR individuals likely reflects deviations during early brain development and could therefore be used as a trait marker.

It remains difficult to exclude the possibility that some of the observed structural and functional impairments (e.g., temporal gyri and insula) may be linked to the presence of a particular symptom, independent of the underlying diagnosis. Beyond psychosis as a trait marker, specific procedures involving more acute states allow enquiries into this specific question. Functional MRI capture studies of hallucinatory experiences pertain to this second category. In such studies, periods "with" and periods "without" hallucinations are compared during scanning. A recent coordinate-based meta-analysis pooling fMRI and PET capture studies of auditory-verbal hallucinations in schizophrenia patients (Jardri, Pouchet, Pins & Thomas, 2011) indicated a large-scale brain network that displays partial overlap with the previously mentioned structural-functional changes observed in FEP (see **Figure 3.1**). Interestingly, the findings from this meta-analysis from Jardri and colleagues (2011) are comparable to the per-hallucinatory activations observed in 20 drug-näive adolescents with FEP (Jardri et al., 2013). Furthermore, some observed brain impairments may be related not only to the symptoms per se (Cachia et al., 2008) but also to their phenomenology (i.e., their detailed descriptive features), as demonstrated in patients with inner versus outer space auditory hallucinations (Plaze et al., 2011) and in patients with only auditory hallucinations versus audio-visual hallucinations (Amad et al., 2014). In addition, the presence of neurological soft signs (NSS) may contribute, at least in part, to some of the structural impairment reported in FEP patients (Gay et al., 2013). Of note, NSS dimensions (i.e., motor coordination, motor integration and sensory integration) have been demonstrated to correlate with the morphology of various cortical areas. Such findings further support the general idea that in addition to the core structural brain deficits in psychosis, the range of possible symptom manifestations relates to distinct structural correlates (Koutsouleris et al., 2008).

Brain Vulnerability and Protective Factors for Psychosis

Crucially, brain imaging allows the differentiation between endogenous and exogenous factors that influence FEP occurrence and temporal evolution. This is particularly the case for supposedly neuroprotective factors, such as antipsychotic medications, or precipitating factors, such as stress or cannabis. Urbanicity is another candidate suggested to be a risk factor for schizophrenia (van Os, Rutten & Poulton, 2008), and with a potential influence on ACC volume (Tost & Meyer-Lindenberg, 2012). Others report that carriers of a genetic polymorphism of the serotonin transporter (5-HTTLPR) exhibit significant changes in functional connectivity between the ACC and amygdala, and in the context of environmental adversity (Pezawas et al., 2005). Such changes in functional connectivity measurable with fMRI may suggest an increased vulnerability to stress due to a gene-environment interaction. Another example of the potential influence of exogenous factors on FEP occurrence is toxic exposure. Indeed, chronic cannabis consumption has been demonstrated to be associated with the thickening of the amygdalar-hippocampal complex (Yucel et al., 2008), a structure also known to be involved in psychosis (Allen et al., 2012).

What about the measurable brain effects of antipsychotic medications in FEP? A longitudinal study of 211 FEP patients from the *Iowa Longitudinal Study* who underwent repeated structural MRI scanning beginning soon after illness onset (scanned on average 3 times over 7.2 years) evaluated the relative contributions of illness duration, antipsychotic treatment, illness severity and substance abuse on brain volume change (Ho et al., 2011). The longest follow-up period correlated with smaller brain tissue volumes and larger cerebrospinal fluid volumes. A greater duration of antipsychotic treatment was associated with brain tissue reduction after controlling for the effects of the other three predictors. In addition, a greater dose of antipsychotic treatment was associated with smaller gray matter volumes. Progressive decreases in white-matter volume were most evident among patients who received a greater dose of antipsychotic treatment. Finally, the results showed that illness severity had relatively modest correlations with tissue volume reduction, and that alcohol/illicit drug misuse had no significant associations when the effects of the other variables were adjusted. In support for Ho and colleague's findings, a recent meta-regression from Radua and colleagues also indicated that treated patients exhibited the most important structural changes in the insula and the ACC (Radua et al., 2012).

Importantly, the previous analyses did not distinguish between first- and second-generation antipsychotics and did not allow for the interpretation of potential confounding factors, such as the use of a larger dosage in the more severe forms of FEP, or for FEP that is already resistant to the first-generation drugs. A recent fMRI study conducted in 34 patients with FEP before/after introducing a second-generation antipsychotic indicated a concomitant reduction in resting-state functional connectivity and increase in parietal-frontal synchrony that were correlated with symptomatic reduction (Lui et al., 2010). Overall, this sensitivity of brain imaging to the pharmacological effects of antipsychotics has been confirmed by studies coupling pharmacogenetics with fMRI to examine individual responses to treatment (Bertolino et al., 2004). However, the interpretation of the antipsychotic effects on the brain of FEP patients is not straightforward because it remains difficult to disentangle physiological effects from artifact effects on the T1 and T2* MRI signals.

Distinction Between FEP and Chronic Schizophrenia

Another crucial aspect concerns the differences and similarities that may exist between the neural bases of FEP (i.e., an episode that may resolve and have several different evolutions) and schizophrenia (i.e., a chronic disorder). A recent multimodal meta-analysis compared the VBM data of 1,999 patients suffering from schizophrenia and 2,180 healthy controls, and the dMRI data of 699 patients and 681 controls (Bora et al., 2011). A significant bilateral reduction in local cortical volume was observed in the schizophrenia patients at the level of the insula, superior temporal gyri, thalami and the ACC, in both its dorsal and rostral portions. A significant reduction in white-matter fractional anisotropy[1] in patients was also observed within the genu of the corpus callosum, the cingulum, the inferior longitudinal fasciculus and the inferior fronto-occipital fasciculus as well as in thalamic radiations. Male gender, illness duration and the presence of negative symptoms were found associated with a greater loss of gray matter, but only chronicity appeared associated with an increased defect of the white-matter compartment.

The existence of strong overlaps between these findings in schizophrenia and those obtained in FEP patients suggest two main points: First, a dimensional approach (i.e., independent of the underlying diagnosis) may help to delimit specific pathophysiological mechanisms within broader heterogeneous disorders, such as FEP or schizophrenia. This is particularly the case for auditory-verbal hallucinations (Allen et al., 2012). Second, beyond cross-sectional measures such as those synthesized by the previously cited meta-analyses, some studies have focused on the patterns of brain change over time in individuals in the earliest stages of psychosis. Takahashi and collaborators demonstrated that gray matter reductions within the insular cortex precede FEP occurrence and may indicate a pre-existing vulnerability for psychosis or the first stages of a pathological process in high-risk individuals who later develop FEP compared with those who do not (Takahashi et al., 2009). By contrast, using MR-spectroscopy, other authors have demonstrated that such frontal-temporal abnormalities occurred during the transition phase to psychosis (Brugger et al., 2011). These data directly question the potential clinical relevance of predictive brain imaging.

Can Brain Imaging Predict the Transition to Psychosis in High Individuals at High Risk?

Most of the brain imaging studies reviewed above rely mostly on univariate statistical analyses, but alternative methods have recently emerged which allow the identification of the finest level of impairments such as distributed functional or structural patterns across the entire brain or within specific regions of interests. The statistical gain is so high that inference at the subject level becomes possible (Pettersson-Yeo et al., in press). These multivariate methods derived from machine learning (e.g., *linear support vector machine*) allow the classification of a given subject based on a structural or functional MRI recording and have been called "(f)MRI classifiers" (Lemm et al., 2011). After adequate training, such classifiers may be used as diagnostic, prognostic or predictive tools (cf. **Figure 3.2a**; e.g., Rish et al., 2013). Few applications have been developed for the detection of high-risk individuals, or patients, or for the prediction of the response to pharmacological or psychotherapeutic treatments (Orru, Pettersson-Yeo, Marquand, Sartori & Mechelli, 2012). Detection algorithms have been applied in individuals at high risk of psychosis and they were shown to be able to distinguish subsequent converters from non-converters, based on local cortical volume measures (Koutsouleris et al., 2009; Sun et al., 2009) or functional patterns during emotional tasks (Modinos et al., 2012). As an example, classifier findings from Koutsouleris et al. are provided in **Figure 3.2b**.

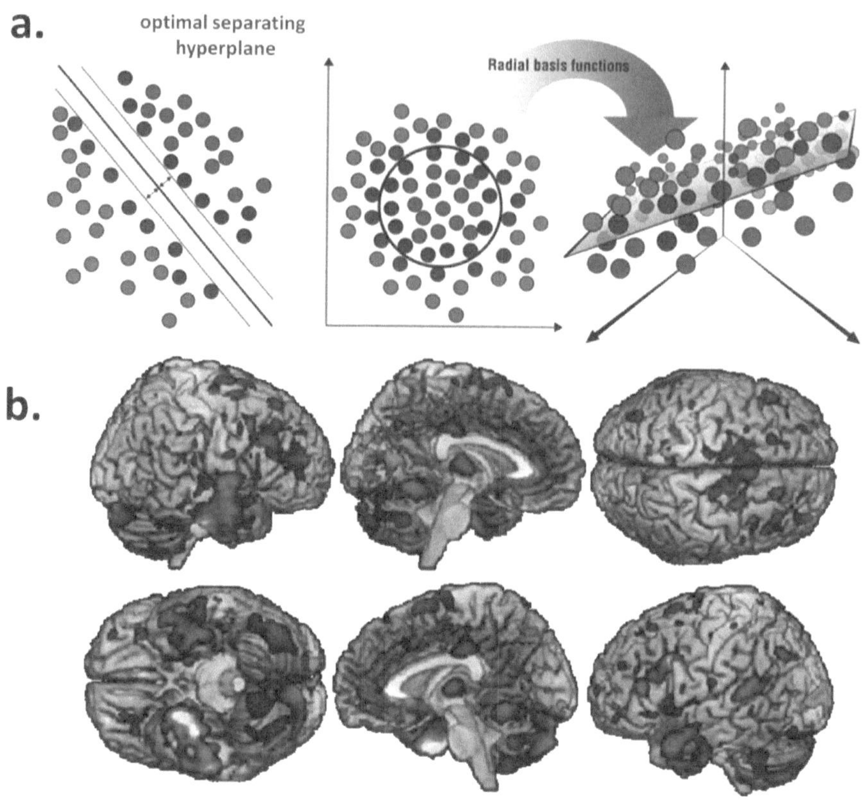

FIGURE 3.2a and b Brain imaging of the transition to psychosis. (a) The principles of a MRI classifier. (Left) Classifiers allow the analysis of MRI data at the individual level and the application of binary classification questions such as "Is this subject a converter or a non-converter?" By considering two populations that need to be dissociated (light and dark gray shapes), a hyperplane can be defined that optimally separates the light and dark gray data. For clarity, this hyperplane is depicted in two dimensions but may be generalized to a multidimensional space. After training the classifier, validation on a second independent sample provides the classifier performances (accuracy, sensitivity, and specificity; right panel). When the relationship between the data and their class labels is nonlinear (dark circle), the use of radial basis functions can map the data into a high-dimensional space where the groups can be separated by means of linear classifiers. (b) Discriminative voxels distinguish at-risk individuals with disease transition (n = 15) from at-risk individuals without disease transition (n = 18) based on their structural MRI. Voxels represent areas that exhibit a significant increase in cortical thickness, whereas blue voxels exhibit a significant reduction in cortical thickness with the occurrence of a FEP. This binary classifier presents an 83% sensitivity and a 80% specificity. These data are adapted from Koutsouleris et al. (2009).

Conclusion

Overall, structural, functional or molecular brain imaging tools provide relevant pathophysiological tracks to understand FEP, far beyond the image of a reductionist localizationism. This chapter mainly reviewed MRI data of psychosis, but readers should remain aware that complementary modalities, such as receptor imaging studies or EEG/MEG, can also provide crucial and complementary information for a broader overview of brain processes of psychosis, although this was judged to be beyond the scope of this review. The exact role of brain imaging in assisting clinicians in the decision-making process, therapy and follow-up will have to be defined and adequately developed within the medical toolbox to significantly improve the healthcare quality for individuals with psychosis.

Note

1 Fractional Anisotropy (FA) is a scalar value between 0 and 1 quantifying the diffusion process within the voxel and providing information regarding the local microstructure of the tissue.

References

Allen, P., Modinos, G., Hubl, D., Shields, G., Cachia, A., Jardri, R., et al. (2012). Neuroimaging auditory hallucinations in schizophrenia: From neuroanatomy to neurochemistry and beyond. *Schizophrenia Bulletin, 38*(4), 695–703.

Amad, A., Cachia, A., Gorwood, P., Pins, D., Delmaire, C., Rolland, B., et al. (2014). The multimodal connectivity of the hippocampal complex in auditory and visual hallucinations. *Molecular Psychiatry, 19*(2), 184–191.

Ashburner, J. (2009). Computational anatomy with the SPM software. *Magnetic Resonance Imaging, 27*(8), 1163–1174.

Bertolino, A., Caforio, G., Blasi, G., De Candia, M., Latorre, V., Petruzzella, V., et al. (2004). Interaction of COMT (Val(108/158)Met) genotype and olanzapine treatment on prefrontal cortical function in patients with schizophrenia. *American Journal Psychiatry, 161*(10), 1798–1805.

Bora, E., Fornito, A., Radua, J., Walterfang, M., Seal, M., Wood, S.J., et al. (2011). Neuroanatomical abnormalities in schizophrenia: A multimodal voxelwise meta-analysis and meta-regression analysis. *Schizophrenia Research, 127*(1/3), 46–57.

Borgwardt, S.J., McGuire, P., Fusar-Poli, P., Radue, E.W., & Riecher-Rossler, A. (2008). Anterior cingulate pathology in the prodromal stage of schizophrenia. *Neuroimage, 39*(2), 553–554.

Bromberg-Martin, E.S., Matsumoto, M., & Hikosaka, O. (2010). Dopamine in motivational control: Rewarding, aversive, and alerting. *Neuron, 68*(5), 815–834.

Brugger, S., Davis, J.M., Leucht, S., & Stone, J.M. (2011). Proton magnetic resonance spectroscopy and illness stage in schizophrenia—A systematic review and meta-analysis. *Biological Psychiatry, 69*(5), 495–503.

Button, K.S., Ioannidis, J.P., Mokrysz, C., Nosek, B.A., Flint, J., Robinson, E.S., & Munafo, M.R. (2013). Power failure: Why small sample size undermines the reliability of neuroscience. *National Revew of Neuroscience, 14*(5), 365–376.

Cachia, A., Borst, G., Vidal, J., Fischer, C., Pineau, A., Mangin, J.F., & Houde, O. (2013). The shape of the AACC contributes to cognitive control efficiency in preschoolers. *Journal of Cognitive Neuroscience, 26*(1), 96–106.

Cachia, A., Paillere-Martinot, M.L., Galinowski, A., Januel, D., de Beaurepaire, R., Bellivier, F., et al. (2008). Cortical folding abnormalities in schizophrenia patients with resistant auditory hallucinations. *Neuroimage, 39*(3), 927–935.

Fischl, B., & Dale, A. M. (2000). Measuring the thickness of the human cerebral cortex from magnetic resonance images. *Proceedings of the National Academy of Science, USA, 97*(20), 11050–11055.

Fusar-Poli, P., Borgwardt, S., Bechdolf, A., Addington, J., Riecher-Rossler, A., Schultze-Lutter, F., Keshavan, M., et al. (2013). The psychosis high-risk state: A comprehensive state-of-the-art review. *JAMA Psychiatry, 70*(1), 107–120.

Gay, O., Plaze, M., Oppenheim, C., Mouchet-Mages, S., Gaillard, R., Olie, J.P., et al. (2013). Cortex morphology in first-episode psychosis patients with neurological soft signs. *Schizophrenia Bulletin, 39*(4), 820–829.

Ho, B. C., Andreasen, N.C., Ziebell, S., Pierson, R., & Magnotta, V. (2011). Long-term antipsychotic treatment and brain volumes: A longitudinal study of first-episode schizophrenia. *Archives of General Psychiatry, 68*(2), 128–137.

Insel, T.R. (2010). Rethinking schizophrenia. *Nature, 468*(7321), 187–193.

Jardri, R., Pouchet, A., Pins, D., & Thomas, P. (2011). Cortical activations during auditory-verbal hallucinations in schizophrenia: A coordinate-based meta-analysis. *Americal Jouranl of Psychiatry, 168*(1), 73–81.

Jardri, R., Thomas, P., Delmaire, C., Delion, P., & Pins, D. (2013). Neurodynamical organization of modality-dependent hallucinations. *Cerebral Cortex, 23*(5), 1108–1117.

Kapur, S. (2003). Psychosis as a state of aberrant salience: A framework linking biology, phenomenology, and pharmacology in schizophrenia. *American Journal of Psychiatry, 160*(1), 13–23.

Koutsouleris, N., Gaser, C., Jager, M., Bottlender, R., Frodl, T., Holzinger, S., Schmitt, G.J., et al. (2008). Structural correlates of psychopathological symptom dimensions in schizophrenia: A voxel-based morphometric study. *Neuroimage, 39*(4), 1600–1612.

Koutsouleris, N., Meisenzahl, E.M., Davatzikos, C., Bottlender, R., Frodl, T., Scheuerecker, J., et al. (2009). Use of neuroanatomical pattern classification to identify subjects in at-risk mental states of psychosis and predict disease transition. *Archives of General Psychiatry, 66*(7), 700–712.

Le Provost, J.B., Bartres-Faz, D., Paillere-Martinot, M.L., Artiges, E., Pappata, S., Recasens, C., et al. (2003). Paracingulate sulcus morphology in men with early-onset schizophrenia. *British Journal of Psychiatry, 182*, 228–232.

Lemm, S., Blankertz, B., Dickhaus, T., & Muller, K.R. (2011). Introduction to machine learning for brain imaging. *Neuroimage, 56*(2), 387–399.

Linden, D.E. (2012). The challenges and promise of neuroimaging in psychiatry. *Neuron, 73*(1), 8–22.

Logothetis, N.K., Pauls, J., Augath, M., Trinath, T., & Oeltermann, A. (2001). Neurophysiological investigation of the basis of the fMRI signal. *Nature, 412*(6843), 150–157.

Lui, S., Li, T., Deng, W., Jiang, L., Wu, Q., Tang, H., Yue, Q., et al. (2010). Short-term effects of antipsychotic treatment on cerebral function in drug-naive first-episode schizophrenia

revealed by "resting state" functional magnetic resonance imaging. *Archive of General Psychiatry, 67*(8), 783–792.
Mangin, J.F., Jouvent, E., & Cachia, A. (2010). In-vivo measurement of cortical morphology: Means and meanings. *Current Opinion in Neurology, 23*(4), 359–367.
Menon, V., & Uddin, L.Q. (2010). Saliency, switching, attention and control: A network model of insula function. *Brain Structure and Function, 214*(5/6), 655–667.
Modinos, G., Pettersson-Yeo, W., Allen, P., McGuire, P.K., Aleman, A., & Mechelli, A. (2012). Multivariate pattern classification reveals differential brain activation during emotional processing in individuals with psychosis proneness. *Neuroimage, 59*(3), 3033–3041.
Orru, G., Pettersson-Yeo, W., Marquand, A.F., Sartori, G., & Mechelli, A. (2012). Using support vector machine to identify imaging biomarkers of neurological and psychiatric disease: A critical review. *Neuroscience & Biobehavioural Review, 36*(4), 1140–1152.
Palaniyappan, L., Marques, T.R., Taylor, H., Handley, R., Mondelli, V., Bonaccorso, S., et al. (2013). Cortical folding defects as markers of poor treatment response in first-episode psychosis. *JAMA Psychiatry, 70*(10), 1031–1040.
Pettersson-Yeo, W., Benetti, S., Marquand, A.F., Dell'acqua, F., Williams, S.C., Allen, P., et al. (in press). Using genetic, cognitive and multi-modal neuroimaging data to identify ultra-high-risk and first-episode psychosis at the individual level. *Psychological Medicine.*
Pezawas, L., Meyer-Lindenberg, A., Drabant, E.M., Verchinski, B.A., Munoz, K.E., Kolachana, B.S., et al. (2005). 5-HTTLPR polymorphism impacts human cingulate-amygdala interactions: A genetic susceptibility mechanism for depression. *Nature Neuroscience, 8*(6), 828–834.
Pierpaoli, C., & Basser, P.J. (1996). Toward a quantitative assessment of diffusion anisotropy. *Magnetic Resonance Medicine, 36*(6), 893–906.
Plaze, M., Paillere-Martinot, M.L., Penttila, J., Januel, D., de Beaurepaire, R., Bellivier, F., et al. (2011). "Where do auditory hallucinations come from?"—A brain morphometry study of schizophrenia patients with inner or outer space hallucinations. *Schizophrenia Bulletin, 37*(1), 212–221.
Radua, J., Borgwardt, S., Crescini, A., Mataix-Cols, D., Meyer-Lindenberg, A., McGuire, P.K., & Fusar-Poli, P. (2012). Multimodal meta-analysis of structural and functional brain changes in first episode psychosis and the effects of antipsychotic medication. *Neuroscience & Biobehavioural Review, 36*(10), 2325–2333.
Rish, I., Cecchi, G., Thyreau, B., Thirion, B., Plaze, M., Paillere-Martinot, M. L et al. (2013). Schizophrenia as a network disease: Disruption of emergent brain function in patients with auditory hallucinations. *PLoS One, 8*(1), e50625.
Smieskova, R., Fusar-Poli, P., Allen, P., Bendfeldt, K., Stieglitz, R.D., Drewe, J., et al. (2010). Neuroimaging predictors of transition to psychosis—A systematic review and meta-analysis. *Neuroscience & Biobehavioural Review, 34*(8), 1207–1222.
Speechley, W.J., Whitman, J.C., & Woodward, T.S. (2010). The contribution of hypersalience to the "jumping to conclusions" bias associated with delusions in schizophrenia. *Journal Psychiatry Neuroscience, 35*(1), 7–17.
Sun, D., van Erp, T.G., Thompson, P.M., Bearden, C.E., Daley, M., Kushan, L., et al. (2009). Elucidating a magnetic resonance imaging-based neuroanatomic biomarker for psychosis: Classification analysis using probabilistic brain atlas and machine learning algorithms. *Biological Psychiatry, 66*(11), 1055–1060.
Takahashi, T., Wood, S.J., Yung, A.R., Phillips, L.J., Soulsby, B., McGorry, P.D., et al. (2009). Insular cortex gray matter changes in individuals at ultra-high-risk of developing psychosis. *Schizophrenia Research, 111*(1/3), 94–102.

Tost, H., & Meyer-Lindenberg, A. (2012). Puzzling over schizophrenia: Schizophrenia, social environment and the brain. *Nature Medicine, 18*(2), 211–213.

van Os, J., & Kapur, S. (2009). Schizophrenia. *Lancet, 374*(9690), 635–645.

van Os, J., Rutten, B.P., & Poulton, R. (2008). Gene-environment interactions in schizophrenia: Review of epidemiological findings and future directions. *Schizophrenia Bulletin, 34*(6), 1066–1082.

Whalley, H.C., Simonotto, E., Moorhead, W., McIntosh, A., Marshall, I., Ebmeier, K.P., et al. (2006). Functional imaging as a predictor of schizophrenia. *Biological Psychiatry, 60*(5), 454–462.

Yucel, M., Solowij, N., Respondek, C., Whittle, S., Fornito, A., Pantelis, C., & Lubman, D.I. (2008). Regional brain abnormalities associated with long-term heavy cannabis use. *Archices of General Psychiatry, 65*(6), 694–701.

Yucel, M., Wood, S.J., Phillips, L.J., Stuart, G.W., Smith, D.J., Yung, A., et al. (2003). Morphology of the anterior cingulate cortex in young men at ultra-high risk of developing a psychotic illness. *British Journal of Psychiatry, 182*, 518–524.

4

NEAR-PSYCHOTIC PHENOMENA IN A CLINICAL CONTEXT

Lennart Jansson

Introduction

Fulminant psychosis is generally recognized in clinical practice, whereas inconspicuous borderline phenomena often cause much more difficulty for the clinician. In the borderland of psychosis we meet a number of phenomena designated as "near-psychotic" or "psychotic-like." Some of these have clear state or occurrent character, others a more habitual or dispositional character (Parnas, Licht & Bovet, 2005a). The definition of "near-psychotic" is directly dependent on the notion of psychosis. In a clinical context, psychosis often refers to an explicit dislocation of reflective propositional "*theoretical rationality*" (Parnas, Nordgaard & Varga, 2010; see also Parnas, *Chapter 2*) presenting as delusions. For practical clinical purposes, near-psychotic symptoms (also known as attenuated psychotic symptoms or psychosis-like experiences, or PLEs) may be seen as phenomena in which the psychotic conviction is less intense and which are formed or elaborated to a lesser extent, or which can be seen as transitory psychotic symptoms.

Psychometric attempts have been made to define the border of psychosis by a simple score. In the CAARMS instrument (Yung et al., 2006) for the assessment of individuals at ultra high risk of psychosis, the risk can be defined as a global rating score of between 3 and 5 on the Unusual Thought Content subscale. The SIPS (McGlashan et al., 2001) also attempts to define near-psychotic symptoms psychometrically. However, such attempts ignore the need for a global contextual assessment of psychosis and often lead to misjudgment. In the DSM-5, some criteria for the diagnosis of "attenuated psychosis syndrome" have been included in the section *Conditions for Further Study*. The categories of symptoms are: delusions, hallucinations, and disorganized speech "in attenuated form, with relatively intact reality testing."

In a broader sense, psychosis also refers to a dislocation of implicit "*practical rationality*" (Parnas et al., 2010; Parnas, *Chapter 2*) revealed through affectivity, expressivity and action as seen in catatonia and in hebephrenic behavioral style. Here, it is more difficult to determine the border of psychosis and it is often ignored in clinical practice, or taken for personality disorder or conduct disorder. Similarly, affective psychoses without "crystallized" hallucinations and delusions are regularly ignored. Rating scales are of little use in examining these areas of psychosis. Psychosis affects the patient's views and attitudes in a global way, as well as his or her affects and behavior which necessitate a global Gestalt assessment of psychosis (see Parnas, *Chapter 2*).

In this chapter we shall examine near-psychotic phenomena like paranoid ideas, overvalued ideas, self-reference, pseudo-obsessions, magical thinking and micro-psychoses, although the list is by no means exhaustive and other phenomena exist.

Near-psychotic phenomena within the schizophrenia spectrum emerge directly from the specific schizophrenic *structure of experience*, that is, they have a solipsistic-autistic character (cf. the schizophrenic delusions; Parnas et al., 2010) and often lack a salient theme. On the other hand, near-psychotic symptoms of other mental disorders will bear the distinct thematic impress of the underlying psychopathological *theme* (e.g., guilt in depression, persecution in delusional disorder). Near-psychotic phenomena are found in the borderland of all categories of psychosis. They appear as trait phenomena in schizotypy, in prodromal and residual phases of schizophrenia as well as in abortive cases, and in affective, organic and toxic states.

Disorders of self-awareness, or self-disorders, have been regarded as constitutive features of schizophrenia for more than a century. These refer to non-psychotic subjective anomalies of self-experience, for example, a profound feeling of emptiness and loss of identity (diminished sense of basic self), or experiencing one's own acts anonymously as from a distance (loss of first-person perspective). These can be collected in a semi-structured psychometric instrument, EASE (Parnas et al., 2005b; see also Parnas & Gram Henriksen, *Chapter 17*). Basic symptoms are subtle subjective experiences that include a great number of the self-disorders but also disorders in the areas of perception (e.g., micropsia), vegetative (e.g., fatigue) and dynamic functions (e.g., impaired tolerance to stress; also see the BSABS instrument, Gross et al., 2008, and the SPI-A instrument, Schultze-Lutter et al., 2007). Self-disorders form the specific structure of psychotic symptoms in schizophrenia. Transition sequences from such non-psychotic experiences through intermediate phenomena into the manifest psychotic first-rank symptoms have been established empirically (Klosterkötter, 1992; also see below). Near-psychotic phenomena can also be experienced in first degree relatives of patients with schizophrenia. Their prevalence in other non-clinical populations, on the other hand, is rather controversial. Some non-psychotic symptoms may be mistaken for psychotic phenomena.

Self-Reference

Self-reference is the experience of people, objects, or events having a direct link to, or personal significance for, the subject. This phenomenon may have a pure, non-psychotic, as-if character, but it may even appear in (near-)psychotic varieties.

Within the schizophrenia spectrum we find the so-called primary self-reference, a state-like athematic experience of an immediate link, not psychologically explicable, between the patient and other people or external events. This experience is considered as an aspect of (quasi)*solipsism*, a position in which the patient feels himself as if being a unique subject in the world, literally or in the sense of centrality (Parnas et al., 2005b). This kind of experience is often linked with transitivistic experience as if people looking at the patient are seeing through him. Non-psychotic self-reference forms one of the criteria of schizotypal personality disorder in the DSM-5.

> *She felt that everybody was looking at her for no reason, or as if she were looking strange in some way, e.g. being 12 feet tall.*
>
> *Having stopped playing the clarinet, he was surprised to read in the newspaper that young people no longer play musical instruments, as if there was some kind of connection with him.*

A different kind of self-reference is seen in initial paranoid schizophrenia as a state phenomenon. Conrad has performed a thorough analysis of the psychopathological process (Conrad, 1958; Broome et al., 2012). In the prodromal phase of the illness, the patient experiences a critical tension, for example, between external obstacles and personal wishes, leading to what Conrad names "trema," which is Greek for stage fright, the "feverish feeling of standing in the spotlight as actors and virtuosi do in real life, and the examinee in a figurative sense."

From this state of mind a referential psychosis will then evolve. Many different contextual meanings may be associated with every perceptual object; for example, trees may mean forestry and in a different context something mysterious or threatening. However, in this phase of initial schizophrenia we find dissolution of the awareness of meaning of such objects resulting in idiosyncratic, referential attribution of meaning, the *delusional perception*:

> *Conrad (1958) describes a case at a field hospital where a soldier was asked to lie down on the couch. Watching the blood stains on the doctor's white coat he was convinced that he was about to be butchered. Blood stains may mean blood drawing but also slaughtering. The patient did not perceive the blood stains in the actual hospital context.*

In delusional perception, a Schneiderian first-rank symptom of schizophrenia, objects attain a personal referential meaning for the patient, although the sensorial perception of the object itself remains unaffected. In the above case, the psychotic theme was persecution, but psychotic self-reference in schizophrenia patients is often associated with grandiosity. For example, one patient believed that everybody was talking about the size of his penis and was sexually attracted by him.

Self-reference in other psychiatric states bears thematic impressions of the underlying state in question: In depression, the referential themes are inferiority, insufficiency, guilt and so forth. The patient experiences that other people are looking at her in a critical, reproaching way. In psychotic depression the patient may believe that she is responsible for her fellow patients' suffering. The manic self-reference will be about other people's admiration, attraction, or expectation of expansive actions. The paranoid variety will have a persecutory theme:

> *A 40-year-old man had the impression that his colleagues were having a grudge against him, showing him an angry attitude and avoiding him. One day he overheard one of them saying in the telephone: "Things are going bad here," to his mind a reference to him.*

Kretschmer (1974) described self-referent psychoses emerging in sensitive personalities with preservation of their personality and a tendency towards remission and thus without indication of a schizophrenic process.

A different non-psychotic form of self-reference with a critical theme may be seen in self-insecure individuals performing in the presence of other people. All these forms of self-reference may be found in schizophrenia, too, but the primary type is seen exclusively here.

Paranoid Ideas

Paranoid ideas comprise a number of not-yet-psychotic phenomena characterized by intense suspiciousness, watchfulness and vague ideas of being persecuted or monitored. Usually, there is no thematization but just some vague ideas of persecution. The patient may be afraid of being assaulted and avoid walking alone in the street or answering the door. Experiences of monitoring do not require—as in self-reference—an object seeming to be directed towards the patient. The patient may just feel as if someone somewhere, e.g., across the street, is watching him, or as if a camera or microphone is hidden somewhere in the room.

A particular *gullible-suspicious paradox* has been described by Meehl (1964, p. 51), in his checklist of schizotypic signs, as

> a peculiar mixture of oversensitivity, suspiciousness or mistrust in some situations with a naive and childlike gullibility such that he is readily "kidded," "taken in," or made the butt of a practical joke or of conversational "stringing along" which would be obvious to most people of his intelligence and social experience.

This paradox should be regarded as a reflection of loss of common sense, by which the patient has difficulty in finding the proper level of confidence.

Delusional Mood

Delusional mood is an ominous feeling of an imminent danger not yet thematized and therefore not yet having the character of delusion. As the psychosis is manifesting itself, the experience undergoes thematization and transformation into delusion. Delusional mood in initial schizophrenia has been analyzed by Conrad (Conrad, 1958; Broome et al., 2012). He presents the case of Rainer, a soldier in the German army during World War II, as an example of delusional mood transforming into self-referent and persecutory psychosis:

> *For some time he had been feeling that there was something in the air. Whatever it was, he could not say; perhaps there was a special assignment ahead. "Rumors" began to go that as the only one in the camp he would be promoted troop leader. It was "rumored" by underhand means. There was no mention of names, but it seemed clear that he was the one they were meaning. Then everybody became very hostile or at least envious towards him.*
>
> *(Conrad 1958, pp. 8–9; my translation)*

One special subtype of delusional mood is the *passivity mood*: a diffuse feeling or mood of being somehow in a passive, dangerously exposed position, at the mercy of the world, in an unspecified and non-concretized manner (Parnas et al., 2005b). The passivity mood may form the basis of passivity phenomena such as thought insertion.

Fleeting paranoid reactions in connection with intense affective stress may be seen in borderline personality disorder (being one criterion of the DSM-5 diagnosis) and other personality disorders. Suspiciousness and paranoid ideation form one of the criteria of schizotypal personality disorder in the DSM-5 and of schizotypal disorder in the ICD-10.

Social Anxiety

The term social anxiety covers, in a broad sense, a number of quite different phenomena whose common denominator is anxiety or discomfort in social situations. They are seen in many different psychiatric states, and not least in the schizophrenia spectrum, motivating the tendency to social isolation. In this spectrum the social anxiety is closely related to the disorders of intersubjectivity. The exploration of the specific quality of social anxiety is an important diagnostic tool.

Some of the phenomena expounded elsewhere in this chapter are associated with social anxiety, first of all self-reference and paranoid ideation. In paranoid anxiety, the patient fears other people and suspects that they follow her or plan to assault her.

Social perplexity is often met with in schizophrenia spectrum cases. The loss of common sense or natural evidence makes it difficult for the patient to relate to other people. The patient is uncertain about unwritten social conventions, and fleeting mutual chatting is replaced by hyper-reflective, forced conversation about well-defined topics. Many patients report a fatigue arising even from informal time together with their friends. After being together with others the patient may ruminate about what was said or obsessively go through the whole conversation.

The concept of ontological insecurity was explored in detail by Laing (1960), who identified three forms of anxiety encountered by the "ontologically insecure person": engulfment, implosion, and petrification. In engulfment the person fears that he is "losing himself," that his autonomy or existence is threatened even by being understood or loved by another person. In that case isolation may be felt as safer. The psychotic presentation of this experience could be being engulfed by fire. In implosion the person feels that any contact with reality threatens to let him "implode" as if he were a vacuum. Petrification denotes a kind of depersonalization, in which the subject experiences himself as the object of others and feels threatened with the possibility of becoming no more than a thing in the world. These types of ontological anxiety, thus characterized by a pervasive sense of insecurity, weakness, inferiority, indecisiveness, low anxiety tolerance, persistent low-grade free-floating (objectless) anxiety, or a subtle, pervasive sense of something ominous impending (Parnas et al. 2005b), also represent a category of social anxiety.

> *In company with other people I feel tense in my body, I can't smile, my heart is knocking, I feel dizzy and I can't breathe. It is not just a matter of feeling vulnerable – it's hard to describe. It is just that other people make me extremely insecure and wrong. I feel that people can see that I am wrong in some way or another.*

A series of phenomena within the schizophrenia spectrum are related to disorders of self-demarcation, the transitivistic phenomena. Passivity phenomena such as thought insertion or withdrawal included in the Schneiderian first-rank symptoms are prominent psychotic examples of transitivism. There are, however, also many near-psychotic or even non-psychotic varieties (see below).

Some patients complain about not tolerating crowds. They avoid pedestrian streets, department stores and the like. They explain that there is too much noise or action, they feel overwhelmed by stimuli (Gross et al., 2008; Schultze-Lutter et al., 2007).

In the DSM-5, there is a new separate diagnosis, social anxiety disorder, broadened from the DSM-IV diagnosis of social phobia, to designate all kinds of chronic anxiety or discomfort in social situations. The ICD-10 diagnosis, social phobia, is apparently more narrowly related to personality disorders associated with low self-esteem and fear of criticism. In the DSM-5, excessive social anxiety is also one of the criteria of schizotypal personality disorder.

Overvalued Ideas

The overvalued idea is an idea that is socially accepted as reasonable in itself but regarded as too excessive by the general population and that preoccupies the individual's mental life. It is ego-syntonic, as opposed to obsessions, and is usually comprehensible with knowledge of the individual's past experience and personality. It is associated with a high degree of affect (e.g., anxiety or anger) when there is a threat to the loss of the person's goal or object of the belief.

> *After watching the trailer of Al Gore's documentary* An Inconvenient Truth, *at age 20 she became frightened and for a year or so she was constantly preoccupied with environmental issues and spent much of her time checking that the electric light and her electronic devices were turned off.*

In dysmorphophobia, patients are preoccupied with bodily change and examine themselves in search of such changes. Anorectic patients are preoccupied with becoming fat and having a perfect body shape. Such cases of preoccupation are regarded as overvalued ideas. But in many cases the dysmorphophobia and the anorectic body concern are expressive of the experience of a more profound bodily dissolution as seen in the schizophrenic process. These patients also experience morphological change (a paroxystic experience as if the size or form of body parts has changed), sometimes search for this change or even perceive it in the mirror (mirror phenomenon). These examples are not to be seen as simple overvalued ideas but as more complex psychopathological phenomena.

Møller and Husby (2000) have expounded the role of overvalued ideas in the initial prodrome of schizophrenia as a preoccupation with and withdrawal to, for example, religious mysticism, philosophy, new concepts for the world and for human existence. They describe a stage-like development into psychosis: first, the new idea, second, the overvaluation, third, the preoccupation and fourth, the withdrawal. The fifth stage is a delusional extension. Parnas and Handest (2003, p. 131) illustrate this development with the case of Peter:

> *January 1985: "strange change is affecting him," feels "self-disgust," has "lost contact to himself." August 1985: increasingly preoccupied by existential themes and Indian philosophy, "perhaps meditation could help." Increasingly isolated. January 1987: feels fundamentally transformed, "something in me has become inhuman," "no contact to his body," "feels empty," has to "find a new path in his life." January 1988: is of the opinion that Indians are superior compared to other human races; they perhaps have a mission to save our planet. September 1992: preoccupied by*

> *recurring thoughts about extraterrestrials. January 1993: convinced that Indians are reincarnated extraterrestrials. April 1994: feels that he is being brought here each day from another planet in order to assist Indians in their salvatory mission. June 1994: first admission to a psychiatric ward, 24 years old.*

The overvalued ideas are prevalent outside clinical psychiatry in areas such as conspiracy theories ("9/11 was a hoax: The twin tower were blown up by the US government") and extreme religious or political movements. Inside psychiatry they are found in schizotypy, anorexia nervosa, body dysmorphic disorder, hypochondriasis, hoarding and morbid jealousy. Body dysmorphic disorder in the DSM-5, whose validity is unknown, is grouped with obsessive-compulsive disorder, and, like this disorder, it is associated with varying degrees of insight (good, poor, and absent/delusional). Overvalued ideas underlie some of the diagnostic criteria of schizotypal disorder in the ICD-10 as well as DSM-5: odd beliefs, paranoid ideas and ruminations without inner resistance, and in the ICD-10 they even form a part of one of the criteria for schizophrenia: "persistent hallucinations . . . accompanied by delusions . . . or persistent overvalued ideas," which should here be read as delusions with lesser degree of organization.

Magical Thinking

Magical thinking is a form of non-causal thinking (i.e., thinking, not following rational cause–effect relationships). An example of causal thinking is that if I strike a match, it will light the fire. In magical thinking, I may try to prevent an accident by counting to 10. Magical thinking is seen as a natural way of thinking in preschool children. A certain magical component is intrinsic to adult thinking as well, reflected in religion as well as the general preoccupation in horoscopes, synchronicity, numerology and "more things in heaven and earth." All this represents culture or subculture-embedded thinking, but without any experience of actual magical powers or magical events. The appearance of omens is considered as possible, but these are relatively rare.

A more pathological near-psychotic form of magical thinking is seen in schizophrenia spectrum cases. It is a criterion of schizotypal personality disorder of the DSM-5 (2013, p. 655): "Odd beliefs or magical thinking that influences behavior and is inconsistent with subcultural norms (e.g., superstitiousness, belief in clairvoyance, telepathy, or "sixth sense"; in children and adolescents, bizarre fantasies or preoccupations)," as well as the ICD-10: "Odd beliefs or magical thinking influencing behavior and inconsistent with subcultural norms" (p. 69). To distinguish between schizotypal and culture-embedded experiences, Meehl (1964, p. 30) states this example:

> *[. . .] if a patient says "I always arrange the books that way before I leave my apartment, just to make sure that nothing happened," and further exploration shows that*

> *he really means this, i.e., he is making sure (rather than merely assuaging a tension by doing something he is perfectly clear is pointless and foolish)—then he has magical ideation and the sign should be checked as present.*

Magical thinking sometimes accompanies pseudo-obsessions (see below). Magical thinking may have the character of a solipsistic experience of being in the center of the world, and thereby bordering on or transforming into solipsistic grandiosity:

> *He believed that he could control the weather because the weather changed with his mood.*
>
> *He believed that he could inflict headache or even a brain tumor to another person by concentrating all his will power staring at him.*

Pseudo-Obsessions

Obsessive-like phenomena are widespread across the diagnostic categories. Obsessions and compulsions proper are found primarily in obsessive-compulsive disorder. Obsessions are thoughts and imaginations, which are experienced as intrusive, ego-dystonic, and absurd by the patient who tries to resist them by the aid of compulsions, and who does not allow them to expand into detailed, frightening imagination. So, the obsessions are not accompanied by strong emotions or impulsions. The anxiety, too, is held in check by compulsions, and the patient's sense of reality is intact. The compulsion is causally related to the obsession: If the patient gets the idea that she may hurt somebody with a knife, she will lock down the knives. Although there may be a component of magical thinking associated with the obsession, the patient does not have magical experiences.

In the pseudo-obsession, several of these characteristics are no longer fulfilled. The patient will begin to consider the thematic contents as plausible, that is to say that the thought is becoming ego-syntonic. Resistance is weakened, and we are no longer dealing with an obsession in the strict sense of the word, but of a sudden, not quite voluntary thought event or even voluntary imagination or rumination. Rather than glimpses of the feared situation, the patient experiences a lifelike, detailed, imaginative sequence, like an "inner movie" (in some cases even with the character of hallucination). The contents may be unpleasant or frightening, but it may also be accompanied by pleasurable or aggressive feelings or impulses:

> *Watching a razor blade he gets a picture of cutting himself in the eye, and the sight of a bolt cutter makes him imagine himself cutting off his fingers, so that he can almost feel it happen.*

> *Meeting a sinister-looking man in the train he saw himself in his mind's eye beating this man up in an adrenaline rush.*

The corresponding compulsive act, or pseudo-compulsion, is no longer causally related to the obsessive thought but has rather the character of a compulsive ritual magically related to the pseudo-obsession:

> *During her school days she always had to wash her hands and shake them over her bed to prevent something terrible to happen, and she had to look under the bed to see if there was some dangerous creature hiding there.*

Where the pseudo-obsession may end up as delusion proper, it may end up as a catatonic ritual. (It must be pointed out that not all kinds of catatonic behavior are pseudo-compulsions, some may be seen as responses to voices or reactions to delusions, and others as repetitious motor acts without any explicit meaning for the patient.)

The DSM-5 allows rating obsessions with "poor insight" or "absent insight/delusional beliefs." The latter no longer belong to the obsessive-compulsive area but to delusions belonging to psychosis. In the Y-BOCS instrument for OCD (Goodman et al., 1989) there are five levels of an insight dimension: excellent, good, fair, poor insight and delusional. Pseudo-obsessions also constitute one of the criteria of schizotypal disorder in the ICD-10 (not present in the DSM-5): "Ruminations without inner resistance, often with dysmorphophobic, sexual or aggressive contents."

Flashback experiences in torture victims are often described in a way resembling pseudo-obsessions, as involuntary lifelike images with frightening contents that comprise the repetitious revival of the torture situation. Often the experience is near-psychotic or even micropsychotic, the victim believing the torture to go on.

Derealization and Depersonalization

Derealization and depersonalization constitute a group of heterogeneous episodic phenomena. In *derealization* the outside world is perceived as changed. In *depersonalization* one's own mind or body appears to be changed. In their basic forms they are non-psychotic phenomena. Derealization is found in several mental disorders. In states of intense anxiety (e.g., panic attacks) the outside world appears as surrealistically changed and distanced from the patient. In severe depression the patient feels separated from the world which, informed by the depressive mood, appears as inanimate and dreary. In the schizophrenia spectrum there are two different types of derealization, a global and an intrusive one (Parnas et al., 2005b). In the global type, the world is experienced as transformed, unreal, strange, or "made."

Everything looks like pieces of scenery, and the trees seem to be made of plastic.

In the intrusive type, there is an increase or accentuation of the physiognomy of the world or of its isolated aspects or components.

At the beach the sea seemed to "address itself" to her, as if it "wanted to draw attention to itself." This was accompanied by an almost religious feeling of something greater than reality.

Depersonalization likewise covers different phenomena. In a state of intense anxiety the patient may feel as if watching herself from outside, perhaps as a double. Hallucinatorily watching oneself is called *heautoscopy*. In severe depression (melancholy) the patient feels inanimate and detached from her emotions and her environment (Fuchs, 2005), the body is experienced as petrified or dead culminating in the nihilistic delusion of being dead, one component of Cotard's syndrome. In less severe depressive states we meet a variety of the same phenomenon. In schizophrenia spectrum we frequently find a manifestation of the loss of selfhood (ipseity) as an experiential distance to one's own intentional acts. The patient then watches herself speaking, acting, or thinking, rather than implicitly experiencing herself as the agent of her own action.

Words are just passing out of her mouth. When eating she watches her arm moving to the plate. When speaking, it seems like listening to a tape recording. She has difficulty in recognizing her own thoughts.

Somatic depersonalization is a different kind of depersonalization seen within the schizophrenia spectrum. There the whole body or some of its parts are perceived as strange, alien, lifeless, or separated from each other, dislocated, or not existing.

She feels "artificial," "stuffed," or as if made of plastic. Her hands seem strange and scary. When her boyfriend was holding her hand she felt jealous as if he was holding somebody else's hand.

This kind of depersonalization may be accompanied by perceptual changes watching one's reflection in the mirror (mirror phenomenon).

Derealization and depersonalization are usually seen as non-psychotic or near-psychotic phenomena. They form part of one diagnostic criteria of schizotypal (personality) disorder in the DSM-5 as well as ICD-10. It is important to distinguish between derealization, in which the outside world seems changed, and loss of primary presence (Parnas et al., 2005b), in which the patient is just not affected by the world or feels separated from it (bell jar experience). In the SCAN

(Wing et al., 1974) some of these phenomena are mixed up. Under the heading of perceptual disorders depersonalization is grouped together with loss of presence.

Hallucination-Like Experiences

Simple, *unformed hallucinatory experiences* of auditory or visual type have been described in organic states (Cummings & Miller, 1987) as well as within the schizophrenia spectrum, here considered basic symptoms (Gross et al., 2008). In the visual field they are experienced as flashes of light or shapes (*photopsias*) and in the auditory field various sounds (*acoasms*). Although hallucinatory by nature they are usually not reckoned as psychotic phenomena, the patients themselves perceiving them as sensory disturbances. Some patients may experience scary shadows or figures in the fringe of their visual field having the impression that there is something or someone there. These are psychotic experiences in spite of low degree of elaboration. A *functional hallucination* is a true hallucination originating in a perception, but independent of perception itself, for example, hearing a voice coming from the sound of running water. *Illusions* are misinterpretations of perceived objects based on the fact that objects are always seen as something. Objects are mistaken for something else, often followed by rapid realization of the mistake. There is no distortion of the perception itself as, for example, in micropsia. Jaspers (1997) listed three different types of illusion: illusions due to inattentiveness, illusions due to affect, and pareidolia. *Pareidolia* is an illusionary experience formed by imagination (e.g., seeing "the man in the moon").

> *Gadelius (1933) states a patient having a series of illusions one night after his father's sudden disappearance (i.e., due to affect): he was seeing a water bottle and the blotter on the desk as a child's skeleton, a vase as a skull, and shirts and towels thrown over a chair as white hands (see* ***Figure 4.1****).*

Illusions are found in many psychotic disorders and they are included in two of the criteria of schizotypal disorder in the ICD-10: bodily illusions (here meaning *cenesthesias*) or other illusions, and intense illusions as quasi-psychotic episodes. In the DSM-5, schizotypal personality disorder only mentions the bodily illusions. Schizophrenia spectrum patients may report episodes of *uncertainty in discriminating between different modes of experiencing*: perception, fantasy, or memory. It seems to the patient as if the cell phone or door bell is ringing, the door is opening or closing, but it might as well be her fantasy. Answering the door or phone, the patient immediately realizes her mistake. The patient may also be in doubt whether she has been thinking out loud or just thinking for herself or whether she did experience this event herself or somebody has told her. One patient living with his parents had episodes as if his father was calling his name but he actually did not hear anything. These phenomena belong to the disorders of self-awareness (Parnas et al, 2005b). They are more expressive of the patient's uncertainty or confusion than of perceptual-like experiences like hallucinations.

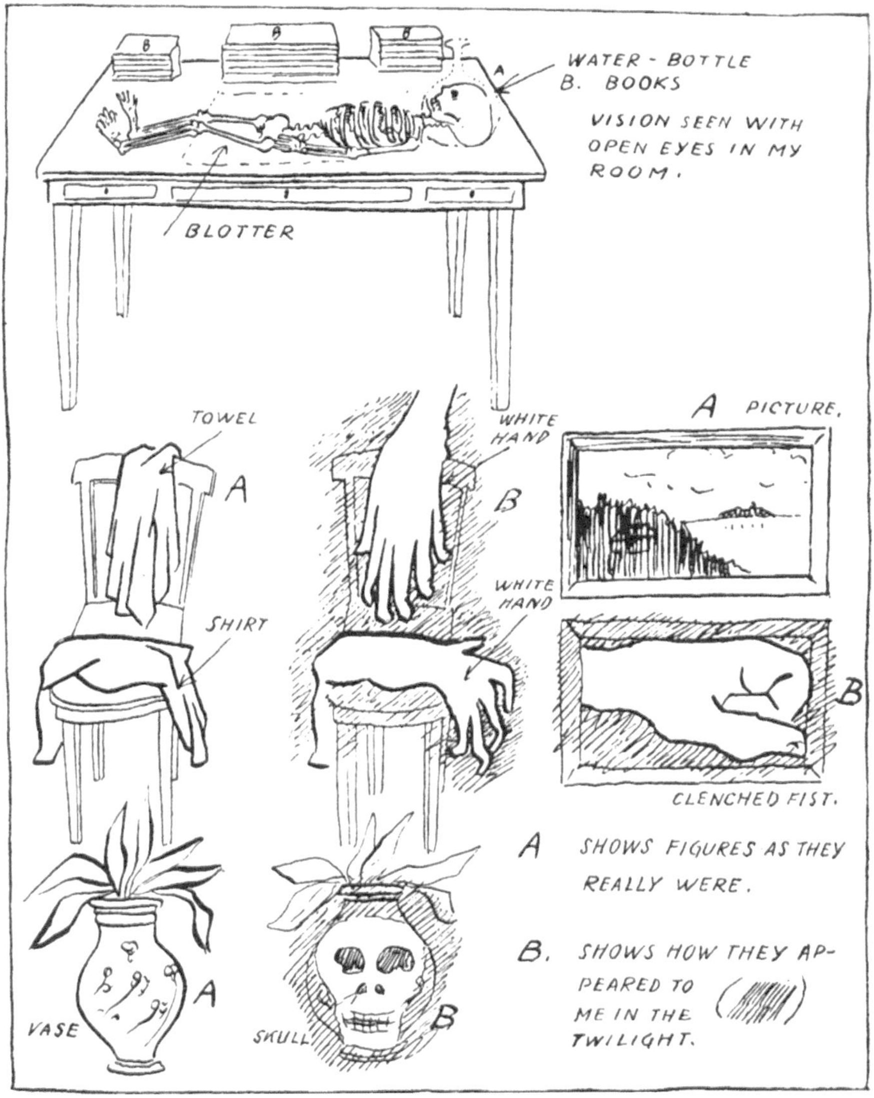

FIGURE 4.1 Drawing 15 from Gadelius (1933): Drawing by the patient in Case VIII to explain how his visions of skeletons, hands and so forth arose (typical illusions)

Disorders of Demarcation

Transitivism is a term coined by Wernicke referring to the experience of a part of the personality detaching itself and then being attached to another person. The term *appersonation* designates the experience of properties of another person being incorporated in the patient. In later-time psychiatry they are both referred to as transitivism, or as loss or permeability of the self-world boundary. Originally reserved for expressive psychotic phenomena later to be included in Schneider's first-rank symptoms as phenomena of influence, the term has also been used for near-psychotic or even subjective non-psychotic phenomena. They are considered pathognomonic for schizophrenia spectrum disorders. They form a veritable spectrum of experiences from diffuse feelings of being exposed and receptive (passivity mood; Parnas et al., 2005b) to psychotic, Schneiderian forms.

One type of transitivistic phenomena concerns the experience of being "read like a book":

> *She feels naked and she feels that everybody can see right through her, and sometimes perceive what she is thinking about. Although she knows very well that they can't possibly do so, she catches herself deliberately thinking of something nice to get rid of the embarrassing feeling.*

This not-yet-psychotic phenomenon is approaching or briefly taking shape of thought broadcast. This type of experience is frequently associated with primary self-reference and may be provoked by eye contact. Another type of transitivism concerns the feeling of mentally fusing or being mixed up with others:

> *When I am getting too close to another person I am losing my boundaries: you think this and I think that. I am in doubt and get confused. Was this something she was feeling or something I was feeling?*

Yet another type is about bodily fusion:

> *I have never been a fan of handshakes. Shaking hands with the doctor the other day I had a distant feeling . . . it felt like two pieces of leather being rubbed together . . . but the scary thing about it was the feeling that it was my own hand, that I was shaking my own hand, and that I was her hand.*

Micropsychoses

The concept of micropsychosis (also referred to as quasi-psychotic episodes) was formed by Hoch and Polatin to refer to short-lived psychotic episodes in pseudo-neurotic (schizotypal) patients with subsequent complete reintegration. In these patients they described a "zig-zag over the reality line":

> *They say "it is as if I were to hear a voice," or "as if I were to be observed." When the emotional charge becomes more intense, they suddenly say, "I hear a voice," or "I am observed."*
>
> (*Hoch & Polatin, 1949*)

In their experience three significant elements of micropsychosis usually appear simultaneously: hypochondriac ideas, ideas of reference, and feelings of depersonalization. To these elements Paul Meehl added "clouded and confusional" states in absence of an organic explanation, which include states of perplexity:

> *I got all fouled up, all mixed up in the head there, I didn't know what the hell was going on, or even hardly who or where I was.*
>
> *(Meehl, 1964)*

One caveat: In American psychiatry the word "perplexity" is often used in a broader sense also to denote organic states of confusion. What is meant here is an anxious state of loss of meaning closely related to loss of common sense and ambivalence (Parnas et al., 2005b). Many of the phenomena described elsewhere in this chapter may assume the character of micropsychosis. The duration of micropsychotic episodes is minutes, hours, or even a couple of days (the micropsychosis thus overlapping with the brief limited intermittent psychotic episodes [BLIPS] of prodromal instruments such as the CAARMS, lasting less than a week; Yung et al., 2006).

Micropsychosis is *never* seen in personality disorder—by definition so to speak. However, during the last decades we have seen a groundless tendency to accept, for example, episodes of hallucinations in borderline patients, and thus, many disorganized patients with schizophrenia who are not capable of forming stable psychotic symptoms have been diagnosed with a borderline personality disorder. Genuine borderline patients may at most experience paranoid-like reactions in connection with strong emotional distress.

Crazy Action

In the absence of manifest delusions a (near-)psychotic state may reveal itself through behavior, through a "crazy action" (in German: *unsinnige Handlung*, and in French: *délire des actes*; see also Parnas, *Chapter 2*).

> *A mother collected her son from school one day to take him on a late cancellation trip to Italy but without informing the school or anybody else. An Interpol notice was issued. After returning home she explained that they just needed a vacation.*

Conrad (1958) presented several cases from the German army of crazy actions in initial schizophrenia. Often such acts were the first indication of imminent psychosis. In a context of ruthless discipline seemingly minor offences might be considered as "crazy." Here is another example of his:

> *A 26-year-old corporal had served as a car driver all through the entry of Russia and in December 1941 he was sent back to Germany to attend a seminar. Affected by*

> *the victorious advance and with the prospect of promotion he was in an elevated state of mind during the 3-day journey, "as if intoxicated." On his arrival he listened to a broadcast speech by the Fuhrer which affected him to the point of bursting into tears. Immediately, he came to the decision to write a letter to the Fuhrer. He went back to his quarters and wrote: "Listening to your speech I burst into tears twice: the first time by the mentioning of the middle section of the Eastern front, where I myself was serving, and the second time by the mentioning of the German legation in Washington where my cousin, once a radio operator on the proud German ship Columbus, is serving. You and the Reichmarschall are the two greatest heads of this nation. All German soldiers hope and wish to spend their next Christmas at home with their mothers." He went to Berlin in order to send this letter but was warned against doing it. On his way back a self-reference psychosis broke out with maniform excitement and flight of ideas.*
>
> *(My translation)*

Such crazy actions in initial schizophrenia emerge, according to Conrad, as the result of an increased field of tension, either in the form of external pressure or hopeful expectations, increasing the basic affectivity. In the above case the radio speech constituted an additional tension.

Transition from Non-Psychotic to Psychotic Symptoms

The Huber group mapped out the steps of the transition from basic symptoms to first-rank symptoms (e.g., Klosterkötter, 1992; see **Figure 4.2**). The basic symptoms, non-psychotic, subjective experiences found in schizophrenia spectrum disorders, were described in the introductory section of this chapter. These symptoms have been divided into non-specific stage-1 basic symptoms and stage-2 basic symptoms that are considerably more specific to the schizophrenia spectrum. Psychotic symptoms may be regarded as "stage-3" symptoms in this sequence. There is an overlap between stage-2 phenomena and the disorders of self-awareness assessed in the EASE instrument (Parnas et al., 2005b). As examples of this transition: cenesthesias (bodily sensations) transform into bodily influence symptoms, thought blocking (sudden interruption of thoughts) into thought withdrawal, and thought interference (irrelevant thoughts breaking in) into thought insertion. Intermediate "near-psychotic" phenomena can be identified. That kind of transition can be illustrated by a case from our clinic:

> *A young woman complains about a simultaneous split between one critical part of her always dragging her down, and another part of her with a normal positive attitude (I split [*Ichspaltung*], a self-disorder). She experiences some kind of inner struggle between the two of them, "like the angel and the devil in a cartoon," but identifies them as two separate sides of her own personality. Two months later she reports that the critical side now has transformed into a strange woman sometimes stepping into*

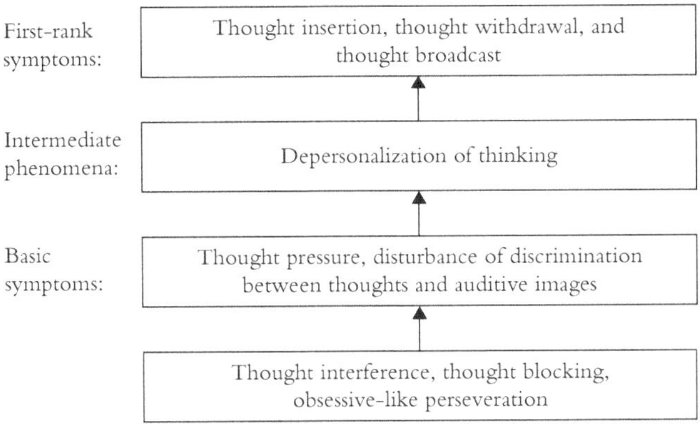

FIGURE 4.2 Example of transition from non-psychotic to psychotic symptoms (adapted from Klosterkötter, 1992)

her whom she can see and feel grapping her shoulders (a bizarre delusion, visual and tactile hallucinations).

In a theoretical study Henriksen, Raballo and Parnas (in press) similarly propose a clinical-phenomenological account of the pathogenesis of verbal hallucinations in schizophrenia suggesting that pathological changes in the experience of space and morbid objectification of inner speech may lead to crystalized verbal hallucinations.

Pitfalls

Double book-keeping in schizophrenia—a term coined by Bleuler (1950; Sass, 1994)—is a phenomenon in which the patient relates to the intersubjective world while at the same time maintaining his private psychotic ideas. In a peculiar way these two views do not seem to collide. This may leave the impression in the clinician of the patient having full medical insight, and therefore of non-psychotic or near-psychotic phenomena even in the presence of true psychotic symptoms. This impression is probably often strongest in structured settings such as clinical interviews.

Dissimulation is another cause of underestimating psychotic symptoms. Here, too, the interviewing technique is crucial for obtaining valid information. Straightforward questioning may be experienced as excessive prying by the sensitive patient causing him to deny pathological phenomena. On the other hand, some clinicians seem to have the habit of playing down or explaining away the psychopathology by psychological interpretation ("the principle of charity"; see Parnas, *Chapter 2*) while questioning the patient, leading to the same result.

Anomalous experiences like the disorders of self-awareness, basically seen as non-psychotic "as-if" phenomena found, for example, in schizotypal personality disorder or prodromal schizophrenia, may appear so alien to some clinicians as to cause them to mistake them for psychotic symptoms. Thus, the "as-if" feeling of morphological bodily change, for example, the fingers swelling up "like water balloons" may give the impression of a "hypochondriac delusion." The solipsistic "as-if" experience of other people resembling mindless zombies may be mistaken for psychotic grandiosity.

Episodic hallucinations may be taken for micropsychoses even in case of repeated episodes during the day. Few psychotic patients hear voices throughout the day. Patients with frequent, daily episodes will usually appear clinical psychotic and fulfill the criteria for a psychotic disorder. Micropsychoses are more infrequent: the proposed DSM-5 criteria for attenuated psychosis syndrome require that symptoms such as unformed hallucinations must have been present (at least) once per week for the past month.

Psychoses with few manifest symptoms but with a loss of implicit rationality are mistaken for non-psychotic or near-psychotic states. This is an old problem as reflected in Wilmanns' complaints that doctors failed to diagnose psychosis in vagabonds and petty criminals who mostly proved to be catatonic and hebephrenic cases (Wilmanns, 1906). A number of such "symptom-poor" (Blankenburg, 1971), abortive, subclinical or "larvated" schizophrenia pictures have been described, and among these the cenesthetic schizophrenia and the endogenous juvenile-asthenic failure syndrome (Gross, Huber & Schüttler, 1982). The hebephrenic (ICD-10) or disorganized (DSM-IV) subtypes of schizophrenia (abolished in the DSM-5 but still lying hidden in the schizophrenia criteria of grossly disorganized behavior and thinking), which are also related to this group, are frequently mistaken for borderline personality disorder. The life history will usually reveal a later adolescence onset than in personality disorder or even an onset into the twenties. In a similar way, moderate mania may be confused with antisocial personality disorder but a state-like, episodic course will indicate an affective episode.

Certain phenomena of normal psychology may be mistaken for (near-) psychotic phenomena. In a comparison of university students with patients with schizophrenia using a self-questionnaire, both groups seemed to describe similar phenomena, but a closer inspection revealed that they were referring to qualitatively different phenomena. For example, to the prompt, "When I look at things they appear strange to me" the clinical sample responded with description of the experience of derealization: "When looking at people, they sometimes seem strange, like they're not real, and the things in the house, too," whereas the non-clinical sample described experiences related to attention or reflection: "After observing the faces of people for a long time, I see them differently. What I mean is that they are not the way I thought they were before" (Stanghellini, et al., 2012).

Conclusive Remarks

Near-psychotic phenomena are widespread in the borderlands of all psychotic disorders. In clinical work, the familiarity with these phenomena is prerequisite for making the differential diagnosis. Their presence in supposedly non-psychotic disorders such as personality disorder or obsessive-compulsive disorder is suggestive of a more severe mental illness, for example, schizotypy or initial psychosis. In research, not least in prodromal and first episode studies, a thorough knowledge of them is the precondition of the proper utilization of psychopathological instruments. Many rating scales apparently covering near-psychotic items or grading psychopathology fail to provide definitions instead listing a number of questions (like, "Do you ever feel that you are a very special or unusual person?") and leave it to the interviewer to interpret the response in psychopathological terms. The validity of such items is dubious. The validity of structured rating scales and operationalized diagnostic systems depend on the user's clinical experience, skills and, when needed, readiness to depart from the structure. There is no shortcut to psychopathology.

References

American Psychiatric Association. (2013). *Diagnostic and statistical manual of mental disorders* (5th ed.). Washington, DC: American Psychiatric Association.

Blankenburg, W. (1971). *Der Verlust der natürlichen Selbstverständlichkeit. Ein Beitrag zur Psychopathologie symptomarmer Schizophrenie*. Stuttgart, Germany: Ferdinand Enke Verlag.

Bleuler, E. (1950). *Dementia praecox or the group of schizophrenias*. New York, NY: International Universities Press.

Broome, M. R., Harland, R., Owen, G. S., & Stingaris, A. (Eds.). (2012). *The Maudsley reader in phenomenological psychiatry*. Cambridge, UK: Cambridge University Press.

Conrad, K. (1958). *Die beginnende Schizophrenie. Versuch einer Gestaltanalyse des Wahns*. Stuttgart, Germany: Thieme.

Cummings, J. L., & Miller, B. L. (1987). Visual hallucinations: Clinical occurrence and use in differential diagnosis. *The Western Journal of Medicine, 146*, 46–51.

Fuchs, T. (2005). Corporealized and disembodied minds: A phenomenological view of the body in melancholia and schizophrenia. *Philosophy, Psychiatry, and Psychology, 12*, 95–107.

Gadelius, B. (1933). *Human mentality in the light of psychiatric experience*. Copenhagen, Denmark: Levin & Munksgaard.

Goodman W. K., Price L. H., Rasmussen S. A., et al. (1989) The Yale-Brown Obsessive Compulsive Scale. I. Development, use, and reliability. *Archives of General Psychiatry, 46*(11), 1006–1011.

Gross, G., Huber, G., Klosterkotter, J., & Linz, M. (2008). *BSABS–Bonn scale for the assessment of basic symptoms*. Berlin, Germany: Shaker Verlag.

Gross, G., Huber, G., & Schüttler, R. (1982). Larvierte Schizophrenie? In *Der Schizophrene außerhalb der Klinik* (pp. 19–33). Bern-Stuttgart-Wien, Germany: Verlag Hans Huber.

Henriksen, M. G., Raballo, A., & Parnas, J. (in press). The pathogenesis of auditory verbal hallucinations in schizophrenia: A clinical-phenomenological account. *Philosophy, Psychiatry & Psychology*.

Hoch, P., & Polatin, P. (1949). Pseudoneurotic forms of schizophrenia. *Psychiatric Quarterly, 23*, 248–276.

Jaspers, K. (1997). *General psychopathology*. Baltimore, MD: Johns Hopkins University Press.

Klosterkötter, J. (1992). The meaning of basic symptoms for the genesis of the schizophrenic nuclear syndrome. *The Japanese Journal of Psychiatry and Neurology, 46*, 609–630.

Kretschmer, E. (1974). The sensitive delusion of reference. In S.R. Hirsch (Ed.), *Themes and variations in European psychiatry: An anthology* (pp. 153–159). Charlottesville, VA: University of Virginia Press.

Laing, R. D. (1960). *The divided self: An existential study in sanity and madness*. London, UK: Penguin Books.

McGlashan, T. H., Tandy, J., Woods, S. W., Hoffman, R. E., & Davidson, L. (2001). Instrument for the assessment of prodromal symptoms and states. *Early Intervention in Psychotic Disorders, 91*, 135–149.

Meehl, P. (1964). Manual for use with checklist of schizotypic signs (Report No. PR-73–5). Minneapolis: University of Minnesota, Research Laboratories of the Department of Psychiatry. Retrieved from www.tc.umn.edu/~pemeehl/061ScChecklist.pdf

Møller, P., & Husby, R. (2000). The initial prodrome in schizophrenia: Searching for naturalistic core dimensions of experience and behavior. *Schizophrenia Bulletin, 26*, 217–232.

Parnas, J., & Handest, P. (2003). Phenomenology of anomalous self-experience in early schizophrenia. *Comprehensive Psychiatry, 44*, 121–134.

Parnas, J., Licht, D., & Bovet, P. (2005a). Cluster A personality disorders: A review. In M. Maj, H. S. Akiskal, J. E. Mezzich, & A. Okasha (Eds.), *Personality disorders* (1–74). New York, NY: John Wiley & Sons.

Parnas, J., Møller, P., Kircher, T., Thalbitzer, J., Jansson, L., Handest, P., & Zahavi, D. (2005b). EASE: Examination of anomalous self-experience. *Psychopathology, 38*, 236–258.

Parnas, J., Nordgaard, J., & Varga, S. (2010). The concept of psychosis: A clinical and theoretical analysis. *Clinical Neuropsychiatry*, 7(2), 32–37.

Sass, L. (1994). *The Paradoxes of Delusion: Wittgenstein, Schreber, and the schizophrenic mind*. Ithaca, NY: Cornell University Press.

Schultze-Lutter, F., Addington, J., Ruhrmann, S., & Klosterkötter, J. (2007). *Schizophrenia proneness instrument, adult version (SPI-A)*. Rome, Italy: Giovanni Fioriti Editore.

Stanghellini, G., Langer, A. I., Ambrosini, A., & Cangas, A. J. (2012). Quality of hallucinatory experiences: Differences between a clinical and a non-clinical sample. *World Psychiatry, 11*, 110–113.

Wilmanns, K. (1906). *Zur Psychopathologie des Landstreichers*. Verlag von Johann Ambrosius Barth.

Wing, J. K., Cooper, J. E., & Sartorius, N. (1974). *The measurement and classification of psychiatric symptoms*. Cambridge, UK: Cambridge University Press.

World Health Organization (1992). *The ICD-10 classification of mental and behavioral disorders: Clinical descriptions and diagnostic guidelines*. Geneva, Switzerland: World Health Organization.

Yung, A., Phillips, L., Simmons, M. B., Ward, J., Thompson, K., French, P., & McGorry, P. (2006). *CAARMS: Comprehensive assessment of at risk mental states*. Melbourne, Australia: PACE Clinic, University of Melbourne.

PART II

Psychosis in Different Population Groups

5

HOW TO ASSESS PSYCHOSIS

A Practical Guide

Peter Bosanac and David J. Castle

Introduction

In this chapter the principles, challenges, techniques and practice of a personalized and patient-orientated approach to the assessment of psychotic disorders are covered. Psychosis is a broad and non-specific term encompassing significant distortion or abnormal inference of reality across a spectrum of diagnostic syndromes. These syndromes, as atheoretically categorized in the *Diagnostic and Statistical Manual of Mental Disorders* (American Psychiatric Association [APA], 2013) and the International Classification of Diseases (World Health Organization [WHO], 1994), include schizophrenia and related disorders, major depressive and bipolar disorder with psychotic features, substance induced and intoxication or withdrawal states, delirium and neuropsychiatric disorders such as dementia. On the other hand, transient psychotic experiences may also occur as part of a continuum in the general population (van Os, 2009) and not necessarily reflect significant underlying psychopathology.

People may require psychiatric assessment for psychotic symptoms when these are at a clinically significant threshold, such that there is significant distress or impact on daily living, interpersonal and vocational functioning. People suffering with psychotic disorders may also experience psychopathology in other domains such as disorganization, cognition or affect, which has been referred to as 'salience dysregulation' (van Os, 2009). In this chapter, there will be focus on psychosis in the context of schizophrenia and related disorders and mood disorders with psychotic features.

The prevalence of psychotic symptoms in the general population is 5 to 8% (van Os et al., 2008). However for schizophrenia and related disorders, which occurs equally in men and women, the lifetime prevalence is considerably less and ranges from less than 1 to over 1.5% (Bourdon et al., 1992). The annual incidence of schizophrenia ranges between 0.1 and 0.5 per 1,000 and the median incidence at 15 per 100,000 population (Hafner, Riechler-Rossler & Maurer, 1992; Wing & Fryers, 1976; Jablensky et al., 1992). For major depressive disorder with psychotic features, the lifetime prevalence rate in the general population is 0.35%; for bipolar disorder with psychosis, 0.24%; for substance-induced psychotic disorder, 0.42 %; and for psychotic disorder due to a general medical condition, 0.21% (Suvisaari et al., 2009).

Changes to the classification of schizophrenia in DSM-5 (APA, 2013) include the requirement for two, as opposed to one, Criterion A symptoms, and that at least one must be a positive symptom (namely a delusion or hallucination) or disorganized thinking. Hence, the centrality of bizarre delusions in DSM-IV is mitigated in DSM-5. Also, DSM-5 deletes previously delineated schizophrenia subtypes such as paranoid, catatonic, residual, disorganized and undifferentiated, and instead creates a catatonic specifier. Additionally, in DSM-5 delusional disorder, there is no longer the requirement that the delusion in Criterion A be nonbizarre, although there are bizarre and nonbizarre specifiers. In ICD 11, due in 2015, schizophrenia, schizotypal and delusional disorders will be renamed Schizophrenia spectrum and other primary psychotic disorders (Gaebel, 2012).

Assessment

Challenges in interviewing individuals with psychosis include suspiciousness, guardedness, thought disorder, a history of trauma or posttraumatic stress, and a culturally and, in many settings, linguistically diverse background. Notwithstanding, rapport building with individuals suffering with psychosis requires a strategic and flexible approach, including: an empathic approach to listening and responding to the symptoms and suffering, assessment of insight, and helping place the features of psychosis into perspective with the view to establishing therapeutic goals and alliance (Othmer et al 2002). Assessment should cover positive and negative symptoms (see below), and it must also encompass the impact of symptoms of psychosis on functioning such as self-care, bathing, diet and cooking, budgeting, shopping, leisure, social, vocational, cultural and spiritual domains.

Mental State

Positive symptoms include delusions and hallucinations, accompanied by impaired insight and disorganized thinking. Delusions may be persecutory, referential, grandiose, erotomanic, somatic, mixed or other—in depressive syndromes: nihilistic, guilt and impoverishment. Delusions are firmly held beliefs, based on an abnormal inference of external reality that cannot be challenged with evidence to the contrary and are out of keeping with the person's cultural and educational background. Hallucinations are false percepts that may occur in any of the sensory modalities. Disorganization encompasses disorganized behaviour and thoughts which could be apparent on direct assessment.

Negative symptoms, which are generally associated with schizophrenia more than with other psychotic disorders, entail a loss or inability in regard to emotion (anhedonia), speech (alogia) or motivation (avolition). These negative symptoms may also manifest on the mental state examination with affective restriction or blunting, impoverishment of thought content, as well as cognitive features such as attentional impairment.

Schizophrenia is associated with a breadth of cognitive dysfunction, which may be relatively independent from positive psychotic phenomena (Harvey, 2007). In other words, the severity of positive symptoms does not predict cognitive functioning. Cognitive impairment in schizophrenia includes impaired attentional processing, reasoning/problem solving, social cognition, processing speed, verbal and visual learning and working memory (Green, 2006).

Comorbidity

In psychotic disorders, particularly schizophrenia, comorbidity is the rule rather than the exception. Such comorbidities include substance misuse, depression and anxiety; and potentially life-threatening physical health problems (sequelae of metabolic disturbances such as cardiovascular diseases, obesity and diabetes). All of these can worsen outcome, including morbidity, engagement in care and mortality (Buckley et al., 2009; Bosanac & Castle, 2012), and therefore require a thorough assessment.

Depressive symptoms are common in people with schizophrenia (Upthegrove, 2009), yet often missed or dismissed. Differentiating depressive from psychotic symptoms in psychosis can be challenging (Bosanac & Castle, 2012). Negative symptoms may be secondary, as opposed to core negative symptoms of apathetic withdrawal, restricted affect and paucity of thought (Carpenter, Heinrichs & Wagman, 1988). People with negative symptoms of schizophrenia may describe their interests in a seemingly bland manner (Bosanac & Castle, 2012).

Similarly, around 50% of people suffering with schizophrenia will experience a concurrent anxiety disorder (Pokos et al., 2006), with these symptoms not being the mere sequelae of psychotic phenomena (e.g., persecutory anxiety). Schizophrenia compounded by anxiety symptoms or disorders is associated with poorer quality of life and work outcomes (Goodwin et al., 2001; Huppert & Smith, 2001; Poyurovsky et al., 2001; Borkowska et al., 2003; Özdemir et al., 2003; Wetherell et al., 2003; Hofer et al., 2004; Pallanti, Quercioli & Hollander, 2004; Braga et al., 2004; Huppert & Smith, 2005). Akathisia, an inner restlessness and fidgetiness, is experienced by up to a third of patients being treated with antipsychotic medication and may be erroneously attributed to anxiety symptoms (Waterreus et al., 2012).

Substance use is markedly over-represented in psychotic disorders, with the prevalence of tobacco smoking at two thirds (Cooper et al., 2012), alcohol abuse/dependence at half and substance abuse/dependence in general at one third to one half (Moore et al., 2012). When assessing comorbid substance use in psychosis, the substances used, their quantity, route of administration, frequency, pattern and duration of current level of use, evidence of dependence (presence of tolerance and symptoms on withdrawal from substance) and impact on the person's life (mental and physical, criminal justice history, social and homelessness) are essential (NICE, 2011).

In the onset of psychosis, clarification of the role of substance use ideally requires assessment and observation whilst abstinent (a 'drug-free' assessment), which in turn may necessitate urine or blood drug assays and more restrictive care.

Risk and Safety

In assessing risk, eliciting feelings of guilt, hopelessness and suicidality may differentiate depression from core negative symptoms. People experiencing psychosis are generally at increased risk of suicide (Warman et al., 2004). In people suffering with schizophrenia, 18% to 55% attempt suicide during the course of their lives and 10% commit suicide (Siris, 2001). Individuals with schizophrenia and schizoaffective disorder who complete suicide generally do so in the setting of depression, hopelessness (Klonsky et al., 2012) and despair, which may be compounded by substance misuse as a disinhibiting factor (Warman et al., 2004). People with psychotic depression are five times more likely to commit suicide than those who experience a depressive disorder without psychotic features (Roose et al., 1983; Wolfersdorf et al., 1987).

Suicide risk assessment in psychosis requires the identification of acute risk, as well as available protective factors. If the patient with psychosis has a past pattern of symptoms associated with self-harm or a suicide attempt, this can serve as a guide to assessing level of suicide risk. The initial steps of evaluation require the establishment of rapport, a calm, empathic and non-judgmental approach and the use of initial open-ended questions (British Medical Journal, BMJ, 2012). In addition, if the person being assessed is not able to directly answer questions or is not cooperative at assessment, possible warning signs for hidden suicidal ideation or plan include anger, agitation, despair, despondence, lack of rapport, guardedness or suspicious injuries on physical examination (BMJ, 2012). The most predictive factors for imminent suicide in psychosis are the presence of a suicide plan and immediate access to lethal means. Delusions of thought insertion, grandeur, and mind reading increase suicide risk in depression with psychotic features over a non-psychotic depressive syndrome (Simon, 2006). Immediate intervention, including invigilation of local Mental Health Act legislation and involvement of emergency services such as the police or ambulance are required if the person with psychosis is threatening or exploring ways or accessing means to kill themselves (BMJ, 2012). Protective factors against suicide, if apparent, may include important relationships and interests. Yet, clinical judgment alone is insufficient and there are no evidence-based risk factors that are unequivocally predictive of imminence, especially if there is no one or a clinical record to provide a collateral history. Moreover, there is no evidence that protective factors mitigate acute factors that may be drivers for suicide.

There is an association between schizophrenia, especially when positive symptoms and substance use are present, and violence (Walsh, Buchanan & Fahy, 2002), as well as hostile behaviour, poor impulse control, involuntary treatment for first episode psychosis, impaired insight and adherence with treatment, criminal history and previous suicide attempts (Witt et al., 2013). A first episode of schizophrenia is also associated with an increased risk of violence prior to treatment (Large & Nielssen, 2011). On the other hand, structured tools for assessing the risk of violence in the community are of little clinical utility (Singh et al., 2011).

Cognition

Whilst the National Institute of Health (NIH) in the US has developed the Measurement and Treatment Research to Improve Cognition (MATRICS) for the assessment of cognitive functioning in clinical trials in schizophrenia (Nuechterlein et al., 2008), this is generally not used for routine clinical assessment and may not adequately cover executive functioning. Practical clinical assessment of cognition in psychosis is more circumspect, and may be generally covered by broad tests contained in the Mini-Mental State Examination (MMSE; Folstein, Folstein & McHugh, 1975) or similar, combined with assessment of executive functioning. The MMSE covers orientation, concentration, language, immediate and short-term memory, calculation and praxis (Folstein, Folstein & McHugh, 1975), but additional assessment of executive functioning is required—sequencing, verbal fluency, trail making, abstraction [similarities/differences]. Luria's test of hand movements (motor-reciprocation) and judgment—and additional assessment of parietal function (construction, calculation) may also be required in more comprehensive assessment.

Medical Assessment and Investigations

Physical examination, including neurological, is essential to confirm or exclude general medical precipitants for (or comorbidity to) the psychosis. These will be impacted by the degree of cooperation and rapport. It is important to assess for, or exclude general medical precipitants or comorbidities. Hence, in this context, baseline blood tests such as serum electrolytes, renal function, liver function tests, thyroid function tests, vitamin B12 and a full blood count are essential. In addition, baseline assessments of metabolic risk factors such as fasting blood glucose and serum lipids (cholesterol and triglycerides) are required. In terms of comorbidity, hepatitis and HIV serology are indicated in patients with a history of intravenous drug use. HIV and syphilis serology are indicated when there is protean presentation or one with a potential neuropsychiatric presentation. Structural neuroimaging, namely CT or MRI brain, is required as a baseline assessment in psychosis to exclude intracranial pathology that may be contributory to the psychosis.

Given the excess mortality in schizophrenia (1.5 to 2 times) and reduced life expectancy by one to two decades compared with the general population (Harris & Barraclough, 1998; Newman & Bland, 1991), continuing metabolic monitoring (National Heart, Lung, and Blood Institute, NHLBI, and the American Heart Association, AHA, Guidelines) of physical health is essential (Grundy et al., 2005) and requires assessment of: metabolic risk (family history, obesity), baseline fasting blood glucose (≤100 mg/dl) and education in regard to diet and exercise. In addition, BMI, abdominal girth (a waist circumference ≥102 cm in men and ≥88 cm in women; in people of Asian heritage ≥90 cm in men and ≥80 cm in women), blood pressure (≤130/85 mm Hg), serum lipids (cholesterol, LDL, HDL [≤40mg/dl in men and ≤50mg/dl in women] and triglycerides [≤150 mg/dl]), urea and electrolytes, renal function tests and liver function tests are required on initial assessment and repeated 6 monthly. Also, repeat fasting blood glucose, at least 6 monthly, is essential if there are additional metabolic risk factors such as age greater than 45 years, obesity, a history of elevated blood glucose or gestational diabetes, a family history of diabetes, and ethnic diathesis (e.g., Indian, African, Aboriginal).

Differential Diagnosis

Multiple general medical conditions may cause psychotic symptoms, including: delirium; dementia, including frontotemporal dementia (characterized by personality and behavioural changes and progressive non-fluent aphasia) and in which symptoms of psychosis can present on average five years earlier than the diagnosis of dementia (Velakoulis et al., 2009); stroke; tumours; epilepsy; Huntington's disease; multiple sclerosis; autoimmune disorders involving the central nervous system; infection; hypoxia; thyroid and parathyroid diseases; altered adrenocortical function; hypoglycaemia; hepatic or renal disease; and autoimmune disorders with central nervous system involvement such as systemic lupus erythematosus. Delusions may be precipitated by neurological conditions involving subcortical structures or the temporal lobe. Features of psychosis due to a general medical disorder may be transient, recurrent or persistent (e.g., after acquired brain injury). Limbic encephalitis represents a group of disorders, with a subacute onset of short-term memory loss, seizures (which may be refractory), confusion and psychiatric symptoms. The latter may include psychotic symptoms (Asztely & Kumlien, 2012). MRI brain and anti-VGKC antibodies may be helpful in discerning the diagnosis (Ahmad et al., 2010). A temporal association between the occurrence of psychosis and general medical condition and 'atypical' features such as late age at onset or presence of visual or olfactory hallucinations may be helpful in delineating the role of medical illness.

Hence assessment is a staged process. There are no pathognomonic features or confirmatory pathology tests to differentiate syndromes of psychosis from those precipitated by general medical causes.

Challenges in Assessment

People who feign psychosis for conscious (malingering) or unconscious (factitious disorder) 'gain' may present for assessment. Inconsistencies in their subjective report of symptoms and observed presentation are helpful in discernment from psychosis. Such presentations are suggested by and include: conflicting reports of symptoms; a clear account of being 'confused'; seemingly disorganized behaviour on direct observation, which is absent when not directly observed; abrupt onset of reported delusions; bizarre content of reported ideation or delusions without observable disorganization; an eagerness to discuss reported delusions; conduct that is inconsistent with reported delusions; the absence of internal distractibility when reporting auditory and visual hallucinations; reporting visual hallucinations in black and white as opposed to colour; continuous or vague and inaudible auditory hallucinations, or stilted 'voices' therein; reported hallucinations alone or not being associated with any delusions; not utilizing any strategies to dampen reported hallucinations, or reporting that all commands of auditory hallucinations must be obeyed; and psychological testing (e.g., MMPI; Hathaway & McKinley, 1943; or cBSASH; Stephane et al., 2006) suggesting exaggeration or feigning (Resnick & Knoll, 2005).

On the one hand, culturally bound syndromes, including those with psychotic features, cover presentations that appear to fall outside conventional Western psychiatric diagnostic categories (Niehaus et al., 2004). On the other hand, psychosis occurs across all cultures, and cultural influences impact on communication of symptoms of psychosis, coping and willingness to seek treatment (Versola-Russo, 2006). In bilingual people, features of psychosis may be more evident when interviewed in their native language (Del Castillo, 1970). Whilst an interpreter may be required for the assessment of an impaired hearing or non-English speaking patient, the clinician must have skill in utilizing the interpreter for the latter in particular and also be mindful of any concerns the patient may have about confidentiality or possible tensions with an interpreter from the same or similar ethnic community. In addition, a patient's capacity to readily communicate in an acquired or second language may be affected by anxiety, thought disorder, depression and delusions (Farooq & Fear, 2003). In assessing psychosis with the use of an interpreter, the following are vital: speaking slowly and clearly, speaking directly to the patient and not the interpreter, concentration on non-verbal behavior, clarification of confusing responses and asking the interpreter about their impression of the normality of the conversation (Farooq & Fear, 2003). At the same time, interpreters may obfuscate the assessment of psychosis by making the following errors: omission or inclusion of information, taking over the interview, incorrect translation of an open into a closed question or vice-versa, shortening of a complex response and normalizing a bizarre response (Farooq & Fear, 2003).

Schizophrenia is overrepresented (in excess of 5%) in people with intellectual disability (Moran et al., 2008). In assessing psychosis in intellectually disabled patients, an accompanying familiar person or carer can not only provide support but invaluable collateral history. Although intellectually disabled patients with psychosis may experience deterioration of their communication skills or coherence of thinking, they are more likely to express symptoms via their behaviour. Examples are: new fears or avoidance, increased agitation or emergent anger, reduced emotional expression and response, loss of energy or motivation, social withdrawal, emergent mannerisms such as staring or responding to objects, talking or appearing to listen to non-existent others, covering their eyes or ears and brushing off unseen material from themselves. The following behaviours are generally not consistent with psychosis in those with intellectual disability: volitional self-talk and self-answering, shouts and screeches (most likely vocal tics) and symptoms modeled from others or that can start or stop at will (Aman, 1991; Ryan & Sunada, 1997).

Utility and Choice of Measures in Psychosis

There are a range of instruments that assess psychopathology in psychosis, including positive, negative, disorganization, mood and comorbid substance domains. Whilst symptom rating scales quantify clinical judgment of current psychopathology and change over time, their utility in routine clinical assessment is the subject of continuing debate (Mortimer, 2007). Most patients with psychosis experience only some of the possible symptoms assessed in scales and generally do not develop too many new symptoms over time. Although scales generally lump clusters of symptoms together, specific subscale scores may have more utility in assessment than a global score (Mortimer 2007).

The following instruments are recommended by the American Psychiatric Association (Rush, First & Blacker, 2008) as able to assess the main features, constructs and premorbid features of psychotic disorders, which are paramount for treatment planning. These instruments were chosen because of their reliability and validity. The items measured are generally related, but not interchangeable constructs of symptoms.

The Brief Psychiatric Rating Scale (BPRS; Overall et al., 1962) to measure the severity of general psychopathology, including positive, negative and mood symptoms. Similarly, the 30 item Positive and Negative Syndrome Scale (PANSS; Kay, Fiszbein & Opler, 1987), which has been partially derived from the BPRS, measures general psychopathology, but is rated by a clinical or semi-structured interview by a trained rater. The Scale for the Assessment of Positive Symptoms (SAPS; Andreasen, 1984) and Scale for the Assessment of Negative Symptoms (SANS; Andreasen, 1983) assess the severity of positive and negative symptoms, respectively, by clinical interview by a trained rater. Also useful, the Insight and Treatment Attitudes Questionnaire (ITAQ; McEvoy et al., 1989) is an 11 item, clinician administered instrument that rates illness awareness and insight, and consequently taps into ambivalence, or worse disavowal, in regard to participating in treatment. The BPRS, PANSS, SAPS and ITAQ are described in *Part 4* of this book.

The deficit syndrome and depression can be assessed with the Schedule for the Deficit Syndrome Scale (SDS; Kirkpatrick et al., 1989) and the Calgary Depression Scale for schizophrenia (CDSS; Addington, Addington & Schissel, 1990) respectively. The SDS rates the presence of the deficit syndrome in schizophrenia via a clinician interview and seeks specifically to differentiate primary from secondary depressive symptoms and has both interview questions and observational items. The CDSS was designed specifically to measure depression in people with schizophrenia. This instrument is helpful in complementing clinical assessment in delineating depression from negative symptoms and medication effects in schizophrenia (Upthegrove, 2009).

Alcohol and drug dependence is often comorbid with psychiatric illness. The Clinician Alcohol Use Scale (AUS; Drake, Mueser & McHugo, 1996) and Clinician Drug Use Scale (DUS; Drake, Mueser & McHugo, 1996) are 1 item, clinician rated scales which rate the severity of substance use disorders. The Drug Attitude Inventory (DAI; Hogan, Awad & Eastwood, 1983) is a 10 item self-report inventory which measures the patient's response to medications. Finally, the Alcohol, Smoking and Substance Involvement Screening Test (ASSIST; WHO, 2002) is a 8 question tool which screens for and stratifies the severity for substance use into low, moderate and high risk. This clinically useful tool may be applied to adults experiencing psychosis and for each substance they use, with the severity determining the levels of intervention—treatment as usual, brief or brief with specialist referral.

Recovery-Orientated Assessment

Flexibly tailored, collaborative and individualized assessment and care form the bedrocks of a recovery or personalized and patient-orientated approach. Recovery approaches to assessment of psychosis, of which there are a number of validated types in clinical use, respect and aim to optimize the patient's sense of self, social inclusion and their relationships, whilst instilling hope, rather than focusing on symptoms and impairments alone (Anthony, 1993; Anthony, 2000; Mueser et al., 2006; Rapp & Goscha, 2006). Recovery-focused approaches to assessment and care in people experiencing psychosis include: the Boston University model, in which the patient's rather than clinician's goals are central (Anthony et al., 1988; Mueser et al., 1998); the manualized approach of the Illness Management and Recovery Program which embraces psychoeducation, cognitive-behavioural approaches to adherence to treatment, relapse prevention plans and social and coping skills training (Mueser et al., 2006); the Collaborative Therapy Model (Gilbert et al., 2003), which is also manualized and utilizes psychoeducation, coping and relapse prevention strategies and a treatment journal recording these strategies (Gilbert et al., 2003; Castle et al., 2006); and the Strengths Model (Chopra et al., 2009; Rapp et al., 2006), which emphasizes the engagement between the clinician and patient to identify their strengths, resources and goals in recovery during the assessment phase and beyond.

The current worldwide ethical and legislative focus represents a shift towards supported decision making away from paternalism. The setting of interview and assessment should be the least restrictive as possible, for example in the community or person's home, where acuity of symptoms and or assessment of imminence of risk permit.

The clinical training required to facilitate a recovery patient-focused approach to assessment requires that assessments of people with psychosis take place by well trained clinicians (mental health and with competency in addiction medicine) in settings in which confidentiality, privacy and dignity can be maintained, with language that the person can understand or with access to independent interpreters who are not related to the person and with sensitivity to people from culturally and linguistically diverse backgrounds. Continuity of care and consistency of assessing clinicians are also paramount in establishing therapeutic alliances.

References

Addington, D., Addington J., & Schissel B. (1990). A depression rating scale for schizophrenics. *Schizophrenia Research, 3*, 247–251.

Ahmad, A., Ramakrishna, S., Meara J., & Doran, M. (2010). Autoimmune limbic encephalitis: A reversible form of rapidly progressive amnesia and seizures. *Journal Royal College Physicians Edinburgh, 40*, 123–125.

Aman, M. G. (1991). *Assessing psychopathology and behaviour problems in persons with mental retardation: A review of available instruments*. Publication No. (ADM) 91-1712. Rockville, MD: U.S. Department of Health and Human Services, Public Health Service, Alcohol, Drug Abuse, and Mental Health Administration, National Institute of Mental Health.

American Psychiatric Association. (2013). *Diagnostic and statistical manual of mental disorders* (5th ed.) Washington, DC: American Psychiatric Association.

Andreasen, N. C. (1983). *The Scale for the Assessment of Negative Symptoms (SANS)*. Iowa City, IA: The University of Iowa.

Andreasen, N. C. (1984). *The Scale for the Assessment of Positive Symptoms (SAPS)*. Iowa City, IA: The University of Iowa.

Anthony, W. (2000). A recovery-oriented service system: Setting some system level standards. *Psychiatric Rehabilitation Journal, 24*, 159–168.

Anthony, W. A. (1993). Recovery from mental illness: The guiding vision of the mental health service system in the 1990s. *Psychiatric Rehabilitation Journal, 16*, 11–23.

Anthony, W. A., Cohen, M. R., Farkas, M., & Cohen, B. F. (1988). Clinical care update: The chronically mentally ill. Case management—more than a response to a dysfunctional system. *Community Mental Health Journal, 24*, 219–228.

Asztely, F., & Kumlien, E. (2012). The diagnosis and treatment of limbic encephalitis. *Acta Neurologica Scandinavica, 126*(6), 365–375.

Borkowska, A., Pilaczyñska, E., & Rybakowski, J.K. (2003). The frontal lobe neuropsychological tests in patients with schizophrenia and/or obsessive-compulsive disorder. *The Journal of Neuropsychiatry and Clinical Neurosciences, 15*(3), 359–362.

Bosanac, P., & Castle, D. J. (2012). Schizophrenia and depression. *Medical Journal Australia* (Suppl. 4), 36–39.

Bourdon, K. H., Rae, D. S., Locke, B. Z., Narrow, W. E., & Regier, D. A. (1992). Estimating the prevalence of mental disorders in U.S. adults from the Epidemiologic Catchment Area Survey. *Public Health Reports, 107*(6), 663–668.

Braga, R. J., Petrides, G., & Figueira, I. (2004). Anxiety disorders in schizophrenia. *Comprehensive Psychiatry, 45*(6), 460–468.

British Medical Journal (BMJ). (2012). *Suicide risk management—Diagnosis step-by-step best practice*. Retrieved from http://bestpractice.bmj.com/ bestpractice/monograph/ 1016/ . . . /step-by-step.html

Buckley, P., Miller, B. J., Lehrer, D. S., & Castle, D. J. (2009). Psychiatric comorbidities and schizophrenia. *Schizophrenia Bulletin, 35*(2), 383–402.

Carpenter, W. T., Heinrichs, D. W., & Wagman, A. M. I. (1988). Deficit and non-deficit forms of schizophrenia: The concept. *American Journal of Psychiatry, 145*, 578–583.

Castle, D., & Gilbert, M. (2006). Collaborative therapy: Framework for mental health. *British Journal of Psychiatry, 189*, 467.

Chopra, P., Hamilton, B., Castle, D., Smith, J., Mileshkin, C., Deans, M., et al. (2009). Implementation of the strengths model at an area mental health service. *Australasian Psychiatry, 17*(3), 202–206.

Cooper, J., Mancuso, S. G., Borland, R., Slade, T., Galletly, C., & Castle, D. (2012). Tobacco smoking among people living with a psychotic illness: The second Australian survey of psychosis. *Australian and New Zealand Journal of Psychiatry, 46*, 851–863.

Del Castillo, J.C. (1970) The influence of language upon symptomatology in foreign born patients. *American Journal of Psychiatry, 127*, 242–244.

Drake, R. E., Mueser, K. T., & McHugo, G. J. (1996). Clinician rating scales: Alcohol use scale (AUS), drug use scale (DUS), and substance abuse treatment scale (SATS). In L. Sederer & B. Dickey (eds.), *Outcomes Assessment in Clinical Practice* (pp. 113–116.). Baltimore, MD: Williams & Wilkins.

Farooq, S., & Fear, C. (2003). Working through interpreters. *Advances in Psychiatric Treatment, 9*, 104–109.

Folstein, M. F., Folstein, S. E., & McHugh, P. R. (1975). "Mini-mental state": A practical method for grading the cognitive state of patients for the clinician. *Journal Psychiatric Research, 12*(3), 189–198.

Gaebel, W. (2012). Status of psychotic disorders in ICD-11. *Schizophrenia Bulletin, 38*(5), 895–898.

Gilbert, M., Miller, K., Berk, L., Ho, V., & Castle, D. (2003). Scope for psychosocial treatments in psychosis: An overview of collaborative therapy. *Australasian Psychiatry, 11*, 220–224.

Goodwin, R., Stayner, D.A., Chinman, M.J., & Davidson, L. (2001). Impact of panic attacks on rehabilitation and quality of life among persons with severe psychotic disorders. *Psychiatric Services, 52*(7), 920–924.

Green, M. F. (2006). Cognitive impairment and functional outcome in schizophrenia and bipolar disorder. *Journal of Clinical Psychiatry, 67*(Suppl. 9), 3–8.

Grundy, S. C., Cleeman, J. I., Daniels, S. R., Donato, K.A., Eckel, R. H., Franklin B.A., et al. (2005). AHA/NHLBI scientific statement diagnosis and management of the metabolic syndrome. An American Heart Association/National Heart, Lung, and Blood Institute scientific statement. *Circulation, 112*, 2735–2752.

Hafner, H., Riechler-Rossler, A., & Maurer K. (1992). First onset and symptomatology of schizophrenia: A chapter of epidemiological and neurobiological research into age and sex differences. *European Archives of Psychiatry and Clinical Neuroscience, 242*, 109–118.

Harris, E. C., & Barraclough, B. (1998). Excess mortality of mental disorder. *British Journal of Psychiatry, 173*,11–53.

Harvey, P. D. (2007). Cognitive outcomes in the CATIE schizophrenia trial: Why do they seem different from previous results? *Psychiatry (Edgmont), 4*(9), 20–23.

Hathaway, S. R., & McKinley, J. C. (1943). *Manual for the Minnesota Multiphasic Personality Inventory*. New York, NY: Psychological Corporation.

Hofer, A., Kemmler, G., Eder, U., Edlinger, M., Hummer, M., & Fleischhacker, W.W. (2004). Quality of life in schizophrenia: The impact of psychopathology, attitude toward medication, and side effects. *The Journal of Clinical Psychiatry, 65*(7), 932.

Hogan, T. P., Awad, A. G., & Eastwood, R. (1983). A self-report scale predictive of drug compliance in schizophrenics: Reliability and discriminative validity. *Psychological Medicine, 13*, 177–183.

Huppert, J., & Smith, T. (2001). Longitudinal analysis of the contributions of anxiety and depression to quality of life in schizophrenia. *Journal of Nervous and Mental Disease, 189*, 669–675.

Huppert, J. D., and Smith, T. E. (2005). Anxiety and schizophrenia: The interaction of subtypes of anxiety and psychotic symptoms. *CNS Spectrums, 10*(9), 721–731.

Jablensky, A., Sartorius, N., Ernderg, G., Anker, M., Korten, A., Cooper J. E., Day, R., & Bertelsen, A. (1992). Schizophrenia: Manifestations, incidence and course in different cultures: A World Health Organization 10 country study. *Psychological Medicine*, (Suppl. 20), 1–97.

Kay, S., Fiszbein, A., & Opler, L. (1987). The Positive and Negative Syndrome Scale (PANSS) for schizophrenia. *Schizophrenia Bulletin, 13*, 262–276.

Kirkpatrick, B., Buchanan, R.W., McKenney, P. D., Alphs, L. D., & Carpenter, W.T. (1989). The schedule for the deficit syndrome: An instrument for research in schizophrenia. *Psychiatric Research, 30*, 119–124.

Klonsky, E. D., Kotov, K., Bakst, S., Rabinowitz, J., & Bromet E.J. (2012). Hopelessness as a predictor of attempted suicide among first admission patients with psychosis: A 10 year cohort study. *Suicide and Life-threatening Behaviour, 42*(1), 1–10.

Large, M. M., & Nielssen, O. (2011). Violence in first-episode psychosis: A systematic review and meta-analysis. *Schizophrenia Research, 125*(2/3), 209–220.

McEvoy, J. P., Apperson, L. G., Applebaum, P. S., Ortlip, P., Brecosky, J., Hammill, K., et al. (1989). Insight in schizophrenia: Its relation to acute psychopathology. *Journal of Nervous and Mental Disease, 177*, 43–47.

Moore, E., Mancuso, S. G., Slade, T., Galletly, C. A., & Castle, D. J. (2012). The impact of alcohol and illicit drugs on people with psychosis: The second Australian national survey of psychosis. *Australian and New Zealand Journal of Psychiatry*, 46, 864–878.

Moran, V., Leonard, H., Bourke, J., & Jablensky, A. (2008). Intellectual disability co-occurring with schizophrenia and other psychiatric illness: Population-based study. *British Journal Psychiatry, 193*, 364–372.

Mortimer, A. M. (2007). Symptom rating scales and outcome in schizophrenia. *British Journal of Psychiatry* (Suppl. 191), 7–14.

Mueser, K. T., Bond, G. R., Drake, R. E., & Resnick, S. G. (1998). Models of community care for severe mental illness: A review of research on case management. *Schizophrenia Bulletin, 34*, 37–74.

Mueser, K. T., Meyer, P. S., Penn, D. L., Clancy, R., Clancy, D. M., & Salyers, M. P. (2006). The Illness Management and Recovery Program: Rationale, development, and preliminary findings. *Schizophrenia Bulletin, 32*(Suppl. 1), 32–43.

Newman, S. C., & Bland, R. C. (1991). Mortality in a cohort of patients with schizophrenia: A record linkage study. *Canadian Journal Psychiatry, 36*, 239–245.

NICE. (2011). Psychosis with coexisting substance misuse. The NICE guideline on assessment and management in adults and young people. Retrieved from www.nice.org.uk/nicemedia/live/13414/53691/53691.pdf

Niehaus, D. J., Oosthuizen P., Lochner, C., Emsley, R. A., Jordaan, E., et al. (2004). A culture-bound syndrome 'amafufunyana' and a culture-specific event 'ukuthwasa': Differentiated by a family history of schizophrenia and other psychiatric disorders. *Psychopathology, 37*(2), 59–63.

Nuechterlein, K. H., Green, M. F., Kern, R. S., Baade, L. E., Barch, D. M., Cohen, J. D., et al. (2008). The MATRICS consensus cognitive battery: Part 1. Test selection, reliability, and validity. *American Journal Psychiatry, 165*, 203–213.

Othmer, E., & Othmer, S. (2002). *The clinical interview using DSM-IV TR, vol. 1: Fundamentals*. Washington, DC: American Psychiatric Association.

Overall, J. E., & Gorham, D. R. (1962). The brief psychiatric rating scale. *Psychological Reports, 10*, 799–812.

Özdemir, Ö., Tükel, R., Türksoy, N., & Üçok, A. (2003). Clinical characteristics in obsessive-compulsive disorder with schizophrenia. *Comprehensive Psychiatry, 44*(4), 311–316.

Pallanti, S., Quercioli, L., & Hollander, E. (2004). Social anxiety in outpatients with schizophrenia: A relevant cause of disability. *American Journal of Psychiatry, 161*(1), 53–58.

Pokos, V., & Castle, D. J. (2006). Prevalence of comorbid anxiety disorders in schizophrenia spectrum disorders: A literature review. *Current Psychiatry Reviews, 2*(3), 285–307.

Poyurovsky, M., Hramenkov, S., Isakov, V., Rauchverger, B., Modai, I., Schneidman M., et al. (2001). Obsessive–compulsive disorder in hospitalized patients with chronic schizophrenia. *Psychiatry Research, 102*(1), 49–57.

Rapp, C., & Goscha, R. C. (2006). *The strengths model* (2nd ed.). New York, NY: Oxford University Press.

Resnick, P. J., & Knoll, J. (2005). Faking it: How to detect malingered psychosis. *Journal of Family Practice, 4*(11), 12–25.

Roose, S. P., Glassman, A. H., Walsh, B. T., Woodring, S., & Vital-Herne, J. (1983). Depression, delusions, and suicide. *American Journal of Psychiatry, 140*, 1159–1162.

Rush, A. R., First, M. B., & Blacker, D. (Eds.). (2008). *Handbook of psychiatric measures* (2nd ed.). Washington, DC: American Psychiatric Association.

Ryan, R., & Sunada, K. (1997). Medical evaluation of persons with mental retardation referred for psychiatric assessment. *General Hospital Psychiatry, 19*(4), 274–280.

Simon, R. I. (2006). Suicide risk assessment: Is clinical experience enough? *Journal of the American Academy of Psychiatry and the Law, 34*(3), 276–278.

Singh, J. P., Serper, M., Reinharth, J., & Fazel, S. (2011). Structured assessment of violence risk in schizophrenia and other psychiatric disorders: A systematic review of the validity, reliability, and item content of 10 available instruments. *Schizophrenia Bulletin, 37*(5), 899–912.

Siris, S. G. (2001). Suicide and schizophrenia. *Journal of Psychopharmacology, 15*(2), 127–135.

Stephane, M., Pellizer, J., Roberts, S., & McClannahan, K. (2006). Computerized binary scale of auditory speech hallucinations (cbSASH). *Schizophrenia Research, 88*(1/3), 73–81.

Suuvisaari, P. J., Perälä, J., Suvisaari, J., Saarni, S. I., Kuoppasalmi, K., et al. (2009). Depression in schizophrenia and early psychosis: Implications for assessment and treatment. *Advances in Psychiatric Treatment, 15*, 372–379.

Upthegrove, R. (2009). Depression in schizophrenia and early psychosis: Implications for assessment and treatment. *Advances in Psychiatric Treatment, 15*, 372–379.

van Os, J., Linscott, R. J., Myin-Germeys, I., Delespaul, P., & Krabbendam, L. (2008). A systematic review and meta-analysis of the psychosis continuum: Evidence for psychosis-proneness-persistence-impairment model of psychotic disorder. *Psychological Medicine, 8*, 1–17.

van Os, J. A. (2009). Salience dysregulation syndrome. *British Journal of Psychiatry, 194*(2), 101–103.

Versola-Russo, J. (2006). Cultural and demographic factors of schizophrenia. *International Journal of Psychosocial Rehabilitation, 10*(2), 89–103.

Velakoulis, D., Walterfang, M., Mocellin, R., Pantelis, C., & McLean, C. (2009). Frontotemporal dementia presenting as schizophrenia-like psychosis in young people: Clinicopathological series and review of cases. *British Journal of Psychiatry, 194*(4), 298–305.

Walsh, E., Buchanan, A., & Fahy T. (2002). Violence and schizophrenia: Examining the evidence. *British Journal of Psychiatry, 180*, 490–495.

Warman, D. M., Forman, E. M., Henriques, G. R., Brown, G. K., & Beck, A. T. (2004). Suicide and psychosis: Beyond depression and hopelessness. *Suicide and Life-Threatening Behaviour, 34*(1), 77–86.

Waterreus, A., Morgan, V., Castle, D., Galletly, C., Jablensky, A., Di Prinzio, P., & Shah, S. (2012). Medication for psychosis—Consumption and consequences: The second Australian national survey of psychosis. *Australian and New Zealand Journal of Psychiatry, 46*, 762–773.

Wetherell, J. L., Palmer, B. W., Thorp, S. R., Patterson, T. L., Golshan, S., & Jeste, D. V. (2003). Anxiety symptoms and quality of life in middle-aged and older outpatients with schizophrenia and schizoaffective disorder. *Journal of Clinical Psychiatry, 64*(12), 1476–1482.

WHO ASSIST Working Group. (2002). The alcohol, smoking and substance involvement screening test: Development, reliability and feasibility (ASSIST). *Addiction, 97*(9), 1183–1194.

Wing J. K., & Fryers T. (1976). *Psychiatric services in Camberwell and Salford.* London, UK: MRC Social Psychiatry Unit.

Witt, K., van Dom, R., & Fazel, S. (2013). Risk factors for violence in psychosis: Systematic review and meta-regression analysis of 110 studies. *PLoS One, 8*(2), e55942. doi:10.1371/journal.pone.0055942.

Wolfersdorf, M., Keller, F., Steiner, B., & Hole, G. (1987). Delusional depression and suicide. *Acta Psychiatrica Scandinavica, 76*, 359–363.

World Health Organization. (1994). *International statistical classification of diseases and health related problems.* Geneva, Switzerland: World Health Organization.

6

PSYCHOSIS-LIKE EXPERIENCES IN NON-CLINICAL POPULATIONS

Frank Larøi, Andrea Raballo and Vaughan Bell

Introduction

Psychosis-like experiences (PLE), also referred to in the literature as "subclinical psychotic experiences" or "attenuated psychotic symptoms," are defined as experiences that resemble the positive symptoms of psychosis as encountered in clinical settings but which do not cause the levels of distress or impairment that would lead to clinically significant distress, disability or loss of functioning. This is usually because these experiences are less frequent, intense or intrusive, or because they are not associated with overwhelming emotional reactions.

It is worth noting that psychosis-like experiences may also be captured by terms such as *schizotypy, anomalous perceptual experiences, delusional ideation* or *magical thinking*, although these latter terms often have their own conceptual associations and traditions, which mean that the overlap is not complete. For example, while schizotypy includes psychosis-like experiences, it may also include characteristics such as subclinical anhedonia and social withdrawal. In contrast, *anomalous perceptual experiences* may, in addition to psychosis-like experiences, also include a range of hallucinatory experiences that are not usually associated with idiopathic psychosis—such as migraine aura or sleep hallucinations. In this chapter we are specifically focusing on experiences that are associated with, or thought to be conceptually related to, psychiatric disorders.

Examples of PLE include: "Do you ever feel as if you are being persecuted in some way?", "Do you ever hear voices when you are alone?", "Do you ever feel as if the thoughts in your head are being taken away from you?", "Do you ever hear your own thoughts spoken aloud in your head, so that someone near might be able to hear them?", "Do you think you could learn to read others' minds if you wanted to?", "Have you ever felt that you have special, almost magical powers?"

As mentioned above, they are not experienced as frequently as in psychosis, nor do they elicit high levels of distress or functional impairments.

Prevalence Rates

PLE are more prevalent in the general population than clinical psychotic disorders (van Os et al., 2009), suggesting that these experiences may occur as part of a non-pathological phenotype which lies on a continuum with psychotic disorder. A recent meta-analysis by van Os et al. (2009) reported a median prevalence of around 5% for PLE in the general population. However, one limitation with basing prevalence rates on meta-analyses for "PLE" as a whole is that important nuances are lost, such as the nature and frequency of specific experiences, as well as their qualitative-experiential prominence. In Johns et al. (2004), 4.2% of the general population who was surveyed answered affirmatively to a general hallucination item ("Over the past year, have there been times when you heard or saw things that other people could not?"), whereas only 0.7% endorsed a more specific item about auditory-verbal hallucinations ("Did you at any time hear voices saying quite a few words or sentences when there was no-one around that might account for it?"). Van Os and colleagues (2000) made a distinction between psychotic symptoms that were clinically relevant (i.e., associated with distress and help-seeking behavior) and symptoms that were subclinical (i.e., no distress or help-seeking behavior). This revealed that prevalence rates for clinically relevant and non-clinically relevant delusions were 3.3% versus 8.7%, respectively, and for hallucinations the equivalent rates were 1.7% versus 6.2%.

In addition, there are differences in the characteristic features of psychotic symptoms reported by healthy people when compared to individuals suffering from psychosis. In the context of auditory-verbal hallucinations, studies that compare these two groups of individuals reveal that differences lie largely in the frequency and duration with which they are experienced and age of onset, with the non-clinical group having an earlier onset, often in childhood, and less frequent experiences of voices. The most significant differentiating factor, however, is the degree of negative voice content, with patients reporting a preponderance of negative voices. By contrast, voices experienced by individuals without need for care are mostly neutral or pleasant in content (Johns et al., 2014).

Clinical Relevance

Research on long-term outcomes suggests that individuals who report PLE are at significantly increased risk of developing a clinical disorder, including psychosis. Poulton et al. (2000) found that 11-year-old children who reported psychotic symptoms were at a 5- to 16-fold specific increased risk of adult psychotic disorder. Welham et al. (2009) have also documented that self-reported PLE at age 14 years were associated with an increased risk for adulthood psychotic disorder, assessed at age 21 years. Hanssen et al. (2005) found that, among a general population sample of 18- to 64-year-olds, the number of those who transitioned to clinical psychotic disorder after 2 years was more than 60 times higher for individuals who had previously reported PSE compared with those without. Individuals who report PLE, then, represent a valuable population for studying the developmental trajectory to schizophrenia and related illnesses. It is important to note, however, that PLE observed early in life (e.g., in children) are in general not pathological when they occur alone but that they may become so when, for example, the experiences are repeated and persistent. Thus, it is not just the presence of PLE per se, but the psychopathological, developmental and psychological context that determines outcomes (Kaymaz & van Os, 2010; also see following sections in this chapter).

The Continuum/Dimensional View

One may distinguish between at least two types of continua (Larøi, 2012): a continuum of experience and a continuum of risk. A continuum of experience is where different kinds of experience are related to the specific PLE in question. For instance, in the case of hallucinations, related experiences, such as vivid daydreams and intrusive and vivid thoughts, may lie on such a continuum. Regarding a continuum of risk, people are seen to differ in (a) their proneness to experiencing PLEs and (b) their risk of developing problematic PLEs (i.e., developing clinical symptoms) with need for care. In general, although there is robust evidence for a continuum of psychotic experiences with a broad distribution in the general population, there is less evidence that this represents a single underlying continuum of risk for psychosis (for more on this, see Johns et al., 2014).

Empirical evidence of a putative continuity between clinical and non-clinical populations in terms of PLE comes from a range of findings. First, more people experience PLEs than individuals who receive psychiatric diagnoses (van Os et al., 2009), suggesting a symptomatic continuum between non-patients in the general population and patients with psychotic disorder. Second, in general population samples, hallucinations are correlated with delusions, just as they are in psychotic disorders (Johns & van Os, 2001). Third, PLE (and the related concept of schizotypy) show a similar pattern of symptom dimensional structure to psychiatric symptoms. That is, both clinical and non-clinical populations show dimensions of positive, negative and disorganized/affective symptoms. Fourth, both PLE and psychotic disorders have similar key risk factors, signifying etiological continuity between them. These include demographic (e.g., male sex, younger age, single marital status, being unemployed, belonging to an ethnic minority group), personality (e.g., neuroticism), environmental (e.g., alcohol and drug use, stressful or traumatic experience, exposure to urbanicity), genetic (e.g., family history of psychotic disorders) and neurocognitive (e.g., executive functions, metalizing abilities) risk factors (Myin-Germeys, Krabbendam & van Os, 2003; van Os et al., 2009).

A dimensional/continuum view also maintains that features of a pathological condition such as schizophrenia lie on a continuum with normal behavior and experience, and that schizotypy (viewed as an attenuated form or phenotype of schizophrenia/psychotic disorder) lies somewhere between these two extremes. Indeed, a large body of evidence examining, for example, cognitive and psychological mechanisms, symptom dimensions, social and genetic factors, and demographic risk factors provide evidence for such a claim (cf. Johns & van Os, 2001). It is important to note in this context that schizotypy plays an integral role in defining high-risk populations. For instance, in the criteria of prodromal syndromes, one of the three prodromal syndromes includes "genetic risk and deterioration syndrome," which involves the person fulfilling criteria for schizotypal personality disorder (in addition to a significant drop in psychosocial functioning). Similarly, the role of schizotypal personality disorder is also prominent in other high-risk criteria, such as the PACE ultra-high-risk ones.

Quasi-Continuous/Continuum-Threshold View

Although partly blurred by the polythetic, descriptive structure of contemporary diagnostic systems (i.e., ICD-10, DSM-5), a fully continuous relationship between PLE and psychiatric disorder can be distinguished from a quasi-continuous/continuum-threshold model. The latter is more consistent with the observed skewed distribution of PLE in the general population (i.e., where the majority of the population have low values), qualitative differences in these experiences along the continuum, and the contribution of various risk factors involved in the "transitions" from non-clinical to clinical states. Furthermore, studies comparing PLE in individuals with and without need for care indicate that, in addition to similarities, there are also specific differences in the qualitative features of the experience, and possibly the underlying mechanisms, of PLE across the continuum, some of which might contribute to clinical status.

Moreover, there is emerging evidence that a latent categorical structure of the population underlies the observed continuum of psychosis experience, with one group that is liable to psychosis and another group that is not (Kaymaz & van Os, 2010). In the former, PLE are associated with cognitive and emotional difficulties and a greater likelihood of need for care; by contrast, in the second group, PLE are associated with reduced morbidity and possibly, a different etiology. This could partly explain why two people with the same level of PLE may differ in their clinical outcome. So, although PLE seem to be continuous and distributed across the general population, the risk for developing psychosis might actually be discontinuous rather than truly continuous in the population.

The Psychosis Proneness-Persistence-Impairment Model

A crucial question is whether the presence of PLE predicts the development of clinical states and/or future need for care. Various outcomes for those with PLE may be observed. The most common outcome in childhood is a discontinuation over time. Alternatively, PLE may continue over time with no negative impact (i.e., they remain subclinical over time). Finally, for others, PLE may persist into adolescence and adulthood, and can develop into a clinical psychotic disorder or other diagnosable mental health problems. For instance, Bartels-Velthuis et al. (2011) reported that as many as 76% of children who reported hearing voices at age 7 and 8 stopped hearing voices by age 12–13. Wiles et al. (2006) also showed that a great majority of individuals with PLE similarly did not persist. Hanssen et al. (2005) reported that among individuals with new, incident, PLE at baseline, only 8% had persistence of the PLE at the subclinical level, whereas 84% no longer presented with any PLE at follow-up. The remaining 8% made the transition to clinical disorder. A number of variables may influence this transition to clinical disorder including the number of PLE, degree and persistence of PLE over time, presence of affective dysregulation, pre-morbid social dysfunction, presence of negative symptoms and the use of functional versus "symptomatic" coping (Kaymaz & van Os, 2010).

The psychosis proneness-persistence-impairment model (van Os et al., 2009) attempts to explain this trajectory for psychosis, maintaining that PLE become pathological when they persist. Persistence causes distress and functional impairment and leads to the development of other symptoms. Further, according to this model, PLE that become more numerous and persistent over time are the consequence of a complex interaction between psychological factors (e.g., cognitive biases, affective dysregulation), environmental exposures (e.g., trauma, cannabis use, high levels of urbanicity) and genetic risk (e.g., familial liability to psychosis or other psychopathological disorders). Another important factor that increases the risk of persistence is the emergence of a combined "hallucinatory-delusional state" (a clustering of these two types of symptoms), which may then elicit negative emotions and maladaptive coping, plus other symptoms, leading to functional impairment and a diagnosable psychotic disorder. Thus, an important aspect of this model is that it is the presence of both symptoms (hallucination and delusion ideation) as opposed to one in isolation, that results in increased symptom severity and persistence, as well as an increased risk of clinical outcome and need for care. It is suggested also that the sequence in which these symptoms arise is such: first, a high level of proneness to hallucinations and/or anomalous perceptual experiences, and second, delusional ideation as a way of explaining these former anomalous experiences (where psychological factors such as cognitive biases play an important role). Thus, the pathway from hallucinatory/anomalous perceptual experiences to clinical psychosis is seen as being mediated, at least in part, by secondary delusional formation (cf. Krabbendam et al., 2005).

Direct Causation

It is worth noting that although PLE are usually discussed in terms of longer-term causes and developmental risk factors, they can be more directly triggered by acute psychological or physiological stress—including fatigue, fever, substance use, sensory deprivation, sleep deprivation, exposure to extreme or personally significant events such as grief, loss, violence or abuse. In these contexts, PLEs are typically transitory and usually abate shortly after the stressful situation ends—although in addition, the episode may add to the longer-term risk for later psychosis or enduring PLE. There is also a long tradition of induced states, which includes voluntary participation in stressful or sensorially intense situations (such as in certain religious rituals), as a specific attempt to alter consciousness and where transitory PLEs can be common. These are particularly found in spiritual, religious or culturally sanctioned rituals and recreational pursuits and may additionally involve substances specifically taken for their hallucinogenic properties. It is worth noting that these situations may lead to more intense hallucinations in people predisposed to PLE, and that intense stress can trigger drug-induced and acute psychotic episodes. More typically, however, these experiences abate after the inducing situation finishes.

The Assessment of Psychosis-Like Experiences

The use of accurate and rapid screening instruments for identifying PLE in the general population is highly valuable to both researchers and clinicians. People with high levels of PLE can be conceptualized as representing a "pre-prodromal" population which provides a complementary approach to the ultra-high-risk prodromal strategy. It is important to note, however, that the assessment strategies outlined in this chapter concern the former type (PLE). Regarding the latter type (i.e., instruments that detect persons fulfilling specific criteria such as for prodromal syndromes), see Tambyraja (*Chapter 8*).

Several brief self-report measures exist which are suitable for screening large non-clinical samples when interview is not feasible. Some of the newer scales include the 32-item Cardiff Anomalous Perceptions Scale (CAPS; Bell et al., 2006), which assesses a range of anomalous perceptual experiences including psychosis-like experiences, phenomena more typically associated with neurological disorders, and changes in the clarity and intensity of sensory experience, and the 42-item Community Assessment of Psychic Experiences (CAPE; Stefanis et al., 2002), which measures severity dimensions of positive, negative and depression symptomatology in the general population. The Oxford Liverpool Inventory of Feelings and Experiences (O-LIFE; Mason et al., 1995) has 104 items assessing several dimensions of schizotypy, including perceptual aberrations, magical thinking, cognitive disorganization, anhedonia, negative schizotypy and impulsive nonconformity. Prior to the development of the CAPE and CAPS, commonly used rating scales included the Magical Ideation Scale (MIS; Eckblad & Chapman, 1983), Perceptual Aberration Scale (PAS; Chapman et al., 1978), the Schizotypal Personality Questionnaire (SPQ; Raine, 1991) and the Structured Interview for Assessing Perceptual Anomalies (Bunney et al., 1999). The Launay-Slade Hallucination Scale (LSHS; Launay & Slade, 1981) and its revisions is also frequently used as a measure of hallucination proneness, although it actually assesses a range of cognitive and perceptual phenomena. These rating scales are reviewed in *Part 4*.

Recently, Kelleher et al. (2011) have shown that it may be possible to screen the general adolescent population for PLE with a high degree of accuracy using a short (7 item) questionnaire: The Adolescent Psychotic Symptom Screener (see Kelleher, *Chapter 9*, for more details on this study, and *Part 4* for the scale description). It was found, for example, that an answer of "Yes, definitely" to a screening item on auditory hallucinations was very predictive of interview-verifiable PLE. Other studies have yielded similar findings. For instance, Konings et al. (2006) and Liraud et al. (2004) both found a good correlation between the Community Assessment of Psychic Experiences (CAPE) and interviewer-rated psychosis.

Key issues for self-report measures include the importance of defining a timeline (e.g., lifetime, within the last month) and excluding experiences associated with drugs, fatigue and so forth. It is preferable to avoid dichotomous response scales and to use dimensional ones (Likert scales) both for statistical purposes (e.g., to increase variation in scores) and to avoid defensive responding. Also, it is preferable to assess a large array of experiences while at the same time being able to extract specific factor scores (e.g., auditory hallucination score, persecutory delusion score, etc.) based on total scores. For instance, in a series of studies (Armando et al., 2010, 2012) that included samples of young adults from the general community, and using the CAPE to assess PLE, they found that specific subtypes of PLE may be more closely related to distress, poor functioning and the emergence of full-threshold disorder than other subtypes of PLE. The results showed that, in particular, the persecutory ideas and bizarre experiences subtypes of the CAPE seemed to have stronger psychopathological significance than other subtypes of PLE as they were found to be strongly associated with distress, depression, poor functioning, poor mental health status and help-seeking behavior. Having participants rate supplementary dimensions (e.g., degree of distress, conviction, intrusiveness, frequency) is additionally extremely informative and increases sensitivity of the measure (e.g., only include those with these experiences that are also distressing or that preoccupy the person). For instance, Kline et al. (2014) observed that including a distress scale within a screener aids in identifying a group more likely to meet clinical high-risk criteria, and further, that PLE that participants described as neutral or positive did not appear to be relevant for clinical high-risk screening. Finally, it may also prove pertinent, for example, in order to increase the sensitivity of the evaluation, to assess with other measures that focus on other aspects, especially those aspects that have been shown to be associated with transition to clinical disorder. This may include measures evaluating coping strategies, affective (e.g., depression, anxiety) and other symptoms (e.g., negative) and general social functioning.

It is additionally important, however, to take into account possible limits of self-report/screening instruments in the context of PLE. Clearly one disadvantage of these measures is that limited detail is recorded about the experiences, or that that may not be able to detect pertinent samples (e.g., high-risk or ultra-high-risk persons). This may be offset by using a self-report scale as a screening measure and then, for those who report these experiences, administering more detailed and sensitive instruments. It is also important to bear in mind that the scales are not a good guide to etiology such that, for example, similar experiences may also present in other etiologies as in idiopathic PLE and in epilepsy with simple partial seizures. However, as rapid and broad assessments, self-report scales of PLE tend to be good instruments for tracking change over time and are often used in clinical work for inter-sessional measures where more complete structured or semi-structured assessments are often used at the beginning or end of intervention.

To summarize, the following are some key points to take into account when choosing a PLE measure:

- Self-report measures correlate highly with interview-based measures, but that it is preferable to use both forms (the former as a screening measure and the latter in order to collect more information and/or to increase sensitivity)
- Be aware of the timeline used in the measure
- Instructions excluding the presence of PLE in particular situations (drugs, fatigue, etc.) are important
- Dimensional response scales are preferable to dichotomous ones
- Supplementary dimensional response scales are highly useful (e.g., associated distress)
- The measure should assess a wide array of PLE and furthermore where sub-scores can be calculated.

Conclusion

Brief self-report measures of PLE, such as those included in this chapter, are both quick and easy to use and are therefore highly useful when screening large samples when interview is not feasible. These PLE measures vary somewhat and therefore it is important to be aware of how they differ and also to consider a number of issues before choosing the measure that is best suited for the context in question. On the other hand, if one requires more detailed information or a more sensitive measure, or if one wishes to detect individuals fulfilling specific (diagnostic) criteria, then other measures should be utilized.

References

Armando, M., Nelson, B., Yung, A. R., Ross, M., Birchwood, M., Girardi, P., & Fiori Nastro, P. (2010). Psychotic-like experiences and correlation with distress and depressive symptoms in a community sample of adolescents and young adults. *Schizophrenia Research, 119*, 258–265.

Armando, M., Nelson, B., Yung, A. R., Saba, R., Monducci, E., Dario, C., et al. (2012). Psychotic experiences subtypes, poor mental health status and help-seeking behavior in a community sample of young adults. *Early Intervention in Psychiatry, 3*, 300–308.

Bartels-Velthuis, A. A., van de Willige, G., Jenner, J. A., van Os, J., & Wiersma, D. (2011). Course of auditory vocal hallucinations in childhood: 5-year follow-up study. *British Journal of Psychiatry, 199*, 296–302.

Bell, V., Halligan, P. W., & Ellis, H. D. (2006). The Cardiff Anomalous Perceptions Scale (CAPS): A new validated measure of anomalous perceptual experience. *Schizophrenia Bulletin, 32*, 366–377.

Bunney, W., Hetrick, W., Bunney, B., Patterson, J., Jin, Y., Potkin, S., & Sandman, C. (1999). Structured interview for assessing perceptual anomalies. *Schizophrenia Bulletin, 25*(3), 577–592.

Chapman, L. J., Chapman, J. P., & Raulin, M. L. (1978). Body-image aberration in schizophrenia. *Journal of Abnormal Psychology, 87*, 399–407.

Eckblad, M., & Chapman, L. J. (1983). Magical ideation as an indicator of schizotypy. *Journal of Consulting and Clinical Psychology, 51*, 215–225.

Hanssen, M., Bak, M., Bijl, R., Vollebergh, W., & van Os, J. (2005). The incidence and outcome of subclinical psychotic experiences in the general population. *British Journal of Clinical Psychology, 44*, 181–191.

Johns, L. C., & van Os, J. (2001). The continuity of psychotic experiences in the general population. *Clinical Psychology Review, 21*, 1125–1141.

Johns, L. C., Cannon, M., Singleton, N., Murray, R. M., Farrell, M., . . . Meltzer, H. (2004). Prevalence and correlates of self-reported psychotic symptoms in the British population. *British Journal of Psychiatry, 185*, 298–305.

Johns, L., Kompus, K., Connell, M., Humpston, C., Lincoln, T., Longden, E., . . . Larøi, F. (2014). Auditory hallucinations in persons with and without a need for care. *Schizophrenia Bulletin, 40*, 255–264.

Kaymaz, N., & van Os, J. (2010). Extended psychosis phenotype—Yes: Single continuum—Unlikely. *Psychological Medicine, 40*, 1963–1966.

Kelleher, I., Harley, M., Murtagh, A., & Cannon, M. (2011). Are screening instruments valid for psychotic-like experiences? A validation study of screening questions for psychotic-like experiences using in-depth clinical interview. *Schizophrenia Bulletin, 37*, 362–369.

Kline, E., Thompson, E., Bussell, K., Pitts, S.C., Reeves, G., & Schiffman, J. (2014). PLEs and distress among adolescents using mental health services. *Schizophrenia Research, 152*, 498–502.

Krabbendam, L., Myin-Germeys, I., Bak, M., & van Os, J. (2005). Explaining transitions over the hypothesized psychosis continuum. *Australian and New Zealand Journal of Psychiatry, 39*, 180–186.

Konings, M., Bak, M., Hanssen, M., van Os, J., & Krabbendam, L. (2006). Validity and reliability of the CAPE: A self-report instrument for the measurement of psychotic experiences in the general population. *Acta Psychiatrica Scandinavica, 114*, 55–61.

Larøi, F. (2012). How do auditory verbal hallucinations in patients differ from those in nonpatients? *Frontiers in Human Neuroscience, 6*, 25.

Launay, G., & Slade, P. D. (1981). The measurement of hallucinatory predisposition in male and female prisoners. *Personality and Individual Differences, 2*, 221–234.

Liraud, F., Droulout, T., Parrot, M., & Verdoux, H. (2004). Agreement between self-rated and clinically assessed symptoms in subjects with psychosis. *Journal of Nervous and Mental Disease, 192*, 352–356.

Mason, O., Claridge, G., & Jackson, M. (1995). New scales for the assessment of schizotypy. *Personality and Individual Differences, 18*, 7–13.

Myin-Germeys, I., Krabbendam, L., & van Os, J. (2003). Continuity of psychotic symptoms in the community. *Current Opinion in Psychiatry, 16*, 443–449.

Poulton, R., Caspi, A., Moffitt, T. E., Cannon, M., Murray, R., & Harrington, H. (2000). Children's self-reported psychotic symptoms and adult schizophreniform disorder: A 15-year longitudinal study. *Archives of General Psychiatry, 57*, 1053–1058.

Raine, A. (1991). The SPQ: A scale for the assessment of schizotypal personality based on DSMIII-R criteria. *Schizophrenia Bulletin, 17*, 555–564.

Stefanis, N. C., Hanssen, M., Smirnis, N. K., Avramopoulos, D. A., Evdokimidis, I. K., Stefanis, C.N., . . . Van Os, J. (2002). Evidence that three dimensions of psychosis have a distribution in the general population. *Psychological Medicine, 32*, 347–358.

van Os, J., Hanssen, M., Bijl, R.V., & Ravelli, A. (2000). Strauss (1969) revisited: A psychosis continuum in the general population? *Schizophrenia Research, 45*, 11–20.

van Os, J., Linscott, R. J., Myin-Germeys, I., Delespaul, P., & Krabbendam, L. (2009). A systematic review and meta-analysis of the psychosis continuum: Evidence for a psychosis proneness-persistence impairment model of psychotic disorder. *Psychological Medicine, 39*, 179–195.

Welham, J., Scott, J., Williams, G., Najman, J., Bor, W., O'Callaghan, M., & McGrath, J. (2009). Emotional and behavioural antecedents of young adults who screen positive for non-affective psychosis: A 21-year birth cohort study. *Psychological Medicine, 39*, 625–634.

Wiles, N. J., Zammit, S., Bebbington, P., Singleton, N., Meltzer, H., & Lewis, G. (2006). Self-reported psychotic symptoms in the general population: Results from the longitudinal study of the British National Psychiatric Morbidity Survey. *British Journal of Psychiatry, 188*, 519–526.

7

PSYCHOSIS IN PSYCHIATRIC DISORDERS

Nicoletta M. van Veelen and Iris E. Sommer

Introduction

Reality testing is impaired in patients suffering from psychosis and is expressed with hallucinations, delusional thoughts or disorganized speech. Psychotic disorders are traditionally classified into non-affective and affective. The first consisting of schizophrenia, schizophreniform disorder, delusional disorder and unspecified psychosis. The latter consists of unipolar and bipolar affective disorders with psychosis. Schizo-affective disorder forms an intermediate diagnosis that lies in between these two groups. However, apart from these traditionally classified psychotic disorders, psychotic symptoms are also prevalent in patients with personality disorders, especially in those with schizotypal and borderline personality disorder, in those with post-traumatic stress disorder (PTSD), in substance use and withdrawal and in patients with dementia and delirium. Many other neurological and medical disorders, such as Parkinson's disease, multiple sclerosis and systemic lupus erythematosus can also be complicated by psychosis (see Massoud, Starkstein & Pahissa, *Chapter 10*). In youth, psychotic symptoms are often observed in those with autism and obsessive-compulsive disorder (OCD).

In this chapter, we will focus on the primary psychotic disorders in adult populations. We will first summarize some epidemiological data and the characteristics of specific psychotic symptoms across different psychotic disorders and then discuss the most common diagnostic tools and rating scales available to assess these disorders.

Epidemiology of Psychotic Disorders

The prevalence estimates of psychotic disorders are not always clear. Epidemiological surveys on psychotic disorders are primarily focused on schizophrenia and affective disorders. In addition, the prevalence estimates differ across cultures and studies. Studies based on community samples may underestimate prevalence, while studies in clinical populations are biased toward the most severe and chronic types of psychotic disorders (Perälä et al., 2007; Saha, Chant & McGrath, 2005).

In a comprehensive study of the general population, Perälä et al. (2007) examined the lifetime prevalence of the most common psychotic disorders. For schizophrenia, they found a lifetime prevalence of 0.87%, roughly in accordance with prior estimates at 7–8/1000 (Saha, Chant & McGrath, 2005). The incidence for schizophrenia is slightly higher in men, with a ratio of approximately 1.1:1 (Aleman et al., 2003). In addition, in males the illness has an earlier age of onset and tends to be more severe (Stilo & Murray, 2010). The clinical course is characterized by social and occupational dysfunction, mostly as a result of negative symptoms, with a median proportion of 13.5% recovery (Jääskeläinen et al., 2013). The prevalence of delusional disorder is considerably lower than schizophrenia or mood disorders. It is relatively uncommon in clinical settings, and population prevalences are not well studied. Lifetime prevalence estimates range from 0.03% (Kendler et al., 1982) to 0.18% (Perälä et al., 2007). The mean age of onset is older than for schizophrenia, and contrary to other psychotic disorders, there is an absence of symptoms other than delusions. With regards to the lifetime prevalence of schizophreniform disorder, Perälä et al.'s study (2007) reported it at 0.07%. The latter diagnosis is rare since two thirds of patients will eventually experience a psychotic relapse and convert to another diagnosis (American Psychiatric Association [APA], 2000).

Mood disorders are among the most prevalent of mental disorders. The lifetime prevalence for schizo-affective disorder was estimated at 0.32% (Perälä et al., 2007). Prevalence estimates for bipolar I disorder range from 0.24% (Perälä et al., 2007) to 2.2% (Schaffer et al., 2006), and for bipolar II 1.1% (Merikangas et al., 2007). Bipolar disorder usually emerges in late adolescence and early adulthood. Rates are equally common in men and women, unlike major depressive disorder, which is more common in women. While the majority of bipolar patients will return to a fully functional level between episodes, relapse rates at more than 70% over 5 years are reported (Gitlin et al., 1995). The lifetime prevalence of major depressive disorder ranges from 2.4% (in a European study, in the general population in 18,980 participants, Ohayon & Schatzberg, 2002) to 16.2% (in a large US epidemiological study, Kessler et al., 2003). The course varies widely, from one episode to chronicity across the lifespan with recurrent episodes. The common age of onset is older than in schizophrenia and bipolar disorder.

Of individuals with borderline personality disorder, about 25%–50% report psychotic symptoms (Schroeder, Fisher & Schäfer, 2013). Psychotic symptoms may occur in 15%–65% of individuals with post-traumatic stress disorder, although these rates reduce significantly if comorbid conditions such as psychosis, schizo-affective disorders, substance use, and borderline personality disorders are removed (Gaudiano & Zimmerman, 2010).

Lifetime prevalence for substance-induced psychotic disorders is not widely studied in community-based samples. Perälä et al. (2007) found a lifetime prevalence of 0.42%. The validity of this diagnosis is sometimes questioned, as it is difficult to assess whether substance abuse is the cause of the psychotic disorder, or associated with the psychotic disorder. Young people with psychosis frequently abuse cannabis or stimulants, or have a comorbid substance diagnosis (Grant et al., 2013) and a substantial proportion of patients convert to a schizophrenia spectrum disorder. In a Finnish study, the 8-year cumulative risk for a schizophrenia spectrum diagnosis was approximately 46% for persons with a diagnosis of cannabis-induced psychosis and 30% for those with an amphetamine-induced psychosis (Niemi-Pynttäri et al., 2013).

Data on the prevalence of psychotic disorders due to a general medical condition are also limited (see Stephane, Starkstein & Pahissa, *Chapter 10*). Perälä et al. (2007) found a lifetime prevalence of 0.21%. Lifetime prevalence increased in older age and was 1.71% among subjects 80 years or older. Most subjects with psychotic disorder in the group of 80 years or older had dementia.

Phenomenology of Psychotic Disorders

There is no single psychotic sign or symptom that is pathognomonic for a particular disorder. There are, however, differences in prevalence rates and characteristic features of psychotic symptoms that can aid in differential diagnosis. Best studied are the psychotic features in schizophrenia and mood disorders.

In a European study with a large sample of 6,523 patients with schizophrenia, 73% experienced delusions, 59% hallucinations and 59% disordered thought (Lecrubier et al., 2007). These figures confirm those of previous studies (Breier & Berg, 1999). The lifetime history of auditory hallucinations may actually be as high as 75% in schizophrenia, as these symptoms are not always correctly reported in a first contact (Shinn et al., 2012). Hallucinations may be rarer in late onset schizophrenia (35%) than in early onset schizophrenia (57%) (Mason, Stott & Sweeting, 2013), and they are particularly high in childhood onset schizophrenia (94.9%; David et al., 2011). Auditory hallucinations characterized by running commentary or voices conversing (first-rank hallucinations) and bizarre delusions were thought to be of specific diagnostic significance for schizophrenia, which was reflected in the fourth edition of the *Diagnostic and Statistical Manual of Mental Disorders* (DSM-IV) criteria. While these features were indeed prominent in schizophrenia (42%–62%), they rarely determined the diagnosis (Shinn, Heckers & Ongur, 2013). In the DSM-5 the special treatment of Schneiderian first-rank symptoms was consequently eliminated.

Psychotic symptoms are common in both the manic and depressive phases of bipolar disorder. More than half of patients with bipolar disorder will experience psychotic symptoms in their lifetime. Grandiose delusions are the most common type of psychotic symptom (78%), but all other psychotic symptoms, including formal thought disorders, can present as part of a manic episode (Dunayevich & Keck, 2000; Canuso et al., 2008). Notably, in the DSM criteria for mood disorders, only hallucinations or delusion are included in the diagnostic criteria for psychosis, but not disordered speech. However, when comparing formal thought disorder in bipolar and schizophrenia patients, Jampala, Taylor and Abrams (1989) found that no category of thought disorders was unique to any diagnostic group: 8% of manic patients had thought disorders usually associated with schizophrenia and 10% of schizophrenic patients exhibited flight of ideas, usually associated with mania. When flight of ideas was included in the definition, 75% of the manic patients had formal thought disorder.

Auditory hallucinations are relatively frequent in bipolar patients. In a study comparing 4,972 patients suffering from bipolar disorder, depression or schizophrenia, a cross-sectional prevalence of current hallucinations ranked: schizophrenia (61.1%), bipolar mixed (22.9%), bipolar manic (11.2%), bipolar depressed (10.5%) and unipolar depressed (5.9%). The most frequent hallucinations across all patients were auditory, followed by somatic and visual hallucinations. Compared with patients diagnosed with schizophrenia, hallucinations among patients with bipolar disorder were less severe, more visual and less often auditory. Characteristics of hallucinations were similar among manic and both bipolar- and unipolar-depressed individuals. In general, individuals with hallucinations had less years of education, had higher anxiety scores and greater duration of hospitalization (Baethge et al., 2005). Of individuals suffering a major depressive episode, 14.7% (Johnson, Horwath & Weissman, 1991) to 18.5% (Ohayon & Schatzberg, 2002) were reported to have psychotic features. Psychotic as compared with non-psychotic depression had a more severe course, as reflected in increased risk of relapse, persistence over 1 year and hospitalization that could not be explained by differences in symptom severity (Rothschild, 2013). It was suggested that patients with psychotic depression, particularly those with an early age of onset, may have a higher risk than non-psychotic depressed patients of subsequently developing bipolar disorder (Akiskal et al., 1983).

Studies comparing borderline personality disorder with schizophrenia (Kingdon et al., 2010; Slotema et al., 2012) showed that the groups were similar in their experiences of voices, but differed in frequency of paranoid delusions and childhood trauma. In a small study with chronic patients with PTSD, half of the sample reported auditory hallucinations (Anketell et al., 2010). A comparative study comparing PTSD and schizophrenia (Hamner et al., 2000) found similar severity of hallucinations but lower scores on delusions and conceptual disorganization in the PTSD group.

BOX 7.1: EXAMPLES OF PSYCHOTIC PHENOMENA IN PSYCHIATRIC POPULATIONS

Mr. A. started to hear voices at an age of 21. The voices resemble those of children that used to bully him at school. They tell him that he is worthless and call him names. He believes that these voices are put in his head by a fortune teller with telepathic powers. When he started to use an antipsychotic drug the voices disappeared.

Diagnosis: schizophreniform disorder

Mrs. B. started to hear music at the age of 77. She is still in good health, apart from her rather severe hearing loss. When she lies in bed and all is quiet, she hears the Ave Maria. She arrived to the conclusion that her neighbors must be trying to irritate her by singing so loud all night.

Diagnosis: late onset schizophrenia

Mrs. C. is a 64-year-old widow who was diagnosed with depression 2 years ago. Apart from her problem with eating and sleeping, she frequently sees visions of persons or animals. She finds it an awful experience.

Diagnosis: psychotic depression

Mr. D. has a private practice for paranormal healing. During a healing he holds his clients, hands and waits for the voices to provide him information. He is convinced that they come from spirits of deceased people.

Diagnosis: schizotypal personality disorder

Assessment of Psychotic Phenomena in Psychiatric Populations

Diagnostic Interviews

The most commonly used interviews for the diagnosis of psychotic disorders are the Mini International Neuropsychiatric Interview (M.I.N.I.; Sheehan et al., 1998), the Schedules for Clinical Assessment in Neuropsychiatry (SCAN; Wing et al., 1990), the Structured Clinical Interview for DSM Axis 1 disorders (SCID-I; Spitzer et al., 1992), the Diagnostic Interview for Psychoses (DIP; Castle et al.. 2006) and the Comprehensive Assessment of Symptoms and History (CASH; Andreasen, 1985; Andreasen et al., 1992). These diagnostic interviews are generally well validated, although generally in small patient groups and for a limited number of diagnoses. The interviews differ in their amount of structure and their extent of coverage of diagnoses. Which instrument provides the most appropriate tool depends largely on the research question or purpose of assessment.

The M.I.N.I. is a highly structured interview and is shorter in its application than the other interviews. It is a user and patient-friendly interview. It is therefore probably more apt for routine use in clinical practice to confirm diagnosis than the more extensive interviews. It is a good diagnostic instrument for diagnostic confirmation of psychotic diagnosis in patients from a study sample. In case a more specific classification is needed, the psychotic disorders section from the more detailed M.I.N.I. Plus can be used. All diagnostic interviews generally require extensive training, and the evaluators generally need to be experienced professionals. The M.I.N.I. however, can also be administered by non-professionals, albeit after extensive training. The interview is however less comprehensive in covering differential diagnoses and comorbidities, symptom characteristics as well as time course.

When addressing differential diagnosis, a general axis I interview that provides broad diagnostic coverage, such as the SCID-I interview, may be considered. The SCID is probably the most used diagnostic interview, and has a good diagnostic reliability, tested in a large multisite sample. The SCID-I was designed to correspond directly to DSM-IV criteria, which simplifies the diagnostic decision making. The use of screenings questions shortens the interview, the downside being that the clinician could incorrectly decide to terminate a diagnostic section. As the interview focuses on diagnoses rather than symptoms, the coverage of symptoms is less circumscribed. The SCAN or the DIP interviews are alternatives that can be used to diagnose according to the DSM as well as to the ICD-10 diagnostic system. The strength of the SCAN interview lies in its in-depth exploration of symptoms or pathology, and the evaluation of the patients' current and "lifetime ever" psychiatric status. The most important limitation to the interview is its length, the amount of detail, and extensive training requirements, which makes the interview less user-friendly. The DIP is derived from the SCAN interview and provides diagnoses (either DSM or ICD) using a computerized diagnostic algorithm (OPCRIT).

The CASH on the other hand, is more confined in its diagnostic focus, covering primarily major psychoses and affective disorders. It is therefore less well suited to address differential diagnosis and cannot be used to cover comorbidities. It explores the psychotic symptoms extensively and has a more elaborate coverage of especially negative symptoms, formal thought disorder and bizarre behavior. Moreover, it provides information on premorbid functioning, cognitive functioning, course of illness and age at onset. The interview is of particular use when symptom characteristics need to be addressed, or in descriptive studies of psychotic patients. In addition, the CASH interview provides severity ratings on symptoms (0–5), and therefore can be used in longitudinal studies, measuring reduction of symptom severity or symptom change in different phases of the illness.

Psychopathology Severity Rating Scales

Severity rating scales for psychosis such as the Positive and Negative Syndrome Scale (PANSS; Kay et al., 1987, 1986), Brief Psychiatric Rating Scale (BPRS; Overall et al., 1962) and the Scale for the Assessment of Positive Symptoms (SAPS; Andreasen 1984) were mainly developed to evaluate symptom severity in schizophrenia. The scales differ largely in their degree of comprehensiveness. Both the PANSS and the BPRS assess a range of psychotic and affective symptoms, although the PANSS contains more items. The BPRS is much briefer and therefore user (and patient) friendly. The coverage of negative symptoms by the BPRS is far less extensive than of the PANSS, and the scale may therefore be less sensitive to detect change in negative symptoms. The BPRS is more broadly applicable for patients with a diagnosis outside the schizophrenia spectrum, for example, in unipolar depression (Zanello et al., 2013) while the PANSS is clearly designed for schizophrenia patients.

The PANSS provides separate scores for the Positive, the Negative and General Psychopathology Scale. Arguably, the items on disturbance of volition and unusual thought content are placed on the general pathology scale. Another point of debate, is whether a 4 or 5 dimensional scale, including disorganization, would in fact not better represent the pathology of schizophrenia. Nevertheless, the PANSS is the most widely used rating scale in the field of psychosis. The major feature of the PANSS is that it is sensitive to change, making it a "gold standard" in treatment studies. Before the introduction of the PANSS, the BPRS was used rather standardly in clinical trials and older trials will therefore list BPRS change ratios instead of PANSS scores. The PANSS and BPRS have both been used extensively in randomized clinical trials. In these trials, a 20% criterion as a definition of response is often used, although a 50% criterion cut-off for some patient groups was proposed (Leucht et al, 2005). Moreover, besides assessing treatment response, the PANSS and (to a lesser extend) the BPRS can also be used to determine remission in schizophrenia, as defined by Andreasen et al. (2005).

The SAPS provides much more detail than the PANSS and the BPRS regarding psychotic symptoms. For instance, on this scale hallucinations in different modalities can be scored, and voices commenting and conversing can be differentiated. This is of particular use for clinical and research interventions that primarily aim to reduce positive symptoms. For example, to monitor the progress of cognitive behavioral therapy (CBT), or to quantify the efficacy of transcranial magnetic stimulation (TMS), the SAPS may actually be preferable over PANSS and BPRS. On the other hand, as important symptoms are not assessed, the SAPS cannot provide a reflection of the patient's full status or functioning, nor can it measure remission.

Concluding Remarks and Limitations

These are a substantial number of validated scales available for the assessment of psychosis. The most appropriate instrument depends largely on the research question or purpose of assessment. The rating scales designed for the diagnosis and quantification of psychotic symptoms discussed above have largely focused on patients with schizophrenia and may therefore be less suitable for other diagnostic groups, which hampers transdiagnostic research into hallucinations and delusions.

References

Akiskal, H. S., Walker, P., Puzantian, V. R., King, D., Rosenthal, T. L., & Dranon, M. (1983). Bipolar outcome in the course of depressive illness: Phenomenologic, familial, and pharmacologic predictors. *Journal of Affect Disorders, 5*, 115–128.

Aleman, A., Kahn, R., Selten, J. P. (2003). Sex differences in the risk of schizophrenia: Evidence from meta-analysis. *Archives of General Psychiatry, 60*(6), 565–571.

American Psychiatric Association. (2000). *Diagnostic and statistical manual of mental disorders* (4th ed., text revision). Washington, DC: American Psychiatric Association.

Andreasen, N. C. (1984). *Scale for the assessment of positive symptoms (SAPS)*. Iowa City: University of Iowa.

Andreasen, N. C. (1985). *Comprehensive assessment of symptoms and history*. Iowa City: University of Iowa.

Andreasen, N., Carpenter, W. Jr, Kane, J., Lasser, R., Marder, S., & Weinberger, D. (2005). Remission in schizophrenia: proposed criteria and rationale for consensus. *American Journal of Psychiatry, 162*(3), 441–449.

Andreasen, N., Flaum, M., & Arndt, S. (1992). The comprehensive assessment of symptoms and History (CASH): An instrument for assessing diagnosis and psychopathology. *Archives of General Psychiatry, 49*(8), 615–623.

Anketell, C., Dorahy, M. J., Shannon, M., Elder, R., Hamilton, G., Corry, M., et al. (2010). An exploratory analysis of voice hearing in chronic PTSD: Potential associated mechanisms. *Journal of Trauma & Dissociation, 11*(1), 93–107.

Baethge, C., Baldessarini, R. J., Freudenthal, K., Streeruwitz, A., Bauer, M., & Bschor, T. (2005). Hallucinations in bipolar disorder: Characteristics and comparison to unipolar depression and schizophrenia. *Bipolar Disorders,* 7(2), 136–145.

Breier, A., & Berg, P. H. (1999). The psychosis of schizophrenia: Prevalence, response to atypical antipsychotics, and prediction of outcome. *Biology Psychiatry, 46*(3), 361–364.

Canuso, C., Bossie, C., Zhu, Y., Youssef, E., & Dunner, D. (2008). Psychotic symptoms in patients with bipolar mania. *Journal of Affective Disorders, 111*(2/3), 164–169.

Castle, D. J., Jablensky, A., McGrath, J., Carr, V., Morgan, V., Waterreus, et al. (2006). The diagnostic interview for psychoses (DIP): Development, reliability and applications. *Psychological Medicine, 1*, 69–80.

David, C., Greenstein, D., Clasen, L., Gochman, P., Miller, R., Tossell, J., et al. (2011). Childhood onset schizophrenia: High rate of visual hallucinations. *Journal of the American Academy of Child and Adolescent Psychiatry, 50*(7), 681–686.

Dunayevich, E., & Keck, P. (2000). Prevalence and description of psychotic features in bipolar mania. *Current Psychiatry Reports, 2*(4), 286–290.

Gaudiano, B., & Zimmerman, M. (2010). Evaluation of evidence for the psychotic subtyping of post-traumatic stress disorder. *The British Journal of Psychiatry, 197*, 326–327.

Gitlin, M., Swendsen, J., Heller, T., & Hammen, C. (1995). Relapse and impairment in bipolar disorder. *American Journal of Psychiatry, 152*(11), 1635–140.

Grant, S., Burgess, P., Malhi, G., Whiteford, H., & Hall, W. (2013). Differences in associations between cannabis and stimulant disorders in first admission psychosis. *Schizophrenia Research, 147*(2/3), 216–222.

Hamner, M. B., Frueh, B. C., Ulmer, H. G., Huber, M. G., Twomey, T. J., et al. (2000). Psychotic features in chronic posttraumatic stress disorder and schizophrenia: Comparative severity. *Journal of Nervous and Mental Disease, 188*(4), 217–221.

Jääskeläinen, E., Juola, P., Hirvonen, N., McGrath, J. J., Saha, S., Isohanni, M., et al. (2013). A systematic review and meta-analysis of recovery in schizophrenia. *Schizophrenia Bulletin, 39*(6), 1296–1306.

Jampala, V., Taylor, M., & Abrams, R. (1989). The diagnostic implications of formal thought disorder in mania and schizophrenia: A reassessment. *American Journal of Psychiatry, 146*(4), 459–463.

Johnson, J., Horwath, E., & Weissman, M. (1991). The validity of major depression with psychotic features based on a community study. *Archives of General Psychiatry, 48*(12), 1075–1081.

Kay, S., Fiszbein, A., & Opler, L. (1987). The positive and negative syndrome scale (PANSS) for schizophrenia. *Schizophrenia Bulletin, 13*(2), 261–276.

Kay, S., Opler, L., & Fiszbein, A. (1986). Significance of positive and negative syndromes in chronic schizophrenics. *British Journal of Psychiatry, 149*, 439–448.

Kendler, K. (1982). Demography of paranoid psychosis (delusional disorder): A review and comparison with schizophrenia and affective illness. *Archives of General Psychiatry, 39*(8), 890–902.

Kessler, R., Berglund, P., Demler, O., Jin, R., Koretz, D., Merikangas, K., et al. (2003). The epidemiology of major depressive disorder: Results from the National Comorbidity Survey-Replication (NCS-R). *JAMA, 289*, 3095–3105.

Kingdon, D., Ashcroft, K., Bhandari, B., Gleeson, S., Warikoo, N., Symons, M., et al. (2010). Schizophrenia and borderline personality disorder: Similarities and differences in the experience of auditory hallucinations, paranoia, and childhood trauma. *Journal of Nervous and Mental Disease, 198*(6), 399–403.

Lecrubier, Y., Perry, R., Milligan, G., Leeuwenkamp, O., & Morlock, R. (2007). Physician observations and perceptions of positive and negative symptoms of schizophrenia: A multinational, cross-sectional survey. *European Psychiatry, 22*(6), 371–379.

Leucht, J., Kane, W., Kissling, J., Hamann, E., Etschel, R., & Engel, R. (2005). What does the PANSS mean? *Schizophrenia Research, 79*, 231–238.

Mason, O., Stott, J., & Sweeting, R. (2013). Dimensions of positive symptoms in late versus early onset psychosis. *International Psychogeriatrics, 25*(2), 320–327.

Merikangas, K., Akiskal, H., Angst, J., Greenberg, P., Hirschfeld, R., Petukhova, M., et al. (2007). Lifetime and 12-month prevalence of bipolar spectrum disorder in the National Comorbidity Survey replication. *Archives of General Psychiatry, 64*(5), 543–552.

Niemi-Pynttäri, J., Sund, R., Putkonen, H., Vorma, H., Wahlbeck, K., & Pirkola, S. (2013). Substance-induced psychoses converting into schizophrenia: A register-based study of 18,478 Finnish inpatient cases. *Journal of Clinical Psychiatry, 74*(1), 94–99.

Ohayon, M., & Schatzberg, A. (2002). Prevalence of depressive episodes with psychotic features in the general population. *American Journal of Psychiatry, 159*(11), 1855–1861.

Overall, J. E., & Gorham, D. R. (1962). The brief psychiatric rating scale. *Psychological Reports, 10*, 790–812.

Perälä, J., Suvisaari, J., Saarni, S., Kuoppasalmi, K., Isometsä, E., Pirkola, S., et al. (2007). Lifetime Prevalence of Psychotic and Bipolar I disorders in a general population. *Archives of General Psychiatry, 64*(1), 19–28.

Rothschild, A. J. (2013). Challenges in the treatment of major depressive disorder with psychotic features. *Schizophrenia Bulletin, 39*(4), 787–796.

Saha, S., Chant, D., & McGrath, J. (2005). A systematic review of the prevalence of schizophrenia. *PLOS Medicine, 31*, 225–228.

Schaffer, A., Cairney, J., Cheung, A., Veldhuizen, S., & Levitt, A. (2006). Community survey of bipolar disorder in Canada: Life time prevalence and illness characteristics. *Canadian Journal of Psychiatry, 51*, 9–16.

Schroeder, K., Fisher, H., & Schäfer, I. (2013). Psychotic symptoms in patients with borderline personality disorder: Prevalence and clinical management. *Current Opinion in Psychiatry, 26*(1), 113–119.

Sheehan, D., Lecrubier, Y., Harnett-Sheehan, K., Janavs, J., Weiller, E., Bonara, L., et al. (1998). Reliability and validity of the M.I.N.I. international neuropsychiatric interview (M.I.N.I.): According to the SCID-P. *European Psychiatry, 12*, 232–241.

Sheehan, D., Lecrubier, Y., Sheehan, K., Amorim, P., Janavs, J., Weiller, E., et al. (1998). The mini-international neuropsychiatric interview (M.I.N.I.): The development and validation of a structured diagnostic psychiatric interview for DSM-IV and ICD-10. *Journal of Clinical Psychiatry, 59*(Suppl. 20), 22–33.

Shinn, A., Heckers, S., & Ongur, D. (2013). The special treatment of first rank auditory hallucinations and bizarre delusions in the diagnosis of schizophrenia. *Comprehensive Psychiatry, 53*(6), 718–726.

Shinn, A., Pfaff, D., Young, S., Lewandowski, K., Cohen, B., & Öngür, D. (2012). Auditory hallucinations in a cross-diagnostic sample of psychotic disorder patients: A descriptive, cross-sectional study. *Comprehensive Psychiatry, 53*(6), 718–726.

Slotema, C. W., Daalman, K., Blom, J. D., Diederen, K. M., Hoek, H. W., & Sommer, I. E. (2012). Auditory verbal hallucinations in patients with borderline personality disorder are similar to those in schizophrenia. *Psychological Medicine, 42*(9), 1873–1878.

Spitzer, R., Williams, J., Gibbon, M., & First, M. (1992). The structured clinical interview for DSM-III-R (SCID). I: History, rationale, and description. *Archives of General Psychiatry, 49*(8), 624–629.

Stilo, S., & Murray, R. (2010). The epidemiology of schizophrenia: Replacing dogma with knowledge. *Dialogues in Clinical Neuroscience, 12*, 305–315.

Wing, J. K., Babor, T., Brugha T., Burke, J., Cooper, J. E., Giel, R., et al. (1990). SCAN: Schedules for clinical assessment in neuropsychiatry. *Archives of General Psychiatry, 47*(6), 589–593.

Zanello, B., Berthoud, L., Ventura, J., & Merlo, M. C. G. (2013). The *Brief Psychiatric Rating Scale (version 4.0) factorial structure* and *its sensitivity* in the *treatment* of *outpatients* with *unipolar* depression. *Psychiatry Research, 210*(2), 626–633.

8

AT-RISK MENTAL STATES

Rabindra Tambyraja

Introduction

The emerging consensus of schizophrenia and psychosis as neurodevelopmental illnesses requires a rethinking of the initial stages of illness. Like any developmental illness, it is expected that risk factors and early signs are present at a young age. However, as in many other conditions, the presence of these early subclinical features does not necessarily result in further progression to clinical psychosis and may overlap with early presentations of other illnesses. Therefore, these early signs are likely to be more common in the general population and in conditions with less clinical severity than the full-blown illness. For example, transient psychotic symptoms, or "psychotic-like experiences," can be relatively common and without progression to persistent psychotic illness (see Larøi, Raballo & Bell, *Chapter 6*). This presents a particular problem for mental health clinicians, as many of the treatments aimed at psychosis carry significant risks. The mere label of "psychosis" or "psychotic" can carry a heavy stigma, and the medications used to treat psychosis carry significant metabolic and neurological risks. Therefore, great care must be taken to ensure that these consequences are avoided in individuals that are unlikely to progress to a frank psychotic illness. Furthermore, in some cultures, psychotic-like experiences can be seen as somewhat normative, as long as they are transient, further clouding an accurate assessment of prevalence and risk.

The above factors have led researchers to attempt the development of clear criteria that indicate elevated risk for developing a psychotic illness, and the reader is referred to a recent comprehensive review by leading researchers in the field that explores this ongoing development (Fusar-Poli et al., 2013). These efforts have generally diverged along two lines, those of the "basic symptom" criteria, and those of the "positive symptoms" criteria.

Basic symptoms have been defined as "subtle, subjectively experienced subclinical disturbances in drive, affect, thinking, speech, (body) perception, motor action, central vegetative functions, and stress tolerance" (Schultze-Lutter, 2009) (also see Parnas, *Chapter 2*; Janssen, *Chapter 4*). A key point is that these are *subjectively* experienced and may not be as readily observable as positive symptoms. Similarly, a successful assessment of these changed experiences requires awareness of the experience (insight), but as the psychotic symptoms develop, the insight into cognitive disturbances is frequently lost (Gross, 1989).

In contrast, the positive symptoms approach focuses on the earliest manifestations of the cardinal positive symptoms of psychosis such as perceptual disturbances, disordered communication, or subclinical disordered or paranoid thought. In developing the research criteria for studying these, investigators have worked to create increasingly precise characterizations of these heterogeneous symptoms, as discussed below.

Several terms are used interchangeably in describing this early state and can create confusion. The *prodrome* refers to a clearly pathologic state that precedes a full-blown illness. Although a useful term, it is by nature retrospective, as it is only true if the individual progresses to the full illness. Therefore, two commonly used terms in the literature are the at-risk mental state (ARMS) and the ultra-high-risk state (UHR), which are essentially identical terms. They usually reflect an evaluation with one of the more commonly used rating scales, discussed below. Throughout this chapter, the UHR and ARMS terms will be used interchangeably.

Prevalence

Meng and colleagues recent study used a "basic symptom" scale (the Bonn Scale for the Assessment of Basic Symptoms; BSABS) to assess symptoms in a general adolescent population (Meng et al., 2009). The authors reported that roughly 30% of the general adolescent population reported at least one basic symptom (although this is not considered sufficient to confer UHR status). This is significantly lower than 81% in those with a non-psychotic psychiatric disorder and 96.5% in those with a psychotic disorder, but it signifies that basic symptoms are present at some level in an otherwise healthy, non-psychiatric population. As Meng's is the only study that applied comprehensive pre-psychotic rating instruments to a large, general population, the next closest comparison, with respect to the "positive symptoms" approach, is that of specific psychotic symptoms at the population levels. Auditory hallucinations are the most commonly studied symptoms in population samples of both children and adults. Beginning with studies conducted in children, van Os et al. (van Os, Linscott, Myin-Germeys, Delespaul & Krabbendam, 2009) completed a meta-analysis which found rates of auditory hallucination in both clinical and non-clinical groups to vary between 5% and 16%, clustering in late childhood and early adolescence (Also see Kelleher, *Chapter 9*). The same analysis found that 75%–90% of these psychotic experiences remitted spontaneously over time. A similar meta-analysis using different datasets of experiences in children and adolescents found roughly similar results, with rates of "hallucinatory experiences" (not limited to auditory) ranging between 4.9% to 9% (Rubio, Sanjuan, Florez-Salamanca & Cuesta, 2012). By contrast, the prevalence of auditory hallucinations in adults without psychosis (incorporating a wide age range) has been estimated to range between 10% to 15% (de Leede-Smith & Barkus, 2013). Several factors can help differentiate these non-clinical hallucinatory experiences from those associated with a psychotic illness. These factors include the frequency, duration, emotional valence and disturbance to daily functioning, among other factors (de Leede-Smith & Barkus, 2013; van Os et al., 2009).

Phenomenology

The phenomenology of psychiatric symptoms can be assessed using both subjective reports, as well as observed features. The early features of psychosis can also be considered from both perspectives, as there are symptoms and disturbances most apparent to the individual and those more apparent to an observer. With regard to the prodrome, the "basic symptom" approach typically asks about subjective experiences, while many aspects of the "positive symptoms" approach may be more apparent to an observer. Auditory hallucinations in the UHR can vary from sounds (scratching, buzzing) to audible voices. Visual hallucinations are less common, but typically begin as shadows or a sensation of real visual stimuli looking "different" or changed. Delusions at this point tend to be less bizarre and less firmly held than in frank psychosis. There is usually some preservation of insight (Olvet, Carrion, Auther & Cornblatt, 2013), and hence patients are more aware of the odd nature of the delusions. Correlates of the negative symptoms, such as decreased motivation and socialization, can be more challenging for the patient to recognize themselves but are frequently noted by caregivers.

As described above, the basic symptoms model begins with those that are experienced internally, and thus is worth considering further in the phenomenology of the UHR state. An interesting premise is that of self-disturbance as a basic symptom (see Parnas & Gram Henriksen, *Chapter 17*). This premise requires a more nuanced use of the term *phenomenology* to include salient features of consciousness rather than an exclusive focus on subjective experiences. The self-disturbance is proposed to take place at the most fundamental level of first-person awareness, of experience and cognition as being "mine" (Nelson et al., 2009). Interestingly, this same work has led to interesting correlations between proposed neurobiological mechanisms of a conception of "self," and dysfunction in these regions related to psychosis.

Clouding the diagnostic picture is the frequent co-occurrence of mood and anxiety symptoms. One of the initial validation studies of UHR rating instruments showed comorbidity rates of 69% for mood/anxiety, 25% for substance abuse/dependence, and 44% for one or more axis II disorders (Woods et al., 2009). It is difficult to state with clarity the causal relationships in these symptom clusters, as cognitive or thought disturbances may precipitate mood or anxiety symptoms and vice versa. Similarly, high rates of comorbidity between thought disorders and substance abuse could be due either to self-medication or primary substance abuse exacerbating an underlying vulnerability to such symptoms. Certainly primary mood and anxiety symptoms can co-occur with early psychotic symptoms. The experience of perceptual disturbances, along with changes in cognition and increased difficulty functioning, may contribute to symptoms of anxiety or depression.

Risk Factors

A challenge in assessing risk factors for the UHR state is attempting a meaningful separation from the UHR as a distinct clinical entity as opposed to only being relevant as high-risk state for progression to a full psychotic illness. In truth, it is not clear if such a distinction would be clinically useful. In the recent development of the DSM-5, one disorder under consideration (though not finally accepted) was the psychosis risk syndrome, roughly parallel to the UHR criteria. This suggests that in the research community around this condition, UHR is viewed more as a risk factor for psychosis rather than an independent condition in need of its own risk assessment literature. Of interest, the researchers in the NAPLS (North American Prodromal Longitudinal Study) group have also followed those who met criteria for UHR but who did *not* progress to a psychotic disorder (which described 65% of the group of over 300 subjects; Addington et al., 2011). The 65% who did not convert to psychosis comprised 24% whose symptoms remitted, 20% whose symptoms improved but did not remit entirely, and 21% who received an antipsychotic and thus could not be used in describing the untreated natural history of the UHR state.

Neuroanatomical Correlates of the UHR State

The complicated presentation of the UHR state, as well as the variability in its prognosis, drives a strong interest in improving the diagnostic and prognostic accuracy, and recent advances in neuroimaging techniques have yielded numerous insights, with promise of more to come as techniques develop further. Although the imaging work in the UHR state is not as robust as that in first-episode, there are still consistent and useful findings. The major modalities have included morphological magnetic resonance imaging (MRI), functional MRI (fMRI) and magnetic resonance spectroscopy (MRS). Positron emission tomography (PET) and diffusion tensor imaging (DTI) have also been used, although the literature remains limited. An important caveat in considering the imaging data is that, given ongoing developments within the field, there has been little standardization of imaging techniques and protocols, and so cross-comparisons remain challenging.

Beginning with morphological, or structural, MRI, a recent review considered roughly 30 imaging trials of UHR subjects up to that point (Smieskova et al., 2010) and found qualitatively similar findings to those in first-episode psychosis, though at reduced severity. Specifically, findings included reduced gray-matter volumes in several regions among those that progressed to psychosis, including frontal, cingulate and temporal cortices. Considering longitudinal data, temporal, frontal and cerebellar regions showed progressive gray-matter reduction in subjects that progressed to psychosis. In conducting a meta-analysis on these studies, the authors concluded that between the anterior cingulate cortex (ACC), the prefrontal cortex (PFC) and cerebellum, "these regions were the most consistently abnormal brain regions associated with later transition to psychosis" (Smieskova, et al., 2010). A large Edinburgh study (162 UHR participants, with longitudinal data on 146) validated the finding of whole-brain, and in particular PFC and temporal lobe volume, reduction (McIntosh et al., 2011). A smaller study of UHR subjects that had a higher number of psychosis conversions found significant contraction of the right PFC among those who converted to psychosis (Sun et al., 2009), further demonstrating the importance of the PFC as a possible structural biomarker; a finding validated in updated reviews as well (Brent, Thermenos, Keshavan, & Seidman, 2013).

As the evolution of UHR theory coincided to some extent with advances in fMRI, there has been considerable interest in this modality for assessing progression and risk in the UHR state. Strengthening this is the possibility that *functional* changes may precede observable *structural* changes in a disordered neurodevelopmental process. An important aspect in considering a thought disorder is how to determine the development of appropriately ordered thought through the lifespan. To this, the default mode network (DMN) imaging provides an interesting contribution. The DMN reflects the brain "at rest" but awake, without particular focus, and was first described in 2001 (Gusnard, Akbudak, Shulman & Raichle, 2001; Raichle et al., 2001). This network is comprised primarily of the posterior cingulate, medial prefrontal, and inferior parietal cortices, and is at its most active when the brain is not focused on any particular external task, but instead is engaged in self-referential and reflective activity (Greicius, Krasnow, Reiss & Menon, 2003). Notably, this network has been shown to develop over time in the maturing brain (Fair et al., 2008; Supekar et al., 2010). Reflecting a compartmentalization of mental "work," the DMN is shown to markedly deactivate during times of intense focus on a salient task (Greicius, et al., 2003). In a rich literature of task-based fMRI, the role of the brain at rest, and its ability to shift focus in response to stimuli as reflecting appropriately ordered thought, is an important consideration.

Studies of the DMN in UHR groups are relatively few, but with interesting findings. Some investigators have found a decreased ability to suppress DMN function during task activation (Fryer et al., 2013; Whitfield-Gabrieli et al., 2009; Wotruba et al., 2013), with a similar finding in unaffected siblings of patients with schizophrenia (de Leeuw, Kahn, Zandbelt, Widschwendter & Vink, 2013; Whitfield-Gabrieli, et al., 2009). For those both at genetic risk and with some signs of psychopathology, a trend towards reduced functional connectivity has been found in the precuneus and anterior cingulate (Jang et al., 2011). Although this is a promising research area, the lack of uniformity in protocols and calculation methods has limited the ability to compare across studies and populations.

Magnetic resonance spectroscopy (MRS) is the last major imaging modality, which looks at functional metabolites. One of the most frequently studied is N-acetyl aspartate (NAA), a metabolite found at high concentrations in neuronal (gray matter) tissue, that is thought to be a marker of neuronal integrity (Moffett, Ross, Arun, Madhavarao & Namboodiri, 2007). Although the theory of MRS is beyond the scope of this chapter, its findings in the UHR population are worth noting. A recent meta-analysis of effect size identified that in UHR subjects, there were reductions in NAA in the thalamus, along with trend-level reductions in the temporal lobe (Brugger, Davis, Leucht & Stone, 2011). No changes were found in frontal lobe metabolite levels in that review, but subsequent authors have found reductions in prefrontal cortex NAA in UHR subjects (Mondino, Brunelin & Saoud, 2013).

Scales

There is significant geographic variation in the usage of the main positive-symptom scales. The Structured Interview for Prodromal Symptoms (SIPS) is commonly used in the United States, due in part to the NAPLS research coalition (Addington et al., 2007), which aligned many of the research instruments for ease of comparison. The SIPS reflects the efforts of McGlashan and colleagues to operationalize the criteria set forth by Yung et al (McGlashan et al., 2003; Yung & McGorry, 1996b). Contained within the SIPS is the Scale of Prodromal Symptoms (SOPS), with the same group following up on further psychometric and reliability data (Miller et al., 2003). The Australian group (of which Dr. Yung was a key member), currently the foundation of the Orygen Youth Health program, has developed the Comprehensive Assessment of the At-Risk Mental State (CA-ARMS; Yung & McGorry, 1996a; Yung et al., 2008; Yung et al., 2005). Recently, this group has published long-term outcomes data that extend as far as 15 years (Nelson et al., 2013), with an overall conversion rate to psychosis of 35%, with most conversions to psychosis occurring in the first 2 years.

Both the SIPS and CA-ARMS assess individuals for both positive symptoms and general functional decline as a proxy for negative symptoms. Three positive results are possible from these scales. The first is the Attenuated Positive Symptoms (APS) criteria, which describes positive symptoms that do not rise to the level of full psychotic criteria. The second is the Brief Limited Intermittent Psychotic

Symptoms (BLIPS) criteria, which describes full-criteria psychotic symptoms that spontaneously resolve after a short time. The third, Genetic Risk and Functional Decline (GRD) parallels negative symptoms, and describes global functional decline along with risk factors such as a family history of psychosis or personal history of schizotypal personality disorder. There is significant overlap in these two scales, and they should be expected to give similar results.

Scales that emphasize the basic symptom approach have also been developed, and primary among these is the Bonn Scale for the Assessment of Basic Symptoms (BSABS) (Klosterkötter, Ebel, Schultze-Lutter & Steinmeyer, 1996). Although elements of this have been included in the CA-ARMS and SIPS, the BSABS focuses on basic symptoms entirely. A subsequent longer-term outcomes study by the authors found an overall sensitivity of 0.98 and specificity of 0.59 over a mean period of 9.6 years (Klosterkötter, Hellmich, Steinmeyer & Schultze-Lutter, 2001). The specificity in this could be improved even further by focusing on specific disturbances "such as thought interference, disturbances of receptive language, or visual distortions" (Klosterkötter et al., 2001). The authors of the BSABS have continued to advance the instrument with the Schizophrenia Proneness Instrument (SPI) (Schultze-Lutter, Addington, Ruhrmann & Klosterkötter, 2007), and a specific version created for children and youth (SPI-CY) (Fux, Walger, Schimmelmann & Schultze-Lutter, 2013). The major findings with the SPI are that of either notable *co*gnitive-*per*ceptive basic symptoms (COPER), or high-risk *cog*nitive *dis*turbances (COGDIS). Meeting the specified criteria for either of these confers status of an at-risk mental state. It is notable that although the SPI-CY can be used from age 8 (commensurate with the theory of basic symptoms emerging earlier), some items are not deemed fully reliable until adolescence, when more robust metacognitive processes and abstraction are likely to be in place (Fux et al., 2013). Clearly there is overlap between the basic symptom and positive symptom approaches, and the scales reflect this. The development of the various scales over time and how they accommodated the findings of the others is an interesting topic in its own right, and the reader is referred to a recent excellent review, which discusses this longitudinal development (Daneault & Stip, 2013).

From the length of these scales, it is clear that they require an experienced interviewer and significant time. To address this, and bring the early detection approach to a larger population, self-report screening instruments that are based on the larger scales have been developed. Although the screening instruments are not as exhaustive as the full SIPS and CA-ARMS, they nonetheless have demonstrated useful sensitivity and specificity (Kline et al., 2012). As screening instruments, it is important to note that, while they can identify patients in need of further assessment, they should not be used in isolation to identify the UHR state. A further caveat is that these scales have generally been validated in help-seeking populations presenting to mental health services, and not a true random population sampling (such as all patients presenting to a general medical or pediatric clinic). As this reflects an "enriched" population, their sensitivity and specificity should be considered in that context.

Limitations and Future Directions

The combined efforts of many researchers as described above represent a desire to bring order out of the chaotic and inchoate process of the development of psychosis. In this early phase of the illness, the goal of assessment is accuracy in predicting who will progress to a full psychotic illness. A further limitation is that the subtlety of the earliest findings makes subjects quite difficult to find in the general population, and so the ability for researchers to collaborate across regions is critical, to allow adequate samples for analysis and prediction. While this goal of perfect accuracy remains elusive, the future of this field will likely involve combined modalities of clinical ratings as presented here, neuropsychological findings and perhaps neuroimaging findings as that technology develops. Currently, the major limitation of neuroimaging is that there is such diversity of technology and analysis methods that it is challenging to analyze findings across studies, reducing the utility of the work. As the field moves toward a consensus on the most effective methods, this will likely improve.

With a complex and multifactorial illness, it is unlikely that any one lens will offer the best picture, and an approach that offers combined perspectives will likely in the end be more accurate. The rating scales cited above offer an excellent opportunity to provide consistent measurements of symptoms as they progress over time, and will thus be a key part of any ongoing assessment efforts.

References

Addington, J., Cadenhead, K.S., Cannon, T.D., Cornblatt, B., McGlashan, T.H., Perkins, D.O., et al. (2007). North American prodrome longitudinal study: A collaborative multisite approach to prodromal schizophrenia research. *Schizophrenia Bulletin, 33*(3), 665–672.

Addington, J., Cornblatt, B.A., Cadenhead, K.S., Cannon, T.D., McGlashan, T.H., Perkins, D.O., et al. (2011). At clinical high risk for psychosis: Outcome for nonconverters. *American Journal of Psychiatry, 168*, 800–805.

Brent, B.K., Thermenos, H.W., Keshavan, M.S., & Seidman, L.J. (2013). Gray matter alterations in schizophrenia high-risk youth and early-onset schizophrenia: A review of structural MRI findings. *Children & Adolescent Psychiatry Clinics of North America, 22*(4), 689–714.

Brugger, S., Davis, J.M., Leucht, S., & Stone, J.M. (2011). Proton magnetic resonance spectroscopy and illness stage in schizophrenia—A systematic review and meta-analysis. *Biological Psychiatry, 69*(5), 495–503.

Daneault, J.G., & Stip, E. (2013). Genealogy of instruments for prodrome evaluation of psychosis. *Frontiers in Psychiatry, 4*, 25.

de Leede-Smith, S., & Barkus, E. (2013). A comprehensive review of auditory verbal hallucinations: Lifetime prevalence, correlates and mechanisms in healthy and clinical individuals. *Frontiers in Human Neuroscience, 7*, 1–25.

de Leeuw, M., Kahn, R.S., Zandbelt, B.B., Widschwendter, C.G., & Vink, M. (2013). Working memory and default mode network abnormalities in unaffected siblings of schizophrenia patients. *Schizophrenia Research, 150*(2/3), 555–562.

Fair, D.A., Cohen, A.L., Dosenbach, N.U., Church, J.A., Miezin, F.M., Barch, D.M., et al. (2008). The maturing architecture of the brain's default network. *Proceedings of the National Academy of Science USA, 105*(10), 4028–4032.

Fryer, S.L., Woods, S.W., Kiehl, K.A., Calhoun, V.D., Pearlson, G.D., Roach, B.J., et al. (2013). Deficient suppression of default mode regions during working memory in individuals with early psychosis and at clinical high-risk for psychosis. *Frontiers in Psychiatry, 4*, 92.

Fusar-Poli, P., Borgwardt, S., Bechdolf, A., Addington, J., Riecher-Rossler, A., Schultze-Lutter, F., et al. (2013). The psychosis high-risk state: A comprehensive state-of-the-art review. *JAMA Psychiatry, 70*(1), 107–120.

Fux, L., Walger, P., Schimmelmann, B.G., & Schultze-Lutter, F. (2013). The schizophrenia proneness instrument, child and youth version (SPI-CY): Practicability and discriminative validity. *Schizophrenia Research, 146*(1/3), 69–78.

Greicius, M.D., Krasnow, B., Reiss, A.L., & Menon, V. (2003). Functional connectivity in the resting brain: A network analysis of the default mode hypothesis. *Proceedings of the National Academy of Science USA, 100*(1), 253–258.

Gross, G. (1989). The 'basic' symptoms of schizophrenia. *British Journal of Psychiatry*, (Suppl. 7), 21–25.

Gusnard, D.A., Akbudak, E., Shulman, G.L., & Raichle, M.E. (2001). Medial prefrontal cortex and self-referential mental activity: Relation to a default mode of brain function. *Proceedings of the National Academy of Science USA, 98*(7), 4259–4264.

Jang, J.H., Jung, W.H., Choi, J.S., Choi, C.H., Kang, D.H., Shin, N.Y., et al. (2011). Reduced prefrontal functional connectivity in the default mode network is related to greater psychopathology in subjects with high genetic loading for schizophrenia. *Schizophrenia Research, 127*(1/3), 58–65.

Kline, E., Wilson, C., Ereshefsky, S., Denenny, D., Thompson, E., Pitts, S.C., et al. (2012). Psychosis risk screening in youth: A validation study of three self-report measures of attenuated psychosis symptoms. *Schizophrenia Research, 141*(1), 72–77.

Klosterkötter, J., Ebel, H., Schultze-Lutter, F., & Steinmeyer, E.M. (1996). Diagnostic validity of basic symptoms. *European Archices of Psychiatry & Clinical Neurosci, 246*(3), 147–154.

Klosterkötter, J., Hellmich, M., Steinmeyer, E.M., & Schultze-Lutter, F. (2001). Diagnosing schizophrenia in the initial prodromal phase. *Archives of General Psychiatry, 58*(2), 158–164.

McGlashan, T.H., Zipursky, R.B., Perkins, D., Addington, J., Miller, T.J., Woods, S.W., et al. (2003). The PRIME North America randomized double-blind clinical trial of olanzapine versus placebo in patients at risk of being prodromally symptomatic for psychosis: I. Study rationale and design. *Schizophrenia Research, 61*(1), 7–18.

McIntosh, A. M., Owens, D. C., Moorhead, W.J., Whalley, H.C., Stanfield, A.C., Hall, J., et al. (2011). Longitudinal volume reductions in people at high genetic risk of schizophrenia as they develop psychosis. *Biological Psychiatry, 69*(10), 953–958.

Meng, H., Schimmelmann, B.G., Koch, E., Bailey, B., Parzer, P., Gunter, M., et al. (2009). Basic symptoms in the general population and in psychotic and non-psychotic psychiatric adolescents. *Schizophrenia Research, 111*(1/3), 32–38.

Miller, T.J., McGlashan, T.H., Rosen, J.L., Cadenhead, K., Cannon, T., Ventura, J., et al. (2003). Prodromal assessment with the structured interview for prodromal syndromes and the scale of prodromal symptoms: Predictive validity, interrater reliability, and training to reliability. *Schizophrenia Bulletin, 29*(4), 703–715.

Moffett, J.R., Ross, B., Arun, P., Madhavarao, C.N., & Namboodiri, A.M. (2007). N-acetylaspartate in the CNS: From neurodiagnostics to neurobiology. *Progress in Neurobiology, 81*(2), 89–131.

Mondino, M., Brunelin, J., & Saoud, M. (2013). N-acetyl-aspartate level is decreased in the prefrontal cortex in subjects at-risk for schizophrenia. *Frontiers in Psychiatry, 4*, 99.

Nelson, B., Fornito, A., Harrison, B.J., Yucel, M., Sass, L.A., Yung, A.R., et al. (2009). A disturbed sense of self in the psychosis prodrome: Linking phenomenology and neurobiology. *Neuroscience and Biobehaviour Reviews, 33*(6), 807–817.

Nelson, B., Yuen, H.P., Wood, S.J., Lin, A., Spiliotacopoulos, D., Bruxner, A., et al. (2013). Long-term follow-up of a group at ultra high risk ("prodromal") for psychosis: The PACE 400 study. *JAMA Psychiatry, 70*(8), 793–802.

Olvet, D.M., Carrion, R.E., Auther, A.M., & Cornblatt, B.A. (2013, August 22). Self-awareness of functional impairment in individuals at clinical high-risk for psychosis (Epub). *Early Intervention in Psychiatry*. doi: 10.1111/eip.12086

Rubio, J.M., Sanjuan, J., Florez-Salamanca, L., & Cuesta, M.J. (2012). Examining the course of hallucinatory experiences in children and adolescents: A systematic review. *Schizophrenia Research, 138*(2/3), 248–254.

Schultze-Lutter, F. (2009). Subjective symptoms of schizophrenia in research and the clinic: The basic symptom concept. *Schizophrenia Bulletin, 35*(1), 5–8.

Schultze-Lutter, F., Addington, A. M., Ruhrmann, S., & Klosterkötter, J. (2007). *The schizophrenia proneness instrument, adult version (SPI-A)*. Rome, Italy: Giovanni Fioriti Editore.

Smieskova, R., Fusar-Poli, P., Allen, P., Bendfeldt, K., Stieglitz, R.D., Drewe, J., et al. (2010). Neuroimaging predictors of transition to psychosis—A systematic review and meta-analysis. *Neuroscience and Biobehavioural Reviews, 34*(8), 1207–1222.

Sun, D., Phillips, L., Velakoulis, D., Yung, A., McGorry, P.D., Wood, S.J., et al. (2009). Progressive brain structural changes mapped as psychosis develops in 'at risk' individuals. *Schizophrenia research, 108*(1/3), 85–92.

Supekar, K., Uddin, L.Q., Prater, K., Amin, H., Greicius, M.D., & Menon, V. (2010). Development of functional and structural connectivity within the default mode network in young children. *Neuroimage, 52*(1), 290–301.

van Os, J., Linscott, R.J., Myin-Germeys, I., Delespaul, P., & Krabbendam, L. (2009). A systematic review and meta-analysis of the psychosis continuum: Evidence for a psychosis proneness-persistence-impairment model of psychotic disorder. *Psychological Medicine, 39*(2), 179–195.

Whitfield-Gabrieli, S., Thermenos, H.W., Milanovic, S., Tsuang, M.T., Faraone, S.V., McCarley, R.W., et al. (2009). Hyperactivity and hyperconnectivity of the default network in schizophrenia and in first-degree relatives of persons with schizophrenia. *Proceedings of the National Academy of Science USA, 106*(4), 1279–1284.

Woods, S.W., Addington, J., Cadenhead, K.S., Cannon, T.D., Cornblatt, B.A., Heinssen, R., et al. (2009). Validity of the prodromal risk syndrome for first psychosis: findings from the North American prodrome longitudinal study. *Schizophrenia Bulletin, 35*(5), 894–908.

Wotruba, D., Michels, L., Buechler, R., Metzler, S., Theodoridou, A., Gerstenberg, M., et al. (2013). Aberrant coupling within and across the default mode, task-positive, and salience network in subjects at risk for psychosis. *Schizophrenia Bulletin.* http://dx.doi.org/10.1093/schbul/sbt161

Yung, A.R., & McGorry, P.D. (1996a). The initial prodrome in psychosis: Descriptive and qualitative aspects. *Australian & New Zealand Journal in Psychiatry, 30*(5), 587–599.

Yung, A.R., & McGorry, P.D. (1996b). The prodromal phase of first-episode psychosis: Past and current conceptualizations. *Schizophrenia Bulletin, 22*(2), 353–370.

Yung, A.R., Nelson, B., Stanford, C., Simmons, M.B., Cosgrave, E.M., Killackey, E., et al. (2008). Validation of "prodromal" criteria to detect individuals at ultra high risk of psychosis: 2-year follow-up. *Schizophrenia research, 105*(1/3), 10–17.

Yung, A.R., Yuen, H.P., McGorry, P.D., Phillips, L.J., Kelly, D., Dell'Olio, M., et al. (2005). Mapping the onset of psychosis: The Comprehensive Assessment of At-Risk Mental States. *Australian & New Zealand Journal in Psychiatry, 39*(11/12), 964–971.

9

PSYCHOSIS IN CHILDREN AND ADOLESCENTS

Ian Kelleher

Introduction

Schizophrenia is a rare disorder in childhood; psychotic experiences, on the other hand, are common. More specifically, hallucinations and delusions—the classic symptoms of psychosis—are prevalent in children and adolescents but largely occur outside of the context of a psychotic disorder. Childhood and adolescence are also important developmental periods during which changes occur in the prevalence and significance of psychotic symptoms. This chapter looks at the prevalence and clinical relevance of psychotic experiences in children and adolescents and describes a number of instruments that can be used to assess these symptoms. It also provides a suggested approach to systematically assessing for psychotic experiences.

Psychotic Experiences in the Population

Many studies have looked at the reported rates of psychotic experiences in the young population. The purported prevalence of symptoms varies in line with the methods of assessment. Unsurprisingly, self-report questionnaire studies tend to produce higher prevalence estimates than those produced by interview studies. In fact, prevalences of greater than 90% have been reported in some questionnaire studies (Wigman et al., 2011), suggesting that the subjective interpretation of questions that ostensibly assess psychotic experiences often does not coalesce with the phenomena intended to be examined by researchers and clinicians. This, in fact, has been demonstrated empirically in a study comparing questionnaire and clinical interview, which found that clinicans often disagreed with questionnaire results on the presence or absence of psychotic experiences in young people (Kelleher et al., 2011). In the study, many items intended to assess psychotic phenomena were endorsed by young people whom clinicans did not subsequently rate as having psychotic experiences. However, a number of questionnaire items performed reasonably well compared to clinical interview. In particular, an item on auditory hallucinations ("Have you ever heard voices or sounds that no one else can hear?") demonstrated very good sensitivity, specificity and positive and negative predictive value for clinician-verified psychotic experiences. In a meta-analysis of both community-based interview studies and questionnaire studies that used this validated item, there was a median psychotic symptom population prevalence of 17% in children aged 9 to 12 years and 7.5% in adolescents aged 13 to 18 years (Kelleher et al., 2011). Psychotic experiences, then, are common in childhood and become less common into adolescence.

Influenced by research from 'high risk for psychosis' clinics (Yung et al., 1996, Addington et al., 2007), psychotic experiences have increasingly been viewed as existing on a number of continua—notably a continuum of psychotic conviction or reality testing (see **Figures 9.1** and **9.2**). With regard to auditory vocal hallucinations, for example, for a symptom to be a true hallucination, the individual must not accept, even when directly challenged, that the voice could possibly arise from their own mind. The same "voice hearing" experience in an individual who has some doubt about the external origin of the voices cannot technically be classified as a hallucination; rather, this is termed an attenuated hallucination (i.e., an experience of hearing voices that is perceived as coming from outside the individual's own mind but with at least some degree of intact reality testing). See **Box 9.1** for a practical example. Psychotic experiences, therefore, may be divided into frank symptoms and attenuated symptoms, with the latter being more common. We use the term *psychotic experiences* in the current chapter to refer to both attenuated and frank psychotic symptoms.

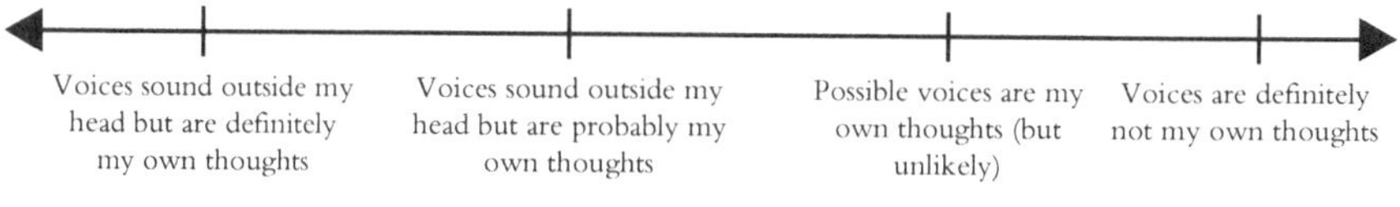

FIGURE 9.1 Continuum of severity of perceptual abnormalities

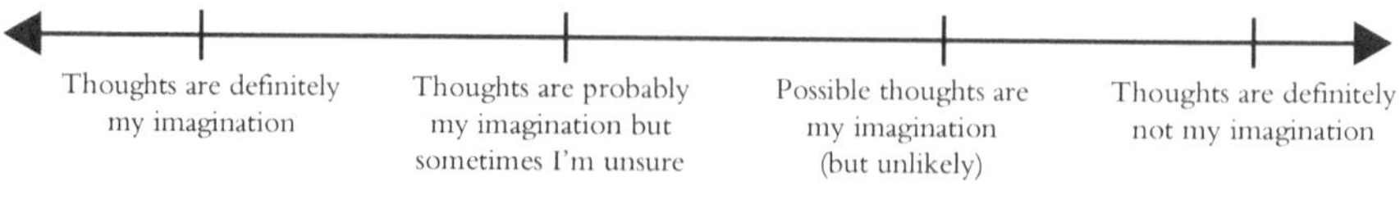

FIGURE 9.2 Continuum of severity of unusual thought content

BOX 9.1: EXAMPLE OF ATTENUATED AND FRANK HALLUCINATORY PHENOMENA IN CHILDREN AND ADOLESCENTS

Example 1

Owen is a 16-year-old boy who reports hearing voices commenting on his behavior. When asked about his attribution for these experiences, he reports that he believes the voices come from a ghost. When asked if there could be any other explanation for hearing these voices other than a ghost, he replies that he does not think so. He is then asked directly if he thinks there is any possibility that the voices could be the product of his own mind. He accepts that this is possible, although he thinks it is unlikely.

Because it was possible to induce some doubt in Owen about the external origin of the voices, his experience is not, technically, a hallucination; rather, it is an attenuated hallucination—a hallucinatory-type experience with (some degree of) intact reality testing. Reality testing varies along a continuum (see **Figure 9.1**).

Example 2

James is a 15-year-old boy who also reports hearing voices commenting on his behavior. Like Owen, when asked about his attribution for these experiences, he states that he believes the voices are those of a ghost. When asked if there could be any other explanation, he replies that there could not. He is then asked directly if he thinks there is any possibility that the voices could be the product of his own mind. He replies that he used to think that the voices could be his imagination but since they have continued to happen he does not believe this anymore and he thinks they are definitely a ghost

In this case, it was not possible to induce any doubt about the external origin of the voices (i.e., reality testing was not intact); James's experience is a formal hallucination.

Clinical Significance of Psychotic Experiences

Initial interest in the pathological significance of psychotic experiences focused largely on the finding that participants in a longitudinal study who had reported psychotic experiences at age 11 had an increased incidence of psychotic disorder in adulthood (Poulton et al., 2000). A number of studies have since replicated this finding (Welham et al., 2009; Kaymaz et al., 2012). However, despite a relatively increased risk, the vast majority of young people who report psychotic experiences do not go on to develop a psychotic disorder. Interestingly, by contrast, more recent research has demonstrated that young people with psychotic experiences are at increased risk for a wide variety of psychiatric disorders, not limited to psychosis (Yung et al., 2007; Scott et al., 2009b; Wigman et al., 2012). In a multicenter Irish study, the majority of children and adolescents who reported psychotic experiences met diagnostic criteria for at least 1 non-psychotic mental disorder (Kelleher et al., 2012a). Psychotic experiences did not predict one single disorder; rather, they were associated with a wide range of depressive, anxiety and behavioral disorders. However, young people with psychotic experiences were at particularly increased risk for multimorbidity, that is, the presence of more than one disorder, with the prevalence of psychotic experiences increasing in a dose-response manner with the number of diagnosable disorders.

The association between psychotic experiences and multimorbidity has also been demonstrated in a clinical setting (Kelleher et al., 2013b). In an Irish adolescent mental health clinic sample, patients who reported psychotic experiences were at significantly higher risk of multimorbid psychopathology than patients who did not report psychotic experiences. Patients with psychotic experiences, in fact, had, on average, three diagnosable mental disorders. What is more, patients with psychotic experiences had poorer socio-occupational functioning than those without, even after adjusting for the number of disorders.

Psychotic experiences have also recently been highlighted as important markers of risk for suicidal behavior in young people (Saha et al., 2011; Kelleher et al., 2012b). In a community-based study, adolescents with psychiatric disorders who reported psychotic experiences (predominantly auditory hallucinations) had a far higher prevalence of suicidal behavior than those with psychopathology who did not report psychotic experiences (Kelleher et al., 2012b). Adolescents with a diagnosis of major depressive disorder who reported psychotic experiences, for example, had a 14-fold increased odds of suicide plans or attempts compared to adolescents with the same diagnosis who did not report psychotic experiences. In a Swedish cohort study, the presence of psychotic experiences was a strong predictor that suicidal ideation, which, usually a transient phenomenon in the population, would persist throughout adolescence (Kelleher et al., 2014). Furthermore, in a prospective Irish cohort study, the incidence of suicide attempts in adolescents with psychopathology who reported psychotic experiences at baseline was 14% at 3-month follow-up and 34% at 1-year follow-up (Kelleher et al., 2013a). By comparison, the incidence of suicide attempts in adolescents with psychopathology who did not report psychotic experiences at baseline was 4% at 3 months and 13% at 1-year follow-up. Similarly, in a long-term follow-up study from age 11 years to age 38 years, researchers in New Zealand found that half of children who reported psychotic experiences had attempted or completed suicide (Fisher et al., 2013). This strong relationship between psychotic experiences and suicidality has also been replicated in clinical settings. In a child and adolescent mental health clinic sample, patients with depressive, anxiety or behavioral disorders who reported psychotic experiences had a far higher odds of suicide plans and attempts than patients with the same disorder who did not report psychotic experiences (Kelleher et al., 2013b). Psychotic experiences, then, whether frank or attenuated, should be recognized as a clinical marker of high risk for multimorbidity, poor functioning and suicidal behavior in population and clinical samples.

A Developmental Perspective

Importantly, the developmental stage of the child reporting the symptom should be taken into account since research has shown that associated psychopathology varies with age. In a Dutch sample of 7- to 8-year-olds, psychotic experiences were associated with only a minor increase in emotional or behavioral symptoms of psychopathology (Bartels-Velthuis et al., 2010). However, at age 12 to 13 years, psychotic experiences were associated with a 3- to 5-fold increased risk of scoring in the abnormal range of the Child Behavior Checklist in the same sample (Bartels-Velthuis et al., 2011). In an Irish population sample of 11- to 13-year-olds, 57% of those who reported psychotic experiences had at least one axis-1 psychiatric disorder (Kelleher et al., 2012a). By comparison, nearly 80% of 13- to 16-year-olds who reported psychotic experiences had at least 1 axis-1 psychiatric disorder. Psychotic experiences, then, may fall within the normal spectrum of experience in childhood but should be expected to discontinue in the course of normal development. Symptoms that persist into adolescence become increasingly predictive of psychopathology.

Assessing Young People for Psychotic Experiences

A number of interview and questionnaire instruments can be used to assess for psychotic experiences in children and adolescents (see assessment scales below). Most interviews involve an assessment of psychotic experiences as part of a broader assessment for mental disorders. However, many of them do not involve a detailed assessment of the characteristics of reported psychotic experiences; rather, they aim to simply establish the presence or absence of psychotic experiences. There are few interviews specifically designed for the purpose of assessing psychotic experiences (e.g., the Auditory Vocal Hallucinations Rating Scale and the SOCRATES Assessment of Perceptual Abnormalities and Unusual Thought Content). The SOCRATES assessment is designed to assess the characteristics of hallucinatory and delusional experiences along a number of dimensions, such as frequency, attributions and associated distress. The AVHRS also assesses the characteristics of vocal hallucinations along a number of dimensions, although it does not assess for non-vocal hallucinations or for delusions.

Questionnaires have also been used to assess for psychotic experiences in many studies (see **Table 9.1**). As described above, endorsement rates of more than 90% for

TABLE 9.1 Questionnaire studies of psychotic experiences in children and adolescents

Instrument	*Source*	*Country of study*	*Age (Years)*
APSS	(Kelleher et al., 2012a)	Ireland	11–13
APSS	(Kelleher et al., 2012a)	Ireland	13–16
CAPE	(Wigman et al., 2011)	Netherlands	10–12
CAPE	(Wigman et al., 2011)	Netherlands	12–16
CAPE	(Yung et al., 2009)	Australia	13–17
CAPE	(Barragan et al., 2011)	Spain	13–17
CAPE	(Armando et al., 2010)	Australia	15–18
DISC	(Kinoshita et al., 2011)	Japan	12–18
DISC	(De Loore et al., 2011)	Netherlands	13–14
DISC	(Lataster et al., 2006)	Netherlands	13–14
PLEQ-C	(Laurens et al., 2012)	UK	9–12
YSR	(Dhossche et al., 2002)	Netherlands	11–18
YSR	(Scott et al., 2009a)	Australia	13–17
YSR	(Kelleher et al., 2014)	Sweden	13–20
YSR	(Scott et al., 2009b)	Australia	14

APSS, Adolescent Psychotic Symptom Screener; CAPE, Community Assessment of Psychic Experiences; DISC, Diagnostic Interview Schedule for Children; PLEQ-C, Psychotic-Like Experiences Questionnaire for Children; YSR, Youth Self Report

"at least one psychotic symptom" have been reported in population-based questionnaire studies (Wigman et al., 2011), raising concerns about the validity of these items. Questionnaires have largely not been invalidated against clinical interview in terms of sensitivity and specificity. Exceptions include specific items that perform well in terms of identifying individuals with genuine psychotic symptoms when compared with gold standard clinical interview (Kelleher et al., 2011). A question on auditory hallucinations—"Have you ever heard voices or sounds that no one else can hear?"—has very good sensitivity, specificity and positive and negative predictive value not just for auditory hallucinations but for psychotic symptoms in general (Kelleher et al., 2011). Furthermore, item response theory analysis in a large population sample of children demonstrated that this question has the strongest psychometric properties for assessing the continuum of psychotic symptoms (Laurens et al., 2012).

How to Assess for Psychotic Symptoms: A Systematic Approach

Any number of questions can be used to "prompt" disclosure of psychotic phenomena. The instruments listed below each contain suggested prompt questions to identify the presence of hallucinations and delusions. The limitation of most instruments, however, is that they provide little guidance in terms of assessing the details of such experiences. The following is a suggested systematic approach that may be applied to the assessment of psychotic symptoms. This approach can be used for both children and adults and may be applied in clinic or community settings.

Hallucinations/Perceptual Abnormalities

i. Source: Enquire whether the experience is perceived as originating inside or outside the head.
ii. Onset: Document when the experiences began.
iii. Duration: Document how long the experiences last. If there are multiple experiences, always note the time length of the longest ever experience as well as an average.
iv. Frequency: Quantify how much time is spent occupied with perceptual abnormalities (e.g., 1 hour per day). Also document if there has been any fluctuation in the frequency of the experiences (becoming more or less frequent).
v. Content: Document the content of the experiences, including how many different voices are heard, what the voices say, whether voices converse/ give commands/comment. In the case of non-vocal hallucinations, document the content (e.g., music, noises etc.).
vi. Character of voices: Note whether voices were male or female, young or old, familiar/non-familiar. Also note if the voice sounds like a normal voice or is different in some way. Note the volume (whispering, shouting, normal) and whether the voice was perceived to be 'good' or 'bad' (emotional valence).
vii. Reality testing and attribution: This is perhaps the most complex part of the assessment. Assessment of attribution should take a stepped approach. First ask an open-ended question about the experience, such as, "When you were hearing [experience], what did you think was going on?" If the individual believes the experience does not arise from their own mind, how convinced are they that this is the case (see **Figure 9.1**)? If the individual does not voluntarily suggest that the experience could be their imagination, challenge them on this by asking, "Do you ever think that [experience] was your imagination or do you think it is definitely [individual's attribution]?"
viii. Timing: Enquire as to whether the experiences occur only at particular times, including whether they are hypnagogic or hypnopompic, only when they are alone, only at night time, only when they have taken alcohol or drugs, only when they had a fever or were peri-ictal.
ix. Functional impact: Assess whether the experiences have impacted on the person's functioning—for example, they are afraid to be alone, they will not go to certain places, they cannot sleep, they cannot concentrate on activities.
x. Severity of distress: Enquire as to whether the experiences are distressing or not. If the experiences are distressing, ask the individual to quantify this on a scale from 1 to 10 in terms of severity.

xi. Assess whether the experience is perceived as originating inside or outside the head.

Delusions/Unusual Thought Content

i. Onset: Document when the unusual thought began.
ii. Duration: If she or he no longer believes [unusual thought content], document how long they held the unusual belief. If there are multiple experiences, always note the time length of the longest ever experience as well as an average.
iii. Frequency: Quantify how much time is spent occupied with unusual thought. Note any recent changes in frequency (e.g., onset 2 months ago, used to spend about 1 hour a day in total thinking about unusual thought content but has been spending at least 3 hours pre-occupied with unusual thoughts per day for past 2 weeks).
iv. Content: Document the unusual thought content.
v. Reality testing and attribution: This is perhaps the most complex part of the assessment. Assessment of attribution should take a stepped approach. First ask an open-ended question, such as, "When you thought [unusual thought], what did you think was going on?" If the individual believes the experience does not arise from their imagination, how convinced are they that this is the case (see **Figure 9.2**)? If the individual does not voluntarily suggest that the experience could have arisen from their imagination, challenge them on this by asking, "Do you ever think that [unusual thought] was your imagination or do you think it is definitely [individual's attribution]?"
vi. Timing: Enquire as to whether they only held the unusual thought at certain times, for example, when febrile or after taking alcohol/drugs.
vii. Functional impact: Assess whether the unusual thought impacted on the person's functioning—for example, they are afraid to be alone, they will not go to certain places, they cannot sleep, they cannot concentrate on activities.
viii. Severity of distress: Enquire as to whether the unusual thought causes distress or not. If the thought is distressing, ask the individual to quantify this on a scale from 1 to 10 in terms of severity.

The description of Elaine's voice in **Box 9.2** can then be described as follows:

Source:	Outside head.
Onset:	3 years ago.
Frequency:	Once a month for past 6 months. Prior to that, once every 3 months.
Duration:	Maximum 3 to 4 minutes but a few seconds on average.

BOX 9.2: PRACTICAL EXAMPLE OF PERCEPTUAL ABNORMALITIES

Elaine is a 14-year-old girl who attends a research study for assessment of psychotic experiences. After rapport-building, and questions about mood and anxiety, she is asked, "Sometimes people hear things or see things and they're not sure where they come from. Does that ever happen to you?" She discloses that sometimes when she is alone she hears a voice speaking. The voice sounds like it is coming from outside her head. She first remembers these experiences occurring when she was 11 years old. These experiences have happened about once a month over the past 6 months. Before that they used to happen about once every 3 months. The experiences have lasted up to 3 to 4 minutes but, on average, last only a few seconds. The voice Elaine hears is always the same: It sounds like a girl around her own age, although it does not sound like anyone she knows. The voice speaks at a normal volume and mainly comments on things Elaine is doing, referring to her in the third person. For example, last week while doing homework, she heard the voice saying "Why is she doing it that *way?" in a critical tone. It is not always critical, however, and usually comments in a more neutral way; for example, "She is wearing a red coat." The voice has never commanded her to do anything. When asked what she thinks is happening when she hears the voice, she says, "I think it's my imagination playing tricks on me." When asked if there could be any other explanation, she says that more recently (in the past 6 months), she has worried that it might be a ghost, although she spontaneously comments that she thinks this is probably not true and it is more likely that it is her imagination. She thinks that the voice does not seem to be either good or bad, although it does frighten her when she hears it (she rates the severity of distress as 6 out of 10). When asked if she is more likely to hear the voice at any particular time or place, she says that it usually happens when she is alone, which is usually in her bedroom. She has never taken any alcohol or drugs when she hears the voice and it has never happened during a fever. In terms of functional impact, Elaine reports that she sometimes cannot get to sleep for hours after hearing the voice because of worry. This has resulted in her being very tired in school the next day and her teacher has reprimanded her on at least three of these occasions for not paying attention (she does not normally get in trouble for inattention). Her grades, however, have not been affected and it has not affected her relationships with her family or friends.*

Content:	One voice only, commenting, third person Examples: "Why is she doing it that way?" "She is wearing a red coat." No conversing voices No commands.

Character:	Teenage, female voice. Sounds like a regular voice. Normal volume. Emotional valence: neutral.
Reality testing and Attribution:	"My imagination playing tricks on me". Over past 6 months has wondered if it could be a ghost but thinks this is unlikely (reality testing score = 2; 6 months ago it was 1).
Timing:	When alone No alcohol/drugs No fever.
Functioning:	Can keep her awake for hours, which has led to her being tired in school and being reprimanded by teacher for inattention. No effect on grades or on functioning with family and friends.
Distress:	6 out of 10.

Assessment Scales

The major assessment scales used to assess for psychotic experiences in children and adolescents are as follows (detailed in *Part 4*).

Structured diagnostic interviews include the Child and Adolescent Psychiatric Assessment (CAPA; Angold, Prendergast, Cox, Harrington, Simonoff & Rutter, 1995), the Schedule for Affective Disorders and Schizophrenia for School-Aged Children (K-SADS; Kaufman, Birmaher, Brent, Rao & Ryan, 1996), and the US National Institute of Mental Health Diagnostic Interview Schedule for Children (DISC; Shaffer, Fisher, Lucas, Dulcan & Schwab-Stone, 2000).

There are several interviews developed to assess psychotic symptoms more specifically. These include the SOCRATES Assessment of Perceptual Abnormalities and Unusual Thought Content (Kelleher & Cannon, 2014), which assesses for the presence of psychotic experiences along several dimensions. Psychotic symptoms can also be assessed using questionnaire. These include the Adolescent Psychotic Symptom Screener (APSS; Kelleher, Harley, Murtagh & Cannon, 2011), the Community Assessment of Psychic Experiences (CAPE; Stefanis, Hanssen, Smirnis, et al., 2002), the Psychotic-Like Experiences Questionnaire for Children (PLEQ-C; Laurens, Hobbs, Sunderland, Green, & Mould, 2012), Youth Self Report (YSR; Achenbach, 1991), and the electronic Multisensory Hallucinations Scale for Children (Jardri et al., in development) which comes as a touch-screen app.

Conclusion

Psychotic experiences are common in children and adolescents. In young children, such experiences may be developmentally appropriate and not necessarily indicate underlying pathology. As children age into adolescence, however, psychotic experiences become increasingly predictive of psychopathology and, in particular, multimorbid psychopathology, characterized by the presence of multiple disorders, poor global functioning and suicidality. Future research to assess specific features of psychotic experiences and how these relate to risk for psychopathology will be valuable. This will necessitate more detailed assessments than have typically been employed in research to date. This chapter gives a suggested systematic approach to the assessment of psychotic experiences in the clinic and in the community.

References

Achenbach, T. (1991). *Manual for the youth self report and profile.* Burlington: University of Vermont, Department of Psychiatry.

Addington, J., Cadenhead, K. S., Cannon, T. D., Cornblatt, B., McGlashan, T. H., et al. (2007). North American prodrome longitudinal study: A collaborative multisite approach to prodromal schizophrenia research. *Schizophrenia Bulletin, 33*, 665–672.

Angold, A., Prendergast, M., Cox, A., Harrington, R., Simonoff, E., & Rutter, M. (1995). The child and adolescent psychiatric assessment (CAPA). *Psychological Medicine, 25*(4), 739–754.

Armando, M., Nelson B., Yung A. R., Ross M., Birchwood M., Girardi P., & Fiori Nastro, P. (2010). Psychotic-like experiences and correlation with distress and depressive symptoms in a community sample of adolescents and young adults. *Schizophrenia Research, 119*, 258–265.

Barragan, M., Laurens K. R., Navarro J. B., & Obiols J. E. (2011). Psychotic-like experiences and depressive symptoms in a community sample of adolescents. *European Psychiatry, 26*(6), 391–401.

Bartels-Velthuis, A. A., Jenner J. A., van de Willige, G., van Os J., & Wiersma D. (2010). Prevalence and correlates of auditory vocal hallucinations in middle childhood. *British Journal of Psychiatry, 196*, 41–46.

Bartels-Velthuis, A. A., van de Willige, G., Jenner, J. A., van Os, J.,& Wiersma, D. (2011). Course of auditory vocal hallucinations in childhood: 5-year follow-up study. *British Journal of Psychiatry, 199*, 296–302. doi:10.1192/bjp.bp.110.086918

De Loore, E., Gunther, N., Drukker, M., Feron, F., Sabbe, B., Deboutte, D., et al. (2011). Persistence and outcome of auditory hallucinations in adolescence: A longitudinal general population study of 1800 individuals. *Schizophrenia Research, 127*, 252–256.

Dhossche, D., Ferdinand, R., Van der Ende, J., Hofstra, M. B., & Verhulst, F. (2002). Diagnostic outcome of self-reported hallucinations in a community sample of adolescents. *Psychological Medicine, 32*, 619–627.

Fisher, H. L., Caspi, A., Poulton, R., Meier, M. H., Houts, R., Harrington, et al. (2013). Specificity of childhood psychotic symptoms for predicting schizophrenia by 38 years of age: A birth cohort study. *Psychological Medicine*, 1–10.

Jardri, R., Demeulemeester, M., Fligans, B., Tabet, A., & Thomas, P. (in development). *Multisensory hallucinations scale for children (MHASC).*

Kaufman, J., Birmaher, B., Brent, D., Rao, U., & Ryan, N. (1996). *The schedule for affective disorders and schizophrenia for school aged children: Present and lifetime version.* Pittsburgh, PA: University of Pittsburgh, Western Psychiatric Institute and Clinic.

Kaymaz, N., Drukker, M., Lieb, R., Wittchen, H. U., Werbeloff, N., Weiser, M., et al. (2012). Do subthreshold psychotic experiences predict clinical outcomes in unselected non-help-seeking population-based samples? A systematic review and meta-analysis, enriched with new results. *Psychological Medicine, 42*(11), 1–15.

Kelleher, I., & Cannon, M. (2014). *SOCRATES assessment of perceptual abnormalities and unusual thought content*. Unpublished manuscript, freely available from authors.

Kelleher, I., Cederlöf, M., & Lichtenstein, P. (2014). Psychotic experiences as a predictor of the natural course of suicidal ideation: A Swedish cohort study. *World Psychiatry, 13*, 184–188. Retrieved from http://onlinelibrary.wiley.com/doi/10.1002/wps.20131/full

Kelleher, I., Corcoran, P., Keeley, H., Wigman, J. T., Devlin, N., Ramsay, H., et al. (2013a). Psychotic symptoms and population risk for suicide attempt: A prospective cohort study. *JAMA Psychiatry, 70*, 940–948.

Kelleher, I., Devlin, N., Wigman, J. T. W., Murtagh, A., Kehoe, A., Fitzpatrick, C., et al. (2013b). Psychotic experiences in an adolescent mental health clinic sample: Implications for suicidality, multimorbidity and functioning. *Psychological Medicine, 12*, 1–10.

Kelleher, I., Harley, M., Murtagh, A., & Cannon, M. (2011). Are screening instruments valid for psychotic-like experiences? A validation study of screening questions for psychotic-like experiences using in-depth clinical interview. *Schizophrenia Bulletin, 37*, 362–369.

Kelleher, I., Keeley, H., Corcoran, P., Lynch, F., Fitzpatrick, C., Devlin, N., et al. (2012a). Clinicopathological significance of psychotic experiences in non-psychotic young people: Evidence from four population-based studies. *British Journal of Psychiatry, 201*, 26–32.

Kelleher, I., Lynch, F., Harley, M., Molloy, C., Roddy, S., Fitzpatrick, et al. (2012b). Psychotic symptoms in adolescence index risk for suicidal behavior: Findings from two population-based case-control clinical interview studies. *Archives of General Psychiatry, 69*, 1277–1283.

Kinoshita, Y., Shimodera, S., Nishida, A., Kinoshita, K., Watanabe, N., Oshima, N., et al. (2011). Psychotic-like experiences are associated with violent behavior in adolescents. *Schizophrenia Research, 126*, 245–251.

Lataster, T., van Os, J., Drukker, M., Henquet, C., Feron, F., Gunther, N., et al. (2006). Childhood victimisation and developmental expression of non-clinical delusional ideation and hallucinatory experiences: Victimisation and non-clinical psychotic experiences. *Society of Psychiatry and Psychiatric Epidemiology, 41*, 423–428.

Laurens, K. R., Hobbs, M. J., Sunderland, M., Green, M., & Mould, G. L. (2012). Psychotic-like experiences in a community sample of 8000 children aged 9 to 11 years: An item response theory analysis. *Psychological Medicine, 42*, 1495–1506.

Poulton, R., Caspi, A., Moffitt, T. E., Cannon, M., Murray, R., & Harrington, H. (2000). Children's self-reported psychotic symptoms and adult schizophreniform disorder: A 15-year longitudinal study. *Archives of General Psychiatry, 57*, 1053–1058.

Saha, S., Scott, J. G., Johnston, A. K., Slade, T. N., Varghese, D., Carter, G. L., & McGrath, J. J. (2011). The association between delusional-like experiences and suicidal thoughts and behaviour. *Schizophrenia Research, 132*(2/3), 197–202.

Scott, J., Martin, G., Bor, W., Sawyer, M., Clark, J., & McGrath, J. (2009a). The prevalence and correlates of hallucinations in Australian adolescents: results from a national survey. *Schizophrenia Research, 107*, 179–185.

Scott J., Martin, G., Welham, J., Bor, W., Najman, J., O'Callaghan, M., et al. (2009b). Psychopathology during childhood and adolescence predicts delusional-like experiences in adults: A 21-year birth cohort study. *American Journal of Psychiatry, 166*, 567–574.

Shaffer, D., Fisher, P., Lucas, C. P., Dulcan, M. K., & Schwab-Stone, M. E. (2000). NIMH diagnostic interview schedule for children version IV (NIMH DISC-IV): Description, differences from previous versions, and reliability of some common diagnoses. *Journal of the American Academy of Child and Adolescent Psychiatry, 39*(1), 28–38.

Stefanis, N., Hanssen, M., Smirnis, N., et al. (2002). Evidence that three dimensions of psychosis have a distribution in the general population. *Psychological Medicine, 32*, 347–358.

Welham, J., Scott, J., Williams, G., Najman, J., Bor, W., O'Callaghan, M., et al. (2009). Emotional and behavioural antecedents of young adults who screen positive for non-affective psychosis: A 21-year birth cohort study. *Psychological Medicine, 39*, 625–634.

Wigman, J.T., van Nierop, M., Vollebergh, W.A., Lieb, R., Beesdo-Baum, K., Wittchen, H. U., et al. (2012). Evidence that psychotic symptoms are prevalent in disorders of anxiety and depression, impacting on illness onset, risk, and severity—Implications for diagnosis and ultra-high risk research. *Schizophrenia Bulletin, 38*, 247–257.

Wigman, J. T., Vollebergh, W. A., Raaijmakers, Q. A., Iedema, J., van Dorsselaer, S., Ormel, J., et al. (2011). The structure of the extended psychosis phenotype in early adolescence—A cross-sample replication. *Schizophrenia Bulletin, 37*, 850–860.

Yung, A. R., Buckby, J. A., Cosgrave, E. M., Killackey, E. J., Baker, K., Cotton, S. M., et al. (2007). Association between psychotic experiences and depression in a clinical sample over 6 months. *Schizophrenia Research, 91*, 246–253.

Yung, A. R., McGorry, P. D., McFarlane, C. A., Jackson, H. J., Patton, G. C., & Rakkar, A. (1996). Monitoring and care of young people at incipient risk of psychosis. *Schizophrenia Bulletin, 22*, 283–303.

Yung, A. R., Nelson, B., Baker, K., Buckby, J. A., Baksheev, G., & Cosgrave, E. M. (2009). Psychotic-like experiences in a community sample of adolescents: Implications for the continuum model of psychosis and prediction of schizophrenia. *Australian & New Zealand Journal of Psychiatry, 43*, 118–128.

10

PSYCHOSIS IN GENERAL MEDICAL AND NEUROLOGICAL CONDITIONS

Massoud Stephane, Sergio Starkstein and Jaime Pahissa

Introduction

Originally considered pathognomonic to diagnostic entities such as schizophrenia and schizoaffective disorders, psychotic symptoms are in fact encountered in many other population groups, including those with neurological and general medical diseases as well as individuals who don't seek clinical care. Psychotic symptoms may not be as unspecific as fever or headache in terms of their etiology, but are widely encountered in medicine. Hence, it is important for medical practitioners to be familiar with the specificities of presentation of psychosis in medical conditions and with the assessment and management of psychosis in these cases.

To denote the origin of psychosis, terminologies such as *primary, secondary, functional* and *organic psychoses* have been used in the literature. In this chapter we will use *primary psychosis* to refer to illnesses where psychotic symptoms are the main features and general medical symptoms and/or signs are sparse. We will use the term *secondary psychosis* when psychotic symptoms are associated with findings suggestive of medical conditions. Although not originally intended, the terms *organic* and *functional psychoses* have been used to refer to psychoses with and without altered brain function, respectively. It is our view that psychotic experiences do not bypass the brain even when altered brain functions cannot be detected or when these symptoms do not require medical care. Psychotic experiences have to be mediated by the brain and psychosis is necessarily organic.

The identification of psychotic symptoms in medically ill patients is not only important for the treatment of the psychological and behavioral repercussion they may have, but also for the management of the underlying medical conditions. For example, while psychosis in mental disorders does not carry ominous information with respect to short-term prognosis, when it is associated with certain medical conditions (e.g., Alzheimer's disease [AD] and Parkinson's disease [PD]), it could indicate a severe or advanced stages of these conditions and is associated with higher mortality (Aarsland et al., 1999). Additionally, the identification of the underlying medical conditions is crucial for a proper treatment of psychosis. In psychosis secondary to vitamin B12 deficiency, antipsychotic medications may not be effective, and vitamin B12 replacement alone could resolve psychosis (Payinda & Hansen, 2000). Furthermore, although psychosis secondary to medical conditions could reflect genetic propensity for psychosis, long-term treatment with antipsychotic medications may not be necessary in some cases such as hypothyroidism (Hall, 1983).

For practical purposes, the acronym TACTICS MDS USE could be handy as a reminder for medical professionals about conditions where psychosis could be encountered (Keshavan & Kaneko, 2013). It refers to: Traumatic brain injury, Autoimmune disease, Congenital/cytogenetic disorders, Toxic/drug induced disorders, Iatrogenic, Cerebrovascular disorders, Space-occupying lesions, Metabolic disorders, Dietary disorders, Sepsis, Unknown medical cause, Seizure disorder, Endocrine disorders. In this chapter, we present an overview of (i) psychosis in general medical conditions, followed by (ii) psychosis in neurological conditions. As the literature in PD is well developed, psychosis in PD is discussed in the most detail. Finally, (iii) assessment methods of psychosis in these conditions. Please note that psychosis related to dementing illnesses is discussed in *Chapter 11* in this book.

Psychosis in General Medical Conditions

It is not uncommon for general medical illnesses to affect brain functions or to result in brain disease. Therefore, theoretically, if these effects involve brain functions that when altered could result in psychosis, medical illnesses could cause psychotic symptoms. In fact, the literature provides numerous instances where psychosis occurs in the course of medical illnesses. We provide below an account of psychosis-related salient features, and of the medical conditions most frequently associated with psychosis. A detailed description of these diseases is beyond the scope of this chapter.

In autoimmune diseases, psychosis is reported in up to 10% of patients with systemic lupus erythematosus (SLE; Appenzeller, Cendes & Costallat, 2008), and to a lesser extent in multiple sclerosis (Kosmidis, Giannakou, Messinis & Papathanasopoulos, 2010) and Hashimoto disease (Keshavan & Kaneko, 2013). In SLE, paranoid and grandiose type delusions as well as auditory and visual hallucinations are described. Interestingly, while immunosuppressive treatment has been observed to induce psychosis in some conditions, it appears to improve psychosis in SLE patients (Appenzeller et al., 2008). With or without autoimmune etiology, hypothyroidism and hyperthyroidism as well as rapid changes of thyroid hormones blood levels, can also result in or exacerbate psychosis (Hall, 1983). No distinctive symptom clusters has been reported in these cases. Multiple case reports also indicate that hypoparathyroidism (Velasco, Manshadi, Breen & Lippmann, 1999), hyperparathyroidism and hypocalcaemia (independently from hyperparathyroidism) could result in psychosis (Papa, Bononi, Sciubba, Ursella & Gentiloni-Silveri, 2003). Generally, the correction of endocrine abnormalities in these conditions resolves psychosis.

Psychosis is associated with about 50% of cases of metabolic disorders resulting from gene mutations, such as adult/adolescent form of Niemann-Pick type C, and Tay Sachs disease (lysosomal storage diseases) (Benes, 1989), and adult form of metachromatic leukodystrophy (mitochondrial disease; Amemiya et al., 2000). There are no distinctive symptoms clusters in these diseases. Psychosis is also a common occurrence (over 10% of cases) in many other genetic disorders such as velocardiofacial (DiGeorge) syndrome (Pulver et al., 1994), and Prader-Willi syndrome (Vogels et al., 2004), which result from deletions of 22q11.2 gene and multiple genes on chromosome 15 (q11–13), respectively. In the former condition, there is a high prevalence of symptoms suggestive of autism, attention deficit, and anxiety disorders in addition to psychotic disorders. In Huntington disease, a trinucleotide repeat disorder at a gene (HTT gene) located on chromosome 4 (4p16.3), paranoia is the most common psychotic symptom and is often associated with depression, irritability, and obsessive compulsive behaviors (Folstein, Chase, Wahl, McDonnell & Folstein, 1987). In Wilson disease, where mutations in the ATP7B gene result in abnormal transport and multi-organ deposition of copper, psychosis is encountered in up to 10% of cases (Rathbun, 1996). Additionally, in Fahr's disease (Bourgeois, 2010), a genetically heterogeneous disease resulting in calcium deposits in vessels and multiple brain structures, persecutory delusions and ideas of reference are sometime reported.

Syphilis (Sobhan, Rowe, Ryan & Munoz, 2004) and acquired immunodeficiency syndrome (AIDS; Dolder, Patterson & Jeste, 2004) are also often associated with psychosis. In the former, psychosis could be the presenting problem, and in these cases is indistinguishable from primary psychosis. In AIDS, persecutory, grandiose and somatic delusions are more prominent. Psychosis is also occasionally encountered in toxoplasmosis (Torrey & Yolken, 2007). Of note, many viral infections were implicated in the pathogenesis of primary psychosis.

Medications and street drugs could induce psychosis by direct effects, withdrawal, or as a long-term complication. Stimulants (amphetamine and cocaine) (Curran, Byrappa & McBride, 2004), phencyclidine (Jansen, 2000) and cannabis (Swain, Gibb, Horwood & Fergusson, 2012) have direct psychogenic effects, while the psychogenic effects of alcohol and benzodiazepine are related to withdrawal (Swain et al., 2012). Hallucinogenic drugs such as Lysergic acid diethylamide (LSD) induce psychosis both by direct effect as well as by long-term complications (Cole & Sumnall, 2003). The medications most commonly associated with psychosis are: glucocotricosteroids (Dubovsky, Arvikar, Stern & Axelrod, 2012), antimalarial (Alisky, Chertkova & Iczkowski, 2006) and antiparkinsonian drugs. Additionally, many other drugs have been sometimes implicated such as benzodiazepine, anticonvulsant and antibiotics.

Reports also link vitamin B12 and folic acid deficiencies to psychosis, with symptoms including persecutory delusions and visual and auditory hallucinations. In the case of vitamin B12, recovery could be obtained with supplementation but not antipsychotic treatment (Payinda & Hansen, 2000). Interestingly, folate and vitamin B12 supplements are also found to be effective treatment for a subtype of schizophrenia with prominent negative symptoms in patients with specific genetic subtype (homozygous for the 484T allele of FOLH1 gene; Roffman et al., 2013).

Finally, individuals with ophthalmic problems may suffer from a well characterized type of psychosis, Charles Bonnet syndrome (CBS; ffytche & Howard, 1999). This syndrome consists of visual hallucinations, ranging from abstract geometric patterns to complex, vivid images such as animals, people or scenes (Santhouse, Howard & ffytche, 2000). Usually, patients have preserved insight that images are not real, and hallucinations are not distressing. The frequency of CBS varies, due to differences in assessment type, age range and ascertainment biases. Among patients with age-related macular degeneration (ARMD), about 40% may have CBS (Abbott, Connor, Artes & Abadi, 2007). Among patients with other ophthalmic diagnoses (e.g., cataract, glaucoma or diabetic retinopathy) the frequency of CBS is about 18% (Khan, Shahid, Thurlby, Yates & Moore, 2008).

Psychosis in Neurological Conditions

Whether in need of treatment or not, psychosis is experienced through the brain, and research providing evidence of altered brain activity in primary psychosis is commonplace. Moreover, psychosis is a well-known complication of neurological disorders, especially among patients with chronic neurodegenerative illness. About half of the patients with Alzheimer's disease (AD) will develop psychosis at some stage of the illness (Jeste & Finkel, 2000). Psychosis is also frequent in Parkinson's disease (PD), the second most frequent neurodegenerative disease (Fernandez et al., 2008), and may also be observed in acute neurological disorders such as epilepsy, stroke and traumatic brain injury, albeit with a lower frequency. Psychoses in AD and PD have received the most attention. AD psychosis is discussed in *Chapter 11*. In this section, we discuss psychosis in neurological conditions other than dementing illnesses.

Parkinson's Disease

A variety of symptoms have been subsumed under the concept of psychosis in PD, ranging from mild illusions to full-blown delusions and hallucinations.

For many years, psychotic symptoms in PD were divided into the categories of "benign psychosis" and "malignant psychosis" (Fenelon, Goetz & Karenberg, 2006). "Benign psychosis" includes illusions, "de passage" hallucinations (vague images of people or objects moving into the peripheral visual field), and "sense of presence" (vivid sensations that somebody is present nearby; Fenelon, Soulas, de Langavant, Trinkler & Bachoud-Levi, 2011). "Malignant psychosis" includes hallucinations, which are most often visual but can involve any sensory modality, and delusions (Holroyd, Currie & Wooten, 2001). Typical visual hallucinations in PD are of animals and people, but without a paranoid component. Hallucinations usually present in a stereotypic way, to the point that patients become familiar with the hallucinatory content. Nevertheless, the concept of "benign hallucinations" in PD has to be discarded, as it was demonstrated that most PD patients with visual hallucinations (and full insight) progress into more severe psychotic states with loss of insight (Fenelon, Mahieux, Huon & Ziegler, 2000). Goetz et al. (Goetz, Fan, Leurgans, Bernard & Stebbins, 2006) demonstrated that in 81% of patients, the transition from "benign" to "malignant" hallucinations occurs over a period of 3 years. In a subsequent study, these authors (Goetz, Fan & Leurgans, 2008) found that early treatment of mild hallucinations resulted in the acute resolution of hallucinations in about half of the patients, and in a reduced rate of progression to psychosis, relative to patients with mild hallucinations who did not receive antipsychotic treatment.

In 2007, the National Institute of Neurological Disorders (NIND), together with the National Institutes of Mental Health (NIMH) convened a workgroup to produce standardized diagnostic criteria for psychosis in PD (Ravina et al., 2007). The workgroup suggested that the diagnosis of psychosis in PD requires the presence of illusions (misinterpretations of a real external stimulus), false sense of presence, hallucinations, and delusions (at least one of these has to be present). These symptoms have to be present in a continuous or recurrent way for at least 1 month. Other criteria include that: patients have to meet the UK Brain bank criteria for PD, all psychotic symptoms must occur after the onset of PD, and psychotic symptoms are not better accounted for by another cause of parkinsonism (e.g., dementia with Lewy bodies, psychiatric disorders). Finally, the diagnostic criteria include the following specifiers: (1) whether preserved insight is present, (2) whether the patient suffers dementia and (3) whether antiparkinsonian medication is being used. Partial validation to these criteria were provided by Mack et al (Mack et al., 2012), who reported that 91% of patients diagnosed with psychosis based on clinical assessments all met the NIND-NIMH criteria.

Frequency: The frequency of hallucinations in PD was reported to range from 16% to 75% (Forsaa, Larsen, Wentzel-Larsen, Goetz, et al., 2010), while delusions were reported to range from 1% to 35% (Forsaa, Larsen, Wentzel-Larsen, Goetz, et al., 2010). This wide discrepancy may be related to ascertainment bias, different instruments used to assess psychosis, different criteria used to diagnose psychosis, lack of rating of "minor" psychotic symptoms, and the presence of depression and cognitive deficits. In a recent study, Fenelon et al. (Fenelon, Soulas, Zenasni & de Langavant, 2010), used a structured questionnaire covering the whole spectrum of PD-associated psychosis. They found hallucinations in 46% of patients, delusions in 4%, and "minor symptoms" in 45%. Using the NIND-NIMH criteria, the frequency of psychosis was 60%. This is consistent with a study by Forsaa et al. (Forsaa, Larsen, Wentzel-Larsen, Goetz, et al., 2010), who recently reported the results from a population-based prospective study that included 137 PD patients with a 12-year follow-up. By the end of the study, the cumulative prevalence of psychosis was estimated at 60%, with cross-sectional prevalence rates ranging between 20% to 40% (Forsaa, Larsen, Wentzel-Larsen, Goetz et al., 2010). Moreover, hallucinations in the context of poor insight are most frequent among PD patients with dementia (Fenelon et al., 2010), and patients may sometimes 'act' the hallucination. Hallucinations with preserved insight are most frequent in earlier stages of PD, and some patients experience these hallucinations as pleasant or comforting (Fenelon et al., 2000).

Functional impact, and risks factors, for psychosis: Psychosis in PD is associated with greater functional impairment, behavioral disturbance, caregiver burden, nursing home placement (Aarsland, Larsen, Tandberg & Laake, 2000), and higher mortality (Aarsland, Larsen, Karlsen, Lim & Tandberg, 1999) as compared to PD patients without psychosis. Moreover, psychosis in PD is a risk factor for the development of dementia (Factor et al., 2003). Lee and Weintraub reported (Lee & Weintraub, 2012) that more severe depression and anxiety, REM behavior disorder and apathy are significantly associated with psychosis in PD. On the other hand, they found no significant association between psychosis and older age and use of antiparkinsonian medication. Mack et al. (2012) reported that PD patients with psychosis were younger, had greater impairments in activities of daily living, more severe depression and cognitive deficits and worse quality of life than PD patients without psychosis. Even "minor" psychotic symptoms were associated with more severe depression and worse quality of life. There were no significant differences on levodopa equivalent dose, which is in agreement with most cross-sectional studies (Fenelon et al., 2010). These findings suggest that levodopa is not sufficient to produce psychosis in PD. There is more evidence for anticholinergic drugs to be related to psychosis in PD, although this association was not always confirmed (Benbir et al., 2006).

Other risk factors identified are PD duration longer than 10 years, presence of REM behavior disorder, higher overall levodopa equivalent dose, increased motor fluctuations, axial rigidity, cognitive impairment, depression and autonomic impairment (Factor et al., 2011; Forsaa, Larsen, Wentzel-Larsen & Alves, 2010). Factor et al. (Factor et al., 2011) found psychosis in PD to be related to longer duration of illness, older age, freezing of gait, depression and cognitive impairment. Whereas psychosis and cognitive decline often co-occur, PD patients with visual hallucinations have a higher risk of developing dementia (Factor et al., 2003). In the context of a longitudinal study, Forsaa et al. (Forsaa, Larsen, Wentzel-Larsen, Goetz et al., 2010) identified older age at onset of PD, higher baseline of levodopa equivalent dose and REM behavior disorder as independent risk factors for incident psychosis. They further suggested that psychosis identified a subgroup of PD patients with a more malignant course of disease.

Epilepsy

The annual incidence of psychosis in epilepsy is twice as high as the annual incidence of schizophrenia in the general population (Tadokoro, Oshima & Kanemoto, 2007). Most frequent symptoms of psychosis in epilepsy include hallucinations, delusions, aggression, and disorganized thought and behavior. Negative symptoms such as alogia, blunted affect, social withdrawal, apathy and inattention are less frequent (Nadkarni, Arnedo & Devinsky, 2007). Psychotic symptoms may occur in the ictal, post-ictal and inter-ictal periods. *Ictal psychosis* is rare and usually consists of visual or auditory hallucinations, emotional changes such as agitation, fear and paranoid thoughts, and other phenomena such as depersonalization, derealization, autoscopy, and out of body experience (Nadkarni et al., 2007).

Post-ictal psychosis (PIP) occurs in about 2% to 8% of patients with epilepsy and is usually associated with temporal lobe epilepsy (Trimble, Kanner & Schmitz, 2010), but it has also been described among patients with primary generalized epilepsy (Devinsky et al., 1995). PIP accounts for about 25% of cases with psychosis in epilepsy (Trimble et al., 2010), but it often goes underdiagnosed. PIP patients show more manic-like symptoms than schizophrenia type symptoms (Kanemoto, Kawasaki & Kawai, 1996). There is usually a lucid interval between the seizure and the onset of psychosis. Diagnostic criteria for PIP are (1) psychosis occurring within 1 week after the seizure, (2) psychosis lasting between 15 hours and 3 months, delusions, hallucinations, disorganized or bizarre behavior, formal thought disorder and/or affective changes and (3) no evidence of anti epileptic drug toxicity, non-convulsive status epilepticus, recent head trauma, alcohol or drug intoxication or withdrawal, and chronic psychotic disorders. Negative symptoms are rarely present. Using the PANSS, Tadokoro et al. (Matsuura et al., 2004; Tadokoro, Oshima & Kanemoto, 2007) reported that negative symptoms are less frequent among epilepsy patients with psychosis as compared to patients with schizophrenia. On the other hand, a factor analysis by Matsuura et al. (Matsuura et al., 2004) showed a similar profile of psychotic symptoms between both groups, although symptoms were more severe among patients with schizophrenia. Finally, *interictal psychosis* may be acute or chronic, and symptoms are similar to those found in PIP (Kanemoto, Tadokoro & Oshima, 2012).

Post-Stroke Psychosis

Psychosis after stroke is a rare phenomenon, with a frequency of about 3% (Kumral & Ozturk, 2004). Psychosis is more frequent among individuals with temporo-parieto-occipital strokes. Patients with post-stroke psychosis have a relatively high frequency of tactile and olfactory hallucinations (Nye & Arendts, 2002) and many patients retain awareness that these hallucinations are not real.

Traumatic Brain Injury

Although a rare cause of psychosis, traumatic brain injury (TBI) may produce psychotic symptoms directly or through secondary seizures. Among war veterans with a TBI, the frequency of psychosis was 9% (Achte, Hillbom & Aalberg, 1969). The risk is increased for patients with a genetic predisposition to psychosis (Harrison et al., 2006), severity of TBI and fronto-temporal lesions (Sachdev, Smith & Cathcart, 2001). Review of case reports shows that Capgras syndrome and reduplicative paramnesia appear within a year of TBI while auditory hallucinations and persecutory delusions appear within 3–4 years after the TBI (Sachdev, Smith & Cathcart, 2001). Negative symptoms are less frequently encountered.

Multiple Sclerosis

In addition to numerous case reports, there is a study showing that short lasting psychosis could occur in up to 4% of patients with Multiple Sclerosis (MS), and delusions are the most frequently observed symptom (Patten, Svenson & Metz, 2005). Psychosis in MS could be related to glucocorticoids treatment and to temporal lobe location of plaques (Keshavan & Kaneko, 2013).

Brain Tumors

Psychosis resulting from brain tumors can be indistinguishable from primary psychosis. Brain tumors should be suspected in new onset psychosis in the elderly, particularly when visual hallucinations are simple and delusions are unelaborate. Secondary psychosis should be also suspected when there is lack of formal thought disorder, and when physical examination reveals focal neurological signs. The location of tumor, rather than type, is a more important determinant of whether psychosis could occur. Generally, tumors located in the temporal or limbic structures are more commonly associated with psychosis than tumors located elsewhere (Galasko, Kwo-On-Yuen & Thal, 1988).

The Assessment of Psychosis in Medical and Neurological Conditions

For a comprehensive management of medical illnesses, all assessments should include an evaluation of mental functioning (here, psychosis); the latter is sometimes omitted by medical practitioners, especially when they are unfamiliar with psychiatric comorbidity of medical conditions. When mental state evaluation is considered, the assessment of psychosis in the medically ill can be challenging. Patients may be unaware of the presence of symptoms, may not readily report them, and may be medically unable to cooperate with lengthy evaluations. Medical practitioners need to seek collateral information from caregivers, rely on observations of the patients' behaviors, and consider the advantages and disadvantages of lengthy comprehensive assessment compared to short and well-tolerated instruments that may offer limited information. The clinical evaluation should include a determination of whether psychosis is primary or secondary and, in the latter case, a differential diagnosis of the underlying medical conditions.

Other than PD (and AD)-specific psychosis assessment instruments, there are no instruments designed to assess psychosis in individual medical conditions and such instruments may not be necessary. Psychosis assessment scales in PD include the SCOPA-Psychiatric Complications (SCOPA-PC; Martinez-Martin, Frades-Payo, Aguera-Ortiz & Ayuga-Martinez, 2012; Visser et al., 2007), the Scale for Evaluation of Neuropsychiatric Disorders in PD (SEND-PD; Martinez-Martin et al., 2012), the University of Miami PD Hallucinations Questionnaire (UM-PDHQ; Papapetropoulos et al., 2008; Santhouse et al., 2000), the Institute of Psychiatry Visual Hallucination Interview (IP-VHI; Santhouse et al., 2000) and the Parkinson's Psychosis Questionnaire (PPQ; Brandstaedter et al., 2005).

The SCOPA-PC provides an assessment of the severity of hallucinations, illusions, paranoid ideation, altered dream phenomena, confusion, sexual preoccupation and compulsive behavior. The SEND-PD evaluates independently the severity and frequency of neuropsychiatric symptoms, including psychosis. As the name implies the UM-PDHQ evaluates aspects of hallucinations such as modality, frequency, duration, insight and emotional burden. The IP-VHI evaluates major and minor visual hallucinations and illusions, and aspects such as insight into the perception, presence and relationship with auditory hallucinations, duration of visual hallucinations, presence of delirium, and use of medications. This instrument has high specificity and positive predictive validity, but other psychometric attributes remain unknown. The PPQ is recommended as a screening instrument for early recognition of psychosis in PD. The PPQ is the only PD psychosis instrument that was validated against the SCID as the gold standard. There was also adequate agreement with the BPRS, suggesting that the PPQ is a valid instrument to assess psychosis in PD.

The Movement Disorders Society (MDS) task force on rating scales organized a special group to provide advice and criticism on existing rating scales to rate psychosis in PD (Fernandez et al., 2008). The task force examined 12 instruments (the above mentioned scales not included) and recommended the four scales for use in PD. Interestingly, all the recommended scales were general psychopathology instruments and none was designed for use in PD. These scales include: The Brief Psychiatric Rating Scale (Overall & Gorham, 1962), the Positive and Negative Syndrome Scale (Kay, Opler & Lindenmayer, 1989), the Neuropsychiatric Inventory (Cummings et al., 1994) and the Schedule for Assessment of Positive Symptoms (Andreasen, 1984). The MDS task force also recommended that a global measure of severity (such as the Clinical Global Impression) be used with the recommended scale (Fernandez et al., 2008). They further suggested that a scale should be specifically designed to assess psychosis in PD to replace the non-specific ones (Fernandez et al., 2008). An approach that we find promising was undertaken by Voss and co-workers (Voss et al., 2013). Based on secondary data, the authors analyzed the stability, reliability and face-validity of a shortened version of the SAPS intended for use in PD. This version includes nine items from the SAPS assessing visual and auditory hallucinations. The SAPS-PD has similar sensitivity to change than the SAPS, but validity and reliability data were not provided.

In conclusion, the current state of the literature suggests that instruments for the assessment of primary psychosis are useful for the assessment of secondary psychosis. For most medical illnesses, other than AD and PD, there are no specific psychosis assessment tools. While disease-specific instruments could be redundant and not clinically useful, future research may design tools more befitting for the setting of secondary psychosis. Research also is needed to provide the psychometric attributes of the most commonly used instruments to assess psychosis in PD.

References

Aarsland, D., Larsen, J.P., Karlsen, K., Lim, N.G. & Tandberg, E. (1999). Mental symptoms in Parkinson's disease are important contributors to caregiver distress. *International Journal of Geriatric Psychiatry, 14*(10), 866–874.

Aarsland, D., Larsen, J.P., Tandberg, E. & Laake, K. (2000). Predictors of nursing home placement in Parkinson's disease: A population-based, prospective study. *Journal of the American Geriatric Society, 48*(8), 938–942.

Abbott, E.J., Connor, G.B., Artes, P.H. & Abadi, R.V. (2007). Visual loss and visual hallucinations in patients with age-related macular degeneration (Charles Bonnet syndrome). *Investigative Opthamology and Visual Science, 48*(3), 1416–1423.

Achte, K.A., Hillbom, E. & Aalberg, V. (1969). Psychoses following war brain injuries. *Acta Psychiatrica Scandinavica, 45*(1), 1–18.

Alisky, J.M., Chertkova, E.L. & Iczkowski, K.A. (2006). Drug interactions and pharmacogenetic reactions are the basis for chloroquine and mefloquine-induced psychosis. *Medical Hypotheses, 67*(5), 1090–1094.

Amemiya, S., Hamamoto, M., Goto, Y., Komaki, H., Nishino, I., Nonaka, I. & Katayama, Y. (2000). Psychosis and progressing dementia: Presenting features of a mitochondriopathy. *Neurology, 55*(4), 600–601.

Andreasen, N. (1984). *Scale for the assessment of positive symptoms (SAPS).* Iowa City: University of Iowa.

Appenzeller, S., Cendes, F. & Costallat, L.T. (2008). Acute psychosis in systemic lupus erythematosus. *Rheumatology International, 28*(3), 237–243.

Benbir, G., Ozekmekci, S., Cinar, M., Beskardes, F., Apaydin, H. & Erginoz, E. (2006). Features associated with the development of hallucinations in Parkinson's disease. *Acta Neurologica Scandinavica, 114*(4), 239–243. doi:10.1111/j.1600-0404.2006.00644.x

Benes, F.M. (1989). Myelination of cortical-hippocampal relays during late adolescence. *Schizophrenia Bulletin, 15*(4), 585–593.

Bourgeois, J.A. (2010). Fahr's disease—A model of neuropsychiatric illness with cognitive and psychotic symptoms. *Acta Psychiatrica Scandinavica, 121*(1), 78.

Brandstaedter, D., Spieker, S., Ulm, G., Siebert, U., Eichhorn, T.E., Krieg, J.C., et al. (2005). Development and evaluation of the Parkinson Psychosis Questionnaire: A screening-instrument for the early diagnosis of drug-induced psychosis in Parkinson's disease. *Journal of Neurology, 252*(9), 1060–1066.

Cole, J.C. & Sumnall, H.R. (2003). Altered states: The clinical effects of ecstasy. *Pharmacology Therapeutics, 98*(1), 35–58.

Cummings, J.L., Mega, M., Gray, K., Rosenberg-Thompson, S., Carusi, D.A. & Gornbein, J. (1994). The Neuropsychiatric Inventory: Comprehensive assessment of psychopathology in dementia. Research Support, U.S. *Neurology, 44*(12), 2308–2314.

Curran, C., Byrappa, N. & McBride, A. (2004). Stimulant psychosis: Systematic review. *British Journal of Psychiatry, 185*, 196–204.

Devinsky, O., Abramson, H., Alper, K., FitzGerald, L.S., Perrine, K., Calderon, J. & Luciano, D. (1995). Postictal psychosis: A case control series of 20 patients and 150 controls. *Epilepsy Research, 20*(3), 247–253.

Dolder, C.R., Patterson, T.L. & Jeste, D.V. (2004). HIV, psychosis and aging: Past, present and future. *AIDS 18*, (Suppl. 1), 35–42.

Dubovsky, A.N., Arvikar, S., Stern, T.A. & Axelrod, L. (2012). The neuropsychiatric complications of glucocorticoid use: Steroid psychosis revisited. *Psychosomatics 53*(2), 103–115.

Factor, S.A., Feustel, P.J., Friedman, J.H., Comella, C.L., Goetz, C.G., Kurlan, R., et al. (2003). Longitudinal outcome of Parkinson's disease patients with psychosis: Comparative study randomized controlled trial research support, *Neurology, 60*(11), 1756–1761.

Factor, S.A., Steenland, N.K., Higgins, D.S., Molho, E.S., Kay, D.M., Montimurro, J., et al. (2011). Disease-related and genetic correlates of psychotic symptoms in Parkinson's disease. *Movement Disorders, 26*(12), 2190–2195. doi:10.1002/mds.23806

Fenelon, G., Goetz, C.G. & Karenberg, A. (2006). Hallucinations in Parkinson disease in the prelevodopa era. *Neurology, 66*(1), 93–98.

Fenelon, G., Mahieux, F., Huon, R. & Ziegler, M. (2000). Hallucinations in Parkinson's disease: Prevalence, phenomenology and risk factors. *Brain, 123 (Pt. 4)*, 733–745.

Fenelon, G., Soulas, T., de Langavant, L.C., Trinkler, I. & Bachoud-Levi, A.C. (2011). Feeling of presence in Parkinson's disease. *Journal of Neurology, Neurosurgery and Psychiatry, 82*(11), 1219–1224.

Fenelon, G., Soulas, T., Zenasni, F. & de Langavant, L.C. (2010). The changing face of Parkinson's disease-associated psychosis: A cross-sectional study based on the new NINDS-NIMH criteria. *Movement Disorders, 25*(6), 763–766.

Fernandez, H.H., Aarsland, D., Fenelon, G., Friedman, J.H., Marsh, L., Troster, A.I., et al. (2008). Scales to assess psychosis in Parkinson's disease: Critique and recommendations. *Movement Disorders, 23*(4), 484–500.

ffytche, D.H. & Howard, R.J. (1999). The perceptual consequences of visual loss: 'Positive' pathologies of vision. *Brain, 122 (Pt. 7)*, 1247–1260.

Folstein, S.E., Chase, G.A., Wahl, W.E., McDonnell, A. M. & Folstein, M.F. (1987). Huntington disease in Maryland: Clinical aspects of racial variation. *American Journal of Human Genetics, 41*(2), 168–179.

Forsaa, E.B., Larsen, J.P., Wentzel-Larsen, T. & Alves, G. (2010). What predicts mortality in Parkinson disease? A prospective population-based long-term study. *Neurology, 75*(14), 1.

Forsaa, E.B., Larsen, J.P., Wentzel-Larsen, T., Goetz, C.G., Stebbins, G.T., Aarsland, D. & Alves, G. (2010). A 12-year population-based study of psychosis in Parkinson disease. *Archives of Neurology, 67*(8), 996–1001.

Galasko, D., Kwo-On-Yuen, P.F. & Thal, L. (1988). Intracranial mass lesions associated with late-onset psychosis and depression. *Psychiatric Clinics of North America, 11*(1), 151–166.

Goetz, C.G., Fan, W. & Leurgans, S. (2008). Antipsychotic medication treatment for mild hallucinations in Parkinson's disease: Positive impact on long-term worsening. *Movement Disorders, 23*(11), 1541–1545.

Goetz, C.G., Fan, W., Leurgans, S., Bernard, B. & Stebbins, G.T. (2006). The malignant course of "benign hallucinations" in Parkinson disease. *Archives of Neurology, 63*(5), 713–716.

Hall, R.C. (1983). Psychiatric effects of thyroid hormone disturbance. *Psychosomatics, 24*(1), 7–11.

Harrison, G., Whitley, E., Rasmussen, F., Lewis, G., Dalman, C. & Gunnell, D. (2006). Risk of schizophrenia and other non-affective psychosis among individuals exposed to head injury: Case control study. *Schizophrenia Research, 88*(1/3), 119–126.

Holroyd, S., Currie, L. & Wooten, G.F. (2001). Prospective study of hallucinations and delusions in Parkinson's disease. *Journal of Neurology, Neurosurgery and Psychiatry, 70*(6), 734–738.

Jansen, K.L. (2000). A review of the nonmedical use of ketamine: Use, users and consequences. *Journal of Psychoactive Drugs, 32*(4), 419–433.

Jeste, D.V. & Finkel, S.I. (2000). Psychosis of Alzheimer's disease and related dementias: Diagnostic criteria for a distinct syndrome. *American Journal of Geriatric Psychiatry, 8*(1), 29–34.

Kanemoto, K., Kawasaki, J. & Kawai, I. (1996). Postictal psychosis: A comparison with acute interictal and chronic psychoses. *Epilepsia, 37*(6), 551–556.

Kanemoto, K., Tadokoro, Y. & Oshima, T. (2012). Psychotic illness in patients with epilepsy. *Therapeutic Advances in Neurological Disorders, 5*(6), 321–334. doi:10.1177/1756285612454180

Kay, S.R., Opler, L.A. & Lindenmayer, J.P. (1989). The positive and negative syndrome scale (PANSS): Rationale and standardisation. *British Journal of Psychiatry*, (Suppl. 7), 59–67.

Keshavan, M.S. & Kaneko, Y. (2013). Secondary psychoses: An update. *World Psychiatry, 12*(1), 4–15.

Khan, J.C., Shahid, H., Thurlby, D.A., Yates, J.R. & Moore, A.T. (2008). Charles Bonnet syndrome in age-related macular degeneration: The nature and frequency of images in subjects with end-stage disease. *Ophthalmic Epidemiology, 15*(3), 202–208.

Kosmidis, M.H., Giannakou, M., Messinis, L. & Papathanasopoulos, P. (2010). Psychotic features associated with multiple sclerosis. *International Review of Psychiatry, 22*(1), 55–66.

Kumral, E. & Ozturk, O. (2004). Delusional state following acute stroke. *Neurology, 62*(1), 110–113.

Lee, A.H. & Weintraub, D. (2012). Psychosis in Parkinson's disease without dementia: Common and comorbid with other non-motor symptoms. *Movement Disorders, 27*(7), 858–863. doi:10.1002/mds.25003

Mack, J., Rabins, P., Anderson, K., Goldstein, S., Grill, S., Hirsch, E.S., et al. (2012). Prevalence of psychotic symptoms in a community-based Parkinson disease sample. *American Journal of Geriatric Psychiatry, 20*(2), 123–132. doi:10.1097/JGP.0b013e31821f1b41

Martinez-Martin, P., Frades-Payo, B., Aguera-Ortiz, L. & Ayuga-Martinez, A. (2012). A short scale for evaluation of neuropsychiatric disorders in Parkinson's disease: First psychometric approach. *Journal of Neurology, 259*(11), 2299–2308.

Matsuura, M., Adachi, N., Oana, Y., Okubo, Y., Kato, M., Nakano, T. & Takei, N. (2004). A polydiagnostic and dimensional comparison of epileptic psychoses and schizophrenia spectrum disorders [Comparative Study]. *Schizophrenia Research, 69*(2/3), 189–201.

Nadkarni, S., Arnedo, V. & Devinsky, O. (2007). Psychosis in epilepsy patients [Review]. *Epilepsia, 48*(Suppl. 9), 17–19.

Nye, E. & Arendts, G. (2002). Intracerebral haemorrhage presenting as olfactory hallucinations. *Emergency Medicine (Fremantle), 14*(4), 447–449.

Overall, J.E. & Gorham, D.R. (1962). The brief psychiatric rating scale. *Psychological Reports, 10*, 799–812.

Papa, A., Bononi, F., Sciubba, S., Ursella, S. &, Gentiloni-Silveri, N. (2003). Primary hyperparathyroidism: Acute paranoid psychosis. *American Journal of Emergency Medicine, 21*(3), 250–251.

Papapetropoulos, S., Katzen, H., Schrag, A., Singer, C., Scanlon, B.K., Nation, D., et al. (2008). A questionnaire-based (UM-PDHQ) study of hallucinations in Parkinson's disease. *BMC Neurology, 8*, 21. doi:10.1186/1471-2377-8-21

Patten, S.B., Svenson, L.W. & Metz, L.M. (2005). Psychotic disorders in MS: Population-based evidence of an association. *Neurology, 65*(7), 1123–1125.

Payinda, G. & Hansen, T. (2000). Vitamin B(12) deficiency manifested as psychosis without anemia. *American Journal of Psychiatry, 157*(4), 660–666.

Pulver, A.E., Nestadt, G., Goldberg, R., Shprintzen, R.J., Lamacz, M., Wolyniec, P.S., et al. (1994). Psychotic illness in patients diagnosed with velo-cardio-facial syndrome and their relatives. *Journal of Nervous and Mental Disease, 182*(8), 476–478.

Rathbun, J.K. (1996). Neuropsychological aspects of Wilson's disease. *International Journal of Neuroscience, 85*(3/4), 221–229.

Ravina, B., Marder, K., Fernandez, H.H., Friedman, J.H., McDonald, W., Murphy, D., et al. (2007). Diagnostic criteria for psychosis in Parkinson's disease: Report of an NINDS, NIMH work group. *Movement Disorders, 22*(8), 1061–1068.

Roffman, J.L., Lamberti, J.S., Achtyes, E., Macklin, E.A., Galendez, G.C., Raeke, L.H., et al. (2013). Randomized multicenter investigation of folate plus vitamin B12 supplementation in schizophrenia. *JAMA Psychiatry, 70*(5), 481–489.

Sachdev, P., Smith, J.S. & Cathcart, S. (2001). Schizophrenia-like psychosis following traumatic brain injury: A chart-based descriptive and case-control study. *Psychological Medicine, 31*(2), 231–239.

Santhouse, A. M., Howard, R.J. & ffytche, D.H. (2000). Visual hallucinatory syndromes and the anatomy of the visual brain. *Brain, 123 (Pt. 10)*, 2055–2064.

Sobhan, T., Rowe, H.M., Ryan, W.G. & Munoz, C. (2004). Unusual case report: three cases of psychiatric manifestations of neurosyphilis. *Psychiatric Services, 55*(7), 830–832.

Swain, N.R., Gibb, S.J., Horwood, L.J. & Fergusson, D.M. (2012). Alcohol and cannabis abuse/dependence symptoms and life satisfaction in young adulthood. *Drug and Alcohol Review, 31*(3), 327–333.

Tadokoro, Y., Oshima, T. & Kanemoto, K. (2007). Interictal psychoses in comparison with schizophrenia—A prospective study. *Epilepsia, 48*(12), 2345–2351. doi:10.1111/j.1528-1167.2007.01230.x

Torrey, E.F. & Yolken, R.H. (2007). Schizophrenia and toxoplasmosis. *Schizophrenia Bulletin, 33*(3), 727–728.

Trimble, M., Kanner, A. & Schmitz, B. (2010). Postictal psychosis [Review]. *Epilepsy & Behavior, 19*(2), 159–161.

Velasco, P.J., Manshadi, M., Breen, K. & Lippmann, S. (1999). Psychiatric aspects of parathyroid disease. *Psychosomatics, 40*(6), 486–490.

Visser, M., Verbaan, D., van Rooden, S.M., Stiggelbout, A. M., Marinus, J. & van Hilten, J.J. (2007). Assessment of psychiatric complications in Parkinson's disease: The SCOPA-PC. *Movement Disorders, 22*(15), 2221–2228. doi:10.1002/mds.21696

Vogels, A., De Hert, M., Descheemaeker, M.J., Govers, V., Devriendt, K., Legius, E., et al. (2004). Psychotic disorders in Prader-Willi syndrome. *American Journal of Medical Genetics, 127A*(3), 238–243.

Voss, T., Bahr, D., Cummings, J., Mills, R., Ravina, B. & Williams, H. (2013). Performance of a shortened scale for assessment of positive symptoms for Parkinson's disease psychosis. *Parkinsonism & Related Disorders, 19*(3), 295–299.

11

PSYCHOSIS IN OLDER ADULTS AND DEMENTIA POPULATIONS

Andrew Ford and Osvaldo P. Almeida

Introduction

Human beings are living longer than ever before, and older adults now make up a considerable proportion of the population (Wiener & Tilly, 2002). Consequently, an increasing proportion of people experiencing psychotic symptoms are elderly. Late-life psychotic symptoms can be broadly classified into those that developed earlier in life and those that have their onset in the context of a disorder of later life. Individuals whose symptoms developed in younger adulthood and persisted into later life most commonly have a schizophrenia-spectrum disorder or severe mood disorder. In contrast, psychotic symptoms developing in later life lack diagnostic specificity and may be the symptomatic expression of various conditions. In this chapter, we will first discuss the epidemiology of psychosis in later life before providing a summary of the clinical features, assessment and management of the most common conditions giving rise to psychotic symptoms in older age. An in depth discussion of the neurobiological underpinnings of these symptoms is beyond the scope of this chapter.

Epidemiology

Prevalence estimates of psychosis in older adults vary depending on whether the sample is community (0.2% to 4.7%) or residential care based (up to 63%) (Zayas & Grossberg, 1998). A retrospective chart review of 1,730 psychogeriatric in-patients experiencing psychotic symptoms indicated that dementia (40%), mood disorders (38%), delirium (7%) and schizophrenia spectrum disorders (4%) accounted for the majority of cases (Webster & Grossberg, 1998), although diagnostic categories will vary depending on the population sampled. Psychotic symptoms are common in dementia sufferers. The Cache County Study reported a point prevalence of 18% for delusions and 10% for hallucinations (Steinberg et al., 2008), but the frequency of those symptoms may be higher in the oldest old (Ostling et al., 2011) and in nursing home settings (Rovner et al., 1990). The overall frequency of psychotic symptoms in Alzheimer's disease (AD) is estimated to be between 30% and 50% (Jeste and Finkel, 2000), while their occurrence in dementia with Lewy bodies (DLB) is considerably higher, with visual hallucinations being a key diagnostic feature in this population (Ballard et al., 2001). Psychosis in vascular dementia has been less studied with some suggesting a similar prevalence to AD (Ballard et al., 2000), while others report lower prevalence (Lyketsos et al., 2000). Estimates of the point prevalence of psychotic symptoms in frontotemporal dementia (FTD) are lower than AD (Mendez et al., 2008). Sensory impairment, dementia severity and type are among the most robust associations (Ballard et al., 1995).

Mood disorders are a frequent cause of psychotic symptoms in later life. Depression affects about 10% of community-dwelling older adults (Beekman et al., 1999), but estimates of the prevalence of psychotic symptoms in this population vary from 7% to nearly half of all cases (Copeland et al., 1999; Ohayon & Schatzberg, 2002). There is limited data available about specific risk factors for psychotic depression in later life but family history, poorer physical health, poorer response to treatment, illness severity, hypothalamic-pituitary-adrenal dysfunction, dopaminergic dysregulation and neuroanatomical abnormalities may play a role (Kim et al., 1999; Nelson & Davis, 1997; Simpson et al., 1999). The prevalence of bipolar disorder appears to decline in later life with an estimated 0.1% 12-month prevalence in adults aged 65 and over (Weissman et al., 1988).

Delirium is a syndrome characterized by a disturbance of consciousness with reduced ability to focus, sustain or shift attention. It has a prevalence of around 15% in hospitalized older patients but is more frequent in certain subpopulations such as those undergoing complex surgery (Bucht et al., 1999). Risk factors are diverse and include advancing age, pre-existing cognitive impairment, medical morbidity, surgery, sensory deprivation, certain medications and metabolic derangement (Fong et al., 2009). Delirium is accompanied by psychotic symptoms in around 40% of cases and these are associated with more active medical conditions and multiple etiologies causing the delirium (Webster & Holroyd, 2000).

The community prevalence of schizophrenia in people older than 65 years is between 0.1% and 0.5% (Copeland et al., 1998), but most individuals would have had the onset of illness in their younger years with only an estimated 4% having the onset of their illness after the age of 60 (Harris & Jeste, 1988). Risk factors for very-late-onset schizophrenia-like psychosis (the proposed term for schizophrenia with onset after 60 years; Howard et al., 2000) include female gender, sensory deficit, social isolation and premorbid schizoid or paranoid personality traits (Harris & Jeste, 1988; Howard et al., 1994). Late-onset cases have also been associated with higher education and better occupational and psychosocial functioning (Castle et al., 1997) compared to those with earlier onset and, to a lesser extent, psychosocial stress, bereavement and physical disability (Castle & Murray, 1993). The community prevalence of delusional disorder in later life is estimated at 0.04% (Copeland et al., 1998).

Dementia

Paranoid ideas are the most frequent type of delusions associated with dementia (Rubin et al., 1988). These often involve suspicions of theft or incursions into the dwelling (e.g., people coming in through the attic or roof). The affected person frequently responds by hiding objects (e.g., money) and subsequently believes these have been stolen. Misidentification syndromes are also common, including the classic mirror delusion, the belief that television characters are real, Capgras delusion and a belief that a "phantom boarder" is living in the house (Forstl et al., 1991). Delusions of infidelity, persecution (often by neighbors) and delusions of reference are not infrequent, but well-systematized delusions are rare (Rubin et al., 1988). Visual hallucinations are the most common perceptual disturbance (often of seeing people/children in the house), particularly in DLB (Tsuang et al., 2009). Auditory and olfactory hallucinations are less common and most hallucinations tend to be fragmented and fleeting.

Psychotic symptoms in dementia show a tendency to resolve spontaneously with only a minority being persistent (Ballard et al., 1997) although the presence of psychosis predisposes to worse long-term outcomes such as higher rates of institutionalization and death, not to mention greater patient and caregiver distress (Scarmeas et al., 2007). The initial focus of management should favor a non-pharmacological approach and a move into more structured and supportive accommodation can be beneficial for some (Spira & Edelstein, 2006). Antipsychotic medications are modestly effective and evidence tends to favor risperidone (Brodaty et al., 2003) and olanzapine (Cummings et al., 2002), although the risk of cerebrovascular events and other side effects are a concern (Ballard & Waite, 2006). Quetiapine or clozapine are the preferred options in patients with DLB and Parkinson's dementia given the risk of worsening motor symptoms with other antipsychotics (Fernandez et al., 2002).

Assessment of psychotic symptoms occurring for the first time in an elderly person should always include a thorough history from the individual and reliable informants, paying special attention to onset, duration and any evidence of associated cognitive impairment. A thorough "organic" screen is essential and is an important aspect of the diagnostic evaluation (Kyomen & Whitfield, 2009).

Structured assessment methods are useful, particularly given the individual's tendency to underreport these symptoms, possible lack of good collateral information and questionable reliability of the history given the associated cognitive deficits. There are a number of assessment tools available that are suited to different health professionals from varying clinical backgrounds. The Neuropsychiatric Inventory (NPI; Cummings et al., 1994) and Behavioral Symptoms in Alzheimer's Disease (BEHAVE-AD; Reisberg et al., 1987) are most widely used in clinical and research settings. Both scales take around 15 minutes to administer and are based on clinician interviews with a reliable informant. The NPI has a nursing home version for individuals in assisted care and also includes ratings of frequency, severity and caregiver distress. The BEHAVE-AD has been strengthened by additions of a frequency and severity weighted version (BEHAVE-AD-FW; Monteiro et al., 2001) and an observer-rated version (E-BEHAVE-AD; Auer et al., 1996).

Other scales developed to assess psychopathology in dementia include several items focusing on psychotic symptoms, such as the Cambridge Mental Disorders of the Elderly Examination (CAMDEX; Roth et al., 1986), Clinical Rating Scale for Symptoms of Psychosis in Alzheimer's Disease (SPAD; Reisberg & Ferris, 1980), Columbia University Scale for Psychopathology in Alzheimer's Disease (CUSPAD; Devanand et al., 1992), Consortium to Establish a Registry for Alzheimer's Disease–Behavioral Rating Scale (CERAD-BRS; Tariot et al., 1995), Dysfunctional Behavior Rating Instrument (DBRI; Molloy et al., 1991), Manchester and Oxford Universities Scale for the Psychopathological Assessment of Dementia (MOUSEPAD; Allen et al., 1996), Neurobehavioral Rating Scale (NRS; Sultzer et al., 1992), and the Present Behavioral Examination (PBE; Hope & Fairburn, 1992).

In older adults more generally, semi-structured interviews to assess psychiatric and psychotic phenomena include the Comprehensive Psychopathological Rating Scale (CPRS; Asberg et al., 1978), Geriatric Mental State Schedule (GMSS; Copeland et al., 1976) and Survey Psychiatric Assessment Schedule (SPAS; Bond et al., 1980).

Mood Disorders

Major depression is the second most common cause of psychotic symptoms in later life, accounting for between 20.4% and 38% of cases (Holroyd & Laurie, 1999; Webster & Grossberg, 1998). The clinical presentation of depression in later life is similar to that in younger adults although with some notable differences. Older adults tend to have more somatic complaints, hypochondriasis, psychomotor disturbance, insomnia, cognitive impairment and a greater likelihood of psychotic symptoms (Kessing, 2006). The psychotic symptoms in depression tend to be mainly delusional in nature and these are mostly mood-congruent, such as delusions of guilt, nihilism and disease (somatic), although mood-incongruent delusions and hallucinations (usually auditory) do occur (Gournellis et al., 2001). Older bipolar patients have a similar presentation to their younger counterparts and psychotic features are present in nearly two thirds of individuals during the active phase of the illness although these patients are less frequently encountered in an old age psychiatry setting (Depp & Jeste, 2004).

Treatment of psychotic depression should include a thorough evaluation of the individual, screening specifically for any contributing medical factors and a comprehensive risk assessment. The presence of psychosis in older adults with depression usually indicates a degree of severity and treatment will invariably need to include an antidepressant medication usually with the addition of an antipsychotic (Broadway & Mintzer, 2007). The presence of psychotic symptoms may also indicate a more favorable response to electroconvulsive therapy (ECT; Dombrovski et al., 2005).

A number of assessment scales have been developed for the assessment of mood disorders but few have been specifically designed for the elderly population. The Geriatric Depression Scale (GDS; Yesavage et al., 1982) and Brief Assessment Schedule Depression Cards (BASDEC; Adshead et al., 1992) are the only two depression screening tools designed specifically for use in elderly populations. Both are relatively brief (around 5 minutes) and screen for the most common symptoms (except psychosis) encountered in this population. The Cornell Scale for Depression in Dementia (CSSD; Alexopoulos et al., 1988) and the Dementia Mood Assessment Scale (DMAS; Sunderland et al., 1988) have been designed for use in dementia patients with comorbid depressive symptoms. Both scales briefly enquire about psychotic symptoms.

Delirium

Delirium is a common cause of psychotic symptoms in the elderly. Common features of delirium include cognitive impairment, sleep disruption, agitation and psychotic symptoms. These symptoms tend to be fluctuating with an acute onset and can persist despite treatment of the presumed underlying cause (Mittal et al., 2011). Delirium can be broadly divided into three clinical subtypes based on motor activity: hypoactive, hyperactive and mixed. Psychotic symptoms can occur in any subtype although are more common and distressing in the hyperactive type (Fong et al., 2009). Visual hallucinations and paranoid delusions predominate, although illusions, other delusional beliefs and auditory and tactile hallucinations do occur (Webster & Holroyd, 2000). Visual hallucinations range from simple, benign, non-threatening dream-like images to complex, terrifying images (e.g., seeing threatening people or animals). Paranoid delusions are most often persecutory in nature and may involve medical staff or fellow patients (Saxena & Lawley, 2009). Mood and anxiety symptoms also tend to predominate with generalized anxiety, depressive symptoms, mood lability and, less commonly, mania. The experience of delirium is an often frightening and threatening experience with psychotic symptoms being the major source of this distress, particularly in the over 50% of patients who recall the delirium experience (Breitbart et al., 2002).

Current approaches to the prevention of delirium in hospitalized patients consist of both non-pharmacological and pharmacological approaches, of which the former are arguably more effective (Siddiqi et al., 2007). Non-pharmacological approaches involve addressing multiple risk factors in a systematic manner together with education and environmental manipulation (Inouye, 2000). Pharmacological approaches may include prophylactic treatment with antipsychotics such as haloperidol (Vochteloo et al., 2011) and cholinesterase inhibitors (Overshott et al., 2008), although evidence for their efficacy is equivocal at best. Emerging data suggest a promising role for melatonin (Al-Aama et al., 2011). Management of established cases of delirium should focus on addressing the likely cause together with appropriate pharmacological and non-pharmacological strategies (Young et al., 2010).

Delirium is unrecognized in 32%–66% of cases (Inouye et al., 1998) and an estimated 30%–40% of delirium cases are preventable (Siddiqi et al., 2006). Assessment includes a thorough history paying special attention to the longitudinal history and onset of symptoms that is essential in trying to differentiate it from other common causes of cognitive impairment in this population (e.g., DLB, AD). Clinical evaluation for the characteristic attention deficits is essential together with a thorough medical screen for likely causes although a clear cause is not always apparent. A number of diagnostic and rating tools have been developed to assist the clinician in diagnosing and rating the severity of delirium. The Confusion Assessment Method (CAM; Inouye et al., 1990) is the most widely used diagnostic tool for delirium and has been incorporated into a number of guidelines worldwide. The CAM is rated by a clinician following a clinical interview and cognitive assessment. Patients are rated on nine domains (item 7 assesses for the presence of perceptual disturbances such as hallucinations, illusions or misinterpretations) but must have had an acute onset and exhibit inattentiveness and fluctuating mental state in addition to either disorganized thinking or altered level of consciousness to warrant a diagnosis of delirium. The CAM has been successfully adapted for use in the ICU (Ely et al., 2001). The Delirium Rating Scale (DRS; Trzepacz et al., 1988) is another popular diagnostic tool. This 10-item scale also relies on investigations and information from hospital staff and relatives perhaps better reflecting usual clinical practice (although neither scale should really be used in isolation). Psychotic symptoms are covered in three items: illusions, hallucinations and delusions. The scale has recently been expanded to include 16 items (DRS-R-98; Trzepacz et al., 2001). Other scales to assess delirium include the Delirium Index (DI; McCusker et al., 1988), Delirium Symptom Interview (DSI; Albert et al., 1992) and the Memorial Delirium Assessment Scale (MDAS; Breitbart et al., 1997).

Late-Onset Schizophrenia and Delusional Disorders

Historically, terminology of later-onset schizophrenia has been confusing but recently this has been classified into two broad groups based on timing of onset: late-onset schizophrenia (onset after 40 years of age) and very-late-onset schizophrenia-like psychosis (onset after 60; Howard et al., 2000). Clinically, there are few differences in the phenomenology and management across the life spectrum of the disorder. Individuals with later onset tend to have more preserved functioning, less thought disorder and less negative symptoms. They also more often present with well-systematized persecutory beliefs (including partition delusions) and multimodal hallucinations (in contrast to younger patients where auditory hallucinations are more common). The auditory hallucinations experienced are often commentary in the third person with abusive or threatening content (Howard et al., 1993a; Howard et al., 1993b; Jeste et al., 1995; Pearlson et al., 1989).

A range of brain imaging abnormalities have been described in late-onset cases including non-specific structural changes, volume reductions of the left temporal lobe and superior temporal gyrus, vascular changes and varying functional imaging changes (Howard et al., 2000). Neuropsychological impairments are similar to those of younger patients. Demonstrating the absence of the typical cognitive deficits seen in dementia plays an essential role in differentiating the two disorders (Almeida et al., 1995).

There are no specific assessment scales for the elderly in the assessment of schizophrenia and related disorders. Scales used in younger patients can readily be used in this population and these are covered elsewhere in this book.

Concluding Remarks

Psychosis in the elderly is relatively common and occurs mainly in the context of dementia, mood disorders and delirium although it can be the result of various other neuropsychiatic conditions (e.g., Parkinson's disease and stroke) that are discussed elsewhere. The clinical presentation of these symptoms varies according to etiology and appropriate diagnosis should guide management. The assessment of psychotic symptoms is complex and should take into account the various potential causes and contributing factors. A number of assessment tools are available to aid in this assessment and these can greatly increase the accuracy and reliability of diagnosis and measurement of severity if used appropriately.

References

Adshead, F., Cody, D.D., & Pitt, B. (1992). BASDEC: A novel screening instrument for depression in elderly medical inpatients. *British Medical Journal, 305*, 397.

Al-Aama, T., Brymer, C., Gutmanis, I., Woolmore-Goodwin, S.M., Esbaugh, J. & Dasgupta, M. (2011). Melatonin decreases delirium in elderly patients: a randomized, placebo-controlled trial. *International Journal of Geriatric Psychiatry, 26*, 687–694.

Albert, M.S., Levkoff, S. E., Reilly, C., Liptzin, B., Pilgrim, D., Cleary, P. D., et al. (1992). The delirium symptom interview: An interview for the detection of delirium symptoms in hospitalized patients. *Journal of Geriatric Psychiatry and Neurology, 5*(1), 14–21.

Alexopoulos, G. S., Abrams, R. C., Young, R. C., & Shamoian, C. A. (1988) Cornell Scale For Depression in Dementia. *Biological Psychiatry, 23*(3), 271–284.

Allen, N. H., Gordon, S., Hope, T., & Burns, A. (1996). The Manchester and Oxford Universities Scale for the Psychopathological Assessment of Dementia (MOUSEPAD). *British Journal of Psychiatry, 169*(3), 293–307.

Almeida, O.P., Howard, R.J., Levy, R., David, A.S., Morris, R.G., & Sahakian, B.J. (1995). Cognitive features of psychotic states arising in late life (late paraphrenia). *Psychological Medicine, 25*, 685–698.

Asberg, M., Perris, C. P., Schalling, D., Sedvall, G. (1978). The CPRS—Development and applications of a psychiatric rating scale. *Acta Psychiatrica Scandinavica*, 1(Suppl. 271), 69.

Auer, S.R., Monteiro, I.M., & Reisberg, B. (1996). The Empirical Behavioral Pathology in Alzheimer's Disease (E-BEHAVE-AD) Rating Scale. *International Psychogeriatrics, 8*, 247–266.

Ballard, C., Bannister, C., Graham, C., Oyebode, F., & Wilcock, G. (1995). Associations of psychotic symptoms in dementia sufferers. *British Journal of Psychiatry, 167*, 537–540.

Ballard, C., Neill, D., O'Brien, J., Mckeith, I.G., Ince, P., & Perry, R. (2000). Anxiety, depression and psychosis in vascular dementia: Prevalence and associations. *Journal of Affective Disorders, 59*, 97–106.

Ballard, C., O'Brien, J., Coope, B., Fairbairn, A., Abid, F., & Wilcock, G. (1997). A prospective study of psychotic symptoms in dementia sufferers: Psychosis in dementia. *International Psychogeriatrics, 9*, 57–64.

Ballard, C.G., O'Brien, J.T., Swann, A.G., Thompson, P., Neill, D., & Mckeith, I.G. (2001). The natural history of psychosis and depression in dementia with Lewy bodies and Alzheimer's disease: Persistence and new cases over 1 year of follow-up. *Journal of Clinical Psychiatry, 62*, 46–49.

Ballard, C., & Waite, J. (2006). The effectiveness of atypical antipsychotics for the treatment of aggression and psychosis in Alzheimer's disease. *Cochrane Database of Systematic Reviews*, CD003476.

Beekman, A.T., Copeland, J.R., & Prince, M.J. (1999). Review of community prevalence of depression in later life. *British Journal of Psychiatry, 174*, 307–311.

Bond, J., Brooks, P., Carstairs, V., & Giles, L. (1980). The reliability of a survey psychiatric assessment schedule for the elderly. *British Journal of Psychiatry, 37*, 148–162.

Breitbart, W., Gibson, C., & Tremblay, A. (2002). The delirium experience: Delirium recall and delirium-related distress in hospitalized patients with cancer, their spouses/caregivers, and their nurses. *Psychosomatics, 43*, 183–194.

Breitbart, W., Rosenfeld, B., Roth, A., Smith, M. J., Cohen, K., & Passik, S. (1997). The Memorial Delirium Assessment Scale. *Journal of Pain and Symptom Management, 13*(3), 128–137.

Broadway, J., & Mintzer, J. (2007). The many faces of psychosis in the elderly. *Current Opinion in Psychiatry, 20*, 551–558.

Brodaty, H., Ames, D., Snowdon, J., Woodward, M., Kirwan, J., Clarnette, R., et al. (2003). A randomized placebo-controlled trial of risperidone for the treatment of aggression, agitation, and psychosis of dementia. *Journal of Clinical Psychiatry, 64*, 134–143.

Bucht, G., Gustafson, Y., & Sandberg, O. (1999). Epidemiology of delirium. *Dementia and Geriatric Cognitive Disorders, 10*, 315–318.

Castle, D.J., & Murray, R.M. (1993). The epidemiology of late-onset schizophrenia. *Schizophrenia Bulletin, 19*, 691–700.

Castle, D.J., Wessely, S., Howard, R., & Murray, R.M. (1997). Schizophrenia with onset at the extremes of adult life. *International Journal of Geriatric Psychiatry, 12*, 712–717.

Copeland, J.R., Beekman, A.T., Dewey, M.E., Hooijer, C., Jordan, A., Lawlor, et al. (1999). Depression in Europe: Geographical distribution among older people. *British Journal of Psychiatry, 174*, 312–321.

Copeland, J.R., Dewey, M.E., Scott, A., Gilmore, C., Larkin, B.A., Cleave, N., et al. (1998). Schizophrenia and delusional disorder in older age: Community prevalence, incidence, comorbidity, and outcome. *Schizophrenia Bulletin, 24*, 153–161.

Copeland, J. R. M., Kelleher, M. J., Kellett, J. M., Gourlay, A. J., Gurland, B. J., Fleiss, J. L., et al. (1976). A semi-structured clinical interview for the assessment of diagnosis and mental state in the elderly: The geriatric mental state schedule: I. Development and reliability. *Psychological Medicine, 6*(3), 439–449.

Cummings, J.L., Mega, M., Gray, K., Rosenberg-Thompson, S., Carusi, D.A., & Gornbein, J. (1994). The Neuropsychiatric Inventory: Comprehensive assessment of psychopathology in dementia. *Neurology, 44*, 2308–2314.

Cummings, J.L., Street, J., Masterman, D., & Clark, W.S. (2002). Efficacy of olanzapine in the treatment of psychosis in dementia with lewy bodies. *Dementia & Geriatric Cognitive Disorders, 13*, 67–73.

Depp, C.A., & Jeste, D.V. (2004). Bipolar disorder in older adults: A critical review. *Bipolar Disord, 6*, 343–367.

Devanand, D. P., Miller, L., Richards, M., Marder, K., Bell, K., Mayeux, R., et al. (1992). The Columbia University Scale for Psychopathology in Alzheimer's disease. *Archives of Neurology, 49*(4), 371–376.

Dombrovski, A.Y., Mulsant, B.H., Haskett, R.F., Prudic, J., Begley, A.E. & Sackeim, H.A. (2005). Predictors of remission after electroconvulsive therapy in unipolar major depression. *Jouranl of Clinical Psychiatry, 66*, 1043–1049.

Ely, E.W., Inouye, S.K., Bernard, G.R., Gordon, S., Francis, J., May, L., et al. (2001). Delirium in mechanically ventilated patients: Validity and reliability of the Confusion Assessment Method for the Intensive Care Unit (CAM-ICU). *JAMA, 286*, 2703–2710.

Fernandez, H.H., Trieschmann, M.E., Burke, M.A., & Friedman, J.H. (2002). Quetiapine for psychosis in Parkinson's disease versus dementia with Lewy bodies. *Journal of Clinical Psychiatry, 63*, 513–515.

Fong, T.G., Tulebaev, S.R., & Inouye, S.K. (2009). Delirium in elderly adults: Diagnosis, prevention and treatment. *National Review of Neurology, 5*, 210–220.

Forstl, H., Burns, A., Jacoby, R., & Levy, R. (1991). Neuroanatomical correlates of clinical misidentification and misperception in senile dementia of the Alzheimer type. *Journal of Clinical Psychiatry, 52*, 268–271.

Gournellis, R., Lykouras, L., Fortos, A., Oulis, P., Roumbos, V., & Christodoulou, G.N. (2001). Psychotic (delusional) major depression in late life: A clinical study. *International Journal in Geriatric Psychiatry, 16*, 1085–1091.

Harris, M.J., & Jeste, D.V. (1988). Late-onset schizophrenia: An overview. *Schizophrenia Bulletin, 14*, 39–55.

Holroyd, S., & Laurie, S. (1999). Correlates of psychotic symptoms among elderly outpatients. *International Journal in Geriatr Psychiatry, 14*, 379–384.

Hope, T., & Fairburn, C.G. (1992). The Present Behavioural Examination (PBE): The development of an interview to measure current behavioural abnormalities. *Psychological Medicine, 22*(1), 223–230.

Howard, R., Almeida, O., & Levy, R. (1994). Phenomenology, demography and diagnosis in late paraphrenia. *Psychological Medicine, 24*, 397–410.
Howard, R., Castle, D., Wessely, S., & Murray, R. (1993a). A comparative study of 470 cases of early-onset and late-onset schizophrenia. *British Journal of Psychiatry, 163*, 352–357.
Howard, R., Castle, D., Wessley, S. & Murray, R. (1993b). Differences in late- and early-onset schizophrenia. *Americal Journal of Psychiatry, 150*, 846–847.
Howard, R., Rabins, P.V., Seeman, M.V., & Jeste, D.V. (2000). Late-onset schizophrenia and very-late-onset schizophrenia-like psychosis: An international consensus. The International Late-Onset Schizophrenia Group. *Americal Journal of Psychiatry, 157*, 172–178.
Inouye, S.K. (2000). Prevention of delirium in hospitalized older patients: Risk factors and targeted intervention strategies. *Annals of Medicine, 32*, 257–263.
Inouye, S.K., Rushing, J.T., Foreman, M.D., Palmer, R.M., & Pompei, P. (1998). Does delirium contribute to poor hospital outcomes? A three-site epidemiologic study. *Journal of General Internal Medicine, 13*, 234–242.
Inouye, S.K., Van Dyck, C.H., Alessi, C.A., Balkin, S., Siegal, A.P., & Horwitz, R.I. (1990). Clarifying confusion: The confusion assessment method. A new method for detection of delirium. *Annals of Internal Medicine, 113*, 941–948.
Jeste, D.V., & Finkel, S.I. (2000). Psychosis of Alzheimer's disease and related dementias: Diagnostic criteria for a distinct syndrome. *American Journal in Geriatric Psychiatry, 8*, 29–34.
Jeste, D.V., Harris, M.J., Krull, A., Kuck, J., McAdams, L.A., & Heaton, R. (1995). Clinical and neuropsychological characteristics of patients with late-onset schizophrenia. *Americal Journal of Psychiatry, 152*, 722–730.
Kessing, L.V. (2006). Differences in diagnostic subtypes among patients with late and early onset of a single depressive episode. *International Journal Geriatric Psychiatry, 21*, 1127–1131.
Kim, D.K., Kim, B.L., Sohn, S.E., Lim, S.W., Na, D.G., Paik, C.H., et al. (1999). Candidate neuroanatomic substrates of psychosis in old-aged depression. *Progress in Neuropsychopharmacol & Biological Psychiatry, 23*, 793–807.
Kyomen, H.H., & Whitfield, T.H. (2009). Psychosis in the elderly. *American Journal of Psychiatry, 166*, 146–150.
Lyketsos, C.G., Steinberg, M., Tschanz, J.T., Norton, M.C., Steffens, D. C., & Breitner, J.C. (2000). Mental and behavioral disturbances in dementia: Findings from the Cache County Study on Memory in Aging. *American Journal of Psychiatry, 157*, 708–714.
McCusker, J., Cole, M., Bellavance, F., & Primeau, F. (1988). The reliability and validity of a new measure of severity of delirium. *International Psychogeriatrics, 10*(4), 421–433.
Mendez, M.F., Shapira, J.S., Woods, R.J., Licht, E.A., & Saul, R.E. (2008). Psychotic symptoms in frontotemporal dementia: Prevalence and review. *Dementia & Geriatric Cognitive Disorders, 25*, 206–211.
Mittal, V., Muralee, S., Williamson, D., Mcenerney, N., Thomas, J., Cash, M. et al. (2011). Review: Delirium in the elderly: A comprehensive review. *American Journal of Alzheimers Disorders and Other Dementias, 26*, 97–109.
Molloy, D.W., McIlroy, W. E., Guyatt, G. H., & Lever, J. A. (1991). Validity and reliability of the Dysfunctional Behaviour Rating Instrument. *Acta Psychiatrica Scandinavica, 84*(1), 103–106.
Monteiro, I.M., Boksay, I., Auer, S.R., Torossian, C., Ferris, S.H., & Reisberg, B. (2001). Addition of a frequency-weighted score to the Behavioral Pathology in Alzheimer's

Disease Rating Scale: The BEHAVE-AD-FW: Methodology and reliability. *European Psychiatry, 16*(Suppl. 1), 5s–24s.

Nelson, J.C., & Davis, J.M. (1997). DST studies in psychotic depression: A meta-analysis. *American Journal of Psychiatry, 154*, 1497–1503.

Ohayon, M.M., & Schatzberg, A.F. (2002). Prevalence of depressive episodes with psychotic features in the general population. *American Journal of Psychiatry, 159*, 1855–1861.

Ostling, S., Gustafson, D., Blennow, K., Borjesson-Hanson, A., & Waern, M. (2011). Psychotic symptoms in a population-based sample of 85-year-old individuals with dementia. *Journal of Geriatric Psychiatry and Neurology, 24*, 3–8.

Overshott, R., Karim, S., & Burns, A. (2008). Cholinesterase inhibitors for delirium. *Cochrane Database of Systematic Reviews*, CD005317.

Pearlson, G.D., Kreger, L., Rabins, P.V., Chase, G.A., Cohen, B., Wirth, J.B., et al. (1989). A chart review study of late-onset and early-onset schizophrenia. *American Journal of Psychiatry, 146*, 1568–1574.

Reisberg, B., Borenstein, J., Salob, S.P., Ferris, S.H., Franssen, E., & Georgotas, A. (1987). Behavioral symptoms in Alzheimer's disease: Phenomenology and treatment. *Journal of Clinical Psychiatry, 48*(Suppl.), 9–15.

Reisberg, B., & Ferris, S. H. (1980). A clinical rating scale for symptoms of psychosis in Alzheimer's disease. *Psychopharmacology Bulletin, 21*(1), 101–104.

Roth, M., Tym, E., Mountjoy, C. Q., Huppert, F. A., Hendrie, H., Verma, S., et al. (1986). CAMDEX: A standardised instrument for the diagnosis of mental disorder in the elderly with special reference to the early detection of dementia. *British Journal of Psychiatry, 149*, 698–709.

Rovner, B.W., German, P.S., Broadhead, J., Morriss, R.K., Brant, L.J., Blaustein, J., et al. (1990). The prevalence and management of dementia and other psychiatric disorders in nursing homes. *International Psychogeriatrics, 2*, 13–24.

Rubin, E.H., Drevets, W.C., & Burke, W.J. (1988). The nature of psychotic symptoms in senile dementia of the Alzheimer type. *Journal of Geriatric Psychiatry and Neurology, 1*, 16–20.

Saxena, S., & Lawley, D. (2009). Delirium in the elderly: A clinical review. *Postgrad Medicine Journal, 85*, 405–413.

Scarmeas, N., Brandt, J., Blacker, D., Albert, M., Hadjigeorgiou, G., Dubois, B., et al. (2007). Disruptive behavior as a predictor in Alzheimer disease. *Archives in Neurology, 64*, 1755–1761.

Siddiqi, N., House, A.O., & Holmes, J.D. (2006). Occurrence and outcome of delirium in medical in-patients: A systematic literature review. *Age Ageing, 35*, 350–364.

Siddiqi, N., Stockdale, R., Britton, A. M., & Holmes, J. (2007). Interventions for preventing delirium in hospitalised patients. *Cochrane Database of Systematic Reviews*, CD005563.

Simpson, S., Baldwin, R.C., Jackson, A., & Burns, A. (1999). The differentiation of DSM-III-R psychotic depression in later life from nonpsychotic depression: Comparisons of brain changes measured by multispectral analysis of magnetic resonance brain images, neuropsychological findings, and clinical features. *Biological Psychiatry, 45*, 193–204.

Spira, A.P., & Edelstein, B.A. (2006). Behavioral interventions for agitation in older adults with dementia: An evaluative review. *International Psychogeriatrics, 18*, 195–225.

Steinberg, M., Shao, H., Zandi, P., Lyketsos, C.G., Welsh-Bohmer, K.A., Norton, M.C., et al. (2008). Point and 5-year period prevalence of neuropsychiatric symptoms in dementia: The Cache County Study. *International Journal of Geriatric Psychiatry, 23*, 170–177.

Sultzer, D. L., Levin, H. S., Mahler, M. E., High, W. M., & Cummings, J. L. (1992). Assessment of cognitive, psychiatric, and behavioral disturbances in patients with dementia: The Neurobehavioral Rating Scale. *Journal of the American Geriatrics Society, 40*(6), 549–555.

Sunderland, T., Alterman, I.S., Yount, D., Hill, J.L., Tariot, P.N., Newhouse, P.A., et al. (1988). A new scale for the assessment of depressed mood in demented patients. *American Journal of Psychiatry, 145*, 955–959.

Tariot, P. N., Mack, J. L., Patterson, M. B., Edland, S. D., Weiner, M. F., Fillenbaum, G., et al. (1995). The behavioral rating scale for dementia of the Consortium to Establish a Registry for Alzheimer's Disease. *American Journal of Psychiatry, 152*(9), 1349–1357.

Trzepacz, P.T., Baker, R.W., & Greenhouse, J. (1988). A symptom rating scale for delirium. *Psychiatry Research, 23*, 89–97.

Trzepacz, P.T., Mittal, D., Torres, R., Kanary, K., Norton, J., & Jimerson, N. (2001). Validation of the Delirium Rating Scale–Revised–98: Comparison with the delirium rating scale and the cognitive test for delirium. *Journal in Neuropsychiatry Clinical Neurosci, 13*, 229–242.

Tsuang, D., Larson, E.B., Bolen, E., Thompson, M.L., Peskind, E., Bowen, J., Mccormick, W., et al. (2009). Visual hallucinations in dementia: A prospective community-based study with autopsy. *American Journal in Geriatric Psychiatry, 17*, 317–323.

Vochteloo, A.J., Moerman, S., Van Der Burg, B.L., De Boo, M., De Vries, M.R., Niesten, D.D., et al. (2011). Delirium risk screening and haloperidol prophylaxis program in hip fracture patients is a helpful tool in identifying high-risk patients, but does not reduce the incidence of delirium. *BMC Geriatrics, 11*, 39.

Webster, J., & Grossberg, G.T. (1998). Late-life onset of psychotic symptoms. *American Journal of Geriatric Psychiatry, 6*, 196–202.

Webster, R., & Holroyd, S. (2000). Prevalence of psychotic symptoms in delirium. *Psychosomatics, 41*, 519–522.

Weissman, M.M., Leaf, P.J., Tischler, G.L., Blazer, D.G., Karno, M., Bruce, M.L. et al. (1988). Affective disorders in five United States communities. *Psychological Medicine, 18*, 141–153.

Wiener, J.M., & Tilly, J. (2002). Population ageing in the United States of America: Implications for public programmes. *International Journal Epidemiology, 31*, 776–781.

Yesavage, J.A., Brink, T.L., Rose, T.L., Lum, O., Huang, V., Adey, M. et al. (1982). Development and validation of a geriatric depression screening scale: A preliminary report. *Journal of Psychiatric Research, 17*, 37–49.

Young, J., Murthy, L., Westby, M., Akunne, A., & O'Mahony, R. (2010). Diagnosis, prevention, and management of delirium: Summary of NICE guidance. *British Medical Journal, 341*, c3704.

Zayas, E.M., & Grossberg, G.T. (1998). The treatment of psychosis in late life. *Journal of Clinical Psychiatry, 59*(Suppl. 1), 5–10.

PART III

The Assessment of Psychotic Symptoms

12

AUDITORY HALLUCINATIONS

Massoud Stephane

Introduction

With the mechanisms of auditory hallucinations (AH) all but known, a definition of these experiences that does not presuppose a certain mechanism is a good starting point as one attempts to evaluate these phenomena for both treatment and research. For this purpose, the adaptation of Esquirol's definition of AH (Esquirol, 1817) would be befitting. From this perspective, AH are experiences whereby auditory perceptions occur without corresponding external sensory stimuli. Yet, and this is the case for all sensory modalities, "normal" perceptions only loosely correspond to external stimuli (Taylor, 1979). For example, speech perception does not depend only on sensory (bottom-up) input, but also on top-down factors such as semantic expectation (Aleman, Bocker, Hijman, de Haan & Kahn, 2003). Esquirol's definition, therefore, encompasses a large spectrum of experiences, from daily mishearing of what someone had said to hearing elaborate conversations when no one is around. From this perspective, hearing "voices" or other sounds without corresponding external stimuli by itself does not carry specific information as far as brain function, pathology, and treatment. For a precise understanding of a given hallucinatory experience, it is crucial to have information about the characteristics of what is heard: the phenomenology of hallucinations.

Indeed, it is currently widely accepted that AH do not have a uniform pathological significance or one mechanism (Jones, 2010; Stephane, Thuras, Nassrallah & Georgopoulos, 2003). While AH have been most often associated with schizophrenia, the literature in the past couple of decades shows that they occur in many other psychiatric illnesses (*Chapter 7*), neurological and general medical diseases (*Chapter 10*) and in non-clinical populations (*Chapter 6*). Surprisingly, the phenomenology of AH in these clinical and non-clinical disorders is far from clear, and it is only recently that the phenomenology of hallucinations has been taken into considerations in clinical research (Daalman et al., 2011; Plaze et al., 2011). In the first meeting of the International Consortium of Hallucinations Research (Waters et al., 2011), both the imaging and phenomenology working groups reported that ignoring hallucinations phenomenology has hindered progress (Allen et al., 2012; Larøi et al., 2012).

An additional implication of this perspective is that it could contribute to demystifying (and rightly so, in my view) these mysterious (dramatic and/or alienating) experiences. Hallucinations may not be as far-fetched as they appear to be. Furthermore, inquiring about the characteristics of the patients' hallucinations has been reported to enhance therapeutic relation with their treatment providers, and help patients develop an understanding and coping with these experiences (Carter et al., 1995; Stephane et al., 2006).

For the purpose of this chapter, I will include in the definition of AH the requirement that the perceptual experiences occur in full sensorium. This would eliminate those perceptual experiences occurring during and around sleep (dreams, and hypnopompic and hypnagogic hallucinations). Although sleep-related perceptual experiences may share, from a neural standpoint, some of the same correlates as hallucinations (given the dissociation between sense and perception), it may be beneficial to separate such experiences from hallucinations occurring in full sensorium. Brain functions are dramatically different during sleep, and sleep-related perceptual experiences have not been described as maladaptive, as often has been AH.

AH can involve linguistic sounds, non-linguistic sounds, and music (with linguistic content or not). Interestingly, the verbal subtype of AH is reported in individuals who were born deaf (Atkinson et al., 2007; du Feu & McKenna, 1999; Esquirol, 1817). Furthermore, hallucinations might share common aspects across sensory modality. For example, hallucinated speech occurs in the auditory modality, in sign language (Atkinson et al., 2007), and in written language (Rousseaux et al., 1994). These observations indicate that while AH are experienced in the auditory sensory modality, they involve operations beyond the auditory modality (language, in these examples). Possibly, because these experiences are endowed of meaning, auditory *verbal* hallucinations have been the main focus for research rather than AH in general. As a result the assessment of auditory verbal hallucinations has been the focus of most assessment instruments. Generally, instruments evaluate non-linguistic AH with lesser details, although this narrow focus might hinder progress in hallucinations research.

In this chapter, I will start by providing a brief review of the phenomenology of AH as well as the cognitive, behavioral and neural models of these symptoms. The review will serve as the foundation for understanding the assessment of AH, which will be discussed at the end of this chapter.

Phenomenology of AH

From a philosophical standpoint, phenomenology is an introspection-based method for the study of consciousness (Husserl, 2001) whereby examining the subjective experiences of participants (first-person perspective) leads to the identification of invariant inter-subjective (shared) phenomena "essences" (third-person perspective) (Zahavi, 2003). From a hetero-phenomenological standpoint (Dennett, 1991), the transition from a first-person perspective to a third-person perspective does not grant objectivity to the phenomena at hand. A third-person perspective could be as deceiving as a first-person perspective. For a sense of how deceptive a third-person perspective (the one you and others share) could be, in the event you have not already done so, I invite you to google "visual illusions." Dennett argues a phenomenon from a third-person perspective is valid only if confirmed by natural science methodologies.

With respect to AH, phenomenology has been based on the hallucinators' (usually patient) reports about the characteristics of his/her experiences (first-person perspective). The literature shows that the characteristics of AH are diverse, and differ from one patient to another (Stephane, 2013). These characteristics (hereafter, phenomenological variables) include, but are not limited to, space location (inside or outside the head), acoustic clarity (similarity to external speech or verbal thoughts), content (systematized involving variable rich topics or repetitive topic, anew or a replay of past experiences), linguistic complexity (hearing individual words, individual sentences, or conversations), concomitancy to normal external speech (hearing voices when alone in silence or while talking to other people), insight or nosognosia into the abnormality of the AH (awareness or not of the perceptions/object dissociation), gender (male or female voices), familiarity (familiar or unfamiliar voices), frequency, loudness, distress and functional impact. (Claude & Ey, 1932; Jaspers, 1959; Nayani & David, 1996; Sedman, 1966; Stephane et al., 2003) (See **Table 12.1**).

Phenomenological research on AH has not just been about marveling about the diversity of these experiences, and attempts to move beyond the first-person perspective of AH have been repeatedly undertaken. Since the early twentieth century, it has been observed that any given characteristic was invariant (shared) only in subsets of individuals with AH, prompting attempts to define subcategories of hallucinations. Based on the presence or absence of variables such as nosognosia (insight) or localization of the hallucinatory experience (outside/inside the head), subcategories such as "true" hallucinations, pseudohallucinations and hallucinosis were defined (Jaspers, 1959; Claude & Ey, 1932; Sedman, 1966). None of these subcategories were validated using neuroscience methods and, as such, the above subcategories of hallucinations were considered a premature closure (Dening & Berrios, 1996). This has not been, however, the end for phenomenological research on hallucinations, and there is now increasing evidence for AH subtypes as valid entities.

TABLE 12.1 The phenomenological variables of AVH (from Stephane et al., 2003)

1) Acoustic qualities:
   a) Clarity:
      i) Clear (like external speech)
      ii) Deep (like internal speech or thinking in words)
   b) Personification:
      i) Man's voice
      ii) Woman's voice
      iii) Robot voices
   c) Loudness (does AVH have loudness)
      i) no
      ii) yes
         (1) Level:
            (a) Like normal conversation
            (b) Louder
            (c) Softer
         (2) Does loudness vary with time?
2) Location:
   a) Inner space:
      i) Head
      ii) Other parts of the body
   b) Outer space (if yes)
      i) Distance:
         (1) Within hearing
         (2) Outside of hearing range
      ii) Relation to the sensation field (through ears)
         (1) yes
         (2) no
3) Number:
   a) One
   b) More than one (if more than one)
4) Direction:
   a) Voices talk among themselves
   b) Voices talk to the patient
5) Linguistics:
   a) Syntax:
      i) First person
      ii) Second person (You, name)
      iii) Third person (he/she, name)
   b) Complexity:
      i) Hearing words
      ii) Hearing sentences
      iii) Hearing conversations
6) Relation to the moment (related to thoughts or action at the moment when heard)
   a) Yes
   b) No
7) Content:
   a) Range:
      i) Repetitive
      ii) Systematized
   b) Focus:
      i) Self
      ii) Non-self
8) Order:
   a) First order (hear)
   b) Second order (talk back to the voices)
   c) Third order (converse with the voices)
9) Replay:
   a) Experiential (previously heard)
   b) Patient speech
   c) Patient thoughts
10) Source attribution:
   a) Self
   b) Other (if yes)
      i) Someone familiar
      ii) God/spiritual being
      iii) Deceased person
11) Time course:
   a) Time dimension:
      i) Constant
      ii) Episodic
   b) Modulation:
      i) worsening modulators
      ii) Improvement modulators
12) Mode of occurrence:
   a) Spontaneous
   b) Triggered (if triggered)
      i) Inducible by will
      ii) Other triggers
13) Concomitance (to):
   a) Speaking
   b) Listening to speech
   c) Listening to non-speech sounds
   d) Activities requiring attention
14) Control strategies:
   a) Listening to speech
   b) Speaking
   c) Listening to non-speech sounds
   d) Activities requiring attention
   e) Other control strategies
15) Safety:
   a) Affect safety
   b) Does not affect safety
16) Affective relatedness:
   a) Comforting
   b) Bothersome
17) Nosognosia
18) Association with other abnormal perceptions
19) Concomitance with other abnormal perceptions
20) Stability of the characteristics over time

Recent studies have examined the patterns of clustering of AH phenomenological variables (McCarthy-Jones et al., 2012; Stephane et al., 2003) (as opposed to the patterns of clustering of patients, which the above mentioned pioneer works attempted, although not statistically), and the dimensionality of the space constructed by these phenomenological variables (Stephane et al., 2003).

In the first cluster analysis study (Stephane et al., 2003), the phenomenological variables clustered as follow: all "control strategies" clustered together, and with the "self attribution.". "Low linguistic complexity, hearing words" clustered with "clear acoustics" and with "outer space location." "Systematized content" clustered with "high linguistic complexity, hearing conversations" and "inner space location," and "multiple voices" clustered with attribution of the voices to others. In the second study involving a larger number of patients (McCarthy-Jones et al., 2012), "command," "second person," "repetitive," "running commentary," "third person" and "constant" hallucinations clustered together. "Similar to memory," "own voice/thought," "first person," "don't address the patient" clustered together. "Nonverbal" hallucinations clustered with hallucinations that "don't make sense," and "identical to memory" was independent from other clusters.

The investigation of the phenomenological space with multidimensional scaling (Kruskal & Wish, 1978) showed a three-dimension solution (Stephane et al., 2003), linguistic complexity (hearing words, hearing sentences, hearing conversations), inner space–outer space locations, and self-other attribution of AH. This dimensionality of the phenomenological space of AH was considered to reflect the dimensionality of the associated neural resources, linguistic processes, sound localization and self-other distinction, respectively.

While insightful and encouraging, these results are not conclusive, and due to methodological differences such as including different sets of the phenomenological variables in the analysis, the two studies are not readily comparable. Phenomenological research on hallucinations could benefit from a number of improvements such as well-defined and agreed upon terminology and standardized phenomenological assessments (Larøi et al., 2012).

Does Phenomenology Matter?

In a sense, phenomenological studies of AH attempt to provide a third-person perspective to the first-person experience of AH. However, as mentioned above, even with more compelling results, a third-person perspective of AH, by itself, may not grant validity to the phenomenological variables, their patterns of clustering or their dimensionality. While indirect evidence for the neural validity of some of these variables (such as anosognosia) could be implied by analogy to other brain symptomatology (see Stephane, 2013, for further information), a third-person perspective of the phenomenology of hallucinations was not put to test until recently.

For example, the pioneer MRI study by Plaze and colleagues (2011) has shown that brain structure abnormalities in schizophrenia patients with AH depend on whether AH were experienced as coming from inside or outside the head. Relative to healthy controls, patients with "outside-the-head" AH had a reduction in the white matter volume in the right temporoparietal junction, whereas patients with "inside-the-head" AH had an increase in the white matter volume in the same area (Plaze et al., 2011). Furthermore, a more recent resting state fMRI study provides consistent findings (Looijestijn et al., 2013), it showed that, in patients, "outside-the-head" hallucinations were associated with higher resting brain activity in a cluster combining the left planum temporale and the right middle frontal gyrus relative to "inside-the-head" hallucinations. In addition to the evidence of differential neural correlates for AH subtypes, research also indicates that AH subtypes differentially respond to treatment. For example, verbal AH with repetitive content could be alleviated by an antiobsessional agent (Stephane et al., 2001), and cognitive behavioral therapy could target specific component of hallucinations such as distress or intensity (Thomas, Rossell, Farhall, Shawyer & Castle, 2011).

Neurocognitive Models of Hallucinations

Earlier models attributed AH to abnormalities of inner speech, a function that could be approximated as "thinking in words." In AH research, inner speech theory is often equated with one model, the forward model (Frith & Done, 1988); however, the literature shows multiple explanatory models based on inner speech. In the mid twentieth century, it was observed that individuals with schizophrenia made soundless lips movements—termed subvocal speech (SVS)—or showed electromyographic (EMG) activity in the speech musculature during hallucinations (Forrer, 1960; Gould, 1948, 1950; Roberts & Solomon, 1952). This prompted researchers to suggest that hallucinating patients are virtually hearing their own self-generated faint SVS (Gould, 1948, 1950); a theory that was abandoned since maneuvers blocking SVS failed to alleviate AH (Stephane, Barton & Boutros, 2001). More recently, it was noted that inner speech is associated not only with a perceptual experience of one's own voice, but also with speech muscle activity that can be detectable with EMG (MacKay, 1992; Sokolov, 1972). On the basis of these observations, our group suggested that hallucinating patients need not hear their SVS through their ears; instead, a central neural disorder of generation of inner speech would result in a perceptual experience (AH) and an epiphenomenon—SVS (Stephane et al., 2001).

To date, all inner speech models suggest variable aberrations of inner speech generation that result in misattribution to other of a self-generated speech. These include deficits such as disconnection between speech generation and speech perception areas (Frith & Done, 1988), altered preconscious planning of discourse (Hoffman, 1986) and meta-cognitive deficits (Bentall, 1990), resulting in a failure to compute the expected sensory experience of self-generated inner speech, unintended verbal messages, and externalizing bias, respectively. Abnormal development of inner speech (Fernyhough, 2004) was also implicated in the pathogenesis of AH. Fernyhough suggested that a reversal of the processes involved in the transformation of social speech into inner speech (i.e., internalization and condensation) (Vygotsky, 1978) would result in an inner speech regaining the characteristics of social speech and attributed to other given that inner speech is necessarily dialogical.

It is also important to note that misattribution to other of self-generated inner speech is not the only disorder that could affect inner speech in relation to AH. Evidence also indicates that hallucinating schizophrenia patients have difficulty in space localization of their own self-generated speech, they confuse self-generated speech experienced inside the head with that experienced outside the head (Stephane et al., 2010). Furthermore, self-other misattribution and inside the head-outside the head confusion are likely to be independent deficits (Larøi & Woodward, 2007; Stephane et al., 2003) .

Even if speech processes have an important role in the verbal type of AH, language does not take place in a cognitive vacuum, it calls upon other cognitive operations such as memory, working memory and executive functions. Additionally, verbal AH contain information about the "voice, identity and affect . . .," and AH could involve non-linguistic sounds. Consistent with these considerations, research also has implicated many other perceptual and cognitive operations in the mechanisms of AH.

Studies report evidence suggesting decreased selective attention in hallucinating patients, which is posited to result in a failure to suppress irrelevant memories (Badcock et al., 2005; Waters et al., 2006), or erroneous percepts (Hugdahl, Løberg & Nygård, 2009). Another study found associations between hallucinations, ruminations and intrusive thoughts (Jones & Fernyhough, 2009). Studies also examined bottom-up and top-down processes involved in normal perception and found evidence for the association of hallucinations with reduced sensory input, increased top-down effect and imbalance between bottom-up and top-down processes.

Reduced sensory input, presumably resulting in over-sensitization of the sensory cortex has been often associated with AH, in particular the non-verbal type. AH has been reported in patients with acquired deafness (Thewissen et al., 2005), in survivors of long solitary ordeals (Logan, 1993), in psychotic patients after periods of social withdrawal (Hoffman, 2008), and during sensory deprivation experiments (Slade, 1988). Furthermore, studies showed that hallucinations were associated with increased facilitation effect of imagery on the perception of pure tones (Aleman et al., 2003), with increased semantic expectation effect on the perception of sentences (Vercammen & Aleman, 2010), with increased propensity to detect meaningful signal from meaningless noise (Bentall & Slade, 1985a), and with hypervigilance (Dodgson & Gordon, 2009). All suggestive of increased top-down effect in hallucinations. Additionally, it has been suggested that imbalance between top-down and bottom-up processing of stimuli could result in erroneous percepts that, when repetitive, would train the network to perceive hallucinations (Aleman et al., 2003). It is also worth noting that trauma has been also associated with the pathogenesis of hallucinations (Hardy et al., 2005) and this could occur via pathways such as intrusive memories or hypervigilance.

Most of these models for AH received empirical support to a variable degree from imaging research. Countless imaging studies support the involvement of language processes in AH (Allen et al., 2012). Research also reports evidence of disconnection between speech generation and speech preception areas directly supporting the forward model (de Weijer et al., 2013; Ford et al., 2001) but, also point to many other mechanisms for self-other misattribution. Studies reported abnormal laterality of the activity of the Supplementary Motor Area (SMA) during the action of speaking (Stephane et al., 2006), and abnormal activity in the left temporal cortex and anterior cingulate (Allen et al, 2007), and abnormal connectivity between these two structures (Mechelli et al., 2007) during operations of self-other distinction of inner speech. Both the SMA and the anterior cingulate have been associated with self-attribution of self-generated actions. Therefore, abnormal laterality or connectivity or function of these areas could result in occasional failure in self-attribution of self-generated speech. Additionally, a number of fMRI and electrophysiological studies support the implication of memory in the pathogenesis of AH. Studies showed deactivation of the parahippocampal gyrus (Diederen et al., 2010; Hoffman et al., 2008), and decrease in theta-band power in the right hippocampus (van Lutterveld et al., 2012) prior to hallucinations, respectively. Unfortunately, the only inner speech model for AH that is based on inner speech development (Fernyhough, 2004) remains empirically untested.

While there is empirical evidence that support, to a variable degree and with occasional inconsistency, most of the above theories about the mechanisms of AH, none explains the wide range of hallucination phenomenology (Larøi et al, 2010), and each of these models explains only a subset of hallucinatory experiences (Stephane, 2013). For over a decade, research has been steadily moving away from a single neural deficit mechanism for AH (Jones, 2010; Stephane 2003). Recently, to account for these considerations, Waters and colleagues (2012) and myself (Stephane, 2013) developed simultaneously and independently two models for hallucinations; although with different details, these two models are conceptually similar. In my own wording, AH result from subject-specific combinatoric associations of multiple neural deficits located at different nodes of distributed neural network involving language, auditory perception and related cognition and with a final common pathway, activation of Wernicke's area when AH are verbal (Stephane, Folstein, Matthew & Hill, 2000), or the primary auditory cortex otherwise. This model accounts for both the specificity of the phenomenology of hallucinations in each subject as well as the variations of hallucinations phenomenology between subjects.

Assessment of Hallucinations

The above review of AH brings an important point to the forefront as one considers the evaluation of these phenomena. What appears like uniform and universal experiences "hearing voices" are in fact very personalized experiences. More importantly, the between-patient (non-patient) variation in these experiences is not a mere curiosity; it reflects the underlying neurobiology and impacts treatment choices. What naturally follows is that the assessment of hallucinations should reflect these personalized aspects of hallucinatory experiences. Although, it is yet to become commonplace, detailed phenomenological assessment of hallucinations is a crucial first step.

Hallucinations assessment tools also address other questions such as how do hallucinations change in response to treatment and how does it correlate with brain activity. Additionally, depending on the clinical setting, questions related to specific treatment or the likelihood to develop hallucinations could be necessary.

Assessment instruments employed questionnaires, semi-structured or structured interviews, and varied in the comprehensiveness of assessment. Most instruments explored verbal type of AH in detail, along with cursory evaluations of AH consisting of non-linguistic sounds and hallucinations in other sensory modalities.

Both binary and continuous scale measurements have been applied to AH, and the use of proper scale is necessary for accurate assessment. Some aspects of hallucinations could be readily coded with binary scale such as whether AH are self- or other-attributed or whether it is experienced inside the head or outside the head, while 'Other' characteristics are better suited for continuous scale measures such as frequency and loudness. With methodological adjustment, the two measurement scales could be employed inter-changeably. For example, the frequency of AH could be assessed with a number of (yes/no) questions, such as, "Do you hear voices all the time?" "Do you hear voices every few minutes?" "Do you hear voices every hour?" and so forth. However one should be careful as these methodological manipulations could lead to inaccurate evaluations. Occasionally, instruments coded the location of AH along a continuous scale (1 = *inside the head*, 2 = *voices inside the head close to the ear*, 3 = *voices outside the head close to the ear* and 4 = *voice outside the head*; Haddock et al, 1999; Lowe, 1973). This coding implies that AH outside the head are more severe than AH inside the head, an assumption that is yet to be confirmed (Copolov et al., 2004).

It is also important to note that AH assessment necessarily relies on the patient's report. Through follow-up questions and with experienced interviewers, structured and semi-structured interviews could offer a sense of the reliability of the patient report about his/her experiences. To date, only one instrument, the computerized binary Scale of Auditory Speech Hallucinations (cbSASH; Stephane et al., 2006), provides psychometric evaluation of the reliability of the subject's report through two subscales designed to detect malingering and inconsistency. The malingering and inconsistency subscales employ commonly used methods for deception detection, the percentage of endorsement of infrequent events, and the percent of mismatch between questions asked twice, differently worded, respectively. These subscales were correlated with corresponding MMPI-II subscales (Butcher et al., 1989), which indicate that, although different in content, the cbSASH and MMPI-II subscales have similar psychometric properties with respect to detection of malingering and inconsistency.

A survey of the literature shows numerous assessment scales for hallucinations, the most comprehensive of which are the Mental Health Research Institute Unusual Perceptions Schedule (MUPS; Carter et al, 1995), and the cbSASH (Stephane et al., 2006), which were developed to address the heterogeneity of schizophrenia and the heterogeneity of hallucinations, respectively. Both employ binary measures for identification of phenomenological subtypes of AH as well as continuous scale measures for evaluation of severity.

Many other assessment tools provide continuous scale measures of a small and variable numbers of the phenomenological characteristics of AH (such as frequency, duration, degree of distress, and amount and degree of negative content) and are used to evaluate the severity of hallucinations in treatment, cognitive and imaging research. These include tools for the assessment of psychosis in general such as the Scale for Assessment of Positive Symptoms (SAPS) (Andreasen, 1984) and the Psychotic Symptom Rating Scales (PSYRATS; Haddock et al., 1999), or for the assessment of hallucinations specifically (Hayashi, Igarashi, Suda & Nakagawa, 2004; Hoffman et al., 2003; Junginger & Frame, 1985; Lowe, 1973; Miller, 1996; Van Lieshout & Goldberg, 2007; Wada-Isoe et al., 2008).

Good interrater reliability was found for the PSYRATS, the scale by Hoffman and colleagues (Hoffman et al., 2003), and the Hamilton Program for Schizophrenia Voices Questionnaire (HPSVQ; Van Lieshout & Goldberg, 2007); good test–retest reliability was also reported in the latter. External criterion validity was reported in some scales. The PSYRATS was validated against the Krawiecka, Goldberg and Vaughn (KGV) psychosis scale (Krawiecka et al., 1977), the Tottori University Hallucinations Rating Scale (TUHRAS; Wada-Isoe et al., 2008) was validated against the Parkinson Psychosis Questionnaire (PPQ; Brandstaedter et al., 2005), and the HPSVQ was validated against the PSYRATS. Furthermore, good internal consistency (high Cronbach's alpha) was reported for the scale by Hoffman and colleagues, the HPSVQ and the TUHRAS.

Another assessment tool, the Launay-Slade Hallucination Scale (LSHS), is posited to evaluate proneness to hallucinations (Launay & Slade, 1981). It includes 12 questions with true/false responses covering hallucinatory and subclinical hallucinatory experience (e.g., vivid or intrusive thoughts, vivid daydreams). Factor analysis showed that these 12 items fall on one dimension, which indicates the continuity of hallucinations and hallucinations-like experiences. This scale was subsequently revised using a continuous scale measurement (LSHS-R; Bentall & Slade, 1985b). Unlike the first version, all studies point to multidimensionality of LSHS-R measures (Aleman et al., 2001; Larøi, Marczewsky & Van der Linden, 2004; Serper et al., 2005; Waters et al., 2003), indicating that hallucinations and "hallucinations like experiences" as measured by this scale are independent.

Few other assessment tools were developed to evaluate aspects of hallucinations that have direct relation to specific treatments to be delivered. For example, the distress and behavioral problems associated with hallucinations were found to be related to the "beliefs about the voices," not to the content of the "voices" (Chadwick & Birchwood, 1994). As such, distress and abnormal behaviors could be treated by cognitive behavioral therapy targeting these beliefs. This lead to the development of the "Beliefs About the Voices" Questionnaire (BAVQ; Chadwick & Birchwood, 1995), which was further revised for better sensitivity (Chadwick et al., 2000). The Maastricht Assessment of Coping Strategies (MACS-I; Bak et al., 2001), the Voices Acceptance and Action Scale (VAAS; Shawyer et al., 2007) and the Voice and You (Hayward, Denney, Vaughan & Fowler, 2008) are conceptually similar scales that were designed to address specific treatment needs, enhancing coping with psychotic symptoms in general, mindful acceptance of the AH and interpersonal therapy, respectively.

In summary, to date, there is a large armamentum to evaluate AH that could fit the multiplicity of purposes of the many disciplines concerned with these phenomena. However, the multiplicity of variable and partially overlapping scales does not go without disadvantages, particularly with respect to comparability of studies. As far as measurement is concerned, AH assessment would benefit greatly from clear definition of what is there to measure in hallucinations, how to measure it, agreed upon terminology and standardized assessment.

References

Aleman, A., Bocker, K.B.E., Hijman, R., de Haan, E.H.F. & Kahn, R.S. (2003). Cognitive basis of hallucinations in schizophrenia: Role of top-down information processing. *Schizophrenia Research, 64*, 175–185.

Aleman, A., Nieuwenstein, M.R., Bocker, K.B.E. & De Haan, E.H.F. (2001). Multidimensionality of hallucinatory predisposition: Factor structure of the Launay–Slade Hallucination Scale in a normal sample. *Personality and Individual Differences, 30*, 287–292.

Allen, P., Amaro, E., Fu, C.H., Williams, S.C., Brammer, M.J., Johns, L.C. & McGuire, P.K. (2007). Neural correlates of the misattribution of speech in schizophrenia. *British Journal of Psychiatry, 190*, 162–169.

Allen, P., Hubl, D., Shields, G., Cachia, A., Jardri, R., Thomas, P., et al. (2012). Neuroimaging auditory hallucinations in schizophrenia: From neuroanatomy to neurochemistry and beyond. *Schizophrenia Bulletin, 38*(4), 695–703.

Andreasen, N. C. (1984). *Scale for the Assessment of Positive Symptoms (SAPS).* Iowa City: University of Iowa Press.

Atkinson, J.R., Gleeson, K., Cromwell, J. & O'Rourke, S. (2007). Exploring the perceptual characteristics of voice-hallucinations in deaf people. *Cognitive Neuropsychiatry, 12*(4), 339–361.

Badcock, J., Maybery, M. & Michie, P.T. (2005). Auditory hallucinations: Failure to inhibit irrelevant memories. *Cognitive Neuropsychiatry, 10*(2), 125–136.

Bak, M., van der Spil, F., Gunther, N., Radstake, S. & Delespaul, P. (2001). Maastricht Assessment of Coping Strategies (MACS-I): A brief instrument to assess coping with psychotic symptoms. *Acta Psychiatrica Scandinavica, 103*(6), 453–459.

Bentall, R.P. (1990). The illusion of reality: A review and integration of psychological research on hallucinations. *Psychological Medicine, 107*(1), 82–95.

Bentall, R.P. & Slade, P.D. (1985a). Reality testing and auditory hallucinations: A signal detection analysis. *British Journal of Clinical Psychology, 24*, 159–169.

Bentall, R.P. & Slade, P.D. (1985b). Reliability of a scale measuring disposition towards hallucination: A brief report. *Personality and Individual Differences, 6*(4), 527–529.

Brandstaedter, D., Spieker, S., Ulm, G., Siebert, U., Eichhorn, T. E., Krieg, J. C., . . . Eggert, K. (2005). Development and evaluation of the Parkinson Psychosis Questionnaire: A screening-instrument for the early diagnosis of drug-induced psychosis in Parkinson's disease. *Journal of Neurology, 252*(9), 1060–1066.

Butcher, J. N., Dahlstrom, W. G., Graham, W. G., Tellegen, A. & Kaemmer, B. (1989). *MMPI-2: Manual for administration and scoring.* Minneapolis: University of Minnesota Press.

Carter, D.M., Mackinnon, A., Howard, S., Zeegers, T. & Copolov, D.L. (1995). The development and reliability of the Mental Health Research Institute Unusual Perceptions Schedule (MUPS): An instrument to record auditory hallucinatory experience. *Schizophrenia Research, 16*(2), 157–165.

Chadwick, P. & Birchwood, M. (1994). The omnipotence of voices: A cognitive approach to auditory hallucinations. *British Journal of Psychiatry, 164*, 190–201.

Chadwick, P. & Birchwood, M. (1995). The omnipotence of voices. II: The Beliefs About Voices Questionnaire (BAVQ). *British Journal of Psychiatry, 166*(6), 773–776.

Chadwick, P., Lees, S. & Birchwood, M. (2000). The revised Beliefs About the Voices Questionnaire (BAVQ-R). *British Journal of Psychiatry, 177*, 229–232.

Claude, H. & Ey, H. (1932). Hallucinations, pseudohallucinations et obsessions. *Annales Medico-Psychologiques, 2*, 279–316.

Copolov, D., Trauer, T., & Mackinnon, A. (2004). On the non-significance of internal versus external auditory hallucinations. *Schizophrenia Research, 69*(1), 1–6.

Daalman, K., Boks, M.P., Diederen, K.M., de Weijer, A. D., Blom, J.D., Kahn, R.S. & et al. (2011). The same or different? A phenomenological comparison of auditory verbal hallucinations in healthy and psychotic individuals. *Journal of Clinical Psychiatry, 72*(3), 320–325.

de Weijer, A. D., Neggers, S.F., Diederen, K.M., Mandl, R.C., Kahn, R.S., Hulshoff Pol, H.E. & et al. (2013). Aberrations in the arcuate fasciculus are associated with auditory verbal hallucinations in psychotic and in non-psychotic individuals. *Human Brain Mapping, 34*(3), 626–634.

Dening, T.R. & Berrios, G.E. (1996). The enigma of pseudohallucinations: Current meaning and usage. *Psychopathology, 29*, 27–34.

Dennett, D.C. (1991). *Consciousness explained*. New York, NY: Little, Brown and Co.
Diederen, K, Daalman, K., Blom, J. D., Goekoop, R., Kahn, R.S. & Sommer, I. E. (2010). Deactivation of the parahippocampal gyrus preceding auditory hallucinations in schizophrenia. *American Journal of Psychiatry, 167*, 427–435.
Dodgson, G. & Gordon, S. (2009). Avoiding false negatives: Are some auditory hallucinations an evolved design flaw? *Behavioral Cognitive Psychotherapy, 37*, 325–334.
du Feu, M. & McKenna, P.J. (1999). Prelingually profoundly deaf schizophrenic patients who hear voices: A phenomenological analysis. *Acta Psychiatrica Scandinavica, 99*(6), 453–459.
Esquirol, E. (1817). *Hallucination* (Vol. 20). Paris, France: Panckoucke.
Fernyhough, C. (2004). Alien voices and inner dialogue: Towards a developmental account of auditory verbal hallucinations. *New Ideas in Psychology, 22*, 49–68.
Ford, J.M., Mathalon, D.H., Heinks, T., Kalba, S., Faustman, W.O. & Roth, W.T. (2001). Neurophysiological evidence of corollary discharge dysfunction in schizophrenia. *American Journal of Psychiatry, 158*, 2069–2071.
Forrer, G.R. (1960). Effect of oral activity on hallucinations. *Archives of General Psychiatry, 2*, 100–103.
Frith, C.D. & Done, D.J. (1988). Toward a neuropsychology of schizophrenia. *British Journal of Psychiatry, 153*, 437–443.
Gould, L.N. (1948). Verbal hallucinations and activity of vocal musculature: And electromyographic study. *American Journal of Psychiatry, 105*, 367–372.
Gould, L.N. (1950). Verbal hallucinations as automatic speech: The reactivation of dormant speech habit. *American Journal of Psychiatry, 107*, 110–119.
Haddock, G., McCarron, J., Tarrier, N. & Faragher, E.B. (1999). Scales to measure dimensions of hallucinations and delusions: The psychotic symptom rating scales (PSYRATS). *Psychological Medicine, 29*(4), 879–889.
Hardy, A., Fowler, D., Freeman, D., Smith, B., Steel, C., Evans, J., et al. (2005). Trauma and hallucinatory experience in psychosis. *Journal of Nervous and Mental Disorder, 193*, 501–507.
Hayashi, N., Igarashi, Y., Suda, K. & Nakagawa, S. (2004). Phenomenological features of auditory hallucinations and their symptomatological relevance. *Psychiatry and Clinical Neurosciences, 58*, 651–659.
Hayward, M., Denney, J., Vaughan, S. & Fowler, D. (2008). The voice and you: Development and psychometric evaluation of a measure of relationships with voices. *Clinical Psychology and Psychotherapy, 15*(1), 45–52.
Hoffman, R.E. (1986). Verbal hallucinations and language production processes in schizophrenia. *Behavioral Brain Science, 9*, 503–548.
Hoffman, R.E. (2008). Auditory/verbal hallucinations, speech perception neurocircuitry, and the social deafferentation hypothesis *Clinical EEG and Neuroscience, 39*(2), 87–90.
Hoffman, R.E., Hawkins, K.A., Gueorguieva, R., Boutros, N.N., Rachid, F., Carroll, K. & et al. (2003). Transcranial magnetic stimulation of left temporoparietal cortex and medication-resistant auditory hallucinations. *Archives of General Psychiatry, 60*(1), 49–56.
Hoffman, R., Varanko, M. Gore, J. C., & Hampson, M. (2008). Time course of regional brain activation associated with onset of auditory/verbal hallucinations. *British Journal of Psychiatry, 193*(5), 424–425.
Hugdahl, K., Løberg, E.M. & Nygård, M. (2009). Left temporal lobe structural and functional abnormality underlying auditory hallucinations in schizophrenia. *Frontiers of Neuroscience, 3*(1), 34–45.

Husserl, E. (2001). *Logical investigations*. London, UK: Routledge.

Jaspers, K. (1959). *Allegemeine psychopathologie* (7th ed.). Manchester, UK: Manchester University Press.

Jones, S.R. (2010). Do we need multiple models of auditory verbal hallucinations? Examining the phenomenological fit of cognitive and neurological models. *Schizophrenia Bulletin, 36*(3), 566–575.

Jones, S.R. & Fernyhough, C. (2009). Rumination, reflection, intrusive thoughts, and hallucination-proneness: Towards a new model. *Behavioral Research and Therapy, 47*(1), 54–59.

Junginger, J. & Frame, C.L. (1985). Self-report of the frequency and phenomenology of verbal hallucinations. *Journal of Nervous and Mental Disease, 173*(3), 149–155.

Krawiecka, M., Goldberg, D. & Vaughan, M. A. (1977). Standardised psychiatric assessment scale for rating chronic psychotic patients. *Acta Psychiatrica Scandinavica, 55*, 299–308.

Kruskal, J.B. & Wish, M. (1978). *Multidimensional scaling*. Newbury Park, CA: Sage.

Larøi, F., de Haan, S., Jones, S. & Raballo, A. (2010). Auditory verbal hallucinations: Dialoguing between the cognitive sciences and phenomenology. *Phenomenology and the Cognitive Sciences, 9*(2), 225–240.

Larøi, F., Marczewski, P. & Van der Linden, M. (2004). Further evidence of the multi-dimensionality of hallucinatory predisposition: Factor structure of a modified version of the Launay-Slade Hallucinations Scale in a normal sample. *European Psychiatry, 19*(1), 15–20.

Larøi, F., Sommer, I.E., Blom, J.D., Fernyhough, C., Ffytche, D.H., Hugdahl, K., et al. (2012). The characteristic features of auditory verbal hallucinations in clinical and non-clinical groups: State-of-the-art overview and future directions. *Schizophrenia Bulletin, 38*(4), 724–733.

Launay, G. & Slade, P. (1981). The measurement of hallucinatory predisposition in male and female prisoners. *Personality and Individual Differences, 2*, 221–234.

Logan, R.D. (1993). *Alone: A fascinating study of those who have survived long, solitary ordeals*. Mechanicsburg, PA: Stackpole Books.

Looijestijn, J., Diederen, K., Goekoop, R., Sommer, I., Daalman, K., Kahn, R., et al. (2013). The auditory dorsal stream plays a crucial role in projecting hallucinated voices into external space. *Schizophrenia Reseach, 146*, 314–319.

Lowe, G.R. (1973). The phenomenology of hallucinations as an aid to differential diagnosis. *British Journal of Psychiatry, 123*(577), 621–633.

MacKay, D.G. (1992). Constraints of theories of inner speech. In D. Reisberg (Ed.), *Auditory imagery* (pp. 121–149). Hillsdale, NJ: Erlbaum.

McCarthy-Jones, S., Trauer, T., Mackinnon, A., Sims, E., Thomas, N. & Copolov, D.L. (2012). A new phenomenological survey of auditory hallucinations: Evidence for subtypes and implications for theory and practice. *Schizophrenia Bulletin*. (First published online, December 23, 2012)

Mechelli, A., Allen, P., Amaro, E.J., Fu, C.H., Williams, S.C., Brammer, M.J., et al. (2007). Misattribution of speech and impaired connectivity in patients with auditory verbal hallucinations. *Human Brain Mapping, 28*, 1213–1222.

Miller, L.J. (1996). Qualitative changes in hallucinations. *American Journal of Psychiatry, 153*(2), 265–267.

Nayani, T.H. & David, A.S. (1996). The auditory hallucination: A phenomenological survey. *Psychological Medicine, 26*(1), 177–189.

Plaze, M., Paillère-Martinot, M.L., Penttilä, J., Januel, D., de Beaurepaire, R., Bellivier, F. & Cachia, A. (2011). Where do auditory hallucinations come from? A brain morphometry study of schizophrenia patients with inner or outer space hallucinations. *Schizophrenia Bulletin, 37*(1), 212–221.

Roberts, B. & Solomon, H. C. (1952). Movement of the vocal apparatus during auditory hallucinations. *American Journal of Psychiatry, 108*, 912–914.

Rousseaux, M., Debrock, D., Cabaret, M., & Steinling, M. (1994). Visual hallucinations with written words in a case of left parietotemporal lesion. *Journal of Neurology, Neurosurgery & Psychiatry, 57*(10), 1268–1271.

Sedman, G. (1966). A phenomenological study of pseudohallucinations and related experiences. *Acta Psychiatrica Scandinavica, 42*, 35–70.

Serper, M., Dill, C.A., Chang, N., Kot, T. & Elliot, J. (2005). Factorial structure of the hallucinatory experience: Continuity of experience in psychotic and normal individuals. *Journal of Nervous & Mental Disease, 193*(4), 265–272.

Shawyer, F., Ratcliff, K., Mackinnon, A., Farhall, J., Hayes, S.C. & Copolov, D. (2007). The voices acceptance and action scale (VAAS): Pilot data. *Journal of Clinical Psychology, 63*(6), 583–606.

Slade, P.D. (1988). *Sensory deception: A scientific analysis of hallucinations*. London, UK: Croom-Helm.

Sokolov, Y.N. (1972). *Inner speech and thought*. New York, NY: Plenum Press.

Stephane, M. (2013). Auditory verbal hallucinations result from combinatoric associations of multiple neural events. *Frontiers of Human Neuroscience, 7*(329), 1–8.

Stephane, M., Barton, S.N. & Boutros, N.N. (2001). Auditory verbal hallucinations and dysfunction of the neural substrates of speech. *Schizophrenia Research, 50*, 63–80.

Stephane, M., Folstein, M., Matthew, E. & Hill, T.C. (2000). Imaging auditory verbal hallucinations during their occurrence. *Journal of Neuropsychiatry and Clinical Neuroscience, 12*(2), 286–287.

Stephane, M., Hagen, M.C., Lee, J.T., Uecker, J., Pardo, P.J., Kuskowski, M. & Pardo, J.V. (2006). About the mechanisms of auditory verbal hallucinations: A positron emission tomographic study. *Journal of Psychiatry and Neuroscience, 31*(6), 396–405.

Stephane, M., Kuskowski, M., McClannahan, K., Surerus, C. & Nelson, K. (2010). Evaluation of inner–outer space distinction and verbal hallucinations in schizophrenia. *Cognitive Neuropsychiatry, 15*, 441–450.

Stephane, M., Pellizzer, G., Roberts, S. & McClannahan, K. (2006). Computerized binary scale of auditory speech hallucinations (cbSASH). *Schizophrenia Research, 88*, 73–81.

Stephane, M., Thuras, P., Nassrallah, H. & Georgopoulos, A.P. (2003). The internal structure of the phenomenology of auditory verbal hallucinations. *Schizophrenia Research, 61*, 185–193.

Taylor, F. K. (1979). The psychopathology of perceptions. In F.K. Taylor (Ed.), *Psychopathology: Its causes and symptoms*. Baltimore, MD: Johns Hopkins University Press.

Thewissen, V., Bentall, R., de Graaf, R., Vollebergh, W. & van Os, J. (2005). Hearing impairment and psychosis revisited. *Schizophrenia Research, 79*(1), 99–103.

Thomas, N., Rossell, S., Farhall, J., Shawyer, F. & Castle, D. (2011). Cognitive behavioural therapy for auditory hallucinations: Effectiveness and predictors of outcome in a specialist clinic. *Behavioral Cognitive Psychotherapy, 39*(2), 129–138.

Van Lieshout, R.J. & Goldberg, J.O. (2007). Quantifying self-reports of auditory verbal hallucinations in persons with psychosis. *Canadian Journal of Behavioural Science/Revue, 39*(1), 73–77.

van Lutterveld, R., Diederen, K. M., Daalman, K., Kahn, R. S., Stam, C. J. & Sommer, I. E. (2012). Oscillatory cortical network involved in auditory verbal hallucinations in schizophrenia. *PLoS One, 7*(7), e41149.

Vercammen, A. & Aleman, A. (2010). Semantic expectations can induce false perceptions in hallucination-prone individuals. *Schizophrenia Bulletin, 36*, 151–156.

Vygotsky, L.S. (1978). *Mind in society, the development of higher psychological processes*. Cambridge, MA: Harvard University Press.

Wada-Isoe, K., Ohta, K., Imamura, K., Kitayama, M., Nomura, T., Yasui, K., et al. (2008). Assessment of hallucinations in Parkinson's disease using a novel scale. *Acta Neurologica Scandinavica, 117*(1), 35–40.

Waters, F., Aleman, A., Fernyhough, C. & Allen, P. (2011). Report on the inaugural meeting of the International Consortium on Hallucination Research: A clinical and research update, and 16 consensus-set goals for future research. *Schizophrenia Bulletin, 38*(2), 258–262.

Waters, F. A., Badcock, J., Michie, P. T. & Maybery, M. (2006). Auditory hallucinations in schizophrenia: Intrusive thoughts and forgotten memories. *Cognitive Neuropsychiatry, 11*, 65–83.

Waters, F., Aleman, A., Fernyhough, C., Woodward, T. S., Badcock, J. C., Barkus, E., et al. (2012). Auditory hallucinations in schizophrenia and nonschizophrenia populations: A review and integrated model of cognitive mechanisms. *Schizophrenia Bulletin, 28*(4), 683–693.

Waters, F. A. V., Badcock, J. C. & Maybery, M. T. (2003). Revision of the factor structure of the Launay-Slade Hallucination Scale (LSHS-R). *Personality and Individual Differences, 35*(6), 1351–1357.

Zahavi, D. (2003). *Husserl's phenomenology*. Paolo Alto, CA: Stanford University Press.

13

VISUAL, OLFACTORY, GUSTATORY AND SOMATIC HALLUCINATIONS

Flavie Waters, Michael H. Connors and Robyn Langdon

Introduction

Everyone has, at one time or other, experienced a sensory deception. Some better known deceptions of the senses include visual or optical illusions that are commonplace experiences in everyday life. Examples include visual after-effects and illusions such as the Müller-Lyer illusion (see **Figure 13.1**). Sensory deceptions such as illusions are the product of a normally functioning brain that has evolved to process sensory information about the world in certain ways. There is no clear demarcation between real perceptions, misperceptions and hallucinations. Rather, there is a gradation, a continuum, of experiences which depends on the relative contribution of sensory input, internal processes, and other biological, psychological and social determinants. All of the sensory modalities can be deceived (visual, auditory, olfactory, gustatory and somatic).

This chapter focuses on hallucinations. Hallucinations occur particularly commonly in the context of medical or organic conditions, although they can also occur in the healthy population. The aim of the current chapter is to briefly review the frequency, clinical characteristics and phenomenology of different types of hallucination, and the tools to assess hallucinations in different modalities. Auditory hallucinations are reviewed separately (see Stephane, *Chapter 12*). The current chapter focuses on hallucinations in the visual, olfactory, gustatory and somatic modalities.

Overview of Assessment Methods

In the assessment of hallucinations, the primary objective is to distinguish hallucinations from other phenomena such as dreams, misperceptions, vivid imagery

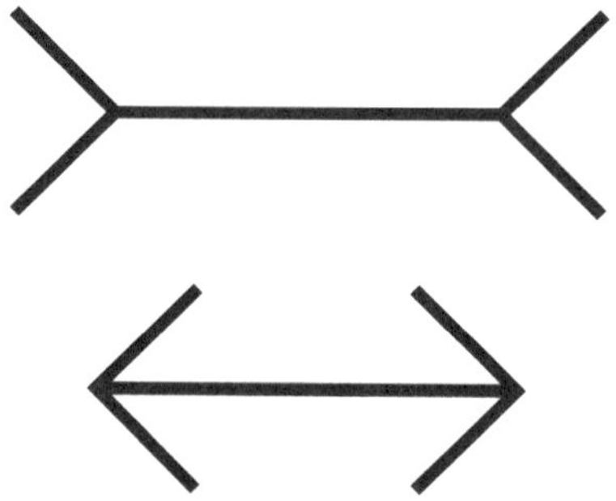

FIGURE 13.1 Müller-Lyer illusion. Consider which line is longer. Most individuals report that the top line is longer, despite the fact that they are metrically the same length. The illusion occurs because the visual system processes the configuration of angles in such a way as to judge concave angles as arising from stimuli which are closer in space than convex angles.

and false beliefs. **Table 13.1** shows a diagnostic algorithm which differentiates the key features of hallucinations from related phenomena (adapted from Blom, 2010). The key features to elicit in any assessment of hallucinations (regardless of the modality) are that:

(i) The experience must be experienced in full consciousness (rules out sleep-related hallucinations, fever, delirium, and hypnosis);
(ii) the experience is not elicited by an external stimulus (excludes visual distortions and illusions);
(iii) the experience has a sense of reality to resemble a veridical perception (must have physical properties of real perceptions and be located in external space: this does not mean that they must be perceived to be real, or that insight must be lacking) and
(iv) the person does not feel s/he has direct and voluntary control over their experience (rules out visual imagery).

An assessment might also characterize hallucinatory experiences in terms of modality, content, phenomenology and temporal history (e.g., first onset, duration, most recent experience and frequency). In clinical settings, the personal meaning and likely cause are also of interest, as is the impact on everyday life and therefore the need for treatment. The methods of assessment vary, and the interviewer must carefully choose his/her instruments according to the purpose of the interview. There are potential weaknesses in all instruments that need to be carefully balanced against the needs of the assessor, study objectives and practical considerations.

When asking broad screening questions, it is important to carefully consider the phrasing of the question. Some questions tend to have clinical implications

TABLE 13.1 A diagnostic algorithm for hallucinations and related phenomena (adapted from Blom, 2010)

Question 1: Are the phenomena experienced (a) during sleep, (b) on the border of waking and sleeping, or (c) while awake?		
During sleep	Rule out hallucinations: (dream)	→ Stop
On the border of waking/sleeping	Hypnagogic or hypnopompic hallucination	→ Go to Question 2
While awake		→ Go to Question 2
Question 2: Are the phenomena perceptual in nature? (i.e., with the physical properties of real perceptions)		
No	Rule out hallucinations: (likely due to thinking, daydream)	→ Stop
Yes		→ Go to Question 3
Question 3: Are the phenomena intentionally elicited? (can they be evoked at will)		
Yes	Rule out hallucinations (imagery)	→ Stop
No		→ Go to Question 4
Question 4: Do they constitute (a) an accurate sensory representation of physical reality, (b) a sensory experience with no corresponding physical reality, or (c) distorted sensory representation of physical reality?		
Accurate sensory representation		→ Stop
No corresponding physical reality	Hallucinations	→ Go to Question 5
Distorted sensory representation	Illusion or distortions	→ Go to Question 6
Question 5: Are the hallucinations (a) simple in nature, (b) complex, or (c) compound (i.e., multimodal) in nature?		
Simple hallucinations[1]	Assess for sensory defect (e.g., eye disease, hearing loss)	→ Determine type and context
Complex hallucinations[2]		→ Determine type and context
Compound hallucinations		→ Determine type and context in each sensory modality
Question 6: Are the illusions/distortions/hallucinations attributable to (a) normal perceptual processing of external stimulus, (b) distortions of the perceptual system, or (c) cognitive reasons?		
Normal processing	Not a hallucination	→ Determine type and context
Perceptual system	Sensory defect causing illusion/distortion but not hallucinations	→ Determine type and context
Cognitive reasons	Cognitive input	→ Determine type and context

[1] Simple hallucinations refer to lights, lines, geometrical shapes or colors.

[2] Complex or "formed" hallucinations are recognizable as figures, animals, faces or objects.

(e.g., "Do you see/hear things that other people cannot see/hear"), while others might normalize the experience (e.g., "It is common for people to see things or hear things that aren't there—have you ever had this experience?"). Clearly, these two types of questions may yield very different answers in psychiatric and non-psychiatric populations. In non-clinical settings, a common approach is to use self-report questionnaires (e.g., see Bell et al.'s 2006 Cardiff Anomalous Perceptions Scale). A common limitation of many self-report questionnaires is that they often do not inquire about hallucinations in different modalities, or subtypes of hallucinations, so it is important to select such tools carefully.

In clinical settings, a variety of instruments might be used. Some instruments have incorporated hallucination questions as part of a larger interview that assesses psychopathology or neuropsychiatric symptoms. The main advantage of such an approach is that such interviews assess symptoms that might commonly co-occur (e.g., delusions, insight). The main limitation in regards to many of these general psychopathology scales is that they do not ask about subtypes (or dimensional features) of hallucinations, nor do they ask about simultaneous/fused hallucinations. In addition, they have often been developed for specific populations or diagnostic groupings and are not easily transferable to individuals with other diagnoses. The most common hallucination assessment instruments (general and specific) appropriate for different clinical settings are listed in *Appendix 3*.

Important considerations in choosing appropriate instruments include: the purpose of the assessment, the specific research or clinical question, time allocated for assessment (5 vs. 60 mins) and the population being studied.

Other instruments have been developed to assess hallucinations in specific modalities. We now present each modality in turn.

Visual Hallucinations

Visual hallucinations refer to visual percepts experienced when awake, and which are not elicited by an external stimulus. Visual hallucinations can be relatively simple (e.g., lights, lines, geometrical shapes or colors) or complex (e.g., people, animals, objects or landscape). In some cases, visual hallucinations can be startling, elaborate, superimposed on the surrounding reality and highly plausible given the situational context.

Visual hallucinations can occur in many different conditions, and are related to a range of biological and psychological factors.

Table 13.2 shows that visual hallucinations are reported in a broad range of population groups, including healthy adults, neurodegenerative conditions, psychiatric disease, and in eye disease. They occur more commonly in neurodegenerative disorders than any other populations. They are particularly frequent in dementia with Lewy bodies (LBD), and Parkinson's disease with dementia (PDD; Mosimann & Collerton, 2010), and they are a core feature of Charles

TABLE 13.2 Most frequent causes of hallucinations (point prevalence: rare < 1%–5%; uncommon 5%–15%; fairly common 15%–50%; very common > 50)

	Auditory	Visual	Olfactory	Gustatory	Somatic
General community					
General population	Uncommon	Uncommon	Uncommon	Rare	Rare
Eye disease	Uncommon	Fairly to very common	Uncommon	?	?
Hearing disorders	Fairly to very common	Uncommon	?	?	?
Migraines	Uncommon	Fairly common	Rare	Uncommon	?
Bereavement	Uncommon	Fairly common	Uncommon	?	Rare
Substance abuse and withdrawal	Very common	Very common	Fairly common	Uncommon	Fairly common
Sleep disorders (Narcolepsy, hypersomnia etc.)	Uncommon	Uncommon	?	?	Common
Neurological and neurodegenerative disorders					
Epilepsy	Uncommon to fairly common	Uncommon to fairly common	Uncommon (TLE), rare (other foci)	Uncommon	?
Brain tumors or lesions	Fairly common	Uncommon	Uncommon	Uncommon	Uncommon
Alzheimer's disease	Uncommon to fairly common	Uncommon to fairly common	Rare to uncommon	?	Rare to uncommon
Dementia with Lewy Bodies	Uncommon	Very common	?	?	?
Parkinson's Disease	Uncommon	Fairly to very common	Uncommon	?	?
Delirium	Uncommon	Fairly to very common	?	?	Rare to uncommon
Huntington's disease	Rare	Rare	?	?	?
Frontotemporal dementia	Rare	Rare	?	?	?
Psychiatric disorders					
Schizophrenia	Very common	Fairly common	Fairly common	Uncommon	Fairly common
Affective psychosis	Uncommon to fairly common	Uncommon to fairly common	Uncommon	Uncommon	Uncommon to fairly common
Tourette syndrome/OCD	?	Uncommon	?	?	Uncommon
PTSD	Uncommon to fairly common	Uncommon	Uncommon		Uncommon

Bonnet syndrome (CBS). They also occur commonly in some neurological conditions; for example localized damage to the midbrain and pons can produce vivid visual hallucinations (peduncular hallucinosis). While originally thought to be atypical or uncommon in psychosis, a recent re-examination of the evidence estimated the mean prevalence of visual hallucinations in schizophrenia to be 27% (based on 29 studies), and in affective psychosis 15% (based on 12 studies) (Waters et al., 2014).

In the general population, visual hallucinations are more commonly reported than hallucinations in any other sensory modality (Sidgwick, 1894; West, 1945). They have been reported by 3% to 14% of community adults (Tien, 1991; Ohayon, 2000) and 10% to 32% of university students (Larøi & Van der Linden, 2003; Waters et al., 2003). Importantly, when research criteria exclude hallucinations arising from drug-taking or physical illness, the prevalence rate of visual hallucinations in the community reduces to 6% (Van Os et al., 2000). In keeping with this observation, visual hallucinations are also common in the context of intoxication and withdrawal from substances such as alcohol, cannabis and cocaine, and other physical states such as physical illness, isolation, loneliness and stress.

Main Dimensional Features

Visual hallucinations are generally classified into "simple" or "complex/formed" types. Simple hallucinations include photopsias (flashes of lights), geometric shapes, or crude or unformed experiences (sparks, etc.). Complex or formed hallucinations present as recognizable figures, animals, faces or objects. These may differ in perceptual quality (detailed, solid, dull, colorful, etc.), location in space, sense of reality, temporal aspects (frequency, evolution over time), degrees of perceived control over the content and appearance, emotional reactions and associated beliefs and appraisals.

There have been no systematic comparisons of these dimensional features across different disorders. There are, however, detailed accounts of visual hallucinations in eye disease, Parkinson's disease, dementia and schizophrenia (Fenelon et al., 2000; ffytche, 2005, 2008, 2009; ffytche et al., 1998; Mosimann & Collerton, 2010; Mosimann et al., 2006). The phenomenological qualities of visual hallucinations vary across disorders. In Charles Bonnet syndrome, simple hallucinations are most common, followed by images of landscapes and people or animals, with faces described as grotesque and cartoon-like (ffytche, 2005). In Parkinson's disease, visual hallucinations of people (alive or deceased), animals and objects are most common, with the contents being fairly stereotyped and repetitive (Fenelon et al., 2000). The content of visual hallucinations in dementia tends to be fairly mundane and of everyday objects or scenes (Mosimann & Collerton, 2010). In schizophrenia and other psychoses, visual hallucinations are detailed and vivid, and have the physical and dynamic properties of real percepts (Baethge et al., 2005; Bowman & Raymond, 1931b; Dudley et al., 2013; Gauntlett-Gilbert & Kuipers, 2003). Complex visual hallucinations mostly consist of human forms (distorted or normal in appearance), faces, spiritual/religious beings, followed by animals and objects. The characteristics that distinguish visual hallucinations in psychosis from those experienced in other diagnoses are their frightening contents, and with patients having strong emotional reactions and appraisals of personal significance (Gauntlett-Gilbert & Kuipers, 2005).

Assessment of Visual Hallucinations

Scales specially developed for visual hallucinations include:

- Institute of Psychiatry Visual Hallucination Interview (IP-VHI; Santhouse et al., 2000)
- North-East Visual Hallucination Interview (NEVHI; Mosimann et al., 2008)
- Queen Square Visual Hallucinations Inventory (QAVHI; Williams et al., 2008)
- Revised Launay Slade Hallucination Scale (RLSHS; Morrison & Haddock, 1997)
- Self-Rated Visual Hallucination Questionnaire for Parkinson's Disease (Barnes & David, 2001)
- Semi-Structured Interview on Complex Visual Hallucinations for Charles Bonnet's Syndrome (Teunisse et al., 1996)
- Semi-Structured Interview about Visions in Psychiatric Patients (Gauntlett-Gilbert & Kuipers, 2005)
- University of Miami Parkinson's Disease Hallucinations Questionnaire (UM-PDHQ; Papapetropoulos et al., 2008)

Olfactory Hallucinations

Olfactory hallucinations are experiences of smell not elicited by an external stimulus (including one's own body). Other terms used to refer to olfactory hallucinations include *phantosmia* (particularly when olfactory hallucinations are the patients' primary presenting symptom) and *olfactory aura* when the experience occurs in the context of epilepsy. The term *olfactory reference syndrome* is used when patients have no insight and believe the odor emanates from themselves. Olfactory hallucinations can occur in the absence of any nasal pathology or odor identification deficit.

The assessment of olfactory hallucinations requires the ruling out of other symptoms and causes. Olfactory hallucinations, for example, can sometimes be confused with olfactory illusions—also known as parosmia and dysosmia—in which an existing smell is misperceived (Leopold, 2002). Olfactory hallucinations can also be mistaken as gustatory hallucinations given the close relationship between taste and smell (Blom, 2010). Finally, other factors that can affect olfaction (e.g., food and drink, smoking, drugs, and medical conditions) need to be ruled out (Blom, 2010).

Olfactory hallucinations can result from many different causes (see **Table 13.2**). They are most frequently observed in schizophrenia, with a lifetime prevalence of 13% to 37% (Goodwin & Jamison, 2007; Langdon et al., 2011; McGrath et al., 2009) and point-prevalence at 6%–26% (Jablensky et al., 1992). Olfactory hallucinations are also observed in neurological conditions such as temporal lobe epilepsy (5%–10% "olfactory auras") (Penfield & Jasper, 1954) and migraines more rarely (in 1% of sufferers; Coleman et al., 2011). Olfactory hallucinations also occur in bipolar disorder, depression, posttraumatic stress disorder, dementia, Parkinson's disease and Charles Bonnet syndrome. Like other hallucinations, olfactory hallucinations also occur in the general, non-clinical, population (3% to 9%) (García-Ptacek et al., 2013; Ohayon, 2000). These experiences may be associated with the use of alcohol, drugs, caffeine, as well as adjustment disorders and lack of sleep.

Main Dimensional Features

The following dimensions may be of particular importance in the assessment of olfactory hallucinations (Coleman et al., 2011; Kopala et al., 1994; Kwapil et al., 1996; Langdon et al., 2011; Stevenson & Langdon, 2011; Stevenson et al., 2011): (1) description of smell, (2) valence (pleasant, unpleasant, neutral), (3) vividness and intensity, (4) frequency, (5) duration, (6) particular triggers, (7) context, (8) beliefs about what caused smell, (9) attribution of cause (internal, external), (10) emotional response (e.g., distress, fear, disgust, confusion), (11) behavioral response (e.g., open window), and (12) ability to control, stop or ignore the smell. While it is usually not possible to distinguish between underlying conditions on the basis of such dimensions, the duration and timing of hallucinations may be more consistent in some disorders. Olfactory auras in epilepsy, for example, are usually brief, lasting several seconds or minutes, and precede an epileptic seizure. In migraine, olfactory hallucinations typically last between 5–60 minutes, usually shortly before or at the same time as a migraine (Coleman et al., 2011). By contrast, olfactory hallucinations in schizophrenia can last from several seconds to several hours and can occur occasionally, several times a week, or even several times a day (Stevenson et al., 2011).

Olfactory hallucinations are typically unpleasant. Frequent descriptions include smelling burning, excrement, decay and body odor, and as a result olfactory hallucinations can often be experienced as intrusive and distressing (Fuller & Guiloff, 1987; Langdon et al., 2011; Meats, 1988). However, they can also be neutral or pleasant (smelling flowers, pine cones and sea air) (Fuller & Guiloff, 1987). Across all disorders, patients tend to experience the same olfactory hallucination repeatedly over time (Diamond et al., 1985). Patients often experience olfactory hallucinations as they would a real odor, and may act on it as if the odor were real (Kopala et al., 1994). For instance, individuals have searched their houses for the source of an odor they believed was a gas leak or rotting fish (Embril et al., 1983). Some may attribute the olfactory hallucinations to their own body odor, typically experienced as offensive (Langdon et al., 2011). As a result, olfactory hallucinations can be associated with social anxiety and depression. Other delusions can also develop around olfactory hallucinations (Bizamcer et al., 2008) and lead to social isolation and distress.

Assessment Scales

There are two rating scales specifically developed to assess olfactory hallucinations:

- Olfactory Hallucinations Phenomenological Survey (Stevenson & Langdon, 2011)
- Scale for Olfactory Hallucinations (Kwapil et al., 1996)

Gustatory Hallucinations

Gustatory hallucinations have not received much research or clinical interest, with a few exceptions (Ohayon, 2000; Tien, 1991). Gustatory hallucinations refer to the perception of taste or flavour that is not elicited by an external stimulus. Often, the taste is unpleasant, and can be long-lasting.

Gustatory hallucinations are most frequent in schizophrenia, with prevalence rates of 1% to 31% (Bauer et al., 2011; Bowman & Raymond, 1931a; Connolly & Gittleson, 1971; Goodwin et al., 1971; Huber et al., 1979). Few studies have studied these experiences outside of schizophrenia. In affective disorders, estimates range from 2.2% to 17% (Baethge et al., 2005; Lewandowski et al., 2009). They have also often been described in the context of epilepsy and seizures.

In the general population, gustatory hallucinations are reasonably common. 1% of individuals experience them at least once a week (Ohayon, 2000; Tien, 1991). They have been linked to a range of clinical contexts, including intoxication, anxiety, depression, and poor sleep (Ohayon, 2000). In Ohayon's study, approximately 66% of subjects with weekly gustatory hallucinations presented with a mental disorder, an organic pathology or intoxication of drugs.

Assessment Scales

There are currently no scales specifically designed for gustatory hallucinations, though it may be possible to adapt the Olfactory Hallucinations Phenomenological Survey (Stevenson & Langdon, 2011) for this purpose.

Somatic Hallucinations

Somatic hallucinations—also known as hallucinations of body sensation, or 'of the body'—refer to a broad range of bodily sensations in the absence of a definite physical cause, including burning, tingling, scraping and heat. Sensations may seem to originate from either within or outside the body. Particular categories include hallucinated pain; sexual hallucinations; thermal hallucinations, tactile (haptic) hallucinations (sensations of being touched or touching a stimulus), proprioceptive hallucinations (related to posture or location of limbs), kinaesthetic hallucinations (sensation of movement), vestibular hallucinations (sense of falling or disorientation), co-enesthetic hallucinations (sensations inside the body and head); for comprehensive conceptual and historical descriptions see Berrios (1982) and Blom and Sommer (2010).

Somatic hallucinations occur in many neurological and psychiatric conditions (see **Table 13.2**). They are common in schizophrenia and other psychoses (Alford et al., 1982; Jenkins & Röhricht, 2007), where they are frequently described as involving touch, stabbing, sexual feelings, distortions of the body, and other sensations arising from the bodily organs. In schizophrenia, they are thought to occur in approximately 19% of individuals (range 1%–53%) (Bauer et al., 2011; Bowman & Raymond, 1931a; Ciompi & Müller, 1976; Connolly & Gittleson, 1971; Goodwin et al., 1971; Huber et al., 1979; Langdon et al., 2011) with similar rates in affective disorders (15%–31%) (Baethge et al., 2005). In psychiatric disorders, they may be associated with a poor prognosis (McCabe et al., 1972; Thomas et al., 2007).

Somatic hallucinations have also been reported in people with brain tumours, sleep disorders such as restless leg syndrome, and neurodegenerative disorders (Brasic, 1998). They occur in approximately 3% of the general population (Ohayon, 2000), especially while falling asleep or waking up (hypnagogic and hypnopompic hallucinations). They are commonly linked to drugs that affect dopaminergic systems such as bupropion (Charuvastra & Yaeger, 2006) and stimulants (particularly cocaine and other amphetamines). They may also be associated with withdrawal from alcohol or benzodiazepines. Drug-related somatic hallucinations are frequently described as bugs crawling over the skin ("cocaine bugs").

Concluding Remarks

Hallucinations can occur in every sensory modality and across many psychiatric and neurodegenerative populations. They also occur surprisingly often in the general population. We have focused on visual, olfactory, gustatory and somatic hallucinations. These represent a fascinating phenomenon for further study and an important target for clinical interventions.

References

Alford, G., Fleece, L., & Rothblum, E. (1982). Hallucinatory-delusional verbalizations: Modification in a chronic schizophrenic by self-control and cognitive Restructuring. *Behavior Modification, 3*, 421–435.

Baethge, C., Baldessarini, R., Freudenthal, K., & Streeruwitz, A. (2005). Hallucinations in bipolar disorder: Characteristics and comparison to unipolar depression and schizophrenia. *Bipolar Disorders, 7*(2), 136–146.

Barnes, J., & David, A.S. (2001). Visual hallucinations in Parkinson's disease: A review and phenomenological survey. *Journal of Neurology, Neurosurgery, and Psychiatry, 70*, 727–733.

Bauer, S., Schanda, H., & Karakula, H. (2011). Culture and the prevalence of hallucinations in schizophrenia. *Comprehensive Psychiatry, 52*, 319–325.

Bell, V., Halligan, P.W., & Ellis, H.D. (2006). The Cardiff Anomalous Perceptions Scale (CAPS): A new validated measure of anomalous perceptual experience. *Schizophrenia Bulletin, 32*(2), 266–366.

Berrios, G. (1982). Tactile hallucinations: Conceptual and historical aspects. *Journal of Neurology, Neurosurgery, and Psychiatry, 45*, 285–293.

Bizamcer, A.N., Dubin, W.R., & Hayburn, B. (2008). Olfactory reference syndrome. *Psychosomatics, 49*, 77–81.

Blom, J.D. (2010). *A dictionary of hallucinations*. New York, NY: Springer.

Blom, J.D., & Sommer, I. (2010). Hallucinations of bodily sensation. In S.I. Blom (Ed.), *Hallucinations: Research and practice*. New York, NY: Springer.

Bowman, K., & Raymond, A. (1931a). A statistical study of hallucinations in the manic-depressive psychoses. *The American Journal of Psychiatry, 88*(2), 299–309.

Bowman, K., & Raymond, A. (1931b). A statistical study of hallucinations in the manic-depressive psychoses. *American Journal of Psychiatry, 11*, 299–309.

Brasic, J.R. (1998). Hallucinations. *Perceptual and Motor Skills, 86*, 851–877.

Charuvastra, A., & Yaeger, D. (2006). Tactile hallucinations associated with therapeutic doses of bupropion in 2 patients. *Journal of Clinical Psychiatry, 67*(11), 1820–1821.

Ciompi, L., & Müller, C. (1976). *Lebensweg und Alter der Schizophrenen*. Berlin, Germany: Springer.

Coleman, E.R., Grosberg, B.M., & Robbins, M.S. (2011). Olfactory hallucinations in primary headache disorders: Case series and literature review. *Cephalalgia, 31*, 1477–1489.

Connolly, F.H., & Gittleson, N.L. (1971). The relationship between delusions of sexual change and olfactory and gustatory hallucinations in schizophrenia. *British Journal of Psychiatry, 119*, 443–444.

Diamond, S., Freitag, F.G., Prager, J., & Gandi, S. (1985). Olfactory aura and migraine. *New England Journal of Medicine, 312*(21), 1390–1391.

Dudley, R., Collerton, D., Nicholson, M., & Mosimann, U. (2013). Clinical characteristics of disclosed visual hallucinations in users of an Early Intervention in Psychosis Service. *Psychosis Research, 5*(2), 127–133.

Embril, J.A., Camfield, P., Artsob, H., & Chase, D.P. (1983). Powassan virus encephalitis resembling herpes simplex encephalitis. *Archives of Internal Medicine, 143*, 341–343.

Fenelon, G., Mahieux, F., Huon, R., & Ziegler, M. (2000). Hallucinations in Parkinson's disease: Prevalence, phenomenology and risk factors [Case Reports]. *Brain, 123 (Pt. 4)*, 733–745.

ffytche, D.H. (2005). Visual hallucinations and the Charles Bonnet syndrome. *Current Psychiatry Reports, 7*(3), 168–179.
ffytche, D.H. (2008). The hodology of hallucinations. *Cortex, 44*(8), 1067–1083.
ffytche, D.H. (2009). Visual hallucinations in eye disease [Review]. *Current Opinion in Neurology, 22*(1), 28–35.
ffytche, D.H., Howard, R.J., Brammer, M.J., David, A., Woodruff, P., & Williams, S. (1998). The anatomy of conscious vision: An fMRI study of visual hallucinations. *Nature Neuroscience, 1*(8), 738–742. doi:10.1038/3738
Fuller, G.N., & Guiloff, R.J. (1987). Migrainous olfactory hallucinations. *Journal of Neurology, Neurosurgery & Psychiatry, 50*, 1688–1690.
García-Ptacek, S., García Azorín, D., Sanchez Salmador, R., Cuadrado, M.L., & Porta-Etessam, J. (2013). Hallucinations and aberrant perceptions are prevalent among the young healthy adult population. *Neurología* (English Edition), *28*, 19–23.
Gauntlett-Gilbert, J., & Kuipers, E. (2003). Phenomenology of visual hallucinations in psychiatric conditions. *Journal of Nervous and Mental Disorders, 191*(3), 203–205.
Gauntlett-Gilbert, J., & Kuipers, E. (2005). Visual hallucinations in psychiatric conditions: Appraisals and their relationship to distress. *British Journal of Clinical Psychology, 44*(1), 77–87.
Goodwin, D., Alderson, P., & Rosenthal, R. (1971). Clinical significance of hallucinations in psychiatric disorders: A study of 116 hallucinatory patients. *Archives of General Psychiatry, 24*, 76–78.
Goodwin, F., & Jamison, K. (2007). *Manic-depressive illness: Bipolar disorders and recurrent depression* (2nd ed.). New York, NY: Oxford University Press.
Huber, G., Gross, G., & Schüttler, R. (1979). *Schizophrenie. Eine verlaufs- und sozialpsychiatrische Langzeitstudie*. Berlin, Germany: Springer.
Jablensky, A., Sartorius, N., Ernberg, G., Anker, M., Korten, A., Cooper, J., et al. (1992). Schizophrenia: Manifestations, incidence and course in different cultures: A World Health Organization ten-country study. *Psychological Medicine Monograph*, (Suppl.), 1–97.
Jenkins, G., & Röhricht, F. (2007). From cenesthesias to cenesthopathic schizophrenia: A historical and phenomenological review. *Psychopathology 40*, 361–368.
Kopala, L.C., Good, K.P., & Honer, W.G. (1994). Olfactory hallucinations and olfactory identification ability in patients with schizophrenia and other psychiatric disorders. *Schizophrenia Research, 12*, 205–211.
Kwapil, T.R., Chapman, J.P., Chapman, L.J., & Miller, M.B. (1996). Deviant olfactory experiences as indicators of risk for psychosis. *Schizophrenia Bulletin, 22*, 371–380.
Langdon, R., McGuire, J., Stevenson, R., Catts, S.V., & Cadoretr, J. (2011). Clinical correlates of olfactory hallucinations in schizophrenia. *British Journal of Clinical Psychology, 50*, 145–163.
Larøi, F., & Van der Linden, M. (2003). Non-clinical participants reports of hallucinatory experiences. *Canadian Journal of Behavioral Science, 37*, 33–43.
Leopold, D. (2002). Distortion of olfactory perception: Diagnosis and treatment. *Chemical Senses, 27*, 611–615.
Lewandowski, K.E., DePaola, J., Camsari, G.B., Cohen, B.M., & Ongür, D. (2009). Tactile, olfactory, and gustatory hallucinations in psychotic disorders: A descriptive study. *Annals Academy of Medicine Singapore, 38*(5), 383–385.
McCabe, M., Fowler, R., Cadoretr, J., & Winokur, G. (1972). Symptom differences in schizophrenia with good and poor prognosis. *American Journal of Psychiatry, 128*, 1239–1243.

McGrath, J., Avramopoulos, D., Lasseter, V., Wolyniec, P., Fallin, D., Liang, K., et al. (2009). Familiality of novel factorial dimensions of schizophrenia. *Archives of General Psychiatry, 66*, 591–600.

Meats, P. (1988). Olfactory hallucinations. *British Medical Journal, 296*(6622), 645.

Morrison, A.P., & Haddock, G. (1997). Cognitive factors in source monitoring and auditory hallucinations. *Psychological Medicine, 27*, 669–679.

Mosimann, U.P., & Collerton, D. (2010). Hallucinations in the context of dementing illnesses. In A.A. Frank Larøi (Ed.), *Hallucinations: A guide to treatment and management*. Oxford, UK: Oxford University Press.

Mosimann, U.P., Collerton, D., Dudley, R., Meyer, T.D., Graham, G., Dean, J.L., et al. (2008). A semi-structured interview to assess visual hallucinations in older people [Validation studies]. *International Journal of Geriatric Psychiatry, 23*(7), 712–718. doi:10.1002/gps.1965

Mosimann, U.P., Rowan, E.N., Partington, C.E., Collerton, D., Littlewood, E., O'Brien, J.T., et al. (2006). Characteristics of visual hallucinations in Parkinson disease dementia and dementia with lewy bodies. *American Journal of Geriatric Psychiatry, 14*(2), 153–160.

Ohayon, M. (2000). Prevalence of hallucinations and their pathological associations in the general population. *Psychiatry Research, 97*, 153–164.

Papapetropoulos, S., Katzen, H., Schrag, A., Singer, C., Scanlon, B., Nation, D., et al. (2008). A questionnaire-based (UM-PDHQ) study of hallucinations in Parkinson's disease. *BMC Neurology, 8*, 21.

Penfield, W., & Jasper, H. (1954). *Epilepsy and the functional anatomy of the human brain*. Boston, MA: Little, Brown.

Santhouse, A., Howard, R., & ffytche, D. (2000). Visual hallucinatory syndromes and the anatomy of the visual brain. *Brain, 123*, 2055–2064.

Sidgwick, H. (1894). Report on the census of hallucinations. *Proceedings of the Society of Psychical Research, 10*, 25–422.

Stevenson, R.J., & Langdon, R. (2011). A preliminary investigation of olfactory function in olfactory and auditory-verbal hallucinators with schizophrenia, and normal controls. *Cognitive Neuropsychiatry, 17*, 315–333.

Stevenson, R.J., Langdon, R., & McGuire, J. (2011). Olfactory hallucinations in schizophrenia and schizoaffective disorder: A phenomenological survey. *Psychiatry Research, 185*, 321–327.

Teunisse, R., Cruysberg, J., Hoefnagels, W., Verbeek, A., & Zitman, F. (1996). Visual hallucinations in psychologically normal people: Charles Bonnet's syndrome. *The Lancet, 247*, 794–796.

Thomas, P., Mathur, P., Gottesman, I.I., Nagpal, R., Rimgaonkar, V.L., & Deshpande, S.N. (2007). Correlates of hallucinations in schizophrenia: A cross-cultural evaluation. *Schizophrenia Research, 92*, 41–49.

Tien, A. (1991). Distributions of hallucinations in the population. *Social Psychiatry and Psychiatric Epidemiology, 26*(6), 287–292.

Van Os, J., Hanssen, M., & Bijl, R.V. (2000). Strauss (1969) revisited: A psychosis continuum in the general population? *Schizophrenia Research, 45*, 11–20.

Waters, F., Collerton, D., Blom, J.D., ffytche, D.H., Jardri, R., Pins, D., et al. (2014). Visual hallucinations in the psychosis-spectrum, and comparative information from neurodegenerative disorders and eye disease. *Schizophrenia Bulletin* (Special Issue 3).

Waters, F.A.V., Badcock, J.C., & Maybery, M.T. (2003). Revision of the factor structure of the Launay-Slade Hallucination Scale (LSHS-R). *Personality and Individual Differences, 35*, 1351–1357.

West, D.J. (1945). A mass observation questionnaire on hallucinations. *Journal of the Society for Psychical Research, 34*, 187–195.

Williams, D. R., Warren, J. D., & Lees, A. J. (2008). Using the presence of visual hallucinations to differentiate Parkinson's disease from atypical parkinsonism. *Journal of Neurology, Neurosurgery and Psychiatry, 79*, 652–655.

14

DELUSIONS

Vaughan Bell and Emmanuelle Peters

Introduction

While humans have a unique ability to consider beliefs as true, false, uncertain or undecided, the concept of delusion implies not just that a belief is wrong but that the process of belief formation itself has become disturbed. Given that beliefs reflect the state of taking something to be the case or regarding it as true (Schwitzgebel, 2014), the assimilation of information to allow us to form beliefs that adequately reflect reality is a central part of presumably healthy adaptive human cognition. Although suboptimal rationality is the norm in human reasoning, delusions reflect a difficulty modifying clearly erroneous or impossible beliefs—particularly beliefs with high emotional salience—resulting in significant disability. Delusions are therefore typically defined as being false, fixed and unswayable by counter-evidence, although, as we shall see, adequately defining delusion is not an easy conceptual task given that a complete definition that adequately and coherently distinguishes pathological from non-pathological beliefs by their characteristics turns out to be remarkably difficult to formulate (David, 1999). Despite not having a perfect definition, the existing criteria mean that, in the clinic, delusions can be diagnosed to an acceptable level of reliability and many scales seek to aid this process by evaluating the dimensions of delusional belief either in its form or content.

Clinical Classification and Definition

There is no universally accepted definition of a delusion but most researchers (somewhat wearily, it must be said) refer to the definition in the *Diagnostic and Statistical Manual*, now recently updated to the DSM-5 (American Psychiatric

Association [APA], 2013). In fact, as with the previous version (the DSM-IV-TR; APA, 2000), the DSM-5 defines delusions in two sections: the glossary (p. 819) and the introduction to the "Schizophrenia Spectrum and Other Psychotic Disorders" section (p. 87). The DSM-5 glossary definition maintains the same definition from the DSM-IV-TR, namely:

> *A false belief based on incorrect inference about external reality that is firmly held despite what almost everyone else believes and despite what constitutes incontrovertible and obvious proof or evidence to the contrary. The belief is not ordinarily accepted by other members of the person's culture or subculture (i.e., it is not an article of religious faith).*
>
> *(APA, 2013, p. 819)*

However, the definition in the "Schizophrenia Spectrum and Other Psychotic Disorders" section has been modified and no longer defines delusions as "false beliefs" and describes them like so: "Delusions are fixed beliefs that are not amenable to change in light of conflicting evidence . . ." (APA, 2013, p. 87). As we shall see, this is probably an advance as not all delusions need be false or falsifiable but, curiously, this creates an inconsistency within the DSM's own definitions.

The glossary definition is clearly much worse conceptually because there are counterexamples to every point (Bell et al., 2003). Delusions are not always false: they may be fortuitously true (e.g., partners of patients with delusional jealousy may begin affairs after the delusion has formed; Sims, 2003) or beliefs may be unfalsifiable either through being a value judgment ("I am a fantastically talented singer") or through being resistant to empirical testing ("Spirits are sending my thoughts to heaven") as noted by Fulford (1994). Delusional themes can also reflect the personal history of the patient (Janssen et al., 2003; Raune et al., 2006) suggesting a level of "truth" at the level of personal meaning that is not reflected in propositional correctness.

With regard to delusions being firmly held, we know that conviction in delusions varies greatly within individuals (Appelbaum et al., 2004; Peters et al., 2012) and that the ability to entertain the possibility of being mistaken has been reported in about 50% of patients (Garety et al., 1997, 2005). Conversely, absolute conviction in personally held beliefs is not, in itself, pathological (Colbert et al., 2010). Indeed, the dimensional nature of conviction and incorrigibility has been recognized in the new DSM-5 definition (introduction to psychotic disorders section): "The distinction between a delusion and a strongly held idea is sometimes difficult to make and depends in part on the degree of conviction with which the belief is held despite clear or reasonable contradictory evidence regarding its veracity." The issue of whether the belief is shared by others is also contentious, considering that beliefs with delusional themes are reported by about 50% of the population (Pechey & Halligan, 2012) and that about 10% of the general population typically score above the mean of inpatients with psychosis on self-report measures of delusional ideation (e.g., Peters et al., 2004).

Despite the inconsistent DSM-5 definitions, as noted above, it is worth highlighting the pragmatic process by which delusions get diagnosed: a patient who is either distressed or impaired appears in front of a clinician and part of their difficulty is judged to be associated with a hard-to-fathom, inflexible and pre-occupying concern which they claim to be true. Perhaps despite the criteria, rather than because of it, clinicians can reliably agree on the presence of delusions (Bell et al., 2006a), suggesting that the implicit pragmatic definition functions quite adequately in most cases. Nevertheless, changes in the latest edition of the DSM-5 to remove the criterion for the presence of a 'bizarre delusion' in the diagnosis of schizophrenia stem from evidence that "bizarreness" could not be adequately agreed upon, even if the presence of a delusion could (Cermolacce et al., 2010). Those wondering how the various DSM definitions compare to the definition in the International Classification of Diseases (ICD-10) may be interested to know that the ICD-10 mentions but does not define delusions.

Psychological models of delusions reflect this pragmatic approach, and consider them to be multi-dimensional in terms of, for example, distress, conviction, preoccupation and interference with functioning (Garety & Hemsley, 1987; Appelbaum et al., 2004; Peters et al., 2004), and operating on a continuum with non-diagnosable or non-clinical beliefs (Bell et al., 2006b; Freeman, 2007). Both population and lab studies have found delusions and delusion-like thinking in non-clinical participants to be associated with higher levels of negative affect and poor psychological well-being (e.g., Freeman et al., 2013; Preti et al., 2012) as well as the presence of cognitive biases in multiple domains (e.g., Moritz et al., 2010; Knowles et al., 2011).

Characteristic Features of Delusions and Association With Disorders

In addition to the diagnostic definition of delusion that focuses on the form of belief, there are also common classifications regarding the content of the belief. Those codified in the DSM-5 include erotomanic delusions (sometimes called De Clérambault's Syndrome—where a person, usually of a higher status, is believed to be in love with the patient; Segal, 1989), grandiose delusions (where the delusion concerns the person having some exceptional talent, status, identity or insight; Knowles et al., 2011), jealous delusions (sometimes called delusional jealousy or the Othello syndrome—where the person believes that their partner is being unfaithful even to the point of impossibility—such as seeing secret lovers in the wardrobe; Easton et al., 2008), somatic delusions (where the delusion concerns bodily shape, functions or sensations; Snaith, 1992) and persecutory delusions (where the delusion centers around the person being persecuted by others; Freeman, 2007). It is worth noting that persecutory delusions are also sometimes called "paranoid" delusions, after the everyday use of the term, although the term *paranoia* has a historical use in psychiatry (Munro, 1999) that has variously implied something akin to the modern-day diagnosis of delusional disorder, or has just meant "delusional" rather than specifically persecutory in nature—hence the use of the term in the diagnosis of "paranoid schizophrenia" in which the person needs only to be delusional and may not have any persecutory delusions. Bizarre delusions, which violate the possibilities of the physical world or seem logically incoherent, are widely discussed in the literature (Cermolacce et al., 2010) although, as noted previously, their diagnostic importance has waned (Shinn et al., 2013).

Further classifications are commonly used in the psychiatric literature and may appear in formal assessments, although are not part of the diagnostic canon. Delusions associated with Schneider's first-rank symptoms are of particular significance due to their traditional importance for the diagnosis of schizophrenia (Waters & Badcock, 2010). It is worth noting that these are as much descriptions of "mental sensations" as delusions although they are usually accompanied by delusional interpretations or as part of a delusional system. They include passivity symptoms or delusions of control (where the person experiences their actions as controlled by an external force), thought insertion or withdrawal (where the person has the experience of thoughts being inserted or removed from their stream of consciousness by an external agent), thought broadcasting (where the person's thoughts feel as if they are being broadcast or available to other people directly from the mind) and thought echo (where the person's thoughts appear to be spoken aloud; see Waters, *Chapter 18*).

Religious delusions are often discussed as a distinct subtype owing to their interaction with cultural factors and personal spirituality (e.g., Mohr et al., 2010). Delusional parasitosis, or Ekbom's syndrome, is the belief that one is infested with parasites and is of particular interest as it tends to present initially to dermatologists rather than mental health professionals and is not uncommonly caused by dopamine-agonist stimulants, such as amphetamine or cocaine, or, in some cases, by levodopa (Freudenmann & Lepping, 2009). The term *delusions of reference* is often used to describe the experience that many things in the world have a personal significance for the person concerned or are an attempt to communicate with them directly—for example, newsreaders making hints about the person's life, or the experience of receiving special messages from the way shops' items are organized (Startup & Startup, 2005).

Another group of delusions, known as delusional misidentification syndromes, concerns the belief that the identity of people or things has changed in some way (Christodoulou et al., 2009). The most well-known is the Capgras delusion, where the person believes that certain people (often close family members) have been replaced by identical or near-identical looking imposters. There is a minor industry in the psychiatric and neuropsychiatric literature of looking for variations within delusional misidentification syndromes, although some common subtypes include the Fregoli syndrome (where the person believes the same person appears to the patient disguised as others) and reduplicative paramnesia, where the person believes that a known person, place, object or location has been duplicated.

Additionally, the Cotard delusion is quite widely discussed (Berrios & Luque, 1995), although seemingly largely because it is so striking rather than because of clinical prevalence as it has very rarely been reported. This delusion is where someone believes themselves to be dead or that their body is rotting.

Epidemiological Information

A recent meta-analysis of general population studies (Linscott & van Os, 2013) suggests that delusions diagnosed by structured clinical interview have a median population prevalence of 4.9% and a median annual incidence of 1.5%. However the frequency of delusional beliefs in non-clinical populations varies according to the methods of assessment and the content of the delusion studied, with paranoid beliefs being the most common (Freeman et al., 2005). The rate of delusional ideation in the general population is much higher than that of psychotic disorders, and can be associated with social and emotional difficulties (Freeman, 2006), although typically they cause less distress and preoccupation than in the clinical population (Peters, Day, McKenna, & Orbach, 1999; Lincoln, 2007).

In terms of psychiatric disorders associated with delusions, it is worth bearing in mind that most include the presence of delusions as a diagnostic criterion and so asking about, for example, the prevalence of delusions in people with schizophrenia, is not particularly informative. However, in terms of the lifetime prevalence of psychotic disorders in general, a study by Perälä et al. (2007) estimated a lifetime prevalence of just over 3%, suggesting that delusions are more common than many assume. It is also worth noting that delusions are typically more common in neurological patients than the general population, with dementia having a particularly high prevalence (see Ford and Almeida, *Chapter 11*). Clearly stage and type of dementia are important for prevalence although a recent review of studies in the area reported an overall prevalence in dementia of about 40% with a range of 15%–76% (Cipriani et al., 2014).

Studies on the risk factors for delusions as an individual symptom are rare, as most reliable epidemiological studies have looked at psychosis as a whole or have focused on specific diagnoses such as schizophrenia. For those studies that have looked at delusions or delusion-like experiences specifically, they seem to be associated with a family history of mental disorder (Varghese et al., 2011), exposure to traumatic events (Scott et al., 2007), low levels of social support (Saha et al., 2012) and higher levels of general psychological distress (Saha et al., 2011). In terms of risk to others, persecutory delusions are a predictor for violence although largely when associated with anger (Coid et al., 2013; Ullrich et al., 2013). Delusions, however, are more reliably associated with self-harm than harm to others (Haddock et al., 2013).

In terms of psychosis and psychosis-like experience in general, genetics, adversity, childhood trauma and abuse, substance misuse, living in an urban environment and social adversity all contribute (Linscott & van Os, 2013). Psychotic states known as acute and transient psychotic disorders have a clear onset directly after an intense emotional stressor and typically resolve with only one in eight people transitioning to receive a diagnosis indicating a longer-term psychotic disorder (Queirazza et al., 2013). In contrast, a significant proportion of cases of first-episode drug-induced psychosis transition to being diagnosed with schizophrenia-spectrum disorders—one third in Crebbin et al. (2009), over half in Komuravelli et al. (2011). Other psychoses are typically linked to measurable disturbance or damage to the brain (so-called organic psychoses) include degenerative brain conditions, epilepsy, cerebrovascular disease, brain tumor, autoimmune or infectious disease and traumatic brain injury (Lautenschlager & Förstl, 2001).

Approaches to Assessing Delusions

Delusions have a special place in psychiatric assessment because they often cannot be self-reported reliably and their presence is usually inferred by the clinician. Because of this, clinician-rated and self-rated scales take a different approach in terms of measurement. Clinician-rated scales rely on the clinician understanding enough about psychopathology to be able to detect the presence of a delusion and then rate it on various dimensions. Self-rated scales typically ask respondents to indicate which of a range of beliefs and ideas linked to common delusional themes they ascribe to before rating these ideas on various dimensions.

For this reason, clinician-rated scales are considered the gold standard for assessment during clinical work or for clinical outcomes studies. Self-rated scales are more commonly used in research on general population studies (on people not being formally treated for mental health conditions and not recruited through clinical channels) or for characterizing psychosis-like experience in studies on clinical populations where formal symptom change is not a main outcome (e.g., measuring levels of paranoia in a group of anxiety disorder patients).

Clinician-Rated Scales of Psychotic Symptoms

The implication of this is that clinician-rated scales typically need to be completed by assessors with sufficient training and experience to be able to identify the presence of a delusion for it then to be rated along its various dimensions. Assessment may be guided by definitions in the scale (e.g., the descriptions that accompany the severity rating in the Scale for Assessment of Positive Symptoms) but this essentially pushes the problem back to a simple clinical diagnostic approach for the initial decision about symptom presence.

At this point, it is worth sounding a note of caution. Agreement on whether a particular belief is a delusion is reliable in statistical terms but is not perfect, meaning that occasionally patients will be diagnosed as delusional when their beliefs are, in fact, justified. This form of mistaken diagnosis is known as the Martha Mitchell effect (Maher, 1988) after the wife of the American Attorney General who claimed there was a conspiracy in the Whitehouse and was diagnosed with mental illness only to be proven correct when the Watergate scandal broke. As Sedler (1995) noted, clinicians are reminded to keep in mind that people can indeed be pursued by the Mafia, kept under surveillance by the police and may be correct in thinking their spouse is being unfaithful in unlikely circumstances. However, as delusions can vary across many dimensions, including their emotional impact, fixity, relation to the person's past history and current circumstances, it is also worth bearing in mind that although the propositional content may not be true (e.g., the person is not being targeted by the CIA) there may be varying degrees of parallel with the person's own life history (e.g., the person was genuinely persecuted by the authorities), meaning that emotional parallels may be apparent.

The three most widely used clinician-rated scales for delusions:

- Positive and Negative Syndrome Scale (PANSS; Kay et al., 2000)
- Psychotic Symptoms Rating Scales (delusions subscale) (PSYRATS; Haddock et al., 1999)
- Scale for Assessment of Positive Symptoms (SAPS; Andreasen, 1984)

The PANSS is most commonly used for clinical outcome studies. The scale has a specific item for rating the presence and severity of delusions (which it defines as "Beliefs which are unfounded, unrealistic and idiosyncratic"), but it is worth noting that delusions can be rated or can affect ratings on many other items. The SAPS and PSYRATS Delusions are more commonly used for the assessment of clinical symptoms and experimental studies.

SAPS items are divided by common themes and include, among other items, persecutory delusions, delusions of jealousy, delusions of sin or guilt, grandiose delusions, religious delusions, somatic delusions, ideas and delusions of reference and delusions of being controlled, alongside a final global rating of severity of delusions, which is based on a rating of "duration and persistence of delusions, the extent of the subject's preoccupation with the delusions, his degree of conviction, and their effect on his actions." The PSYRATS Delusions scale is the only one of the three that specifically focuses on delusions and therefore may be a considerably quicker option if this is the main focus of assessment. It is also the only clinician-rated scale to assess the various dimensions of delusions such as conviction, preoccupation and distress, as separate items. However, while it requires the clinician to record the theme of the delusions the scale does not separately rate individual delusions and requires the highest rating for each dimension for any delusion to be recorded and included in the final score. This makes it unsuitable for a broader or more phenomenological assessment for which the SAPS would be the scale of choice. The SAPS and PANSS are designed to be rated on both patient interviews and additional information from case notes and informants, while the PSYRATS is designed to be rated purely from the interview and focuses only on the last week of experience, making it better for tracking symptom change. The SAPS was developed for measuring symptoms over the past month, although the manual suggests clinicians can define their own period for rating, while the PANSS gives no specific time period but is generally rated for the previous week.

Self-Rated Scales of Delusion

In terms of self-report scales for delusions and delusion-like ideas, or self-report scales relevant to assessing patients with delusions, it is worth noting that there are many of which only a few will be discussed here (see Peters, 2010, for a thorough review):

- Green et al. Paranoid Thought Scales (GPTS; Green et al., 2008).
- Paranoia Checklist (Freeman et al., 2005)
- Peters et al. Delusions Inventory (PDI; Peters, Joseph, & Garety, 1999; Peters et al., 2004)
- Persecutory Ideation Questionnaire (PIQ; McKay et al., 2006)
- State Social Paranoia Scale (Freeman et al., 2007).

The Peters et al. Delusions Inventory (PDI) has been widely researched in recent years. Originally published as a 40-item scale (Peters, Joseph, & Garety, 1999) with content based on the Present State Examination (Wing, Cooper, & Sartorius, 1974), the more commonly used scale is the 21-item version (Peters et al., 2004), which was derived from the original using a principal components analysis. Containing questions on a wide range of common delusional themes, it also asks respondents to rate each endorsed belief on distress, preoccupation and conviction. Although one of the most complete and focused scales for delusional ideation, it has the disadvantage of being more complex than most questionnaire measures meaning that more impaired respondents may need some assistance in completing it.

For measuring paranoid ideation, there are a number of options. Partly due to its history as a concept in psychoanalysis there is a remarkably wide range of paranoia scales in the literature stretching back to the 1970s. The most widely used in contemporary research are those by Freeman and his colleagues, such as The

Paranoia Checklist (Freeman et al., 2005), the State Social Paranoia Scale (Freeman et al., 2007), and the Green et al. Paranoid Thought Scales (GPTS; Green et al., 2008). The GPTS is the most comprehensive and contains two 16-item sections rated on a 1–5 Likert scale: The first section focuses on beliefs about social distrust and reference, and the second on beliefs about other people wanting to cause the respondent harm. There is some overlap in items with the Persecutory Ideation Questionnaire (PIQ; McKay et al., 2006), but the latter tends to focus on beliefs less concerned with direct harm to the respondent. The PIQ is somewhat shorter, consisting of 10 items rated on a 0–4 Likert scale. The Beliefs About Paranoia Scale (Morrison et al., 2005) is a 31-item questionnaire that aims to evaluate metacognitive beliefs about paranoia ("My paranoia protects me," "Everybody is paranoid on some level" etc.) that is particularly relevant for psychological therapists wanting to target unhelpful assumptions. An 18-item short-form has recently been published (Gumley et al., 2011) which retains good psychometric properties.

Schizotypy scales have also been used to measure delusions:

- Magical Ideation Scale (MIS; Eckblad & Chapman, 1983)
- Maudsley Assessment of Delusions Schedule (Buchanan et al., 1993)
- Oxford–Liverpool Inventory of Feelings and Experiences (O-LIFE; Mason et al., 1995)
- Schizotypal Personality Questionnaire (SPQ; Raine, 1991).

There are various schizotypy scales that aim to either measure a similar dimension of magical or delusional ideation, such as the Magical Ideation Scale (Eckblad & Chapman, 1983), or include a wider range of experiences capturing a broader range of experiences linked to a diagnosis of schizophrenia. Perhaps the most comprehensive is the Oxford–Liverpool Inventory of Feelings and Experiences (O-LIFE; Mason et al., 1995), which is a 150-item scale that breaks down into four subscales measuring unusual experiences, cognitive disorganization, introvertive anhedonia and impulsive non-conformity. Extended norms are published in Mason and Claridge (2006) and a short-form consisting of 42 items but maintaining the four subscales is available (Mason et al., 2005). The Schizotypal Personality Questionnaire (SPQ; Raine, 1991) takes a similar approach, but is drawn more directly from the diagnostic criteria of schizotypal personality disorder and so focuses more on interpersonal and cognitive aspects of schizotypy rather than psychosis-like experience. The Schizotypal Personality Questionnaire–Brief (SPQ-B) is a shorter version although it has been noted to be less robust in terms of psychometric properties (Compton et al., 2007).

Recent years have seen a proliferation in 'at risk mental state' or psychosis prodrome self-report screening questionnaires, all of which include coverage of delusional thinking and themes although all seem to be broadly equivalent in their validity and reliability (reviewed in Kline et al., 2012), and are probably best selected by pragmatic considerations of their content and completion.

Conclusion

An adequate definition of delusions remains elusive, although they can be classified clinically and rated relatively reliably. Different approaches to assessing delusions have arisen out of the different traditions in understanding and researching pathological beliefs. What this methodological diversity has provided, however, is a range of scales for capturing different aspects of delusions and delusion-like thinking, and a range of tools that stretch from 5-minute questionnaires to extensive medical history and interview rating instruments. It is perhaps worth noting what is missing. While persecutory delusions are well served, few scales exist for misidentification delusions, which are some of the most widely studied in neurological disorders. There is a similar picture for common delusions that tend to present initially to non-psychiatric specialties, such as delusional parasitosis. Similarly, scales for assessing risk and other factors specifically related to delusions are scarce, with the Maudsley Assessment of Delusions Schedule (Buchanan et al., 1993) being a notable (but lengthy) exception. Nevertheless, the psychological approach to delusions as multidimensional and lying on a continuum with beliefs in the general population has spawned a wide range of scales in the last 15 years that have shown utility in both the clinical and research arenas.

References

American Psychiatric Association. (2000). *Diagnostic and statistical manual of mental disorders* (4th ed., text rev.). Washington, DC: American Psychiatric Association.

American Psychiatric Association. (2013). *Diagnostic and statistical manual of mental disorders* (5th ed.). Washington, DC: Author.

Andreasen, N. C. (1984). *Scale for the Assessment of Positive Symptoms (SAPS).* Iowa City: University of Iowa.

Appelbaum, P. S., Robbins, P. C., & Vesselinov, R. (2004). Persistence and stability of delusions over time. *Comprehensive Psychiatry, 45*(5), 317–324.

Bell, V., Halligan, P. W., & Ellis, H. D. (2003). Beliefs about delusions. *The Psychologist, 16*(8), 418–423.

Bell, V., Halligan, P. W. & Ellis, H. D. (2006a). Diagnosing delusions: A review of inter-rater reliability. *Schizophrenia Research, 86*(1/3), 76–79.

Bell, V., Halligan, P. W. & Ellis, H. D. (2006b). Explaining delusions: A cognitive perspective. *Trends in Cognitive Sciences, 10*(5), 219–226.

Berrios, G. E. & Luque, R. (1995) Cotard's syndrome: Analysis of 100 cases. *Acta Psychiatrica Scandinavica, 91*(3), 185–188.

Buchanan, A., Reed, A., Wessely, S., Garety, P., Taylor, P., Grubin, D., et al. (1993). Acting on delusions. II: The phenomenological correlates of acting on delusions. *British Journal of Psychiatry, 163*, 77–81.

Cermolacce, M., Sass, L., & Parnas, J. (2010). What is bizarre in bizarre delusions? A critical review. *Schizophrenia Bulletin, 36*(4), 667–679.

Christodoulou, G. N., Margariti, M., Kontaxakis, V. P., & Christodoulou, N. G. (2009). The delusional misidentification syndromes: Strange, fascinating, and instructive. *Current Psychiatry Reports, 11*(3), 185–189.

Cipriani, G., Danti, S., Vedovello, M., Nuti, A., & Lucetti, C. (2014). Understanding delusion in dementia: A review. *Geriatrics & Gerontology International, 14*(1), 32–39.

Coid, J. W., Ullrich, S., Kallis, C., Keers, R., Barker, D., Cowden, F., et al. (2013). The relationship between delusions and violence: Findings from the East London first episode psychosis study. *JAMA Psychiatry, 70*(5), 465–471.

Colbert, S. M., Peters, E. R., & Garety, P. A. (2010). Delusions and belief flexibility in psychosis. *Psychology and Psychotherapy: Theory, Research and Practice, 83*(1), 45–57.

Compton, M. T., Chien, V. H., & Bollini, A. M. (2007). Psychometric properties of the Brief Version of the Schizotypal Personality Questionnaire in relatives of patients with schizophrenia-spectrum disorders and non-psychiatric controls. *Schizophrenia Research, 91*(1/3), 122–131.

Crebbin, K., Mitford, E., Paxton, R., & Turkington, D. (2009). First-episode drug-induced psychosis: A medium term follow up study reveals a high-risk group. *Social Psychiatry and Psychiatric Epidemiology, 44*(9), 710–715.

David, A. (1999). On the impossibility of defining delusions. *Philosophy, Psychiatry and Psychology, 6*(1), 17–20.

Easton, J. A., Shackelford, T. K. & Schipper, L. D. (2008). Delusional disorder-jealous type: How inclusive are the DSM-IV diagnostic criteria? *Journal of Clinical Psychology, 64*(3), 264–275.

Eckblad, M., & Chapman, L. J. (1983). Magical ideation as an indicator of schizotypy. *Journal of Consulting and Clinical Psychology, 51*(2), 215–225.

Freeman, D. (2006). Delusions in the nonclinical population. *Current Psychiatry Reports, 8*(3), 191–204.

Freeman, D. (2007) Suspicious minds: The psychology of persecutory delusions. *Clinical Psychology Review, 27*(4), 425–457.

Freeman, D., Garety, P.A., Bebbington, P. E., Smith, B., Rollinson, R., Fowler, D., et al. (2005). Psychological investigation of the structure of paranoia in a non-clinical population. *British Journal of Psychiatry, 186*, 427–435.

Freeman, D., Pugh, K., Green, C., Valmaggia, L., Dunn, G., & Garety, P. A. (2007). A measure of state persecutory ideation for experimental studies. *Journal of Nervous & Mental Disease, 195*, 781–784.

Freeman, D., Startup, H., Dunn, G., Wingham, G., Cernis, E., Evans, N., et al. (2013). Persecutory delusions and psychological well-being. *Social Psychiatry and Psychiatric Epidemiology*. (First published online December 3, 2013)

Freudenmann, R. W., & Lepping, P. (2009). Delusional infestation. *Clinical Microbiology Reviews, 22*(4), 690–732.

Fulford, K. W. M. (1994). Value, illness and failure of action: Framework for a philosophical psychopathology of delusions. In G. Graham & G. L. Stephens (Eds.), *Philosophical psychopathology*. Cambridge, MA: MIT Press.

Garety, P.A., Freeman, D., Jolley, S., Dunn, G., Bebbington, P.E., Fowler, D.G., et al. (2005). Reasoning, emotions, and delusional conviction in psychosis. *Journal of Abnormal Psychology, 114*, 373–384.

Garety, P., Fowler, D., Kuipers, E., Freeman, D., Dunn, G., Bebbington, P., et al. (1997). London–East Anglia randomised controlled trial of cognitive-behavioural therapy for psychosis. II: Predictors of outcome. *British Journal of Psychiatry, 171*, 420–426.

Garety, P. A. & Hemsley, D. R. (1987). Characteristics of delusional experience. *European Archives of Psychiatry and Neurology 987*, 236(5), 294–298.

Green, C. E., Freeman, D., Kuipers, E., Bebbington, P., Fowler, D., Dunn, G., et al. (2008). Measuring ideas of persecution and social reference: The Green et al. Paranoid Thought Scales (GPTS). *Psychological Medicine, 38*(1), 101–111.

Gumley, A. I., Gillan, K., Morrison, A. P., & Schwannauer, M. (2011). The development and validation of the Beliefs About Paranoia Scale (Short Form). *Behavioural and Cognitive Psychotherapy, 39*(1), 35–53.

Haddock, G., Eisner, E., Davies, G., Coupe, N., & Barrowclough, C. (2013). Psychotic symptoms, self-harm and violence in individuals with schizophrenia and substance misuse problems. *Schizophrenia Research, 151*(1/3), 215–220.

Haddock, G., McCarron, J., Tarrier, N., & Faragher, E.B. (1999). Scales to measure dimensions of hallucinations and delusions: The psychotic symptom rating scales (PSYRATS). *Psychological Medicine, 29*, 879–889.

Janssen, I., Hanssen, M., Bak, M., Bijl, R.V., de Graaf, R., Vollebergh, W., et al. (2003). Discrimination and delusional ideation. *British Journal of Psychiatry, 182*, 71–76.

Kay, S. R., Opler, L. A., & Fiszbein, A. (2000). *The Positive and Negative Syndrome Scale (PANSS) manual.* Toronto, ON: Multi-Health Systems.

Kline, E., Wilson, C., Ereshefsky, S., Denenny, D., Thompson, E., Pitts, S.C., et al. (2012). Psychosis risk screening in youth: A validation study of three self-report measures of attenuated psychosis symptoms. *Schizophrenia Research, 141* (1), 72–77.

Knowles, R., McCarthy-Jones, S., & Rowse, G. (2011). Grandiose delusions: A review and theoretical integration of cognitive and affective perspectives. *Clinical Psychology Review, 31*(4), 684–696.

Komuravelli, A., Poole, R., & Higgo, R. (2011). Stability of the diagnosis of first-episode drug-induced psychosis. *Psychiatric Bulletin, 35*, 224–227.

Lautenschlager, N. T. & Förstl, H. (2001). Organic psychosis: Insight into the biology of psychosis. *Current Psychiatry Reports, 3*(4), 319–325.

Lincoln, T. M. (2007). Relevant dimensions of delusions: Continuing the continuum versus category debate. *Schizophrenia Research, 93*, 211–220.

Linscott, R. J., & van Os, J. (2013). An updated and conservative systematic review and meta-analysis of epidemiological evidence on psychotic experiences in children and adults: On the pathway from proneness to persistence to dimensional expression across mental disorders. *Psychological Medicine, 43*(6), 1133–1149.

Maher, B. (1988). Anomalous experience and delusional thinking: The logic of explanations. In T. F. Oltmanns & B. A. Maher (Eds.), *Delusional beliefs*. Chichester, UK: Wiley.

Mason, O., Claridge, G., & Jackson, M. (1995). New scales for the assessment of schizotypy. *Personality and Individual Differences, 18*, 7–13.

Mason, O., Linney, Y., & Claridge, G. (2005). Short scales for measuring schizotypy. *Schizophrenia Research, 78*(2/3), 293–296.

Mason, O., & Claridge, G. (2006). The Oxford-Liverpool Inventory of Feelings and Experiences (O-LIFE): Further description and extended norms. *Schizophrenia Research, 82*(2/3), 203–211.

McKay, R., Langdon, R., & Coltheart, M. (2006). The persecutory ideation questionnaire. *Journal of Nervous and Mental Disease, 194*(8), 628–631.

Mohr, S., Borras, L., Betrisey, C., Pierre-Yves, B., Gilliéron, C., & Huguelet, P. (2010). Delusions with religious content in patients with psychosis: How they interact with spiritual coping. *Psychiatry, 73*(2), 158–72.

Moritz, S., Vitzthum, F., Randjbar, S., Veckenstedt, R., & Woodward, T. S. (2010). Detecting and defusing cognitive traps: Metacognitive intervention in schizophrenia. *Current Opinion in Psychiatry, 23*(6), 561–569.

Morrison, A.P., Gumley, A.I., Schwannauer, M., Campbell, M., Gleeson, A., Griffin, E., et al. (2005). The Beliefs about Paranoia Scale: Preliminary validation of a metacognitive approach to conceptualising paranoia. *Behavioural & Cognitive Psychotherapy, 33*, 153–164.

Munro, A. (1999) *Delusional disorder: Paranoia and related illnesses*. Cambridge, UK: Cambridge University Press.

Pechey, R., & Halligan, P. (2012). Prevalence and correlates of anomalous experiences in a large non-clinical sample. *Psychology and Psychotherapy: Theory, Research and Practice, 85*(2), 150–162.

Perälä, J., Suvisaari, J., Saarni, S. I., Kuoppasalmi, K., Isometsä, E., et al. (2007). Lifetime prevalence of psychotic and bipolar I disorders in a general population. *Archives of General Psychiatry, 64*(1), 19–28.

Peters, E., Day, S., McKenna, J., & Orbach, G. (1999). The incidence of delusional ideation in religious and psychotic populations. *British Journal of Clinical Psychology*, 38, 83–96.

Peters, E., Joseph, S., Day, S., & Garety, P. (2004). Measuring delusional ideation: The 21-item Peters et al. Delusions Inventory (PDI). *Schizophrenia Bulletin, 30*(4), 1005–1022.

Peters, E., Lataster, T., Greenwood, K., Kuipers, E., Scott, J., Williams, S., et al. (2012). Appraisals, psychotic symptoms and affect in daily life. *Psychological Medicine, 42*(5), 1013–1023.

Peters, E. R. (2010). Assessment in psychosis. In R. Hagen, D. Turkington, B. Torkil & R. W. Graw (Chapter 4), *CBT for psychosis: A symptom-based approach*. New York, NY: ISPS Routledge.

Peters, E. R., Joseph, S. A., & Garety, P. A. (1999). Measurement of delusional ideation in the normal population: Introducing the PDI (Peters et al. Delusions Inventory). *Schizophrenia Bulletin, 25*(3), 553–576.

Preti, A., Cella, M., Raballo, A., & Vellante, M. (2012). Psychotic-like or unusual subjective experiences? The role of certainty in the appraisal of the subclinical psychotic phenotype. *Psychiatry Research, 200*(2/3), 669–673.

Queirazza, F., Semple, D. M., & Lawrie, S. M. (2013). Transition to schizophrenia in acute and transient psychotic disorders. *British Journal of Psychiatry*. (First published online December 19, 2013)

Raine, A. (1991). The SPQ: A scale for the assessment of schizotypal personality based on DSM-III-R criteria. *Schizophrenia Bulletin, 17*(4), 555–564.

Raune, D., Bebbington, P., Dunn, G., & Kuipers, E. (2006). Event attributes and the content of psychotic experiences in first-episode psychosis. *Psychological Medicine, 36*(2), 221–230.

Saha, S., Scott, J. G., Varghese, D., & McGrath, J. J. (2011). The association between general psychological distress and delusional-like experiences: A large population-based study. *Schizophrenia Research, 127*(1/3), 246–251.

Saha, S., Scott, J., Varghese, D., & McGrath, J. (2012). Social support and delusional-like experiences: A nationwide population-based study. *Epidemiology and Psychiatric Sciences, 21*(2), 203–212.

Scott, J., Chant, D., Andrews, G., Martin, G., & McGrath, J. (2007). Association between trauma exposure and delusional experiences in a large community-based sample. *British Journal of Psychiatry, 190*, 339–343.

Schwitzgebel, E. (2014). Belief. In E. N. Zalta (Ed.), *The Stanford encyclopedia of philosophy* (Spring 2014 ed.). Available from http://plato.stanford.edu/archives/spr2014/entries/belief/

Sedler, M. J. (1995). Understanding delusions. *Psychiatric Clinics of North America, 8*(2), 251–262.

Segal, J. H. (1989). Erotomania revisited: From Kraepelin to DSM-III-R. *American Journal of Psychiatry, 146*(10), 1261–1266.

Shinn, A. K., Heckers, S., & Öngür, D. (2013). The special treatment of first rank auditory hallucinations and bizarre delusions in the diagnosis of schizophrenia. *Schizophrenia Research, 146*(1/3), 17–21.

Sims, A. (2003). *Symptoms in the mind: An introduction to descriptive psychopathology* (3rd ed.). Edinburgh, UK: Elsevier Science.

Snaith, P. (1992). Body image disorders. *Journal of Psychotherapy and Psychosomatics, 58*(3/4), 119–124.

Startup, M., & Startup, S. (2005). On two kinds of delusion of reference. *Psychiatry Research, 137*(1/2), 87–92.

Varghese, D., Saha, S., Scott, J. D., Chan, R. C., & McGrath, J. J. (2011). The association between family history of mental disorder and delusional-like experiences: A general population study. *American Journal of Medical Genetics, Part B, 156B*(4), 478–483.

Ullrich, S., Keers, R., & Coid, J. W. (2013). Delusions, anger, and serious violence: New findings from the MacArthur Violence Risk Assessment Study. *Schizophrenia Bulletin*. (First published online September 18, 2013)

Waters, F. A., & Badcock, J. C. (2010). First-rank symptoms in schizophrenia: Re-examining mechanisms of self-recognition. *Schizophrenia Bulletin, 36*(3), 510–517.

Wing, J. K., Cooper, J. E., & Sartorius, N. (1974). *Measurement and classification of psychiatric symptoms* (9th ed.). Cambridge, UK: Cambridge University Press.

15

LANGUAGE DISORDER

Mujeeb Uddin Shad

Introduction

Language is the method of human communication, consisting of the use of words in a structured and conventional way. The ability to communicate effectively through spoken and written language is compromised in psychotic disorders such as schizophrenia, and this impairment contributes to frequently observed deficits in social and vocational functioning (Hoffman & Kuper, 1997; Norman et al., 1999). This underscores the significance of, and the need to assess, language dysfunction during psychosis. Before a discussion of the assessment of language disorder can commence, it is important to review perspectives on both thought and language deficits observed during psychosis as well as the cognitive and neurobiological correlates of language/thought dysfunction.

Thought Disorder

Deficits in expression of thought have been documented for decades. While Kraepelin (1919) coined the term *dementia praecox* to describe cognitive deficits in schizophrenia, Bleuler (1911) included loosening of association as one of the fundamental symptoms of schizophrenia. Thought disorder has been difficult to define because speech provides the only objective measure to assess language dysfunction as well as thought disorder. Thus, a patient may have a normal thought process but may have difficulty in language expression as would be expected in a case of primary language dysfunction. Another patient may have a thought disorder but does not want to talk despite having an intact primary language function. Historically, thought disorder in schizophrenia was attributed to regressive behavior (Gardner, 1931) and a lack of conceptual boundaries and deficits in causal links

(Cameron, 1944). However recent language research in schizophrenia provides some insight into thought disorder encountered in this illness.

A review of language studies in schizophrenia (Covington et al., 2005) has described at least two kinds of impairment: thought disorder and schizophasia. In this review, thought disorder is described as a failure at the discourse level and appears to be primarily a disruption of executive function and pragmatics, perhaps with impairment of the syntax-semantics interface, while schizophasia is stated to involve disruption primarily at the lexical level comprising various dysphasia-like impairments, such as clanging, neologism and unintelligible utterances. In a similar view, some studies have classified language dysfunction on the basis of microlinguistic and macrolingusitic abilities in individuals with schizophrenia (Marini et al., 2008). Microlinguistic abilities refer to lexical and morpho-syntactic skills, whereas macrolinguistic abilities relate to pragmatic and discourse level processing, which appear similar to the description of thought disorder by Covington et al. (2005). The study reported macrolinguistic abilities to be more significantly impaired in schizophrenia individuals than microlinguistic abilities (Marini et al., 2008). Poor performance on some semantic tasks (i.e., Peabody Picture Vocabulary Test, the Speed and Capacity of Language-Processing Test and the Boston Naming Test) is particularly impaired in individuals with thought disorder (Goldberg et al., 1998).

A thought disorder can present itself in the content of the speech (i.e., thought content, which is simply what the patient is talking about) or the process of speech (i.e., thought process, which is how a patient expresses his or her ideas, sentences and words together; Taylor, 1981). However, disorders of thought content and process are not mutually exclusive and sometimes it is difficult to distinguish between the two (Berenbaum & Barch, 1995). Preoccupation with a disorder of thought content (i.e., delusion) may be expressed as a disorder of thought process, such as perseveration or circumstantiality and vice versa. Although early researchers reported thought disorder only in schizophrenia individuals (Bleuler, 1911), with time it has become clear that thought disorder can occur in individuals with mood disorders, especially during the manic phase of a bipolar affective disorder (Andreasen, 1979a; Johnston & Holtzman, 1979; Solovay et al., 1987). However, thought disorder in schizophrenia as compared to manic individuals is often more severe, with an increased use of peculiar words and phrases (Solovay et al., 1987). Additionally, there may be noticeable differences between thought content of individuals with schizophrenia and bipolar disorder. Delusional beliefs in bipolar disorder are more likely to have an element of grandiosity, while schizophrenia individuals' delusions are more likely to have persecutory connotations (Solovay et al., 1987). Of note, some symptoms of thought disorder, such as derailment, loss of goal-directed activity, poverty of content of speech, tangentiality and illogicality were particularly more characteristic of schizophrenia than other symptoms such as neologism and thought blockade (Andreasen, 1979b).

In summary, thought disorder is a complex phenomenon, which varies within and across psychiatric diagnoses and which is not clearly understood. In the past, thought disorder was classified on a conceptual basis and only the individual's thinking was inferred. This approach was followed by an empirical approach of grouping phenomena constituting thought disorder based on frequency of their co-occurrence to enhance our understanding of thought disorder. More recently, a psycholinguistic approach has been utilized for further understanding of thought disorder and the complex relationship it has with language disorder.

Language and Speech Deficits in Schizophrenia

Language processing involves a multilevel and multi-component dynamic system (Caplan, 1992). The levels (sublexical, lexical, sentential and discourse) refer to processes of linguistic material of corresponding linguistic complexity, and the components (phonology, syntax and semantics) represent processes of human speech sounds, structure or order of words and sentences, and meaning of language, respectively.

Individuals with schizophrenia often display language anomalies in simple words (the lexical level), sentences (the sentential level), and discourse (the discourse level) levels of language (Kuperberg, 2010). At the lexical level, Chaika (1974) reported pronounceable non-words and confusion of antonyms in schizophrenia along with impairment of clear access to the words as suggested by observation of clang association, word approximation and neologism in schizophrenia individuals. At the sentential level, incompatibilities between subject and verb, failures to pronominalize or delete, and errors in tense and article choice have been documented (Chaika, 1974). Other anomalies at sentential level include lack of discourse markers for sequencing or transitions (e.g., finally, thus), announcing contradiction (e.g., but, however) and similarity (e.g., and; Chaika, 1974), grammatical deviance (Hoffman & Sledge, 1988), incoherent discourse (Hoffman et al., 1986), and failure of reference in individuals with schizophrenia (Wykes & Leff, 1982) as well as their unaffected siblings and parents (Docherty et al., 2004). Hoffman et al. (1985) reported misrepresentation of the meanings of the sentences from a controlled set of input sentences in schizophrenia individuals. Finally, at the discourse level, many syntactic peculiarities have been reported such as more use of passive voice, perfect tense and state verbs but less use of achievement verbs and qualifying subordinators (Pylyshyn, 1970). In addition, the association between sentences in schizophrenia individuals was shown to be more dependent on phonetic and semantic features rather than the topic (Chaika, 1974).

Language deficits in schizophrenia have also been observed in other aspects of language such as deficit in rate, rhythm and tone of speech, flat intonation or unusual voice quality (phonetics). Schizophrenia individuals have also been reported to have reduction in the syntactic complexity and syntactical deviance (syntax) (Morice & Ingram 1983; Shedlack et al., 1997).

Although language abnormalities in schizophrenia, as described above, have been documented across all language levels and components, language research in schizophrenia has largely focused at one level or one component at a time. In addition, levels and components are inter-connected and inter-dependent. Therefore, it is not only necessary to understand language disorders in schizophrenia at specific levels and components, but also the dynamics and interactions across levels and components. A recent study has reported abnormal dynamics between levels and components of language in schizophrenia (Stephane et al., 2014). Based on study findings, the authors have proposed a model for interface between various language levels and components. This model suggests reduced between level top-down (discourse to lexical level) flow of linguistic information as well as alteration of the relationship between phonology and semantics but not between syntax and semantics.

Language disorder has also been implicated in the pathogenesis of auditory hallucinations (AHs), a frequent symptom in schizophrenia (Stephane et al., 2001). Studies have shown activation of Wernicke's area to auditory hallucinations and this activation was considered to constitute the final common pathway for the hallucinatory experience (Stephane et al., 2000). Furthermore, another study showed that different individuals may have differential hearing experience of single words, sentences or conversation (Stephane et al., 2003), which probably indicates dysfunction at multiple levels of language processing in schizophrenia including language comprehension.

Language and Cognitive Processes

High-order cognitive functions are required to maintain effective human interaction through language. These include selective attention (Schwartz, 1982), working memory (Goldman-Rakic, 1994), access to internal representation of context (Cohen & Servan-Schreiber, 1992), use of strategy (Iddon et al., 1998), verbal memory (Stevens et al., 2000) and executive functions (Just & Carpenter, 1992; Shallice, 1988). The majority of these cognitive functions are compromised in schizophrenia individuals and have been linked to specific speech deficits. For example, severity of disorganized speech in schizophrenia has been correlated with distractibility (Docherty & Gordinier, 1999), deficits in short-term verbal memory (Nestor et al., 1998), selective attention (Barch et al., 1999), sustained attention (Pandurangi et al., 1994, Strauss et al., 1993), executive functions (Nestor et al., 1998) and lower-level information processing such as prepulse inhibition (Dawson et al., 2000).

More specifically, some studies have linked various levels and components of language processing with specific cognitive functions, which adds further complexity to this subject. For example, a deficit in rehearsal component of working memory might compromise encoding of semantic information (Brebion et al., 1997). Impaired working memory in schizophrenia may also explain decreased contextual recall, resulting in increased repetition in speech, a feature associated with formal thought disorder in schizophrenia (Manschreck et al., 1991). The association between performance on working memory and language tasks in schizophrenia is strongest at sentential and discourse levels but not the lexical level (Barch et al., 1999). Studies also showed that verbal working memory deficits are correlated with language comprehension deficits (Condray et al., 1996). In addition, disturbances in referential communication were associated with distractibility (Docherty & Gordinier, 1999; Harvey et al., 1986), working memory and attention (Docherty et al., 1996) and poor performance on tasks of immediate auditory memory (Docherty & Gordinier, 1999). Deficits in working memory and attention have also been associated with syntactic errors in a study of written language in schizophrenia subjects (Thomas et al., 1993). Furthermore, studies of semantic memory in schizophrenia that were based on a neuropsychological model that distinguishes between storage and access/retrieval deficits have shown that the problem appears to be one of access and/or retrieval and of using semantic knowledge effectively (Shallice, 1988). These observations suggest that impaired memory and disordered speech may have a common pathogenesis.

While informative, it is important to mention that the results from these studies do not clearly define the complex relationships between language dysfunction and specific cognitive functions. Reasons for lack of clarity include non-specific and broad definitions of some of the cognitive functions implicated, such as working memory and attention. Therefore, current efforts are being focused to classify cognitive systems conceptually and empirically in relation to language system, such as studies utilizing tasks for working memory that include linguistic domains with different levels of behavioral as well as neurobiological assessments.

In this context, a psycholinguistic approach is being utilized to investigate language processing at different levels (i.e., lexical, sentential and discourse; Kuperberg, 2010). This approach provides a comprehensive analysis of language dysfunction in individuals with thought disorder and allows assessment of interactions between different types of cognitive processes that are involved in language processing such as nonverbal semantic processing, attention, and working memory. For example, a recent study investigated individuals' linguistic performance on tests designed to explore sublexical, lexical, sentence and discourse processing (Stephane et al., 2007). This study investigated processes specific to each level of language separately, and allowed study of linguistic operations without being affected by symptomatology as well as the examination of the relationship between linguistic operations and symptoms. The study results showed that schizophrenia individuals performed as well as healthy control subjects in recognizing correct linguistic stimuli but were impaired in recognizing incorrect linguistic stimuli and exhibited a bias to consider incorrect stimuli as correct (Stephane et al., 2007). The authors concluded that this lack of awareness of incorrect linguistic information would prevent individuals from correcting their abnormal speech and may provide one of the explanations for abnormal speech in schizophrenia.

Neurobiology of Language Dysfunction in Schizophrenia

Early neuroscientists discovered that two areas in the brain play a crucial role in language processing; Wernicke's and Broca's cortex (Wernicke, 1995). People with a lesion in Wernicke's area develop receptive aphasia in which there is a major impairment of language comprehension but the speech retains normal speech rhythm and a relatively normal sentence structure (Saygin et al., 2003). While lesions in Broca's area result in expressive aphasia meaning that they cannot speak despite knowing what they want to say and understanding what is being said to them (Poeppel et al., 2008). These lesions in Broca's area may also be associated with problems with articulation, word-finding, word repetition and producing and comprehending complex grammatical sentences, both verbal and written. Those with expressive aphasia also exhibit non-grammatical speech and are unable to use syntactic information to determine the meaning of sentences. Development of non-invasive techniques, including functional magnetic resonance imaging (fMRI) and electrophysiology such as event-related potential (ERP) has facilitated investigation of language processing in human subjects (Phillips & Kuniyoshi, 2005) and have shown a neural network that extends beyond Broca's and Wernicke's areas.

Neuroanatomical studies have reported small reductions in the volume of several regions of interest, particularly within the temporal and prefrontal cortices containing Wernicke's and Broca's area, respectively in individuals with schizophrenia (Shenton et al., 2001). One study suggested that, within a group of schizophrenic individuals, the degree of atrophy within the left temporal cortex was correlated with the severity of thought disorder (Shenton et al., 1992). It is therefore possible that subtle temporal and frontal gray matter atrophy may contribute to some of the abnormalities in language function discussed in this chapter. Functional MRI studies have provided additional insights and have shown that language processing is not simply localized to the frontal and temporal regions but involves perturbations of brain activity in neural networks comprising multiple cortical regions, such as anterior cingulate and parietal and subcortical structures, such as the cerebellum and thalamus (Kuperberg & Heckers, 2000). However, most functional neuroimaging studies in schizophrenia that have used linguistic stimuli have been at the level of individual words rather than whole sentences or discourse. Studies that have used cognitive measures, such as verbal fluency (Frith et al., 1995) and semantic categorization (Curtis et al., 1998) have reported abnormal patterns of activity within frontal and temporal regions. Some of the studies have also reported greater activity in the parietal cortex of schizophrenia individuals was found than controls in response to covert word production (Curtis et al., 1998) as well as learning and recalling word lists (Fletcher et al., 1998). While increased activation of the inferior temporal cortex and/or fusiform cortex has also been reported in schizophrenia individuals in response to cued stem recall of semantically encoded words (Heckers et al., 1998), the recognition of novel words (Crespo-Facorro et al., 2001), the completion of sentences (Kircher et al., 2001) and during speech production (McGuire et al., 1998; Kircher et al., 2001).

Event-related potentials (ERPs) are recordings of brain electrical activity to provide a measure of neurophysiological events associated with a particular stimulus of interest in a cognitive task. In this context, one of the most consistent findings in schizophrenia is a reduction in the amplitude of the P300, which represents the process of updating of contextual information within memory (Donchin & Coles, 1988). However, this finding is not specific for schizophrenia and not all studies have reported an increased latency of the P300 in schizophrenia (Ford, 1999). Another common electrophysiological finding in schizophrenia is prolonged N400 latency and abnormal N400 amplitude in response to target words (Niznikiewicz et al., 1997) and unprimed words in word-pair semantic priming paradigms (Holcomb, 1988). Another study showed N400 congruence to target words preceded by indirectly related words was reported only in schizophrenia individuals but not in healthy participants (Spitzer et al., 1997). Other studies have also reported an abnormally reduced N400 effect in both sentence (Salisbury et al., 2000) and word-pair paradigms (Condray et al., 1999). However, not all studies have shown a smaller N400 amplitude in response to unprimed than primed words in semantic priming word-pair paradigms (Koyama et al., 1994; Olichney et al., 1997) and to words preceded by incongruent rather than congruent contexts in sentence paradigms (Nestor et al., 1997; Niznikiewicz et al., 1997; Sitnikova et al., 2002). Heterogeneity in patient samples used in these studies may explain contradictory findings.

Assessment of Language/Thought Disorder

There are many formal scales for the assessment of speech and thoughts abnormalities in schizophrenia and other psychotic illnesses, of which the most common are: Scale for Assessment of Thought, Language and Communication (TLC; Andreasen, 1979b), Thought Disorder Index (TDI; Johnston & Holtzman, 1979; Solovay et al., 1986), and Thought and Language Index (TLI; Liddle et al., 2002). Given the inter-dependence between language and other cognitive functions, it is important to evaluate the cognitive functions most closely associated with language such as working memory and attention. Therefore, the Brief Assessment of Cognition in Schizophrenia (BACS; Keefe et al., 2004) will also be reviewed. This cognitive battery will provide a cognitive basis of language processing and will improve assessment of language dysfunction observed during psychosis.

Scale for Assessment of Thought, Language and Communication (TLC; Andreasen, 1979a) is derived from the Scale to Assess Negative Symptoms (SANS; Andreasen, 1983) and Scale to Assess Positive Symptoms (SAPS; Andreasen, 1984). This instrument allows assessment of formal thought disorder through the examination of verbal output with respect to 20 symptom items of schizophrenia. The scale has been shown to provide diagnostic specificity within and across psychotic disorders. Severity of disorganized speech differentiated schizophrenia and mania from schizoaffective disorder (Andreasen et al., 1986), while associative loosening and abnormalities of thought, such as neologism and blocking, have little diagnostic value (Andreasen, 1979a). Overall, the TLC scale offers a comprehensive measure with consistency from one study to another and stable rates of thought disorder across different samples with cross validation (Andreasen et al., 1986; Harvey et al., 1997; Mazumdar et al., 1995).

Thought Disorder Index (TDI; Johnston & Holtzman, 1979; Solovay et al., 1986) assesses, classifies and measures instances of formal thought disorder. The TDI has good psychometric properties and it provides a highly sensitive tool to assess subtle anomalies in thought disorder (Straube & Oades, 1992), including those observed in a high risk population (Goldstein, 1985).

Thought and Language Index (TLI; Liddle et al., 2002) offers one of the quickest assessment tools to assess formal thought disorder based on standard stimuli. In addition, the TLI has the ability to detect subtle abnormalities of thought disorder making it a reliable and sensitive measure for capturing attenuated to severe speech disorders in schizophrenia as well as minor and subclinical speech changes in healthy and high risk populations.

The Brief Assessment of Cognition in Schizophrenia (BACS; Keefe et al., 2004) is a measure to assess cognitive function in schizophrenia. Although primarily developed for clinical trials, BACS provides an effective tool to examine the relationship between language dysfunction and cognition in schizophrenia. The scale offers a standardized measure to assess cognitive functions that are most commonly compromised in psychotic disorders and are frequently associated with language dysfunction in schizophrenia. These cognitive functions and their respective measures include verbal memory, working memory, motor speed, verbal fluency, attention, speed of information processing and executive function. The BACS is a reliable measure to assess cognitive function in schizophrenia individuals, which can be utilized to assess the relationship between language dysfunction and cognitive function in this patient population.

Conclusions

In summary, schizophrenia is a complex disorder where language and related brain and cognitive dysfunction are encountered. Studies have identified abnormalities in both language output and comprehension in schizophrenia individuals. These abnormalities have been described at multiple levels of language processing, including lexical level, sentential level and discourse level and at multiple components of language processing, including phonetic, semantic and syntactic. The neurocognitive basis of language dysfunction in schizophrenia has been investigated using structural and functional neuroimaging as well as electrophysiological techniques. In general, these techniques have given complementary information. ERP studies suggest neurophysiological deficits in using semantic context, while neuroimaging studies suggest widespread structural and functional neuroanatomical abnormalities, particularly in, but not limited to, the temporal and frontal cortices.

References

Andreasen, N. C. (1979a). Thought, language and communication disorders: II. Diagnostic significance. *Archives of General Psychiatry, 36*, 1325–1330.

Andreasen, N. C. (1979b). Thought, language and communication disorders: II. Clinical assessment, definition of terms, and evaluation of their reliability. *Archives of General Psychiatry, 36*, 1315–1321.

Andreasen, N. C. (1983). *Scale for the assessment of negative symptoms*. Iowa City: University of Iowa Press.

Andreasen, N. C. (1984). *Scale for the assessment of positive symptoms*. Iowa City: University of Iowa Press.

Andreasen, N. C. (1986). Scale for the assessment of thought, language, and communication (TLC). *Schizophrenia Bulletin, 12*, 473–482.

Andreasen, N. C., & Grove, W. M. (1986). Thought, language, and communication in schizophrenia: Diagnosis and prognosis. *Schizophrenia Bulletin, 12*(3), 348–359.

Barch, D. M, Carter, C. S, Perlstein, W., Baird, J., Cohen. J. D., & Schooler, N. (1999). Increased Stroop facilitation effects in schizophrenia are not due to increased automatic spreading activation. *Schizophrenia Research, 39*, 51–64.

Berenbaum, H., & Barch, D. (1995). The categorization of thought disorder. *Journal Psycholinguist Research, 24*, 349–376.

Bleuler, E. (1911). *Dementia praecox: Or the group of schizophrenias*. New York, NY: International University Press.

Brebion, G., Amador, X., Smith, M. J., & Gorman, J. M. (1997). Mechanisms underlying memory impairment in schizophrenia. *Psychological Medicine, 27*, 383–393.

Cameron, N. (1944). Experimental analysis of schizophrenic thinking. In J. Kasanin (Ed.), *Language and thought in schizophrenia*. Berkeley: University of California Press.

Caplan, D. (1992). Language structure, processing and disorders. Cambridge, MA: MIT Press.

Chaika, E. (1974). A linguist looks at schizophrenic language. *Brain and Language, 1*, 257–276.

Cohen, J. D., & Servan-Schreiber, D. (1992). Context, cortex, and dopamine: A connectionist approach to behaviour and biology in schizophrenia. *Psychological Review, 99*, 45–77.

Coleman, M. J., Carpenter, J. T., Waternaux, C., Levy, D. L., Shenton, M. E., Perry, J., et al. (1993). The thought disorder index: A reliability study. *Psychological Assessment: A Journal of Consulting and Clinical Psychology, 3*(3), 336–342.

Condray, R., Steinhauer, S. R., van Kammen, D. P., & Kasparek, A. (1996). Working memory capacity predicts language comprehension in schizophrenic individuals. *Schizophrenia Research*, 20, 1–13.

Condray, R., Steinhauer, S. R., Cohen, J. D., van Kammen, D. P., & Kasparek, A. (1999). Modulation of language processing in schizophrenia: Effects of context and haloperidol on the event-related potential. *Biological Psychiatry, 45*, 1336–1355.

Covington, M. A., He, C., Brown, C., Naci, L., McClain, J. T., Fjordbak, B. S., et al. (2005). Schizophrenia and the structure of language: The linguist's view. *Schizophrenia Research, 77*(1), 85–98.

Crespo-Facorro, B., Wiser, A. K., Andreasen, N.C., O'Leary, D.S., Watkins, G. L., et al. (2001). Neural basis of novel and well-learned recognition memory in schizophrenia: A positron emission tomography study. *Human Brain Mapping, 12*, 219–231.

Curtis, V. A., Bullmore, E. T, Morris., R. G., Brammer, M. J., Williams, S. C., Simmons, A., et al. (1998). Attenuated frontal activation in schizophrenia may be task dependent. *Schizophrenia Research, 37*, 35–44.

Dawson, M. E., Schell, A. M., Hazlett, E. A., Nuechterlein, K. H., & Filion, D. L. (2000). On the clinical and cognitive meaning of impaired sensorimotor gating in schizophrenia. *Psychiatry Research, 96*, 187–197.

Docherty, N. M., Gordinier, S. W., Hall, M. J., & Dombrowski, M. E. (2004). Referential communication disturbances in the speech of nonschizophrenic siblings of schizophrenia individuals. *Journal of Abnormal Psychology, 113*, 399–405.

Docherty, N. M., & Gordinier, S. W. (1999). Immediate memory, attention and communication disturbances in schizophrenia individuals and their relatives. *Psychological Medicine, 29*, 189–197.

Docherty, N. M., Hawkins, K. A., Hoffman, R. E., Quinlan, D. M., Rakfeldt, J., & Sledge, W. H. (1996). Working memory, attention, and communication disturbances in schizophrenia. *Journal of Abnormal Psychology, 105*, 212–219.

Donchin, E., & Coles, M. G. H. (1988). Is the P300 component a manifestation of context updating? *Behavior and Brain Sciences, 11*, 355–372.

Fletcher, P. C., McKenna, P. J., Frith, C. D., Grasby, P. M., Friston, K. J., & Dolan, R. J. (1998). Brain activations in schizophrenia during a graded memory task studied with functional neuroimaging. *Archives of General Psychiatry, 55*, 1001–1008.

Ford, J. M. (1999). Schizophrenia: The broken P300 and beyond. *Psychophysiology, 36*, 667–682.

Frith, C. D., Friston, K. J., Herold, S., Silbersweig, D., Fletcher, P., Cahill, C., et al. (1995). Regional brain activity in chronic schizophrenic individuals during the performance of a verbal fluency task. *British Journal of Psychiatry, 167*(3), 343–349.

Gardner, G. E. (1931). The measurement of psychotic age: A preliminary report. *American Journal of Psychiatry, 10*, 963–975.

Goldberg, T. E., Aloia, M. S., Gourovitch, M. L., Missar, D., Pickar, D., & Weinberger, D. (1998). Cognitive substrates of thought disorder, I: The semantic system. *American Journal of Psychiatry, 155*, 1671–1676.

Goldman-Rakic, P. S. (1994). Working memory dysfunction in schizophrenia. *Journal of Neuropsychiatry and Clinical Neurosciences, 6*, 348–357.

Goldstein, M. J. (1985). Family factors that antedate the onset of schizophrenia and related disorders: The results of a fifteen year prospective longitudinal study. *Acta Psychiatrica Scandinavica* (Suppl. 319), 7–18.

Green, M. F., Nuechterlein, K. H., Gold, J. M., Barch, D. M., Cohen, J., Essock, S., et al. (2004). Approaching a consensus cognitive battery for clinical trials in schizophrenia: The NIMH-MATRICS conference to select cognitive domains and test criteria [Review]. *Biological Psychiatry, 56*(5), 301–307.

Hain, C., Maier, W., Hoechst-Janneck, S., & Franke, P. (1995). Subclinical thought disorder in first-degree relatives of schizophrenic individuals: Results from a matched-pairs study with the Thought Disorder Index. *Acta Psychiatrica Scandinavica, 92*(4), 305–309.

Harvey, P. D., Earle-Boyer, E. A., & Levinson, J. C. (1986). Distractibility and discourse failure: Their association in mania and schizophrenia. *Journal of Nervous and Mental Disease,* 174, 274–279.

Harvey, P. D., Lombardi, J., Leibman, M., Parrella, M., White, L., Powchik, P., et al. (1997). Age-related differences in formal thought disorder in chronically hospitalized schizophrenic individuals: A cross-sectional study across nine decades. *American Journal of Psychiatry, 154*, 205–210.

Heckers, S., Rauch, S. L., Goff, D., Savage, C. R., Schacter, D. L., Fischman, A. J., et al. (1998). Impaired recruitment of the hippocampus during conscious recollection in schizophrenia. *Nature Neuroscience, 1*, 318–323.

Hoffman, R. E., Hogben, G. L., Smith, H., & Calhoun, W. F. (1985). Message disruptions during syntactic processing in schizophrenia. *Journal of Communication Disorders, 18*, 183–202.

Hoffman, R. E., & Sledge, W. (1988). An analysis of grammatical deviance occurring in spontaneous schizophrenic speech. *Journal of Neurolinguistics, 3*, 89–101.

Hoffman, R. E., Stopek, S., & Andreasen, N. C. (1986). A comparative study of manic vs. schizophrenic speech disorganization. *Archives of General Psychiatry, 43*, 831–8.

Hoffmann, H., & Kuper, Z. (1997). Relationships between social competence, psychopathology and work performance and their predictive value for vocational rehabilitation of schizophrenic individuals. *Schizophrenia Research, 23*, 69–79.

Holcomb, P. J. (1988). Automatic and attentional processing: An event-related brain potential analysis of semantic priming. *Brain and Language, 35*, 66–85.

Holzman, P. S., Shenton, M. E., & Solovay, M. R., (1986). Quality of thought disorder in differential diagnosis. *Schizophrenia Bulletin, 12*(3), 360–372.

Horn, H., Jann, K., Federspiel, A., Walther, S., Wiest, R., Müller, T., et al. (2012). Semantic network disconnection in formal thought disorder. *Neuropsychobiology, 66*, 14–23.

Iddon, J. L., McKenna, P. J., Sahakian, B. J., & Robbins, T. W. (1998). Impaired generation and use of strategy in schizophrenia: Evidence from visuospatial and verbal tasks. *Psychological Medicine, 28*, 1049–1062.

Johnston, M. H., & Holtzman, P. S. (1979). *Assessing schizophrenic thinking*. San Francisco, CA: Jossey-Bass.

Just, M. A., & Carpenter, P. A. (1992). A capacity theory of comprehension: Individual differences in working memory. *Psychological Review, 99*, 122–149.

Keefe, R. S., Goldberg, T. E., Harvey, P. D., Gold, J. M., Poe, M. P., & Coughenour, L. (2004). The Brief Assessment of Cognition in Schizophrenia: Reliability, sensitivity, and comparison with a standard neurocognitive battery. *Schizophrenia Research, 68*(2/3), 283–297.

Keefe, R. S., Poe, M., Walker, T. M., & Harvey, P. D. (2006). The relationship of the Brief Assessment of Cognition in Schizophrenia (BACS) to functional capacity and real-world functional outcome. *Journal of Clinical and Experimental Neuropsychology, 28*(2), 260–269.

Kircher, T. T., Bulimore, E. T., Brammer, M. J., Williams, S. C., Broome, M. R., Murray, R. M., et al. (2001). Differential activation of temporal cortex during sentence completion in schizophrenic individuals with and without formal thought disorder. *Schizophrenia Research, 50*(1/2), 27–40.

Kircher, T. T., Liddle, P. F., Brammer, M. J., Williams, S. C., Murray, R. M., & McGuire, P. K. (2001). Neural correlates of formal thought disorder in schizophrenia: Preliminary findings from a functional magnetic resonance imaging study. *Archives of General Psychiatry, 58*(8), 769–774.

Koyama, S., Hokama, H., Miyatani, M., Ogura, C., Nageishi, Y., & Shimokochi, M. (1994). ERPs in schizophrenic individuals during word recognition task and reaction times. *Electroencephalography Clinical Neurophysiology, 92*, 546–554.

Kraepelin, E. (1919). *Dementia praecox and paraphasia* (Trans. B. M. Barclay). Edinburgh, UK: Livingstone.

Kuperberg, G., & Heckers, S. (2000). Schizophrenia and cognitive function. *Current Opinion in Neurobiology, 10*, 205–210.

Kuperberg, G. R. (2010). Language in schizophrenia, Part 1: An introduction. *Linguistics and Language Compass, 4*(8), 576–589.

Liddle, P. F., Elton, T. C. N., Caissie, S. L., Anderson, C. M., Bates, D. J., Quested, D. J., et al. (2002). Thought and Language Index: An instrument for assessing thought and language in schizophrenia. *British Journal of Psychiatry, 181*, 326–330.

Manschreck, T. C., Maher, B. A., Rosenthal, E., & Berner, J. (1991). Reduced primacy and related features in schizophrenia. *Schizophrenia Research, 5*, 35–41.

Marini, A., Spoletini, I., Rubino, I. A., Ciuffa, M., Bria, P., Martinotti, G., et al. (2008). The language of schizophrenia: An analysis of micro and macrolinguistic abilities and their neuropsychological correlates. *Schizophrenia Research, 105*(1/3), 144–155.

Mazumdar, P. K., Chaturvedi, S. K., & Gopinath, P. S. (1995). A comparative study of thought disorder in acute and chronic schizophrenia. *Psychopathology, 28*, 185–189.

McGuire, P. K., Quested, D. J., Spence, S. A., Murray, R. M., Frith, C. D., & Liddle, P. F. (1998). Pathophysiology of 'positive' thought disorder in schizophrenia. *British Journal of Psychiatry, 173*, 231–235.

Metsänen, M., Wahlberg, K. E., Saarento, O., Hakko, H., Tarvainen, T., Koistinen, P., et al. (2005). Stability of Thought Disorder Index among high-risk and low-risk adoptees in the Finnish adoptive family study of schizophrenia. *European Psychiatry, 20*(1), 35–40.

Morice, R. D., & Ingram, J. C. (1983). Language complexity and age of onset of schizophrenia. *Psychiatry Research, 9*, 233–242.

Murray, H. A. (1943). *The Thematic Apperception Test manual.* Cambridge, MA: Harvard University Press.

Nestor, P. G., Kimble, M. O., O'Donnell, B. F., Smith, L., Niznikiewicz, M. A., Shenton, M. E, et al. (1997). Aberrant semantic activation in schizophrenia: A neurophysiological study. *American Journal of Psychiatry, 154*, 640–666.

Nestor, P. G., Shenton, M. E., Wible, C., Hokama, H., O'Donnell, B. F., Law, S., et al. (1998). A neuropsychological analysis of schizophrenic thought disorder. *Schizophrenia Research, 29*, 217–225.

Niznikiewicz, M. A., O'Donnell, B. F., Nestor, P. G., Smith, L., Law, S., Karapelou, M., et al. (1997). ERP assessment of visual and auditory language processing in schizophrenia. *Journal of Abnormal Psychology, 1*, 85–94.

Norman, R. M., Malla, A. K., Cortese, L., Cheng, S., Diaz, K., McIntosh, E., et al. (1999). Symptoms and cognition as predictors of community functioning: A prospective analysis. *American Journal of Psychiatry, 156*, 400–405.

Olichney, J. M., Iragui, V. J., Kutas, M., Nowacki, R., & Jeste, D.V. (1997). N400 abnormalities in late life schizophrenia and related psychoses. *Biological Psychiatry, 42*, 13–23.

Pandurangi, A. K., Sax, K.W., Pelonero A. L., & Goldberg, S. C. (1994). Sustained attention and positive formal thought disorder in schizophrenia. *Schizophrenia Research, 13*, 109–116.

Phillips, C., & Kuniyoshi L. S. (2005). Language and the brain. In *Yearbook of science and technology* (pp. 166–169). New York, NY: McGraw-Hill.

Poeppel, D., Idsardi, W. J., & van Wassenhove, V. (2008). Speech perception at the interface of neurobiology and linguistics. *Philosophical Transactions of the Royal Society, B, 363*(1493), 1071–1086.

Pylyshyn, Z.W. (1970). Clinical correlates of some syntactic features of individuals' speech. *Journal of Nervous and Mental Disease, 150*, 307–16.

Rorschach, H. (1942). *Psychodiagnostik.* Bern, Germany: Hans Huber.

Salisbury, D. F., O'Donnell, B. F., McCarley, R.W., Nestor, P. G., & Shenton, M. E. (2000). Event-related potentials elicited during a context-free homograph task in normal versus schizophrenic subjects. *Psychophysiology, 37*, 456–463.

Saygin, A. P, Dick, F., Wilson, S. M., Dronkers, N. F., & Bates, E. (2003). Neural resources for processing language and environmental sounds: Evidence from aphasia. *Brain: A Journal of Neurology, 126*, 928–945.

Schwartz, S. (1982). Is there a schizophrenic language? *Behavior and Brain Sciences, 5*, 579–626.

Shallice, T. (1988). *From neuropsychology to mental structure.* Cambridge, UK: Cambridge University Press.

Shedlack, K., Lee, G., Sakuma, M., Xie, S. H., Kushner, M., Pepple, J., et al. (1997). Language processing and memory in Ill and well siblings from multiple families affected with schizophrenia. *Schizophrenia Research, 25*, 43–52.

Shenton, M. E., Dickey, C. C., Frumin, M., & McCarley, R.W. (2001). A review of MRI findings in schizophrenia. *Schizophrenia Research, 49*(1/2), 1–52.

Shenton, M. E, Kikinis, R., Jolesz, F. A., Pollak, S. D., LeMay, M., Wible, C. G., et al. (1992). Abnormalities of the left temporal lobe and thought disorder in schizophrenia. *New England Journal of Medicine, 327*, 604–612.

Sitnikova, T., Salisbury, D. F., Kuperberg, G., & Holcomb, P. I. (2002). Electrophysiological insights into language processing in schizophrenia. *Psychophysiology, 39*(6), 851–860.

Solovay, M. R, Shenton, M. E, Gasperetti, C., Coleman, M., Kestnbaum, E., Carpenter, J. T., et al. (1986). Scoring manual for the Thought Disorder Index. *Schizophrenia Bulletin, 12*(3), 483–496.

Solovay, M. R., Shenton, M. E., & Holzman, P. S. (1987). Comparative studies of thought disorders. *Archives of General Psychiatry, 44*, 13–20.

Spitzer, M., Weisbrod, M., Winkler, S., & Maier, S. (1997). Event-related potentials in semantic speech processing by schizophrenic individuals. *Nervenarzt, 68*, 212–225.

Stephane, M., Barton, S., & Boutros, N. N. (2001). Auditory verbal hallucinations and dysfunction of the neural substrates of speech. *Schizophrenia Research, 50*, 61–78.

Stephane, M., Folstein, M., Matthew, E., & Hill, T. C. (2000). Imaging auditory verbal hallucinations during their occurrence. *Journal of Neuropsychiatry and Clinical Neurosciences, 12*, 286–287.

Stephane, M., Pellizer, G., Fletcher, C. R., & McClannahan, K. (2007). Empirical evaluation of language disorder in schizophrenia. *Journal of Psychiatry and Neuroscience, 32*(4), 250–258.

Stephane, M., Thuras, P., Nassrallah, H., & Georgopoulos, A. P. (2003). The internal structure of the phenomenology of auditory verbal hallucinations. *Schizophrenia Research, 61*, 185–193.

Stephane, M., Kuskowski, M., & Gundel, J. (2014). Abnormal dynamics of language in schizophrenia. *Psychiatry Research*. (First published online February 18, 2014)

Stevens, A. A., Donegan, N. H., Anderson, M., Goldman-Rakic, P. S., & Wexler, B. E. (2000). Verbal processing deficits in schizophrenia. *Journal of Abnormal Psychology, 109*, 461–471.

Straube, E. R., & Oades, R. D. (1992). *Schizophrenia: Empirical research and findings*. New York, NY: Academic Press.

Strauss, M. E., Buchanan, R.W., & Hale, J. (1993). Relations between attentional deficits and clinical symptoms in schizophrenic individuals. *Psychiatric Research, 47*, 205–213.

Taylor, M. A. (1981). *The neuropsychiatric mental state examination*. New York, NY: Spectrum Publications.

Thomas, P., Leudar, I., Newby, D., & Johnston, M. (1993). Syntactic processing in the written language output of first episode psychotics. *Journal of Communication Disorders, 26*, 209–230.

Wechsler, D. (1958). *The measurement and appraisal of adult intelligence* (4th ed.). Baltimore, MD: Williams & Wilkins.

Wernicke, K. (1995). The aphasia symptom-complex: A psychological study on an anatomical basis (1875). In P. Eling (Ed.), *Reader in the history of aphasia: From Franz Gall to Norman Geschwind* (pp. 69–89). Amsterdam, Netherlands: John Benjamins.

Wykes, T., & Leff, J. (1982). Disordered speech: Differences between manics and schizophrenics. *Brain and Language, 15*, 117–124.

16
INSIGHT

Adrian Preda, Keira James and Theo G. M. van Erp

> *You just said that I am insane. In that case my belief is not a delusion, but a correct idea. Therefore I have no delusion. Therefore I am not, after all, insane. It is only a delusion that I am insane, hence I have a delusion, hence I am insane, hence I am right, hence I am not insane. Isn't psychiatry a magnificent science? (Frigyes Karinthy, cited by David, 1990, pp. 166–167)*

Introduction

The lack of insight is one of the most common symptoms in schizophrenia, and may be associated with reduced quality of life (Wiffen et al., 2010), poor treatment adherence, increased number of hospitalizations, as well as poor social cognition (Quee et al., 2011; Weiler, Fleisher & McArthur-Campbell, 2000). Despite its clinical importance, it remains a complex and poorly understood phenomenon in psychosis and other clinical conditions in which it occurs. The current chapter focuses on insight in psychosis, although we start with definitions and description of insight deficits in different population groups.

The definition of insight varies depending on clinical setting and clinical condition. Within the area of psychoanalysis and cognitive psychology, the term refers to a sudden gain in understanding of a previously unclear relationship or problem—informally referred to as a "eureka" moment. More specifically, it refers to the restructuring of a problem that allows a rapid understanding of a solution that has been "unseen" prior to that moment in time (Gilhooly & Murphy, 2005). Similarly, from a psychodynamic perspective, insight is understood within the general framework of self-awareness (Osatuke et al., 2008), and is conceptualized as a sudden understanding of a previously unconscious process. Collectively these definitions of the term imply that insight is an all-or-nothing, one-dimensional mental state, where one does not have insight until one achieves it.

Within the literature of neurological disorders, insight has a slightly different meaning. A lack of insight, or anosognosia, is often used to convey a lack of awareness of disability or neurological deficits (Mullen et al., 1996). For example, with localized brain lesions to the parietal lobe, some patients deny having (and behave as though they do not have) difficulty moving affected body parts in the context of hemiparesis and sensory deficits. Similarly, with bilateral occipital lobe lesions causing cortical blindness, the term *visual anosognosia* refers to a phenomena where patients lack awareness of their blindness and behave as though they can see (Anton's syndrome; Baier & Karnath, 2005; David, Owen & Förstl, 1993). Anosognosia of cognitive deficits within neurodegenerative conditions such as Alzheimer's disease is also common (Stewart et al., 2010), although the clinical presentation is quite heterogenous and level of awareness of specific cognitive deficits can vary between patients (Stewart et al., 2010).

Poor insight (or denial that one is ill) is very common in, and considered an essential feature of, psychotic spectrum disorders (Amador et al., 1993; David, 1999). The concept of insight in relation to psychosis is traditionally expressed as a relational term: There is a lack of insight *into something* (David et al., 2012). In 1896, Kraeplin described how his patients with schizophrenia often seemed unaware of the fact that they suffered from a mental condition and were in need of care, but did not see this as a pathognomonic feature of schizophrenia (Kraepelin, 1920). Disease awareness and attribution deficits remained relatively un-appreciated until 1934 when Aubrey Lewis defined insight as "the correct attitude to morbid change in oneself, and moreover, the realization that the illness is mental" (Lewis, 1934, p. 496). As discussed by David (1999), Lewis (1934) was also the first psychiatrist to point to the similarities between the lack of insight displayed by psychotic patients and the lack of awareness of disability displayed by neurological patients with right-hemisphere damage: "Failure to appreciate blindness, deafness or paralysis . . . has its own name among neurologists." Nowadays, poor insight is described as "one of the most common symptoms" of, and "may be one of the best predictors of poor outcome" in schizophrenia according to the fifth edition of the *Diagnostic and Statistical Manual of Mental Disorders* (DSM-5; American Psychiatric Association, 2013). It lays the foundations for classical differential diagnosis separating primary psychotic from non-psychotic/neurotic disorders. Clinicians specializing in the treatment of severe psychosis have met their fair share of patients who claim that their condition is non-existent. As supportive evidence they may present information conveyed via special messages and hallucinated voices, or they may interpret their psychiatric commitment to a locked unit as proof that the government is indeed all powerful and clearly out to get them.

The Construct of Insight

Following these historical developments, psychiatrists in the early 20th century tended to equate psychosis with lack of insight (Lewis, 1934). However, later evidence emerged which forced authors to revise this view. Specifically (a) not all patients with acute psychosis had a lack of insight; (b) positive clinical change did not always correlate with improvements of insight (McEvoy et al., 1989); (c) insight did not appear to have any clear relationship with other clusters of symptoms (Preda, Bota & Harvey, 2011); (d) some aspects of insight are more amenable to change with treatment than others (Wiffen et al., 2010), and finally (e) good insight into one domain does not predict insight into another (David, 2012). This suggests that, while insight is related to psychopathology, it is likely to be best understood as a multidimensional construct (Amador et al., 1993; Beck et al., 2004; David, 1990; David et al., 2012; Koren et al., 2013) with "modality-specific, overlapping dimensions or awareness systems" (Koren et al., 2013, p. 245).

For example, one distinction has been made between the lack of "broad" awareness that one is ill ("broad deficits," or *anautognosia)*, and the lack of focused awareness of symptoms, impairments, and performance (Narrow deficits: *dysautognosia)* (Amador et al., 1993; Shad et al., 2007) (see **Table 16.1**). In addition, a number of theories have been proposed to conceptualize the different dimensions of insight in relation to psychosis (David, 1990; Amador et al., 1993). The first came from David (1990), who proposed three dimensions of insight: (a) the recognition that one has a mental illness, (b) the recognition of the need for treatment and (c) the ability to label unusual mental events (such as hallucinations or delusions) as pathological. Amador and colleagues (1993) subsequently suggested a further distinction between dimensions of *awareness* and *attribution*. According to Amador et al. (1993), insight has five dimensions, including four dimensions relating to awareness (having a mental disorder, need of medication, consequence of illness and of specific symptoms), and one to attribution (attributing symptoms to illness).

TABLE 16.1 Illustration of the different insight deficits dimensions

Insight Deficits	*Broad*	*Narrow*
Deficits of Awareness	"I don't have a mental disorder.""I don't need medication."	"I don't hallucinate.""There is nothing wrong with my leg."
Deficits of Attributions	"They put me in the hospital for no good reason."	"The voices are real."

Epidemiology and Clinical Correlates

The majority of patients with schizophrenia have (at least partial) insight into their illness, with rates ranging between 50% and 89% (Sevy et al., 2004), a finding that remains robust across cultures (Wilson, Ban & Guy, 1986). A multisite study (*n* = 412; Amador et al., 1993) using rigorous assessments found that insight deficits were more pervasive and severe in individuals with schizophrenia than in individuals with schizoaffective disorder and other mood disorders. While this finding was replicated by Weiler et al. (2000; *n* = 187), contradictory findings also exist (e.g., David et al., 1995). No clear association exists between generalized or specific insight dimensions and demographic variables such as age, sex or ethnicity (Arduini et al., 2003; David et al., 1995; Schwartz, 1998).

Enduring questions exist regarding the influence of insight on clinical state. A number of studies have shown that poor insight is linked to exacerbation of illness in individuals with schizophrenia and bipolar disorder, and that some improvements of insight are seen in patients after treatment (Weiler et al., 2000). Wiffen et al. (2010) also found improvements of insight with treatment, but did not find that insight was closely related to improvements in psychotic symptoms. Instead, trait-like qualities of insight have been linked to factors such as premorbid functioning and education (Wiffen et al., 2010), or sociopathic and schizoid personality traits (Campos et al., 2011).

Etiology of Insight

While insight is now well understood as a multidimensional construct, questions remain regarding the underlying cause of poor insight. The etiology of insight has been conceptualized according to a number of different and contrasting theories. It has been viewed as (a) a psychological defense (or a coping process); (b) a type of "delusion" regarding physical and mental health (and thus part of the positive symptoms cluster); (c) a decrease in normal mental function of awareness—a "mental withdrawal" (thus part of the negative symptoms cluster); (d) a type of cognitive impairment or a metacognitive deficit (David et al., 2012; Osatuke et al., 2008; Preda et al., 2011; Shad et al., 2006); and (e) a specific brain abnormality—similar in concept to anosognosia described in patients with well-defined cortical lesions.

There is mixed evidence for proposals that insight belongs to either positive or negative symptom clusters (Lincoln, Lüllmann & Rief, 2007; Osatuke et al., 2008; Preda et al., 2011). In a recent meta-analysis of 40 relevant studies, small associations were found between insight and positive and negative symptoms, suggesting a modest influence of positive and negative symptoms on insight with shared variance ranging between 5.2% and 7.2% (Mintz et al., 2003). This finding was replicated in a review of the cross-sectional and longitudinal relationship between insight and depression in 88 studies (Lincoln et al., 2007; see also Chan et al., 2012). A more consistent finding is that of a positive correlation between insight and low mood or depression (Mintz et al., 2003; Lincoln et al., 2007), although caution must be taken in drawing causal links based on these associations (Osatuke et al., 2008).

Studies into the cognitive correlates of insight have also been mixed (see the review in Osatuke et al., 2008). Recent studies involving large patient cohorts or meta-analyses have tended to point to low IQ and prefrontal cortex dysfunctions. Specifically, Keshavan et al. (2004) reported a relationship between lack of insight and low IQ in a cohort involving 500 patients with psychosis. The finding was partly replicated in a systematic review and meta-analysis based on 35 studies (n = 2354 individuals with psychosis; Aleman et al., 2006). In Aleman et al.'s study, five cognitive domains were examined: total cognition, IQ, verbal and visual memory, frontal executive functions (excluding the Wisconsin Card Sorting Test) and one construct captured specifically by the Wisconsin Card Sorting Test. In addition to the relationship between insight and lower IQ (particularly found in people with schizophrenia), Aleman et al. also showed association between insight and performance on the Wisconsin Card Sorting Test with a medium effect size (Aleman et al., 2006). This latter result suggests a cognitive explanation of insight that involves reduced flexibility in abstract set-shifting, perseveration and reduced error-monitoring (see also Chan et al., 2012; Shad et al., 2006; Spalletta et al, 2014). In a systematic review of 34 studies, Shad et al. (2006) also found that frontal cortical function was strongly linked to insight (particularly perseverance, response inhibition, conceptual flexibility, and error-monitoring), but that IQ was inconsistently related to insight.

With regards to brain structure and functions, it has been suggested that different neural networks may be involved with different aspects of insight (Chan et al., 2012; Spalletta et al, 2014). Abnormalities have been shown in distributed networks at the level of the prefrontal cortex, cingulate, superior and inferior parietal areas, insula, putamen and temporal cortex, in addition to defective connections between these areas (Antonius et al., 2011; Torey, 2013; Spalletta et al., 2014). Studies have demonstrated an association between lack of insight and reduced gray matter and white matter brain volume in the frontal lobe, possibly reflecting its role in self-processing and self-monitoring (e.g., Spalletta et al., 2014). Functional imaging studies in healthy people using tasks requiring self-awareness and self-referencing are consistent with these observations, where findings of cortical midline involvement predominate, encompassing the medial frontal and cingulate cortex (Northoff et al., 2006). However, there are also several studies that have failed to report any brain abnormalities associated with poor insight, and it is likely that differences in sample characteristics, imaging methodologies and methods used to assess insight contributed to these variations in results.

In summary, a single explanation of insight is unlikely and multiple etiologies (possibly in different combinations depending on condition and phase of illness) may best explain lack of insight in psychosis (Baier, 2010; David et al., 2012; Osatuke et al., 2008; Quee et al., 2011). In fact, it has been suggested that the conceptual heterogeneity of insight might be in part the reason for the inconsistent correlations found between poor insight and global severity of psychopathology, treatment compliance and prognosis, and more recently neuropsychological deficits, brain structure and function abnormalities (Aleman et al., 2006; Lysaker et al., 2006; Marková et al., 2003; Mintz, Dobson & Romney, 2003; Pijnenborg, van Donkersgoed, David & Aleman, 2013; Shad et al., 2007). However, few studies have examined the profile of performance in different subtypes of insight and more research is needed to explore how dimensional aspects of insight in psychosis and other population groups relate to clinical and cognitive characteristics and brain structure and function.

Assessment of Insight

The conceptual complexity of insight has resulted in a spectrum of assessment tools.

Comprehensive Mental State Assessments

The Present State Examination (PSE; Luria & McHugh, 1974) has been widely used internationally. The PSE assesses insight with an initial open-ended question, followed by questions assessing the severity of poor insight, ranging from denial or severely impaired insight to full insight (scored 0–3). Its advantage is its comprehensiveness—complementing the focused assessment of insight within the broader context of a patient's psychopathology. The result is an increase in convergent validity for any specific measured item. However, its comprehensiveness is costly in terms of time and resources. Moreover, the assessment of insight is limited in its ability to distinguish between different dimensions (such as awareness versus attribution).

The Positive and Negative Syndrome Scale in Schizophrenia (PANSS; Kay, Fiszbein, & Opler, 1987) consists of 30 items across three symptoms scales: positive, negative, and general psychopathology. The latter scale addresses lack of judgment and insight in G12. This is defined as a "failure to recognize past or present psychiatric illness or symptoms, denial of need for psychiatric hospitalization or treatment, decisions characterized by poor anticipation of consequences, and unrealistic short-term and long-range planning" (Kay et al., 1987, p. 261), and is rated on a 7-point scale, ranging from 1 (*full or unimpaired insight and judgment*) to 7 (*extreme deficits*; Kay et al., 1987). The PANSS assesses the patient's awareness of diagnosis, disorder attribution, and insight about need for treatment. Social insight is also assessed via questions about future plans and longer-term goals. Present as well as past beliefs are assessed within the measure; and scoring is based on the patient's responses only (collateral information is not utilized). Similar to the PSE, the PANSS is comprehensive, assessing insight in the context of the patient's broader psychopathology. It is also brief, with the total interviewing time generally under 30 minutes. However, the measure lacks distinction between poor insight and judgment, takes into consideration only thought content expressed during the examination and loses detail of the specific dimensional deficits (such as need for treatment) within the global deficit score.

Stand-Alone Assessments of Insight

The Schedule for Assessing the Components of Insight (SACI; David, 1990) is a brief, rater- or self-administered multidimensional 7-items scale examining three aspects of insight (recognizing the need for treatment, awareness of illness and attribution of symptoms) as well as a supplementary question probing hypothetical contradiction. The SACI focuses on symptoms over the month prior to examination. All items are scored on a 3-point scale (0 = *poor insight* to 2 = *intact insight*). The supplementary question is a 4-point scale with intermediate ratings reflective of partial levels of insight. The global score indicates severely impaired insight (a score of 0) to full insight (a score of 14).[1] While the SACI is multidimensional, it does not differentiate between "deficits of awareness" versus "deficits of attribution," Furthermore, the interpretation of the hypothetical question is loaded heavily on a patient's affective state, possibly reducing the inter-subscale validity as well as the overall global validity of the measure.

The Beck Cognitive Insight Scale (BCIS; Beck et al., 2004) is a 15-item self-report scale aimed at discriminating between the dimensions of self-reflectiveness versus self-certainty. Both are reported to measure separate components of "cognitive insight": "(a) the patients' capacity and willingness to observe their mental productions and to consider alternative explanations; and (b) their overconfidence in the validity of their beliefs" (Beck et al., 2004, p. 327). Subscale scores are used to calculate a "cognitive insight" composite score by subtracting the self-certainty score from the self-reflectiveness score (Beck et al., 2004). While the scale has been found to show good psychometric properties, the two components show inconsistent associations with pathological delusions (Engh et al., 2007).

The Insight Scale (IS-B; Birchwood et al., 1994;) is a brief, self-administered, multidimensional 8-item scale rating three different aspects of insight: attribution (relabeling) of symptoms, awareness of illness and recognizing the need for treatment (Birchwood et al., 1994). This has been found to be easy to administer with good psychometric properties.

The Insight and Treatment Attitudes Questionnaire (ITAQ; McEvoy et al., 1989) contains 11 open-ended questions that assess a patient's awareness of their illness, need for admission and need for treatment. The assessment places heavy emphasis on the patient's insight about need for treatment, does not differentiate between awareness versus attribution deficits and does not assess social insight deficits.

The Marková and Berrios Insight Scale (IS-MB-2003; Marková et al., 2003) is a re-standardized version of the original IS-MB-1992 (Marková & Berrios, 1992). The IS-MB-2003 excludes some original items, rephrases some and adds some (Marková et al., 2003). The revised version includes 30 items (instead of the original 32). Despite the conceptual and pragmatic refinements it is not clear if the IS-MB-2003 has improved on the validity and reliability of the IS-MB-1992.

The Scale to Assess Unawareness of Mental Disorder (SUMD; Amador et al., 1993) has two versions—the original 17-item scale (SUMD-17) and the revised abridged 9-item scale (SUMD-A). The composition of the SAUMD-17 combines general and discrete items, reflecting the three common perspectives on insight deficits—awareness of mental illness, awareness of the consequences of mental illness, and awareness of the treatment effects. Both current and past periods (retrospective insight) can be assessed. The SUMD-A evaluates global awareness of the mental disorder, awareness of the effect of medications, awareness of the social consequences of having the illness and specific items assessing the awareness of specific signs and symptoms (Amador, Flaum & Andreasen, 1994).

The Self-Appraisal of Illness Questionnaire (SAIQ; Marks et al., 2000) is a 17-item self-administered, multidimensional insight scale rating concepts such as awareness of illness, beliefs about the outcome of the illness, worry about the illness, worry about related issues and recognition of the need for treatment. Based on factor analysis, the 17-item scores can be organized along the dimensions of Presence/Outcome of Disease, Worry, and Need for Treatment.

Overall, good intercorrelations are found between insight assessment scales. High correlations between the items that assess global insight on the PSE, the PANSS, the ITAQ, and the SUMD suggest that these measures have a common target (Lincoln et al., 2007). However, scales or subscales targeting specific types of insight (e.g., cognitive insight) show lower correlations, both between scales and to global insight, suggesting that insight is not a homogeneous concept (Lincoln et al., 2007). In addition, while self-report scales show similar consistency and reliability, correlations between observer-rated and self-rated assessment are low (Lincoln et al., 2007)

Finally, while there is broad agreement that insight is a multidimensional concept, there is less consensus when defining the specific dimensions of insight (Marková & Berrios, 1995; Marková et al., 2003) and how different perspectives and assessments of insight compare with one another (Young et al., 2003).

Conclusion

Insight deficits are an important symptom domain of psychosis, yet they remain a poorly understood construct. There is a lack of consistency in correlations between insight and clinical course, response to treatment, other symptom domains, and structural or functional abnormalities. The complexity in defining and measuring insight has led many to conclude that it is a multidimensional construct, and that a number of etiologies must contribute to poor insight in psychosis, including a combination of (a) clinical symptoms, (b) illness stage, (c) cognitive deficits and (e) brain dysfunction (Quee et al., 2011). Clinicians and academics alike must pay careful attention to the definition of insight, the choice of rating scales, potential correlates, and study design. Future research is recommended to address standardization of the operating definitions and categories of insight.

Note

1 Scores can reach 18 if the supplementary question is included.

References

Aleman, A., Agrawal, N., Morgan, K.D., & David, A.S. (2006). Insight in psychosis and neuropsychological function: Meta-analysis. *The British Journal of Psychiatry, 189*, 204–212. doi:10.1192/bjp.189.3.204

Amador, X.F., Flaum, M., & Andreasen, N.C. (1994). Awareness of illness in schizophrenia and schizoaffective and mood disorders. *Archives of General Psychiatry, 51*, 826–836.

Amador, X.F., Strauss, D.H., Yale, S.A., Flaum, M.M., Endicott, J., & Gorman, J.M. (1993). Assessment of insight in psychosis. *The American Journal of Psychiatry, 150*(6), 873–879.

American Psychiatric Association. (2013). *Diagnostic and statistical manual of mental disorders* (5th ed.). Washington, DC: American Psychiatric Association.

Antonius, D., Prudent, V., Rebani, Y., D'Angelo, D., Ardekani, B.A., Malaspina, D., et al. (2011). White matter integrity and lack of insight in schizophrenia and schizoaffective disorder. *Schizophrenia Research, 128*, 76–82.

Arduini, L., Kalyvoka, A., Stratta, P., Rinaldi, O., Daneluzzo, E., & Rossi, A. (2003). Insight and neuropsychological function in patients with schizophrenia and bipolar disorder with psychotic features. *Canadian Journal of Psychiatry. Revue Canadienne de Psychiatrie, 48*(5), 338–341. Retrieved from www.ncbi.nlm.nih.gov/pubmed/12866340

Baier, B., & Karnath, H.-O. (2005). Incidence and diagnosis of anosognosia for hemiparesis revisited. *Journal of Neurology, Neurosurgery, and Psychiatry, 76*(3), 358–361. doi:10.1136/jnnp.2004.036731

Baier, M. (2010). Insight in schizophrenia: A review. *Current Psychiatry Reports, 12*, 356–361.

Beck, A.T., Baruch, E., Balter, J.M., Steer, R.A., & Warman, D.M. (2004). A new instrument for measuring insight: The Beck Cognitive Insight Scale. *Schizophrenia Research, 68*(2/3), 319–329. doi:10.1016/S0920-9964(03)00189-0

Birchwood, M., Smith, J., Drury, V., Healy, J., Macmillan, F., & Slade, M. (1994). A self-report insight scale for psychosis: Reliability, validity and sensitivity to change. *Acta Psychiatrica Scandinavica, 89*, 62–67. doi:10.1111/j.1600-0447.1994.tb01487.x

Campos, M.S., Garcia-Jalon, E., Gilleen, J.K., David, A.S., Peralta, V., & Cuesta, M.J. (2011). Premorbid personality and insight in first-episode psychosis. *Schizophrenia Bulletin, 37*(1), 52–60.

Chan, S.K.W., Chan, K.K.S., Lam, M.M.L., Chiu, C.P.Y., Hui, C.L.M., Wong, G.H.Y., et al. (2012). Clinical and cognitive correlates of insight in first-episode schizophrenia. *Schizophrenia Research, 135*, 40–45.

David, A., Owen, A. M., & Förstl, H. (1993). An annotated summary and translation of "On the self-awareness of focal brain diseases by the patient in cortical blindness and cortical deafness" by Gabriel Anton (1899). *Cognitive Neuropsychology, 10*(3), 263–272. doi:10.1080/02643299308253464

David, A., Van Os, J., Jones, P., Harvey, I., Foerster, A., & Fahy, T. (1995). Insight and psychotic illness: Cross-sectional and longitudinal associations. *The British Journal of Psychiatry, 167*, 621–628.

David, A.S. (1990). Insight and psychosis. *The British Journal of Psychiatry, 156*(6), 798–808. doi:10.1192/bjp.156.6.798

David, A.S. (1999). "To see oursels as others see us": Aubrey Lewis's insight. *The British Journal of Psychiatry, 175*(3), 210–216. doi:10.1192/bjp.175.3.210

David, A.S., Bedford, N., Wiffen, B., & Gilleen, J. (2012). Failures of metacognition and lack of insight in neuropsychiatric disorders. *Philosophical Transactions of the Royal Society B, 367*, 1379–1390.

Engh, J.A., Friis, S., Birkenaes, A., Jonsdottir, H., Ringen, P., Ruud, T., et al. (2007). Measuring cognitive insight in schizophrenia and bipolar disorder: A compararative study. *BMC Psychiatry, 7*, 71–77.

Gilhooly, K., & Murphy, P. (2005). Differentiating insight from non-insight problems. *Thinking & Reasoning, 11*(3), 279–302. doi:10.1080/13546780442000187

Kay, S.R., Fiszbein, A., & Opler, L.A. (1987). The positive and negative syndrome scale (PANSS) for schizophrenia. *Schizophrenia Bulletin, 13*, 261–276. doi:10.1093/schbul/13.2.261

Keshavan, M.S., Rabinowitz, J., DeSmedt, G., Harvey, P.D., & Schooler, N. (2004). Correlates of insight in first-episode psychosis. *Schizophrenia Research, 70*, 187–194.

Koren, D., Viksman, P., Giuliano, A. J., & Seidman, L.J. (2013). The nature and evolution of insight in schizophrenia: A multi-informant longitudinal study of first-episode versus chronic patients. *Schizophrenia Research, 151*, 245–251.

Kraepelin, E. (1920). Translated in part by Barclay, R. M. (1971). *Dementia praecox and paraphrenia*. Huntington, NY: Robert E. Krieger.

Lewis, A. (1934). The psychopathology of insight. *British Journal of Medical Psychology, 14*(4), 332–348. doi:10.1111/j.2044-8341.1934.tb01129.x

Lincoln, T.M., Lüllmann, E., & Rief, W. (2007). Correlates and long-term consequences of poor insight in patients with schizophrenia: A systematic review. *Schizophrenia Bulletin, 33*(6), 1324–42. doi:10.1093/schbul/sbm002

Luria, R.E., & McHugh, P.R. (1974). Reliability and clinical utility of the "Wing" Present State Examination. *Archives of General Psychiatry, 182*(6), 866–871.

Lysaker, P., Whitney, K., & Davis, L. (2006). Awareness of illness in schizophrenia: Associations with multiple assessments of executive function. *The Journal of Neuropsychiatry and Clinical Neurosciences, 18*(4), 516–520.

Marková, I., & Berrios, G. (1992). The assessment of insight in clinical psychiatry: A new scale. *Acta Psychiatrica Scandinavica, 86*(2), 159–164.

Marková, I., Roberts, K., Gallagher, C., Boos, H., McKenna, P., & Berrios, G. (2003). Assessment of insight in psychosis: A re-standardization of a new scale. *Psychiatry Research, 119*(1/2), 81–88.

Marková, I.S., & Berrios, G.E. (1995). Insight in clinical psychiatry revisited. *Comprehensive Psychiatry, 36*(5), 367–376. doi:10.1016/S0010-440X(95)90118-3

Marks, K.A., Fastenau, P.S., Lysaker, P. H, & Bond, G.R. (2000). Self-Appraisal of Illness Questionnaire (SAIQ): Relationship to researcher-rated insight and neuropsychological function in schizophrenia. *Schizophrenia Research, 45*(3), 203–211.

McEvoy, J.P., Apperson, L.J., Appelbaum, P.S., Ortlip, P., Brecosky, J., Hammill, K., et al. (1989). Insight in schizophrenia. Its relationship to acute psychopathology. *The Journal of Nervous and Mental Disease,* 177(1), 43–47.

Mintz, A.R.A., Dobson, K.K.S., & Romney, D.D.M. (2003). Insight in schizophrenia: a meta-analysis. *Schizophrenia Research, 61*(1), 75–88. doi:10.1016/S0920-9964(02)00316-X

Mullen, R., Howard, R., David, A., & Levy, R. (1996). Insight in Alzheimer's disease. *International Journal of Geriatric Psychiatry, 11,* 645–651.

Northoff, G., Heinzel, A., de Greek, M., Bermpohl, F., Dobrowolny, H., & Panksepp, J. (2006). Self-referential processing in our brain—A meta-anaylsis of imaging studies on the self. *Neuroimage, 30,* 440–457.

Osatuke, K., Ciesla, J., Kasckow, J.W., Zisook, S., & Mohamed, S. (2008). Insight in schizophrenia: A review of etiological models and suppoting research. *Comprehensive Psychiatry, 49,* 70–77.

Pijnenborg, G.H.M., van Donkersgoed, R.J.M., David, A.S., & Aleman, A. (2013). Changes in insight during treatment for psychotic disorders: A meta-analysis. *Schizophrenia Research, 144*(1–3), 109–117. doi:10.1016/j.schres.2012.11.018

Preda, A., Bota, R., & Harvey, P. (2011). Neurocognitive deficits, negative symptoms, and insight in schizophrenia. In M. Ritsner (Ed.), *Handbook of schizophrenia spectrum disorders* (Vol. 2). Netherlands: Springer. doi:10.1007/978-94-007-0831-0

Quee, P.J., van der Meer, L., Bruggeman, R., de Haan, L., Krabbendam, L., Cahn, W., et al. (2011). Insight in psychosis: Relationship with neurocognition, social cognition and clinical symptoms depend on phase of illness. *Schizophrenia Bulletin, 37*(1), 29–37.

Schwartz, R.C. (1998). Insight and illness in chronic schizophrenia. *Comprehensive Psychiatry, 39*(5), 249–254. Retrieved from www.ncbi.nlm.nih.gov/pubmed/9777275

Sevy, S., Nathanson, K., Visweswaraiah, H., & Amador, X. (2004). The relationship between insight and symptoms in schizophrenia. *Comrehensive Psychiatry, 45,* 16–19.

Shad, M.U., Keshavan, M.S., Tamminga, C.A., Cullum, C.M., & David, A. (2007). Neurobiological underpinnings of insight deficits in schizophrenia. *International Review of Psychiatry, 19*(4), 437–446. doi:10.1080/09540260701486324

Shad, M.U., Tamminga, C.A., Cullum, M., Haas, G.L., & Keshavan, M.S. (2006). Insight and frontal cortical function in schizophrenia: A review. *Schizophrenia Research, 86,* 54–70.

Spalletta, G., Piras, F., Piras, F., Caltagirone, C., & Orfei, M. D. (2014). The structural neuroanatomy of metacognitive insight in schizophrenia and its psychopathological and neuropsychological correlates. *Human Brain Mapping, 35,* 4729–4740.

Stewart, G., McGeown, W.J., Shanks, M.F., & Venneri, A. (2010). Anosognosia for memory impairment in Alzheimer's disease. *Acta Neuropsychiatrica, 22,* 180–187.

Torey, E.F. (2013). The Anatomical Basis of Anosognosia. Retrieved from www.treatmentadvocacycenter.org/about-us/our-reports-and-studies/2143

Weiler, M.A., Fleisher, M.H., & McArthur-Campbell, D. (2000). Insight and symptom change in schizophrenia and other disorders. *Schizophrenia Research, 45,* 29–36.

Wiffen, B.D.R., Rabinowitz, J., Lex, A., & David, A.S. (2010). Correlates, change and 'state or trait' properties of insight in schizophrenia. *Schizophrenia Research, 122*, 94–103.
Wilson, W.H., Ban, T.A., & Guy, W. (1986). Flexible system criteria in chronic schizophrenia. *Comprehensive Psychiatry, 27*(3), 259–265.
Young, D.A., Campbell, Z., Zakzanis, K.K., & Weinstein, E. (2003). A comparison between an interview and a self-report method of insight assessment in chronic schizophrenia. *Schizophrenia Research, 63*(1/2), 103–109. doi:10.1016/S0920-9964(02)00378-X

17

DISTURBANCE OF THE EXPERIENCE OF SELF

A Phenomenologically-Based Approach

Josef Parnas and Mads Gram Henriksen

Introduction

This chapter is devoted to a specific kind of disorders of self-experience occurring selectively in the schizophrenia spectrum disorders. This is a topic that is currently a target of vigorous research (Parnas & Henriksen, 2014). Self-disorders appear to be a fundamental, perhaps even constitutive experiential phenotype of the schizophrenia spectrum disorders. This clinical intuition and nosological idea was ventilated more or less explicitly in all classical texts on schizophrenia (e.g., Kraepelin, 1913; Bleuler, 1911/1950; Jaspers, 1913/1997; Schneider, 1950/1959). In the following, we present a summary of the empirical research, the clinical picture of self-disorders and a theoretical conceptualization of self-disorders.

Methodological Issues

The issues of subjectivity and self have all but vanished from the canonical discourse on the nature of psychosis in general and on schizophrenia in particular (see Parnas, *Chapter 2*). Therefore, some introductory remarks concerning the nature of subjective experiences are required. In short, it is quintessential to realize that the patient never manifests a series of mutually independent, isolated symptoms or signs, individuated, like in somatic medicine, by their reference to an underlying anatomo-physiological substrate (e.g., like sneezing indicates rhinitis) and devoid of meaning. Rather, as it was already pointed out (Parnas, *Chapter 2*), symptoms and signs are best considered as certain Gestalts of interwoven experience, feeling, expression, belief, and actions—all permeated by biographical and not only by biological detail. Most importantly, a symptom does not need to exist as a fully articulated, introspectible "mental object" but may sometimes consist of specific changes in the *structure* or *form* of consciousness, it may exhibit a quasi-habitual, pre-reflective quality and the patient's report of it will usually involve recollection, imagination and reflection. With regard to the issue of disordered self-experience, an adequate assessment presupposes here an adequate phenomenological interview (Nordgaard et al., 2013), and, a fortiori, a knowledgeable, skilled, and reliability-trained interviewer (see below). Finally, it is important to stress that the phenomenological approach to explore self-disorders should not be conflated with introspectionism. The introspective data constitutes only a fraction of what is at stake in a phenomenological assessment. The patient's comportment to and experience of his world, objects, meanings and social life usually constitute the core of the phenomenological investigation. Moreover, phenomenology and introspectionism are epistemologically fundamentally different. Like the epistemological approach of empiricism, introspectionism considers mental phenomena as simple objects, lending themselves to a description from an ordinary layman perspective.

Self-Disorders: Historical Aspects

The earliest, quite rich psychopathological descriptions of anomalous self-experience appeared in French psychiatry (e.g., Janet, 1903; Hesnard, 1909), but these were never specifically linked to schizophrenia, because it did not have a foothold in the French nosology at that time. However, explicit references to a disordered experience of self in schizophrenia, considered as its fundamental phenotype, are present in nearly all foundational texts on schizophrenia, though in various terms and with variable clarity. For example, Kraepelin (1913) considered "disunity of consciousness" to be the core feature of schizophrenia. Bleuler (1911/1950) considered "ego disorders" among the "fundamental" symptoms of schizophrenia. Jaspers observed that for the patient with schizophrenia, the sense of self-presence was fundamentally weakened: "Descartes' 'cogito ergo sum' may still be superficially cogitated but it is no longer a valid experience" (Jaspers, 1913/1997, p. 122). Schneider (1950/1959) considered the formative matrix of the "first rank symptoms" to be a "radical qualitative change" of the field of consciousness, involving a disturbed first-personal "givenness" ("*Ichheit*") and a disturbed sense of "mineness" of experience ("*Meinhaftigkeit*"). The interest in the self in schizophrenia continued in phenomenological psychiatry (e.g., Kimura, 1992; Sass, 1992; Fuchs 2005) and in some psychodynamically oriented theoretical contributions and case studies.

Self-Disorders: Summary of Empirical Results

The contemporary interest in and research on disorders of the self in the schizophrenia spectrum disorders began with the publication of two, independent, explorative-qualitative studies of first-admission schizophrenia spectrum patients in Denmark (Parnas et al., 1998) and Norway (Møller & Husby, 2000), which were followed by more systematic empirical studies (Parnas et al., 2003, 2005a, 2011; Raballo & Parnas 2011; Raballo et al., 2011). Collectively, these studies demonstrated that the sense of self in schizophrenia often is very fragile and unstable. In 2005, we published a semi-structured psychometric instrument for a qualitative and quantitative Examination of the Anomalies of Self-Experience (EASE; Parnas et al., 2005b).

The research employing these scales demonstrates jointly the following results: (1) Self-disorders aggregate selectively in schizophrenia and schizotypal disorders but not in the disorders outside the schizophrenia spectrum (Parnas et al., 2005a; Raballo et al., 2011; Nordgaard & Parnas, in press). (2) There is no significant difference in self-disorders among patients with schizophrenia and patients with schizotypal disorder (Raballo & Parnas, 2012; Nordgaard & Parnas, in press). (3) Self-disorders occur more frequently in residual schizophrenia than in remitted bipolar psychosis (Parnas et al., 2003), and differentiate between first-admitted cases with bipolar psychosis and schizophrenia, even after adjusting for the differences in the scores on the PANSS-derived positive and negative symptom scales (Haug et al., 2012). (4) Self-disorders occur in individuals who are biologically related to probands with schizophrenia and who themselves suffer from a schizophrenia spectrum disorder (Raballo & Parnas, 2011). (5) Prospective studies indicate that self-disorders are identifiable among non-psychotic help-seeking adolescents (Koren et al., 2013), that self-disorders predict transition to psychosis in an ultra-high-risk sample (Nelson et al., 2012) and, in a 5-year follow-up study of first-admitted *non-schizophrenia spectrum* patients, high initial levels of self-disorders were predictive of a subsequent diagnostic transition to the schizophrenia spectrum (Parnas et al., 2011).

Clinical Manifestations of a Disordered Self in Schizophrenia

In phenomenological terms, the foundational, pre-reflective articulation of the subject-object intentional relation is disturbed, unstable and threatened in the schizophrenia spectrum disorders (Parnas & Sass, 2011). On the *world-pole* this disturbance may manifest itself as a lack of immersion in the surrounding world and failing immediate grasp of the world's self-evidentness (e.g., questioning what others take for granted, with questions such as "Why is the grass green?" or "Why do people say 'hello' to each other?"), varieties of derealization, and alienation from the social world. The disturbance of experience at its world-pole is nearly always associated with disorders at the *self-pole* of the experience.

The majority of young patients with schizophrenia spectrum disorders complain of not feeling truly alive, not fully existing, lacking their innermost identity, being fundamentally, though often ineffably, different from others. What distinguishes this pervasive feeling of being different or, as these patients frequently express it, "wrong,"[1] cannot be articulated in terms of *concrete, mundane properties or predicates* (e.g., feeling stupid, too fat, not well-dressed or having other interests than one's peers). Rather, there seems to be a very basic sense of being *ontologically* different (*different in kind*) or of living in another ontological dimension (e.g., one of our patients said: "I do not feel like a spiritual being, it is as if I am a physical object, e.g., like this radiator"). Or to put it differently, it is a sense of being different in which one's own humanity is alarmingly at stake. This is sometimes associated with quasi-solipsistic attitudes or experiences (see below).

There is typically a deficient sense of "mineness" of the field of awareness, in which the sense of self no longer seamlessly permeates the acts and the contents of awareness. There is a hyper-reflective attitude directed to one's own experiencing: thoughts, feelings, or sense impressions, are being regarded or *inspected* from afar as *objects of awareness* rather than simply "lived through." One patient distinguished between "being thoughts" and "having thoughts" when the latter was experienced as introspectible, thing-like objects. There may also be distortions of the first-person perspective (e.g., "my point of view seems to tremble slightly, etc."; also see Saks, 2007, p. 12). Often, the field of awareness loses its natural transparency and becomes populated with objectified and *spatialized* sensations, feelings and thoughts.[2] Thus the patient may report that it feels *as if* his thoughts were (spatially) located to a particular part of his head. The qualification "as if" is frequently used when the patients describe their anomalies of self-experience. This qualification testifies to the fact that the patient's *reflective reality judgment is still intact*. Thought pressure, that is, rapid, parallel thought tracks or rapidly changing thoughts with a loss of meaning, is often associated with spatialization of these experiences (e.g., a sense of pressure on the inside of the skull). In acts of fantasy and imagination (relevant in the differential diagnosis of the obsessive compulsive disorder), an experiential distance creeps in between the subject and his object of imagination. In the schizophrenia spectrum disorders, the image becomes increasingly reified, spatialized, and *pictorial*, transforming obsession into a pseudo-obsessive, quasi-hallucinatory experience (see Jansson, *Chapter 4*). The process of spatialization and objectivation of thoughts is implicated in the beginning stages of the "internal" *Gedankenlautwerden* ("thoughts aloud," confined to the patient's interiority). Normal sense of "mineness" implies an experiential unity or fusion between the thinking act, namely, the thought and the thinking subject. In schizophrenia, however, this unity often gives way to a situation where the patient somehow *inspects*, listens to or perceives his own thoughts *in order to know* what he is thinking.

The diminished sense of being a self is also often disordered in its bodily corporeal dimension (Fuchs, 2005). There may be different forms of disembodiment, for example, the patient may complain of "a split between my mind and my body" or that "it feels as if my body does not really fit" or the patient may describe a hyper-reflective predicament "I live only in my head." There may be various cenesthetic sensations, sense of morphological change, motor disturbance and even bodily disintegration.

This unstable and often failing sense of "mineness" of experience is often associated with an inadequate sense of the privacy of one's own consciousness or interiority, that is, a compromised sense of me–not/me demarcation, or "ego-boundaries" (transitivism). For example, the patient may feel that he is radically exposed (Henriksen et al., 2010) and transparent to others' gaze, he may feel "naked" and have fleeting experiences that others have access to his thoughts (qualified at this stage with the "as if" conditional; see also Jansson, *Chapter 4*).

Finally, some patients have quasi-solipsistic experiences which are inaccessible to others (Henriksen & Parnas, 2014). Hence, the patient may observe a sense of grandiosity, in which others may be seen as being only exhibited with everyday banalities of life. The solipsistic dimension may also manifest itself by short-lived feelings of being the center of universe (or *being the universe*) or a feeling that one's experiential field is the only extant reality. In our view, the solipsistic dimension plays a crucial role in the lack of insight and treatment non-compliance characteristic of schizophrenia (Henriksen & Parnas, 2014).

Self-disorders, as described above, are sometimes enacted through altered or strange existential patterns, for example, solipsistic grandiosity, bizarre actions, "double book-keeping," mannerist behaviors or a search for a new existential or metaphysical meaning, for example, adherence to sectarian political or religious groups (Møller, 2000; Henriksen & Parnas, 2012; Parnas & Henriksen, 2013).

A few additional clinical observations merit emphasis here. First, self-disorders have mainly a persisting "trait-like" character. The notion of "trait phenotype" is usually applied to the expressive or behavioral features. In the case of experiential (subjective) phenomena such as self-disorders, the trait-like character manifests itself through their articulation as a constant or recurring *infrastructure* of the patient's conscious life, operating *more as forms of experience* (the *how* of experience) *than as particular contents* (the *what* of experience). For example, the distinctive features of thought pressure are not the particular thought content, but what the patient regularly experiences, say, several thematically unrelated and uncontrollable trains of thoughts occurring chaotically at the same time and devoid of meaning. In sum, self-disorders are, to a large extent, structural aspects of subjective life, and they are never far away (as a potentiality) from the ongoing stream of experience.

Very often, patients report that their self-disorders date back to childhood or early adolescence, and, at the time of their first admission, many self-disorders have become almost indistinctly interwoven into the patients' mode of experiencing. At least partly for this reason, patients seldom seem to experience their initial self-disorders as "symptoms" of an illness but rather as intrinsic features of their existence. Moreover, self-disorders tend to persist after remission of a psychotic episode. It must be stressed, we are not dealing here with *psychotic* phenomena: self-disorders do not simply become elaborated at a psychotic level, although the articulation of psychosis in schizophrenia *is* related to the initial self-disorders. Many patients consider self-disorders as the very core of their suffering, contributing more to their suffering than the symptoms of psychosis (Møller & Husby, 2000). Not infrequently, patients are surprised to learn that the psychiatrist is familiar with their experiences and they may become profoundly relieved that others share similar experiences.

It is also worthwhile to note that the patient's initial complaints often have a character of *quite vague or non-specific clichés* that may cover over much more specific and characteristic complaints. Blankenburg (1968, 1971) described this phenomenon with the expression "non-specific specificity." Often it is only when the patient is asked for a concretely lived example of his (non-specific) complaint that a more characteristic (specific) configuration of anomalous experience emerges. For example, a patient complaining of "fatigue," may, upon prompting, report a constant, oppressive burden of a reflective, energy-consuming, *effort* to decode and understand the meanings of ordinary everyday conversations (in this case "fatigue" covers loss of common sense, perplexity and hyper-reflection). The psychiatrist's acquaintance with the phenomenon of "non-specific specificity" (Blankenburg, 1968, 1971) is, in our view, crucial in the context of early diagnostic assessment.

Phenomenological Account of Self-Disorders

It is important to emphasize that the instability of the very basic sense of self does not equal a *lack* or *dissolution* of the self (which perhaps only occur in severe cases of catatonia). Thus, the patient continues of course to be a subject of awareness and to affirm herself with the first-personal pronoun, namely, "I." In other words, no matter how vulnerable the patients may be or how many self-disorders they are exposed to, their lives remain full and complete forms of human existence. The terms "instability" or "dis-order" indicate, however, that the normally tacit, taken-for-granted, pre-reflective, and pre-conceptual sense of being the subject of awareness no longer saturates one's experiences in the usual, unproblematic way. Rather, the basic sense of self appears to be fragile, oscillating and constantly threatened.

But what does this basic sense of self more specifically refer to? The basic sense of self signifies that we live our conscious life as a self-present, single, temporally persistent, bodily and demarcated (bounded) subject of experience and action (Jaspers, 1913/1997; Albahari, 2006). To articulate the most basic or irreducible dimension of selfhood, phenomenology (Zahavi, 2005) and neuroscience (Damasio, 2010) operate with the notions of a "minimal" or "core" self, that is, a necessary structure that *must be in place* in order for any experience to be experienced as *someone's* experience (in contrast to, say, existing in a free-floating state and only post-hoc appropriated by the subject in an act of reflection). The basic (or minimal) sense of self is experientially, but pre-reflectively, manifest (i.e., it is not "unconscious"). It refers to the first-personal articulation of experiencing, typically called "mineness," "myness," "for-me-ness" or *ipseity* (Zahavi, 2005; Sass & Parnas, 2003; Parnas & Sass, 2011). The term *ipseity* (from the Latin *ipse*, "self") conveys that all experiences are tacitly or pre-reflectively lived as *my* experiences, that is, from my first-person perspective. Ipseity has also a more substantial aspect of the sense of "I-me-myself" that persists across the passage of time and across different and changing modalities of conscious life. It is immediately, pre-reflectively, and non-inferentially given or present as a founding stratum of our experiential life. This sense of "I-me-myself" is propertyless, that is, it cannot be *further* described with a series of adjectives or attributes. From a phenomenological perspective, ipseity or the self does not "show up" in our experiences as a sort of object or quasi-object, which we may direct our attention towards. *Ipseity cannot be defined or grasped independently from the stream of consciousness in which it manifests itself as a specific structural (first-personal) configuration of that stream.*

Ipseity is a pre-condition of more rich and complex feelings of identity, that is, ipseity signifies that I am *always already* aware of myself and have therefore no need for introspection, self-observation or self-reflection to assure myself of being myself or being the one who entertains these thoughts or undergoes these experiences. Ipseity conveys a foundational, immutable core that is necessary for our sense of existing as a self-present, bodily, demarcated and persisting subject of awareness. Thus, ipseity exhibits a paradoxical nature: It may be considered as a general, universal *form* of consciousness while also, notwithstanding its lack of properties, founding the most intimate, *individuated* core of our personal identity (Hart, 2009). In that sense, we may, though obviously in a somewhat artificial way, distinguish ipseity from more complex levels of selfhood (e.g., the so-called narrative, extended or personal self).

Our major claim is that schizophrenia spectrum disorders involve a selective disturbance of ipseity (Sass & Parnas, 2003; Parnas & Sass, 2011), which, however, may also impact more complex levels of selfhood (such as narrative levels of selfhood). In contrast, the personality disorders outside the schizophrenia spectrum seem, in our view, to reflect disturbances at more sophisticated, self-representational or narrative levels of selfhood (Nelson et al., 2013), leaving ipseity largely unaffected.

Conclusions

This chapter presented specific disturbances of self-experience as an important experiential phenotype of the schizophrenia spectrum disorders. Although the founders of the concept of schizophrenia considered self-disorders as a constitutive feature of schizophrenia, systematic empirical studies only emerged in the recent decade. Notably, the foundational definition of schizophrenia was not based on a number of particular psychotic symptoms but relied on the identification of a characteristic trait-like Gestalt, marked by the peculiarities or strangeness in the expressive, communicative, and symbolic space (Parnas, 2011). In grasping the Gestalt, we do not only apprehend the "external" features or "signs"—we perceive a certain whole, *jointly constituted* by its "outer" and the "inner" aspects; that is, we do not only register the "signs" but also sense a profound "inner change" (what might be called the "symptoms"). In this particular context, the phenomenological notion of a disorder of the self, itemized into its empirical aspects in the EASE scale, permits a more focused, targeted, and explicitly articulated (reliable) investigation and description of the psychopathological aspects of schizophrenia. However, it needs to be reiterated that psychopathological research targeting self-disorders cannot be carried out within a standard contemporary epistemological-methodological framework (i.e., by non-psychiatrist interviewers, selectively trained in the application of a specific structured interview schedule) but requires significant clinical experience, a certain level of psychopathological scholarship, and reliability-training in the phenomenological use of the EASE-interview. Finally, the notion of self-disorder has, of course, important implications for early detection and differential diagnosis, perhaps by allowing for the strategies of "closing in" with detection measures with few false positives (Nelson et al., 2008). Finally, it seems to us that psychotherapies, which are intimately informed about the specific nature of the patient's suffering are likely to improve their therapeutic efficacy (Škodlar et al., 2013).

Funding

Carlsberg Foundation (#2012010195 to M.G.H.).

Notes

1 The term "wrong" is a translation of the Danish *forkert*, a polysemic term, which in this particular context refers to "not really fitting," "being strangely different" (etymologically, *forkert* is linked to the old Germanic *vorkeren*, which means something like "not turning the right way," "inverted"). In German psychopathology, this feeling has a specific name in the context of schizophrenia, namely, *Anderssein* (being different).

2 Note that mental phenomena are by their essence experientially *non-spatial*, which was one of the fundamental insights of the French philosopher René Descartes, who contrasted "*res cogitans*" ("thinking thing" [the mind]) and "*res extensa*" ("extended thing" [all spatial objects]).

References

Albahari, M. (2006). *Analytical Buddhism: The two-tiered illusion of self.* Basingstoke, UK: Palgrave Macmillan.

Blankenburg, W. (1968). Der Versagenszustand bei latenten Schizophrenien. *Deutsche Medizinische Wochenschrift, 93*, 67–71.

Blankenburg, W. (1971). *Der Verlust der natürlichen Selbstverständlichkeit. Ein Beitrag zur Psychopathologie symptomarmer Schizophrenien.* Stuttgart, Germany: Enke.

Bleuler, E. (1911/1950). *Dementia Praecox oder Gruppe der Schizophrenien.* In G. Aschaffenburg (Ed.), Handbuch der Psychiatrie. Spezieller Teil, 4. Abteilung, 1. Häfte. Leipzig, Germany: Deuticke. Trans. J. Zinkin & N. D. C. Lewis, *Dementia Praecox or the Group of Schizophrenias.* New York, NY: International University Press.

Damasio, A. R. (2010). *Self comes to mind: Constructing the conscious brain.* New York, NY: Pantheon Books.

Fuchs, T. (2005). Corporealized and disembodied minds: A phenomenological view of the body in melancholia and schizophrenia. *Philosophy, Psychiatry, and Psychology, 12,* 95–107.

Hart, J. G. (2009). *Who one is. Book 1. Meontology of the 'I': A transcendental phenomenology.* Berlin, Germany: Springer.

Haug, E., Lien, L., Raballo, A., Bratlien, U., Oie, M., Andreasen, O. A., et al. (2012). Selective aggregation of self-disorders in first-treatment DSM-IV schizophrenia spectrum disorders. *Journal of Nervous and Mental Disease, 200,* 632–636.

Henriksen, M. G., & Parnas, J. (2012). Clinical manifestations of self-disorders and the gestalt of schizophrenia. *Schizophrenia Bulletin, 38,* 657–660.

Henriksen, M.G., Parnas, J. (2014). Self-disorders and schizophrenia: A phenomenological reappraisal of poor insight and noncompliance. *Schizophrenia Bulletin,* 40: 542–547.

Henriksen, M. G., Škodlar, B., Sass, L. A., & Parnas, J. (2010). Autism and perplexity: A qualitative and theoretical study of basic subjective experiences in schizophrenia. *Psychopathology, 43,* 357–368.

Hesnard, A.-L. M. (1909). *Les troubles de la personalité dans les états d'asthénie psychique. Étude de Psychologie Clinique. Thèse de médecine.* Bordeaux, France: Université de Bordeaux.

Janet, P. (1903). *Les Obsessions et la psychasthénie.* Paris, France: Alcan.

Jaspers K. (1913/1997). *General psychopathology.* Translation by J. Hoenig and M. W. Hamilton. London: The Johns Hopkins University Press.

Kimura, B. (1992). *Réflexion et soi chez le schizophréne.* Paris, France: Presses Universitaires de France.

Koren, D., Reznik, N., Adres, M., Scheyer, R., Apter, A., Steinberg, T., et al. (2013). Disturbances of basic self and prodromal symptoms among nonpsychotic help seeking adolescents. *Psychological Medicine, 43,* 1365–1376.

Kraepelin, E. (1913). *Psychiatrie. Ein Lehrbuch für Studierende und Ärzte.* Aufl 8, vollständig umgearbeitet. Leipzig, Germany: Johann Ambrosius Barth.

Møller, P. (2000). First-episode schizophrenia: do grandiosity, disorganization, and acute initial development reduce duration of untreated psychosis? An exploratory naturalistic case study. *Comprehensive Psychiatry, 41,* 184–190.

Møller, P., & Husby, R. (2000). The initial prodrome in schizophrenia: Searching for naturalistic core dimensions of experience and behavior. *Schizophrenia Bulletin, 26,* 217–232.

Nelson, B., Thompson, A., Chanen, A. M., Amminger, G. P., & Yung, A. R. (2013). Is basic self-disturbance in ultra-high risk for psychosis ("prodromal") patients associated with borderline personality pathology? *Early Intervention in Psychiatry,* 7, 306–310.

Nelson, B., Thompson, A., & Yung, A. R. (2012). Basic self-disturbance predicts psychosis onset in the ultra high risk for psychosis "prodromal" population. *Schizophrenia Bulletin, 38,* 1277–1287.

Nelson, B., Yung, A. R., Bechdolf, A., & McGorry, P. D. (2008). The phenomenological critique and self-disturbance: Implications for ultra-high risk ("prodrome") research. *Schizophrenia Bulletin, 34,* 381–392.

Nordgaard, J., & Parnas, J. (in press). Self-disorders and schizophrenia-spectrum: A study of 100 first hospital admissions. *Schizophrenia Bulletin*. doi: 10.1093/schbul/sbt239

Nordgaard, J., Sass, L. A., & Parnas, J. (2013). The psychiatric interview: Validity, structure, and subjectivity. *European Archives of Psychiatry and Clinical Neuroscience, 263*, 353–364.

Parnas, J. (2011). A disappearing heritage: The clinical core of schizophrenia. *Schizophrenia Bulletin, 37*, 1121–1130.

Parnas, J., Handest, P., Jansson, L., & Saebye, D. (2005a). Anomalous subjective experience among first-admitted schizophrenia spectrum patients: empirical investigation. *Psychopathology, 38*, 259–267.

Parnas, J., Handest, P., Saebye, D., & Jansson, L. (2003). Anomalies of subjective experience in schizophrenia and psychotic bipolar illness. *Acta Psychiatrica Scandinavica, 108*, 126–133.

Parnas, J., & Henriksen, M. G. (2013). Subjectivity and schizophrenia: Another look at incomprehensibility and treatment non-adherence. *Psychopathology, 46*, 320–329.

Parnas, J., & Henriksen, M. G. (2014). Disordered self in the schizophrenia spectrum: A clinical and research perspective. *Harvard Review of Psychiatry*. doi: 10.1097/HRP.0000000000000040

Parnas, J., Jansson, L., Sass, L. A., & Handest, P. (1998). Self-experience in the prodromal phases of schizophrenia. *Neurology, Psychiatry, and Brain Research, 6*, 97–106.

Parnas, J., Møller, P., Kircher, T. Thalbitzer, J., Jansson, L., Handest, P., et al. (2005b). EASE: Examination of anomalous self-experiences. *Psychopathology, 38*, 236–258.

Parnas, J., Raballo, A., Handest, P., Jansson, L., Vollmer-Larsen, & A., Saebye, D. (2011). Self-experience in the early phases of schizophrenia: 5-year follow-up of the Copenhagen Prodromal Study. *World Psychiatry, 10*: 200–204.

Parnas, J., & Sass, L. A. (2011). The Structure of Self-consciousness in Schizophrenia. In S. Gallagher (Ed.), *The Oxford handbook of the self* (pp. 521–546). Oxford, UK: Oxford University Press.

Raballo, A., Parnas, J. (2011). The silent side of the spectrum: schizotypy and the schizotaxic self. *Schizophrenia Bulletin, 37*, 1017–1026.

Raballo, A., & Parnas, J. (2012). Examination of anomalous self-experience: Initial study of the structure of self-disorders in schizophrenia spectrum. *Journal of Nervous and Mental Disease, 200*, 577–583.

Raballo, A., Sæbye, D., & Parnas, J. (2011). Looking at the schizophrenia spectrum through the prism of self-disorders: An empirical study. *Schizophrenia Bulletin, 37*, 344–351.

Saks, E. R. (2007). *The center cannot hold*. New York, NY: Hyperion.

Sass, L. A. (1992). *Madness and modernism: Insanity in the light of modern art, literature, and thought*. Cambridge, MA: Harvard University Press.

Sass, L. A., & Parnas, J. (2003). Schizophrenia, consciousness, and the self. *Schizophrenia Bulletin, 29*, 427–444.

Schneider, K. (1950/1959). *Klinische Psychopathologie*. Stuttgart, Germany: Thieme. Trans. M. W. Hamilton, *Clinical psychopathology*. New York, NY: Grune & Stratton.

Škodlar, B., Henriksen, M. G., Sass, L.A., Nelson, B., & Parnas, J. (2013). Cognitive-behavioral therapy for schizophrenia: A critical evaluation of its theoretical framework from a clinical-phenomenological perspective. *Psychopathology, 46*, 249–265.

Zahavi, D, (2005). *Subjectivity and Selfhood: Investigating the first-person perspective*. Cambridge, MA: MIT Press.

18

PASSIVITY SYMPTOMS (EXPERIENCE OF ALIEN CONTROL)

Flavie Waters

Introduction

Individuals with passivity symptoms ("experience of alien control") report that their actions are no longer under their own control and that their will is replaced by the intentions of another force or agency. Passivity symptoms belong to a larger group of symptoms originally described by the German psychiatrist Kurt Schneider. He identified nine symptom dimensions which he thought had "first-rank" importance for the diagnosis of schizophrenia (Schneider, 1946). These first-rank symptoms have had critical importance as diagnostic criteria for schizophrenia in the 10th revision of the WHO International Classification of Diseases (ICD-10), and the fourth edition of the *Diagnostic and Statistical Manual of Mental Disorders* (DSM-IV). In the DSM-5, however, their diagnostic weight has been downgraded due to concerns about their diagnostic utility and specificity to schizophrenia (Jablensky, personal communication).

First-rank symptoms have received considerably less attention in research settings than in clinical practice. A key contributing factor is the lack of homogeneity among the nine symptom dimensions. The diversity of symptom dimensions subsumed under this one construct points instead to diverse phenomena, and researchers have favored constructing a new classification with more restrictive and homogeneous symptom dimensions that could be examined and used for experimentation. This new classification has targeted a subset of symptoms that share a clear phenomenological feature of "passivity" or ego-boundary disturbance—that is, the subjective experience of disturbed body ownership alongside replaced will. Other first-rank symptoms that could not be brought into this group without speculative elaborations (delusional mood, perception and idea and thought echo) have been left out of this "passivity" grouping. This new classification has allowed subgroups (individuals with, and without, passivity symptoms) to be constructed for the purpose of psychological, biological and social research. In the past 10 years, this symptom cluster has been the focus of steady research interest. They are frequently and readily elicited in people diagnosed with schizophrenia, and are a fascinating set of phenomena to observe and study. The aim of the current chapter is to briefly review the frequency, clinical characteristics and phenomenology of passivity symptoms and the rating scales that assess them.

Characteristic Features of Passivity Symptoms

Passivity symptoms signify a qualitative change in the thought process, characterized by a lack of normal sense of ownership for thoughts and actions, disturbed sense of boundary between the self and others, and the experience of one's will as replaced or influenced by that of some external agent. Passivity symptoms are not delusions (i.e., fixed false beliefs): The primary experience is a *perceptual* (rather than cognitive) change in self-awareness and self-concepts. Thoughts and actions are experienced as alien and no longer as one's own. Perceptual change occurs first, and is passively experienced in the sense that it is not under conscious control. Cognitive interpretation follows, and, in some cases, delusional elaboration ensues due to the person's effort to make sense of these mental experiences ("my will is controlled using telepathy"). However, delusional interpretation is not a necessary feature of the experience and some patients may claim not to know the origins of foreign thoughts or actions. Passivity symptoms may therefore occur in a delusional or non-delusional form, but explanatory delusions must not be taken as evidence for passivity symptoms. Care must also be taken to differentiate passivity symptoms from delusions of religious influence. The belief that God controls everything, including them and their fate, will strengthen (and not replace) the person's will (Jablensky, personal communication).

Passivity symptoms refer to a cluster of thought interference and replaced will experiences. Some suggest that they cannot be considered or defined in isolation from each other, nor independently from one another (Niedenthal et al., 2005). Instead, they are to be considered as interrelated facets of a more comprehensive change in the person's subjective experience. In other words, something makes these symptoms "hang together," perhaps through a disturbance of the basic sense of self (Sass & Parnas, 2003) or in brain function (Fletcher & Frith, 2009; also see Parnas, *Chapter 2*).

The passivity symptoms that are most commonly used in research, together with their definitions (adapted from Wing et al., 1990), are as follow's:

Loud thoughts: Individuals report that their thoughts sound "loud" in their head, so loud that someone standing nearby could hear them. Thinking, which is normally a silent process, now takes the form of sound.

Thought insertion: Thoughts are experienced as alien, and not the person's own. Typically, thoughts are said to have been placed in their mind by an outside force, often by means of telepathy requiring an explanatory delusion.

Thought broadcast: Individuals experience their thoughts as accessible to others, and even diffusing out of their mind so that they may be available by others. Thoughts are no longer a private experience. The experience is passive. The rater needs to distinguish this symptom from the ability to transmit thoughts voluntarily, which is a delusion of grandiose ability.

Thought withdrawal: Thoughts have been taken out, forcibly removed, of one's mind by others. Interviewers need to distinguish this experience from delusions that the person's thoughts are being read, which is an explanatory delusion. Thought withdrawal may be an elaboration of thought broadcast, thought insertion, loud thoughts or experience of replaced control.

Thought commentary: There is more than one stream of thought in the mind. Thoughts recognized as non-self or alien may comment on the person's thoughts, or on something that the person is doing or reading.

Passivity/replacement of will by external force: The essence of this cluster of symptoms is that the person experiences his/her will as replaced, or influenced, by the intention of some other force or agency. The experience occurs most commonly through overt motor behaviors. For instance, a person may report that his or her speech is produced without a sense of intention or that his/her voice now speaks someone else's words. Else, individuals report that their movements or handwriting are not their own but someone else's, or that actions such as eating or walking are not the product of their intention. In addition to motor behaviors, emotions may be replaced such that individuals may report that their emotions are no longer under their volitional control, and that these emotions do not belong to them. The basic experience may be elaborated in different ways. Individuals may report that they are the victim of a possession, and that they feel like a robot or zombie controlled by an external force.

Auditory hallucinations: Some empirical studies have, at times, included specific subtypes of auditory hallucinations in the passivity symptoms cluster. Schneider's original descriptions suggested that first-rank symptoms included two subtypes of auditory hallucinations: hallucinated voices giving a running commentary on the patient's behavior, or discussing the patient between themselves. These hallucinated voices are alien and unbidden, and passively experienced. The inclusion of these auditory hallucinations in the passivity symptoms cluster has been inconsistent in the empirical literature, with some studies preferring to focus exclusively on thought interference experiences and passivity/replacement of will by external force, and omitting auditory hallucinations from this cluster.

Of note, passivity symptoms have at times been defined in wider or narrower terms. Wide definitions refer to the experience of *influence* of sensations over thoughts and actions. Here, a person's will is merely influenced by an external agent. By contrast, narrow definitions propose that that thoughts and actions are *replaced* and controlled by an external agent. The proposal is of a continuum of severity ranging from influenced sensations through to inserted/replaced experiences, with the distinction perhaps of clinical relevance with narrow definitions having greater specificity to schizophrenia (Mellor, 1970a; Taylor & Heiser, 1971; Wing et al., 1974). However, the debate regarding whether to rate symptoms in the strictest sense did not quite reach a consensus, and the differentiation between experiences of "influence" and "control" has not been consistently applied in the literature. Exceptions include studies that have used the Scale for the Assessment of Passivity Phenomena (see below), which assigns greater scoring weights for inserted, than replaced, experiences.

Epidemiology

Passivity (and first-rank) symptoms are thought to be largely characteristic of schizophrenia, although schizophrenia can be diagnosed in their absence. Approximately 40% to 80% of persons diagnosed with schizophrenia have at least one passivity symptom (Carpenter et al., 1973; Mellor, 1970a; O'Grady, 1990; Peralta & Cuesta, 1999; Thorup et al., 2007). Differences in prevalence estimates likely reflect variations in populations and ascertainment methods. The most rigorous studies, with large sample sizes and interview methods, have tended to show prevalence rates between 57% (Carpenter & Strauss, 1974) and 79% (Mellor, 1970a). Epidemiological evidence also shows that these symptoms are "culturally robust," occurring with comparable frequency in different countries and cultures. In the WHO studies (Jablensky et al., 1992), the prevalence of first-rank symptoms amongst patients with ICD-defined schizophrenia ranged from 38% in a rural India area, to 84% in Nigeria, with description of first-rank symptoms showing striking similarities (Jablensky, 1992). Across studies, the more commonly reported symptoms are loud thoughts, thought insertion, and replaced will (Carpenter et al., 1973; Chopra & Gunter, 1987; Mellor, 1970b; O'Grady, 1990), and the median number of symptoms per person is two (O'Grady, 1990).

Passivity (and first-rank) symptoms occur in psychiatric disorders other than schizophrenia. For example, they can be found in affective psychosis (mania, depression, bipolar disorder), personality disorders, alcoholic states and temporal lobe epilepsy (Marneros, 1988), although prevalence rates are notably lower than in schizophrenia. Prevalence estimates range between 5% to 16% of individuals with major depression (Carpenter & Strauss, 1974; Tandon & Greden, 1987; Wing & Nixon, 1975), 9% to 23% in mania (Carpenter & Strauss, 1974; Carpenter et al., 1973; Taylor, 1972; Wing & Nixon, 1975), 9% to 23% in other affective disorders (Carpenter et al., 1973; Chopra & Gunter, 1987; O'Grady,

1990; Wing & Nixon, 1975) and 12% in personality disorders and neuroses (Carpenter & Strauss, 1974).

Functional Impact of Passivity Symptoms

The functional impact of passivity symptoms has not been comprehensively studied, although the quality of patients' communicative behavior may be affected. According to the theory of "embodied cognition," there is a close relationship between internal self-representations and the expression of social behaviors and emotions (Niedenthal et al., 2005). We recently tested this hypothesis in individuals with schizophrenia with (at least two) passivity symptoms, predicting that disturbed self-representation would be associated with functional impairments in social interpersonal behaviors (Waters et al., 2012). Data were analyzed from 227 patients with first-episode psychosis who took part in the WHO multicenter study on the determinants of outcome of severe mental disorders. The results showed that everyday interpersonal behaviors were affected in individuals with passivity symptoms, relative to individuals without these symptoms. Specifically, there were difficulties in social interactions, abnormalities in facial expressions, and in body language, which were not explained by other clinical symptoms. Furthermore, these social dysfunctions remained two years after the first experience of a psychotic illness, pointing to abnormalities that remain stable over time.

Explanatory Accounts of Passivity Symptoms

Early explanatory models of passivity symptoms focused on three neuropsychological domains, specifically, memory deficits (Trimble, 1990), reduced cerebral lateralization (Crow, 1997) and self-monitoring deficits (Frith & Done, 1989). Passivity symptoms however, are not so easily explained in terms of traditional cognitive domains (Waters et al., 2009). Later models suggested that passivity symptoms arise because of difficulties in motor control processes, and particularly deficits in the mechanisms that give rise to the sense of agency (Frith, 2005). Evidence provided in support includes studies showing abnormalities in processing internal actions (Blakemore et al., 2000; Lindner et al., 2005) and in self-monitoring mechanisms of voluntary actions in the absence of visual feedback (Frith & Done, 1989; Turken et al., 2003). Patients with passivity symptoms also show difficulties making decisions based on whether the visual feedback of an action corresponds to their own movements, or to another person, as demonstrated on self/other attribution tasks (Daprati et al., 1997).

An alternate view suggests that a range of other processes, including low-level perceptual deficits, may affect the ability to judge one's actions accurately. Recent conceptualizations are challenging the views that passivity symptoms arise exclusively because of a dysfunction in action control mechanisms (Pacherie, 2007;

Spence, 2001; Synofzik et al., 2008a). Instead, there may be several other sources of information within the domains of sensory, perceptual, cognitive and motor processes which are necessary prerequisites for a coherent sense of self. We recently proposed that passivity symptoms arise due to abnormalities at the level of body awareness and representations ("self-centers"), alongside other psychological processes which play a pivotal role in the way the body is experienced (Waters & Badcock, 2010). This includes deficits in body ownership, body structural description and body image, in addition to deficits in body agency. These subtypes of body representations (de Vignemont, 2007) are domains that are intrinsically linked to one's sense of identity, self-concept and sense of uniqueness (Synofzik et al., 2008b), and they are needed for the performance of purposeful and errorless actions, and they underlie the ability to reflect on ourselves and our actions. These body representations remain to be fully explored in patients with passivity symptoms, and current work is underway examining the general versus specific profile of individuals with and without passivity symptoms (Graham et al., 2014).

Other powerful psychological effects such as internal timing mechanisms may be involved (Decety & Chaminade, 2003; Haggard & Cole, 2007; Knoblich, 2002; Pacherie, 2007). Impaired timing processes have been well documented in schizophrenia, and recent studies have linked these timing deficits more specifically to the presence of passivity symptoms. Here, internal timing impairments extend beyond those relating to overt motor control, as shown on tasks of motor imagery (Danckert et al., 2004; Maruff et al., 2003) and auditory discrimination (Waters & Jablensky, 2009). Given the role of timing precision for shaping the sensory awareness of movements and for generating the subjective perception that some events belong together (Haggard & Cole, 2007), these abnormalities in timing awareness may contribute to a breakdown in the perceived relations between actions and their effects in individuals with passivity symptoms (Franck et al., 2005; Spence, 2002) and lead to self–other attribution errors (Waters, 2013; Graham et al., 2014).

Altogether, several theoretical models exist but they are not necessarily mutually exclusive. It is likely that impairments reflect abnormalities in distributed networks. Functional magnetic resonance imaging (fMRI) studies also support the idea of a distributed network in passivity symptoms involving self-referential processing, body awareness and social cognition, and involving the medial prefrontal cortex, anterior cingulate, inferior temporal gyrus and the right parietal cortex (Farrer & Franck, 2007; Franck et al., 2002; Ganesan et al., 2005; Maruff et al., 2003; Suzuki et al., 2005). This evidence however, leaves open the question of what triggers a given cortical area to activate a series of other brain systems and regions.

The Assessment of Passivity Symptoms

Experienced interviewers will know that eliciting and rating symptoms with certainty in individuals with psychosis is sometimes difficult. Passivity symptoms are no exception. The symptoms must be carefully elicited and reliably assessed, and the rater needs to ensure that informants understand the question and provide clear symptom descriptions. Often, respondents are not able to provide a sufficiently clear description of symptoms and errors may occur. Given the risk of false positive ratings, it is common practice in research to use a criterion of two or more symptoms in order to decide whether passivity symptoms are present in any given individual. The rater must also be able to distinguish these symptoms from other psychotic symptoms such as delusions.

Passivity symptoms have sometimes been assessed using general psychopathology scales, such as the Scale for the Assessment of Positive Symptoms (SAPS; Andreasen, 1984), but this scale is limited in that it only assesses a small subset of passivity symptoms. For example, loud thoughts (the most common type of passivity symptoms) are not included, nor is thought commentary. The most comprehensive psychopathology scale, and with the most reliable descriptions of passivity symptoms, is the SCAN (Schedules for Clinical Assessment in Neuropsychiatry), or its precursor the Present State Examination (PSE; Wing et al., 1974), although both are fairly lengthy if administered in their entirety.

Few scales have been designed to assess passivity symptoms exclusively. Exceptions include the Passivity Symptoms Interview (PSI; Waters et al., 2009), which is derived from the SCAN item questions and definitions, and with passivity symptoms rated as present if two or more symptoms are present in the past month (Present State) or at any time in the past (Lifetime). The Scale for the Assessment of Passivity Phenomena (Spence et al., 1997) is also very comprehensive, although it takes a very different approach by providing different weights to wide and narrow definitions of symptoms.

Concluding Remarks

Altogether, passivity symptoms are fascinating phenomena to study. The research community has brought these symptoms together as a family of symptoms, but the fact remains that they are poorly understood and underresearched. Questions remain regarding their core underlying mechanisms, diagnostic boundaries, and functional impact. The rating scales cited above offer an excellent opportunity to provide consistent measurement of symptoms and should remain an important part of any ongoing assessment efforts.

References

Andreasen, N.C. (1984). *Scale for the Assessment of Positive Symptoms (SAPS)*. Iowa City: The University of Iowa.

Blakemore, S.-J., Smith, J., Steel, R., Johnstone, E., & Frith, C. (2000). The perception of self-produced sensory stimuli in patients with auditory hallucinations and passivity experiences: Evidence for a breakdown in self-monitoring. *Psychological Medicine, 30*, 1131–1139.

Carpenter, W., & Strauss, J. (1974). Cross-cultural evaluation of Schneider's first-rank symptoms of schizophrenia: A report from the International Pilot Study of Schizophrenia. *American Journal of Psychiatry, 131*(6), 682–687.

Carpenter, W., Strauss, J., & Muleh, S. (1973). Are there pathognomonic symptoms in schizophrenia? An empiric investigation of Schneider's first-rank symptoms. *Archives of General Psychiatry, 28*, 847–852.

Chopra, H., & Gunter, M. (1987). Diagnostic value of Schneider's first rank symptoms in schizophrenia. *British Journal of Psychiatry, 150*, 132.

Crow, T. (1997). Schizophrenia as failure of hemispheric dominance for language. *Trends in Neurosciences, 20*(8), 339–343.

Danckert, J., Saoud, M., & Maruff, P. (2004). Attention, motor control and motor imagery in schizophrenia: Implication for the role of the parietal cortex. *Schizophrenia Research, 70*, 241–261.

Daprati, E., Franck, N., Georgieff, N., Proust, J., Pacherie, E., Dalery, J., et al. (1997). Looking for the agent: An investigation into consciousness of action and self-consciousness in schizophrenic patients. *Cognition, 65*, 71–86.

de Vignemont, F. (2007). How many representations of the body? *Behavioral and Brain Sciences, 30*(2), 1–3.

Decety, J., & Chaminade, T. (2003). When the self represents the other: A new cognitive neuroscience view on psychological identification. *Consciousness and Cognition, 12*, 577–596.

Farrer, C., & Franck, N. (2007). Self-monitoring in schizophrenia. *Current Psychiatry Reviews, 3*, 243–251.

Fletcher, P. C., & Frith, C. D. (2009). Perceiving is believing: A Bayesian approach to explaining the positive symptoms of schizophrenia. *Nature Review Neuroscience, 10*(1), 48–58.

Franck, N., O'Leary, D., Flaum, M., Hichwa, R., & Andreasen, N. (2002). Cerebral blood flow changes associated with Schneiderian first-rank symptoms in schizophrenia. *The Journal of Neuropsychiatry and Clinical Neurosciences, 14*(3), 277–282.

Franck, N., Posada, A., Pichon, S., & Haggard, P. (2005). Altered subjective time of events in schizophrenia. *The Journal of Nervous and Mental Disease, 193*(5), 350–353.

Frith, C. (2005). The self in action: Lessons from delusions of control. *Consciousness and Cognition, 14*, 752–770.

Frith, C., & Done, D. (1989). Experiences of alien control in schizophrenia relfect a disorder in the central monitoring of action. *Psychological Medicine, 19*, 359–363.

Ganesan, V., Hunter, M., & Spence, S. (2005). Schneiderian first-rank symptoms and right parietal hyperactivation: a replication using fMRI. *American Journal of Psychiatry, 162*, 1454.

Graham, K., Martin-Iverson, M.T., Holmes, N.P., Jablensky, A., & Waters, F. (2014). Deficits in agency in schizophrenia, and additional deficits in body image, body schema, and internal timing in passivity symptoms. *Frontiers in Psychiatry.* doi: 10.3389/fpsyt.2014.00126.

Haggard, P., & Cole, J. (2007). Intention, attention and the temporal experience of action. *Conscious and Cognition, 16*(2), 211–220.

Jablensky, A. (1992). Schizophrenia: manifestations, incidence and course in different cultures: A World Health Organization ten-country study. *Psychological Medicine, Monograph* (Suppl. 20), 1–97.

Jablensky, A., Sartorius, N., Ernberg, G., Anker, M., Korten, A., Cooper, J., et al. (1992). Schizophrenia: Manifestations, incidence and course in different cultures. A World Health Organization Ten-Country Study. *Psychological Medicine* (Monograph Suppl.), 1–97.

Knoblich, G. (2002). Self-recognition: Body and action. *Trends in Cognitive Sciences, 6*(11), 447–449.

Lindner, A., Thier, P., Kircher, T., Haarmeier, T., & Leube, D. (2005). Disorders of agency in schizophrenia correlate with an inability to compensate for the sensory consequences of actions. *Current Biology, 15*(12), 1119–1124.

Marneros, A. (1988). Schizophrenic first-rank symptoms in organic mental disorders. *British Journal of Psychiatry, 152*, 625–628.

Maruff, P., Wilson, P., & Currie, J. (2003). Abnormalities of motor imagery associated with somatic passivity phenomena in schizophrenia. *Schizophrenia Research, 60*, 229–238.

Mellor, C. (1970a). First-rank symptoms of schizophrenia. *British Journal of Psychiatry, 117*, 15–23.

Mellor, C. (1970b). First-rank symptoms of schizophrenia. I. The frequency in schizophrenics on admission to hospital. II. Differences between individual first-rank symptoms. *British Journal of Psychiatry, 117*, 15–23.

Niedenthal, P., Barsalou, L., Winkielman, P., Krauth-Gruber, S., & Ric, F. (2005). Embodiment in attitudes social perception and emotion. *Personality and Social Psychology Review, 9*, 184–211.

O'Grady, J. (1990). The prevalence and diagnostic significance of schneiderian first rank symptoms in a random sample of psychiatric in patients. *British Journal of Psychiatry, 156*, 496–500.

Pacherie, E. (2007). The sense of control and the sense of agency. *Psyche, 13*(1), 1–30.

Peralta, V., & Cuesta, M. (1999). Diagnostic significance of Schneider's first-rank symptoms in schizophrenia. *British Journal of Psychiatry, 174*, 243–248.

Sass, L.A., & Parnas, J. (2003). Schizophrenia, consciousness, and the self. *Schizophrenia Bulletin, 29*(3), 427–444.

Schneider, K. (1946). *Klinische Psychopathologie.* Trans., 1959, *Clinical psychopathology*. Stuttgart, Germany: Georg Thieme Verlag.

Spence, S. (2001). Alien control: From phenomenology to cognitive neurobiology. *PPP, 8*(2/3), 163–172.

Spence, S. (2002). Alien motor phenomena: A window to agency. *Cognitive Neuropsychiatry, 7*(3), 211–220.

Spence, S., Brooks, D., Hirsch, S., Liddle, P., Meehan, J., & Grasby, P. (1997). A PET study of voluntary movement in schizophrenia patients experiencing passivity phenomena (delusions of alien control). *Brain, 120*, 1997–2011.

Suzuki, M., Zhou, S., Hagino, H., Niu, L., Takahashi, T., Kawasaki, Y., et al. (2005). Morphological brain changes associated with Schneider's first-rank symptoms in schizophrenia: a MRI study. *Psychological Medicine, 35*(4), 549–560.

Synofzik, M., Vosgerau, G., & Newen, A. (2008a). Beyond the comparator model: A multifactorial two-step account of agency. *Consciousness & Cognition, 17*(1), 219–239.

Synofzik, M., Vosgerau, G., & Newen, A. (2008b). I move, therefore I am: A new theoretical framework to investigate agency and ownership. *Consciousness & Cognition, 17*, 411–424.

Tandon, R., & Greden, J. (1987). Schneiderian first-rank symptoms: Reconfirmation of high specificity for schizophrenia. *Acta Psychiatrica Scandinavica, 75*, 392–294.

Taylor, M. (1972). Schneiderian first-rank symptoms and clinical prognostic features in schizophrenia. *Archives of General Psychiatry, 26*, 64–67.

Taylor, M., & Heiser, J. (1971). Phenomenology: An alternative approach to diagnosis of mental disease. *Comprehensive Psychiatry, 12*(5), 480–487.

Thorup, A., Petersen, L., Jeppesen, P., & Nordentoft, M. (2007). Frequency and predictive values of first rank symptoms at baseline among 362 young adult patients with first-episode schizophrenia: Results from the Danish OPUS study. *Schizophrenia Research, 97*(1/3), 60–67.

Trimble, M. (1990). First-rank symptoms of Schneider: A new perspective? *British Journal of Psychiatry, 156*, 195–200.

Turken, A., Vuilleumier, P., Mathalon, D., Swick, D., & Ford, J. (2003). Are impairments of action monitoring and executive control true dissociative dysfunctions in patients with schizophrenia? *American Journal of Psychiatry, 160*(10), 1881–1883.

Waters, F. (2013). Time perception and discrimination in individuals with auditory hallucinations. In T.P.R. Jardi & D. Pines (Ed.), *The Neuroscience of Hallucinations* (pp. 185–199). New York, NY: Springer.

Waters, F., & Badcock, J. (2010). First-rank symptoms in schizophrenia: Reexamining mechanisms of self-recognition. *Schizophrenia Bulletin, 36*(3), 510–517.

Waters, F., Badcock, J., Dragovic, M., & Jablensky, A. (2009). Neuropsychological functioning in schizophrenia patients with first-rank (passivity) symptoms. *Psychopathology, 42*(1), 47–58.

Waters, F., & Jablensky, A. (2009). Timing judgment deficits in patients with first-rank (passivity) symptoms. *Psychiatry Research, 167*, 12–20.

Waters, F., Rock, D., Dragovic, M., & Jablensky, A. (2012). 'Social dysmetria' in first-episode psychosis patients. *Acta Psychiatrica Scandinavica, 123*(6), 475–484.

Wing, J., Babor, T., Brugha, T., Burke, J.I., Cooper, J.E., Giel, R., et al. (1990). Schedules for clinical assessment in neuropsychiatry (SCAN). *Archives of General Psychiatry, 47*, 589–593.

Wing, J., Cooper, J., & Sartorius, N. (1974). *Measurement and classification of psychiatric symptoms*. Cambridge, MA: Cambridge University Press.

Wing, J., & Nixon, J. (1975). Discriminating symptoms in schizophrenia: A report from the international pilot study of schizophrenia. *Archives of General Psychiatry, 32*, 853–859.

PART IV

Rating Scales for Psychosis and Psychotic Symptoms

APPENDIX 1

Index of Rating Scale Names

ADOLESCENT PSYCHOTIC SYMPTOM SCREENER (APSS)

Reference:

Kelleher, I., Harley, M., Murtagh, A., & Cannon, M. (2011). Are screening instruments valid for psychotic-like experiences? A validation study of screening questions for psychotic-like experiences using in-depth clinical interview. *Schizophrenia Bulletin, 37*(2), 362–369.

Administration time: 5 minutes
Rating instructions: Self-report
Population groups: Children, adolescents and adults

DESCRIPTION:

The scale has seven items designed to screen for psychotic symptoms. Questions are rated 0 (*no, never*), 0.5 (*maybe*) or 1 (*yes, definitely*). Total scores are summed and higher scores indicate a greater number of psychotic symptoms. Validation was conducted in a sample of 334 adolescents aged 11–13 years who underwent detailed clinical interviews. Sensitivity and specificity in identifying young people with psychotic symptoms varied among items. The question on auditory hallucinations (item 4 below) had the strongest positive predictive value for interview-verified auditory hallucinations (71.4%) and for any psychotic-like experiences (100%). Negative predictive value was 90.4% and 88.4% respectively.

Items are as follows:

1. Some people believe that their thoughts can be read by another person. Have other people ever read your mind?
2. Have you ever had messages sent just to you through TV or radio?
3. Have you ever felt that you were under the control of some special power?
4. Have you ever heard voices or sounds that no one else can hear?
5. Have you ever seen things that other people could not see?
6. Have you ever felt you have extra-special powers?
7. Have you ever thought that people are following or spying on you?

CORRESPONDENCE:

A/Professor Mary Cannon, Royal College of Surgeons in Ireland, Department of Psychiatry, Education and Research Center, Beaumont Hospital, Dublin 9, Ireland. Email: marycannon@rcsi.ie

---

AUDITORY VOCAL HALLUCINATIONS RATING SCALE (AVHRS)

Reference:

Jenner, J. A., van de Willige, G. University Medical Centre Groningen, University Centre for Psychiatry, Groningen, The Netherlands

Administration time: 20–30 minutes
Rating instructions: Structured interview by a clinician or experienced rater
Population groups: Psychiatric populations

DESCRIPTION:

This structured interview has 16 sections assessing for the presence and descriptive features of auditory verbal hallucinations ("voices") experienced in the past month. Questions include: Number of voices heard, time of day, frequency, duration, location of voices, loudness, cause of voices, positive and negative content, emotional impact, emotional interference, control, anxiety related to voices, interference with thoughts, loud thoughts, third-person hallucinations. There is no corresponding component for non-verbal hallucinations. Scoring is on a 5-point rating scale and a description is provided for each score. Internal consistency was good (Chronbach's $\alpha = 0.84$ and 0.77, $n = 62$), as was inter-rater reliability (correlation coefficient = 0.84 and 0.88) (Bartels-Velthuis et al., 2012).

CORRESPONDENCE:

Jenner J. A., University Medical Center Groningen, University Center for Psychiatry, 9700 RB Groningen, The Netherlands. Email: rgoc@umcg.nl

Source: Available by contacting the corresponding author.

Additional Reference:

Bartels-Velthuis, A. A., Van de Willige, G., Jenner, J. A., & Wiersma, D. (2012). Consistency and reliability of the Auditory Vocal Hallucination Rating Scale (AVHRS). *Epidemiology and Psychiatric Sciences, 21*, 305–310.

BECK COGNITIVE INSIGHT SCALE (BCIS)

Reference:

Beck, A.T., Baruch, E., Balter, J.M., Steer, R.A., & Warman, D.M. (2004). A new instrument for measuring insight: the Beck Cognitive Insight Scale. *Schizophrenia Research, 68*(2–3), 319–329.

Administration time: 15–20 minutes
Rating instructions: Self-report
Population groups: Psychiatric populations

DESCRIPTION:

This 15-item questionnaire assesses "cognitive" insight, specifically referring to flexibility as a cognitive style or metacognitive ability. The BCIS measures cognitive insight in two empirically derived factors: Self-certainty (6-items, e.g., At times, I have misunderstood other people's attitudes towards me) and self-reflectiveness (9-items, e.g., I can trust my own judgment at all times). Items are rated on a 4-point scale from 0 (*do not agree at all*) to 3 (*agree completely*). A cognitive insight composite index score is calculated by subtracting the self-certainty from the self-reflectiveness scale scores. Validation was conducted in 150 adults with psychosis. Both subscales have adequate internal consistency (Chronbach's α = 0.60–0.68) and convergent validity with the Scale to Assess Unawareness of Mental Disorder (SUMD; correlation coefficient = 0.62–0.67). The literature however shows an inconsistent association with pathological delusions.

CORRESPONDENCE:

Professor A. T. Beck, Department of Psychiatry, University of Pennsylvania. Email address: becka@mail.med.upenn.edu

Source: Available commercially through Pearson Assessment publishers: www.pearsonassessments.com

BEHAVIORAL SYMPTOMS IN ALZHEIMER'S DISEASE (BEHAVE-AD)

Reference:

Reisberg, B., Borenstein, J., Salob, S. P., Ferris, S. H., Franssen, E., & Georgotas, A. (1987). Behavioral symptoms in Alzheimer's disease: Phenomenology and treatment. *Journal of Clinical Psychiatry, 48*(Suppl. 5), 9–15.

Administration time: 15–20 minutes
Rating instructions: Structured interview by a clinician or experienced rater
Population group: Alzheimer's disease

DESCRIPTION:

The interview assesses psychopathology in Alzheimer's disease (AD) across seven domain areas. There are 25 items in total, rated from 0 (*not present*) to 3 (*present with behavioral or emotional response*). The timeframe for symptom assessment is the preceding 2 weeks. Psychotic symptom items include: persecutory delusions, delusional misidentification (e.g., spouse is an imposter), delusions of abandonment and infidelity, paranoid ideation (e.g., people are stealing things). Hallucinations in all modalities are also assessed. Clear descriptions are provided for each score. Internal consistency was excellent (Chronbach's $\alpha = 0.96$), and interrater reliability for the seven behavioral domains was found to be 0.65–0.91.

CORRESPONDENCE:

Professor Barry Reisberg, Aging and Dementia Research program, Department of Psychiatry, NYU Medical Center, 560 First Avenue, New York, NY 10016. Email: barry.reisberg@med.nyu.edu

Source: Available by contacting the corresponding author.

Further Reference:

Sclan, S. G., Saillon, A., Franssen, E., Hugonot-Diener, L., Saillon, A., & Reisberg, B. (1996). The behavior pathology in Alzheimer's disease rating scale (BEHAVE-AD): Reliability and analysis of symptom category scores. *International Journal of Geriatric Psychiatry, 11*(9), 819–830.

BELIEFS ABOUT PARANOIA SCALE (BAPS)

References:

Gumley, A. I., Gillan, K., Morrison, A. P. & Schwannauer, M. (2011). The development and validation of the Beliefs about Paranoia Scale (Short Form). *Behavioural and Cognitive Psychotherapy, 39*(1), 35–53.

Morrison, A.P., Gumley, A.I., Schwannauer, M., Campbell, M., Gleeson, A., Griffin, E., & Gillan, K. (2005). The Beliefs about Paranoia Scale: Preliminary validation of a metacognitive approach to conceptualising paranoia. *Behavioural & Cognitive Psychotherapy, 33*, 153–164.

Administration time: 10–15 minutes
Rating instructions: Self-report
Population groups: General population

DESCRIPTION:

This scale assesses metacognitive beliefs about paranoia in the general population. The original 50-item version (Morrison et al., 2005) was revised into a 18-item version (Gumley et al., 2011). The latter version comprises three dimensions: Negative Beliefs about Paranoia (e.g., My paranoia gets out of control), Paranoia as a Survival Strategy (e.g., If I were not paranoid, others would take advantage of me), and Normalizing beliefs (e.g., Most people get paranoid sometimes). Each item is rated on a four-point scale ranging from 1 (*not at all*) to 4 (*very much*). It is particularly aimed at understanding cognitions related to paranoid thinking and has been used in clinical settings to assess change in paranoia. Validation was conducted with 185 non-clinical participants. The internal consistency was excellent (Chronbach's $\alpha = 0.89$).

CORRESPONDENCE:

Professor Tony Morrison, School of Psychological Sciences, The University of Manchester, Oxford Rd., Manchester M13 9PL, UK. Email: anthony.p.morrison@manchester.ac.uk

Source: In the original publication.

BELIEFS ABOUT VOICES QUESTIONNAIRE (BAVQ-R)

References:

Chadwick, P., & Birchwood, M. (1995). The omnipotence of voices. II: The Beliefs About Voices Questionnaire (BAVQ). *British Journal of Psychiatry, 166*, 773–776.
Chadwick, P., Lees, S., & Birchwood, M. (2000). The revised Beliefs About Voices Questionnaire (BAVQ-R). *British Journal of Psychiatry, 177*, 229–232.

Administration time: 10–15 minutes
Rating instructions: Self-report
Population groups: Psychiatric populations

DESCRIPTION:

This questionnaire is often used in clinical settings to assess change in beliefs about auditory verbal hallucinations ("voices") as a cause of distress and behavioral problems. The original questionnaire (1995) had binary measurements. This was changed in 2000 to a continuous scale measurement. The revised scale (BAVQ-R) is a 35-item questionnaire rated on a 4-point scale. There are five subscales, evaluating beliefs about: Malevolence (e.g., My voice is evil), Benevolence (e.g., My voice wants to protect me), and Omnipotence (e.g., My voice is very powerful) and actions: Resistance (e.g., When I hear my voice, usually I tell it to leave me alone) and Engagement reactions (I seek the advice of my voice). Informants are asked to base their responses on their dominant voice. Internal consistency was adequate (Chronbach's α = 0.74–0.88, n = 71). Test–retest reliability was found to be 0.80. There was convergent validity with the Hospital Anxiety and Depression Scale (HADS) and strong correlations between the Resistance subscale and the Belief about malevolence subscales.

CORRESPONDENCE:

Professor Paul Chadwick, King's College London, Institute of Psychiatry, DeCrespigny Park, London SE5 9AF, UK. Email: paul.chadwick@kcl.ac.uk

Source: In the initial publication.

BONN SCALE FOR THE ASSESSMENT OF BASIC SYMPTOMS (BSABS)

Reference:

Gross, G., Huber, G., Klosterkötter, J., & Linz, M., (1987). *Bonner Skala fur die Beurteilung von Basissymptomen* (BSABS; *Bonn Scale for the Assessment of Basic Symptoms*). Berlin, Germany: Springer.

Administration time: Approximately 2–3 hours
Rating instructions: Semi-structured interview by a clinician or experienced rater
Population groups: Adolescents and adults (pre-clinical, residual and at risk)

DESCRIPTION:

This semi-structured interview assesses basic symptoms. Operational definitions of experiences are provided, along with examples of questions to allow assessment in a semi-structured interview format. It contains 178 items in five main categories: Dynamic Deficiencies (both with and without symptoms), Anomalies of Cognitive, Perceptual, Motor Experiences and Cenesthesias. Items assess disturbances of thought, language, perception, self-awareness, body perception, affect, concentration, energy, social contacts and non-verbal expressions. Although very comprehensive, there has been a recent increase in the use of the shorter Schizophrenia Proneness Instrument–Adult (SPI-A), which is derived from the BSABS.

CORRESPONDENCE:

Dr. Frauke Schultz-Lutter, University Hospital of Child and Adolescent Psychiatry and Psychotherapy, University of Bern, Bolligenstr. 111, Haus A, 3000 Bern 60, Switzerland. Email: frauke.schultze-lutter@kjp.unibe.ch

Source: BSBS–Bonn Scale for the Assessment of Basic Symptoms: First Complete English Edition: Manual Commentary, References, Index and Documentation sheet, may be purchased on Amazon.com.

Additional Reference:

Klosterkötter, J. (1988). Basic symptoms and end phenomena of schizophrenia: An empirical study of psychopathologic transitional signs between deficit and productive symptoms of schizophrenia. *Monograph Gesamtgeb Psychiatric Psychiatry Services, 52*, 1–267.

BRIEF ASSESSMENT OF COGNITION IN SCHIZOPHRENIA (BACS)

Reference:

Keefe, R. S, Goldberg, T. E, Harvey, P. D, Gold, J. M, Poe, M. P,. & Coughenour, L. (2004). The Brief Assessment of Cognition in Schizophrenia: Reliability, sensitivity, and comparison with a standard neurocognitive battery. *Schizophrenia Research, 68*(2/3), 283–297.

Rating instructions: Individuals with experience in cognitive assessment methods
Administration Time: Less than 35 minutes
Population group: Schizophrenia

DESCRIPTION:

This scale offers an assessment of multiple cognitive functions that are robustly correlated with schizophrenia and functional outcomes. The tests are as follows: Verbal Learning (verbal memory), Digit Sequencing Task (working memory), Token Motor Task (motor speed), Controlled Word Association Test and Semantic Fluency Test (verbal fluency), Symbol Coding (attention and motor speed) and the Tower of London (executive functions). The scale has a high completion rate probably due to its ease of administration and brevity. Two versions are used to avoid practice effect during repeated administrations in clinical trials. The BACS is also one of several cognitive measures constituting the NIMH-sponsored MATRICS Consensus Cognitive Battery (MCCB; Green et al., 2004). Interclass correlation coefficients were significant at $p < .05$ for all but three of the 42 measures. The test–retest reliability was found to be 0.86–0.92.

CORRESPONDENCE:

Professor Richard Keefe, Director, Schizophrenia Research Group Psychiatry & Behavioral Sciences, Division of Medical Psychology, School of Medicine, Hospital South; Box 3270, Duke University Medical Center, Durham, NC 27710. Email: Richard.keefe@duke.edu

Source Available by contacting the corresponding author, or available as part of the larger MATRICS battery MCCB: www.matricsinc.org/MCCB.htm

Additional Reference:

Green, M. F., Kern, R. S., & Heaton, R. K. (2004). Longitudinal studies of cognition and functional outcome in schizophrenia: Implications for MATRICS. *Schizophrenia Research, 72*(1), 41–51.

BRIEF PSYCHIATRIC RATING SCALE (BPRS)

Reference:

Overall, J. E., & Gorham, D. R. (1962). The Brief Psychiatric Rating Scale. *Psychological Reports, 10*, 790–812.

Administration time: 20–25 minutes
Rating instructions: Semi-structured interview by a clinician or experienced rater
Population groups: Psychiatric populations

DESCRIPTION:

This interview assesses the presence and severity of psychiatric symptoms, and is often used to evaluate treatment response. Ratings are on a 1–7 or 0–6 scale. The BPRS was developed in 1962, but many different versions have become available since. The 24-item scale (BPRS-E) has a stable four-factor structure including negative affect, positive symptoms, negative symptoms, resistance and activation/

tension. The reliability and validity of the BPRS has been established. Crippa et al. (2001) created a structured version which was shown to improve reliability of ratings in interviewers with little clinical experience. Other versions of the BPRS include a nursing modification (McGorry et al., 1988) and a 21-item BPRS version for children (BPRS-C) (Lachar et al., 2001).

Source: In the public domain

Further References:

Crippa, J. A., Sanches, R. F., Hallak, J. E., Loureiro, S. R., & Zuardi, A. W. (2001). A structured interview guide increases Brief Psychiatric Rating Scale reliability in raters with low clinical experience. *Acta Psychiatrica Scandinavica, 103*(6), 465–470.

Lachar, D., Randle, S. L., Harper, R. A., Scott-Gurnell, K. C., Lewis, K. R., Santos, C. W., et al. (2001). The Brief Psychiatric Rating Scale for Children (BPRS-C): Validity and reliability of an anchored version. *Journal of the American Academy of Child and Adolescent Psychiatry, 40*(3), 333–340.

McGorry, P. D., Goodwin, R. J., & Stuart, G. W. (1988). The development, use, and reliability of the brief psychiatric rating scale (nursing modification)—An assessment procedure for the nursing team in clinical and research settings. *Comprehensive Psychiatry, 29*(6), 575–587.

BROWN ASSESSMENT OF BELIEFS SCALE (BABS)

Reference:

Eisen, J. L., Phillips, K. A., Baer, L., Beer, D.A., Atala, K. D & Rasmussen, S. A. (1998). The Brown Assessment of Beliefs Scale: Reliability and validity. *American Journal of Psychiatry, 155*(1), 102–108.

Administration time: 15–30 minutes
Rating instructions: Semi-structured interview by a clinician or experienced rater
Population groups: Psychiatric populations

DESCRIPTION:

This interview assesses conviction, cognitive flexibility and insight with regards to pathological beliefs. These might refer to delusions, overvalued ideas, obsessions and phobias. Informants are first asked to state their belief as specifically as possible (i.e., If I go in the garden, I will be bitten by a snake and die), and then the BABS is used to assess this belief across the following dimensions: Conviction (e.g., How convinced are you these beliefs?), Perception of others' views of beliefs, Explanation of differing views, Fixity of ideas, Attempt to disprove beliefs (e.g., Have you tried to convince yourself that your beliefs are wrong?), Insight and Ideas/delusions of reference. Each item is rated from 0 to 4, based on how much this characteristic was present on average during the past week for the dominant belief (from least to most severe). If there are more than one belief related to the same disorder (two different obsessions or delusions), these beliefs should be rated as composite; however, if the beliefs are connected to two distinct disorders (e.g., body distortion and obsessions about contamination), beliefs are rated separately for each. Validation was conducted in 16 psychiatric patients (Kaplan et al., 2006). Internal validity was excellent (Chronbach's α = 0.89). There was convergent validity with insight scales but not with measures of general psychopathology.

CORRESPONDENCE:

Dr. Eisen, Butler Hospital, 345 Blackstone Boulevard, Providence, RI 02906. Email: Jane_Eisen@brown.edu

Source: Available by contacting the corresponding author.

Additional Reference:

Kaplan, G., Phillips, K., & Vaccaro, A. (2006). Assessment of insight into delusional beliefs in schizophrenia using the Brown Assessment of Beliefs Scale. *Schizophrenia Research, 82*(2/3), 279–281.

CAMBRIDGE MENTAL DISORDERS OF THE ELDERLY EXAMINATION (CAMDEX)

Reference:

Roth, M., Tym, E., Mountjoy, C. Q., Huppert, F. A., Hendrie, H., Verma, S., & Goddard, R. (1986). CAMDEX. A standardised instrument for the diagnosis of mental disorder in the elderly with special reference to the early detection of dementia. *British Journal of Psychiatry, 149*, 698–709.

Administration time: 30 minutes
Rating instructions: Structured interview by a clinician or experienced rater
Population groups: Dementia

DESCRIPTION:

The primary aim of the CAMDEX is to assist in the detection and diagnosis of dementia, with four types of dementia being assessed. There are 92 questions which include a structured interview with the patient to obtain systematic information about the present mental state and history, a structured interview with an informant, and a cognitive section (CAMCOG). Questions assess a broad range of domains including depressed mood, sleep, general functions, and a few questions about delusions and hallucinations. Interrater reliability on different aspects of the tool was good (correlation coefficient = 0.83–0.94, n = 92). A cut-off of 79/80 on the CAMCOG yielded 92% sensitivity and 96% specificity for a clinical diagnosis of dementia.

CORRESPONDENCE:

Dr. Felicia Huppert, Department of Psychiatry, Level E4, Box 189, Addenbrooke's Hospital, Cambridge CB2 2QQ, UK. Email: fah2@cus.cam.ac.uk

Source: The book, computer disk, test battery and form are available commercially from Cambridge University Press.

CARDIFF ANOMALOUS PERCEPTIONS SCALE (CAPS)

Reference

Bell, V., Halligan, P.W., & Ellis, H.D. (2006). The Cardiff Anomalous Perceptions Scale (CAPS): A new validated measure of anomalous perceptual experience. *Schizophrenia Bulletin, 32*(2), 266–366.

Administration time: 10–15 minutes
Rating instructions: Self-report
Population group: General population

DESCRIPTION:

This is a 32-item questionnaire assesses anomalous perceptual experiences that include psychosis-like experiences, phenomena more typically associated with neurological disorders and changes in the clarity and intensity of sensory experience. It takes differing levels of insight into account and asks about experiences from several perspectives, including shared and non-shared perceptual experience. It also includes ratings for distress, intrusiveness and frequency. For example: Item six, "Do you ever hear noises or sounds when there is nothing about to explain them?" (No/Yes). If a yes answer is recorded, respondents are required to provide a rating from one to 5 on each of the following domains: Distress (*not distressed at all–very distressed*); Intrusiveness (*not at all distracting–completely intrusive*); and Frequency (*happens hardly at all–happens all the time*). Validation was conducted in samples of 336 healthy participants and 20 psychotic patients. A three-factor solution was revealed, comprising: Chemosensation (largely olfactory and gustatory items), Clinical Psychosis (first-rank symptoms) and Temporal lobe related ("microseizures"). Internal reliability was good (Chronbach's α = 0.87), and test–retest reliability was 0.77–0.79. There was convergent validity with the Peters Delusion Inventory (PDI) and Launey Slade Hallucination Scale Revised (LSHR).

CORRESPONDENCE:

Dr. Vaughan Bell, Institute of Psychiatry, Box P078, DeCrespigny Park, London, SE5 8AF, UK. Email: Bell@iop.kcl.ac.uk

Source: *In the original publication.*

CHILD AND ADOLESCENT PSYCHIATRIC ASSESSMENT (CAPA)

Reference:

Angold, A., Prendergast, M., Cox, A., Harrington, R., Simonoff, E., & Rutter, M. (1995). The Child and Adolescent Psychiatric Assessment (CAPA). *Psychological Medicine, 25*(4), 739–754.

Administration time: 1½–2 hours
Rating instructions: Semi-structured interview by a clinician or experienced rater
Population groups: Children and adolescents

DESCRIPTION:

This is a structured diagnostic interview for the assessment of axis-1 psychiatric disorders in children and adolescents, including psychotic disorders. The interview is to be administered to the child (9–18) and their parents, and the timeframe for symptom assessment is the preceding three months. The psychotic disorders section is divided into three parts: Disorders of perception and hallucinations, psychotic thought abnormalities and delusional ideas. These sections enquire about a broad range of psychotic experiences. The assessment scale comes with a codebook and an extensive glossary with definitions. Internal validity in affective disorders was shown to be excellent (Chronbach's α = 0.89–0.90).

CORRESPONDENCE:

Dr. Adrian Angold, Developmental Epidemiology Department of Psychiatry and Behavioral Sciences, Duke University Medical Center, Box 3454, Durham, NC 27710, USA. Email: adrian.angold@duke.edu

Source: *Available from the original publication and on the internet:* https://devepi.duhs.duke.edu/capa.html; to be used with permission from the authors

CLINICAL ASSESSMENT OF THE AT-RISK MENTAL STATE (CA-ARMS)

Reference

Yung, A., Yuen, H., McGorry, P., Philips, L., Kelly, D., Dell'Olio, M., et al. (2005). Mapping the onset of psychosis: The Comprehensive Assessment of At-Risk Mental States. *Australian and New Zealand Journal of Psychiatry, 39*(11/12), 964–971.

Administration time: 60–90 minutes
Rating instructions: Structured interview by a clinician or experienced rater
Population groups: Adolescents and adults (pre-clinical)

DESCRIPTION:

This structured interview incorporates and operationalizes the Scale of Prodromal Symptoms (SOPS). It assists the user in providing a comprehensive assessment of psychopathology thought to indicate imminent development of first-episode of psychotic disorder, and to determine if individuals meet any of the three 'Ultra High Risk' (UHR) status subcategories: Attenuated Positive Symptoms, Brief Intermittent Psychotic Symptoms, and Genetic Risk and Deterioration syndromes. It also includes a checklist for Schizotypal Personality Disorder, a detailed family history questionnaire, and a global assessment of functioning. A validation study in 49 UHR young people showed a predictive validity of 40.8% for psychosis at 12 months follow-up. Interrater reliability was 0.85. Concurrent validity as established with measures of general psychopathology.

CORRESPONDENCE:

Professor Alison Yung, University of Manchester, Oxford Road, Manchester, M13 9PL, UK; alison.yung@manchester.ac.uk

Source: Training packages or DVDs available from: http://oyh.org.au/training-resources/training-mental-health-clinicians/caarms-training

CLINICAL CHARACTERISTICS OF AUDITORY HALLUCINATIONS (CCAH)

Reference:

Oulis, P., Mavreas, V., Mamounas, J., & Stephanis, N. (1995). Clinical characteristics of auditory hallucinations. *Acta Psychiatrica Scandinavica, 92*, 97–102.

Administration time: 30 minutes
Rating instructions: Structured interview by a clinician or experienced rater
Population groups: Psychiatric populations

DESCRIPTION:

This interview assesses 25 clinical characteristics of auditory hallucinations on a three-point rating scale. The following domains are assessed: loudness, identification, clarity of content, conviction, location, duration, prominence, lack of volitional control, frequency, and lack of insight. Interrater reliability on the basis of interviews with 60 patients with psychosis was > 0.70, except for 2 items with correlation coefficient = 0.6.

CORRESPONDENCE:

Dr. Panagiotis Oulis, Eginition Hospital, Department of Medicine, National and Kapodistrian University, Athens, Greece. Email: oulisp@med.uoa.gr

Source: Available by contacting the corresponding author

CLINICAL RATING SCALE FOR SYMPTOMS OF PSYCHOSIS IN ALZHEIMER'S DISEASE (SPAD)

Reference:

Reisberg, B., & Ferris, S.H. (1980). A clinical rating scale for symptoms of psychosis in Alzheimer's disease. *Psychopharmacology Bulletin, 21*(1), 101–104.

Administration time: 10 minutes
Rating instructions: Carer interview by trained interviewer
Population groups: Alzheimer's disease

DESCRIPTION:

This brief carer-interview was an earlier development of the BEHAVE-AD. It is the only assessment scale for Alzheimer's Disease with a predominant focus on psychotic symptoms. The SPAD comprises nine items, with scores ranging from zero (not present) to three (severe). Six of the nine items enquire about psychotic symptoms, including delusions of theft (e.g. People are stealing things), misidentification (e.g. Spouse is an imposter), delusions of abandonment, and auditory and visual hallucination experiences. Psychometric properties are not known.

CORRESPONDENCE:

Professor Barry Reisberg, Aging and Dementia Research program, Department of Psychiatry, NYU Medical Center, 560 First Avenue NY 10016, Email: barry.reisberg@med.nyu.edu

Source: Available by contacting the corresponding author

COLUMBIA UNIVERSITY SCALE FOR PSYCHOPATHOLOGY IN ALZHEIMER'S DISEASE (CUSPAD)

Reference:

Devanand, D.P., Miller, L., Richards, M., Marder, K., Bell, K., Mayeux, R., et al. (1992). The Columbia University Scale for Psychopathology in Alzheimer's Disease. *Archives of Neurology, 49*(4), 371–376.

Administration time: 10–20 minutes
Rating instructions: Carer interview by lay or experienced interviewer
Population groups: Alzheimer's Disease

DESCRIPTION:

This carer-interview assesses neuropsychiatric symptoms in Alzheimer's Disease. It was developed as an alternative to clinician-only rated instruments. The timeframe of enquiry is generally the past month. The scale covers five areas of behavioral disturbances with an emphasis on psychotic symptoms. Dimensions include delusions (general, paranoid, abandonment, somatic, misidentification, other), illusions and hallucinations (voices, visions, smells, somatic, other), and other symptoms. Items are rated zero (no), one (yes, vague), and two (yes, clear). Based on 20 interviews, interrater reliability between a psychiatrist and lay interviewer ranged between 0.74 and 1.0.

CORRESPONDENCE:

Dr. D.P. Devanand, New York State Psychiatric Institute, 722 West 168 Street NY 10032, USA. Email: dpd3@columbia.edu

Further References:

Devanand, D.P., Miller, L., Richards, M., Marder, K., Bell, K., Mayeux, R., et al. (1992). The Columbia University Scale for Psychopathology in Alzheimer's disease. *Archives of Neurology, 49*(4), 371–376.

Source: Available by contacting the corresponding author

COMMUNITY ASSESSMENT OF PSYCHIC EXPERIENCES (CAPE)

Reference:

Stefanis, N.C., Hanssen, M., Smirnis, N.K., Avramopoulos, D.A., Evdokimidis, I.K. Stefanis, C.N., et al. (2002). Evidence that three dimensions of psychosis have a distribution in the general population. *Psychological Medicine, 32*, 347–358.

Administration time: Approximately 20–30 minutes
Rating instructions: Self-rated
Population group: General population

DESCRIPTION:

This questionnaire contains 42 items rated on a four-point scale from zero (Never) to three (Always). The three dimensions of the CAPE are Positive (18 items), Negative (14 items), and Depressive (8 items) symptom categories. A total score can be calculated, in addition to scores for these three dimensions. A supplementary dimension assesses distress, and a distress score can be calculated by adding up the scores of the distress questions. Good convergent validity was demonstrated with scales assessing positive, negative and depressive experiences of psychosis (n = 932 young men).

CORRESPONDENCE:

Professor Jim van Os, Department of Psychiatry and Psychology, South Limburg Mental Health Research and Teaching Network, EURON, Maastricht University Medical Centre, Maastricht, The Netherlands. Email: j.vanos@sp.unimaas.nl

Source: A copy of the CAPE in 8 languages may be obtained from the following internet: www.cape42.homestead.com

COMPREHENSIVE ASSESSMENT OF SYMPTOMS AND HISTORY (CASH)

References:

Andreasen, N., Flaum, M., & Arndt, S. (1992). The Comprehensive Assessment of Symptoms and History (CASH): An instrument for assessing diagnosis and psychopathology. *Archives of General Psychiatry, 49*(8), 615–623.

Administration time: 120 minutes
Rating instructions: Semi-structured interview by a clinician or experienced rater

Population groups: Psychiatric populations (major psychosis and affective disorders)

DESCRIPTION:

This elaborate interview contains nearly 1000 items. The items are given detailed definitions, and interview probes are provided. Most of the items are rated on a six-point scale (0–5). The interview is divided into three main sections. The interview starts with socio-demographic information and current psychopathology. The past history section records information concerning previous episodes of the illness. The life-time section addresses other disorders such as alcohol or drug abuse, and summarizes premorbid adjustment, personality traits and functioning. Additional information such as laterality data and global assessment of functions is recorded. Diagnostic validation was conducted in a group of 30 psychiatric individuals.

Interrater reliability was 0.86. More than three quarters of the variables had intra-class correlations coefficient >.65. Test retest reliability for all diagnosis was 0.79. For most items, correlations between patients scores and either informants or gold standard scores (consensus based on patients, family members, medical charts) were greater than 0.70.

CORRESPONDENCE AND PERMISSIONS:

Professor Nancy C. Andreasen, c/o MH-CRC Administrator. Department of Psychiatry. Mental Health Clinical Research Center. University of Iowa Hospitals & Clinics. 200 Hawkins Drive, 2911 JPP, Iowa City, Iowa, USA.

Source: Training manual and tapes are available by contacting the corresponding author

Further References:

Andreasen, N. C. (1985). *Comprehensive Assessment of Symptoms and History*. Iowa City: the University of Iowa.

COMPREHENSIVE PSYCHOPATHOLOGICAL RATING SCALE (CPRS)

Reference:

Asberg, M., Perris, C. P., Schalling, D., & Sedvall, G. (1978). The CPRS—Development and applications of a psychiatric rating scale. *Acta Psychiatrica Scandinavica* (Suppl. 271), 69.

Administration time: Up to 60 minutes
Rating instructions: Semi-structured interview by a clinician or experienced rater
Population groups: Psychiatric populations: adults and older adults

DESCRIPTION:

This interview assesses the severity of psychiatric symptoms and observed behaviors. It consists of 65 items divided into symptoms and observations. Items are rated from zero to three. Two additional items assess global and reliability ratings. Items on psychotic symptoms include delusions of control, thought blocking, persecutory delusions, grandiose delusions, jealous delusions, and hallucinations. Whilst the scale was not primarily intended for use in the elderly, a subscale has been adapted for use in the assessment of dementia (Bucht et al., 1983). Inter-rater reliability of the scale in individuals with schizophrenia was 0.70 to 0.97 (Jacobsson et al., 1978).

CORRESPONDENCE:

Umea Dementia Research Group, Department of Geriatric Medicine and Geriatric Psychiatry, University Hospital, Umea, Sweden, www.clinsci.umu.se/english/units/psychiat/

Additional References:

Bucht, G., & Adolfsson, R. (1983). The Comprehensive Psychopathological Rating Scale in patients with dementia of Alzheimer type and multiinfarct dementia. *Acta Psychiatrica Scandinavica, 68*(4), 263–270.

Jacobsson, L., von Knorring, L., Mattsson, B., Perris, C., Edenius, B., Kettner, B., et al. (1978). The Comprehesive Psychopathological Rating Scale–CPRS–in patients with schizophrenic syndromes: Interrater reliability and in relation to Martens' S-scale. *Acta Psychiatrica Scandinavica*, (Suppl. 271), 39–44.

COMPUTERIZED BINARY SCALE OF AUDITORY SPEECH HALLUCINATIONS (CBSASH)

Reference

Stephane, M., Pellizzer, G., Roberts, S., & McClannahan, K. (2006). Computerized binary scale of auditory speech hallucinations (cbSASH). *Schizophrenia Research, 88*, 73–81.

Administration time: 30–45 minutes
Rating: Self-report, assisted by a mental health professional
Population groups: Psychiatric groups

DESCRIPTION:

The scale was primarily designed for the identification of phenomenologically-defined subtypes of auditory verbal hallucinations. This scale also provides measures of the severity of hallucinations on variables such as frequency and loudness, outlined in chapter 12 (Table 1). The cbSASH investigates the association of verbal hallucination with other modalities of hallucinations and with other perceptual abnormalities (e.g. tinnitus, derealization, and depersonalization). The cbSASH includes three subscales: phenomenology (127 questions), malingering (30 questions), and inconsistency (24 questions). The malingering and inconsistency subscales were validated against the Psychiatric Infrequency Scale (Fp) and Variable Response Inconsistency Scale (VRIN) in the MMPI-II as the external criterions. The phenomenology and malingering subscales have face validity and high internal consistency; internal consistency does not apply for the inconsistency subscale.

CORRESPONDENCE:

Dr. Massoud Stephane. Department of Psychiatry. Oregon Health & Science University. mail code: UHN 80. 3181 SW Sam Jackson Park Road. Portland, Oregon 97239, USA. Email: Stephane@ohsu.edu

Source: Available by contacting the corresponding author

CONFUSION ASSESSMENT METHOD (CAM)

Reference:

Inouye, S. K., van Dyck, C. H., Alessi, C. A., Balkin, S., Siegal, A. P., & Horwitz, R. I. (1990). Clarifying confusion: The confusion assessment interview. A new method for detection of delirium. *Annals of Internal Medicine, 113*(12), 941–948.

Administration time: 5–10 minutes
Rating instructions: Interview by a clinician
Population group: Delirium

DESCRIPTION:

The interview is a brief assessment tool for the detection of delirium according to DSM-III-R criteria. The scale is rated following a clinical interview that should ideally include a cognitive assessment (the authors recommend the Modified Mini-Cog and Digit Span tests). Patients are rated on nine domains, and must have had an acute onset and exhibit inattentiveness and fluctuation in mental state in addition to either disorganized thinking or altered level of consciousness to warrant a diagnosis of delirium. The 7th domain covers perceptual disturbances such as hallucinations and illusions with the following question: "Did the patient have any evidence of perceptual disturbances, such as hallucinations, illusions or misinterpretations, for example, thinking something was moving when it was not". Delusional beliefs are not assessed. The authors reported a sensitivity ranging from 90%

to 100% in two different clinical sites when tested against a consultant psychiatrist's diagnosis of delirium.

CORRESPONDENCE:

Dr. Sharon K. Inouye, Hebrew Senior Life, 1200 Centre Street, Boston MA 02131, Email: agingbraincenter@hrca.harvard.edu

Source: Available by contacting the corresponding author

CONSORTIUM TO ESTABLISH A REGISTRY FOR ALZHEIMER'S DISEASE—BEHAVIORAL RATING SCALE (CERAD-BRS)

Reference:

Tariot, P. N., Mack, J. L., Patterson, M. B., Edland, S. D., Weiner, M. F., Fillenbaum, G., et al. (1995). The Behavioral Rating Scale for Dementia of the Consortium to Establish a Registry for Alzheimer's Disease. *American Journal of Psychiatry, 152*(9), 1349–1357.

Mack, J. L., Patterson, M. B., & Tariot, P. N. (1999). Behavior Rating Scale for Dementia: Development of test scales and presentation of data for 555 individuals with Alzheimer's disease. *Journal of Geriatry, Psychiatry and Neurology, 12*(4), 211–23.

Administration time: 20-45 minutes
Rating instructions: Structured interview by a clinician or experienced rater
Population groups: Alzheimer's Disease

DESCRIPTION:

This interview comprises 46 questions (there is also a 17-item shorter version) covering the following domains: depression, psychosis, self-regulation, irritability/agitation, vegetative features, apathy, aggression and liability. There is a psychotic symptoms subscale with six questions (total score of 30). Questions about delusions refer to themes of infidelity, persecution, misidentification and reference, and takes into account degree of conviction. Auditory and visual hallucinations are also included. Validation conducted in 303 patients with probable AD showed interrater reliability ranging from 0.77 to 1.00, and test–retest correlation coefficients of 0.70 to 0.89.

CORRESPONDENCE:

Dr. Pierre Tariot, Banner Alzheimer's Institute, 901 E Willetta St, Phoenix AZ 85006, Email: pierre.tariot@bannerhealth.com

Source: Available for purchase from http://cerad.mc.duke.edu/Scale.htm

CONVICTION OF DELUSION BELIEFS SCALE (CDBS)

Reference:

Combs, D., Adams, S., Michael, C., Penn, D., Basso, M., & Gouvier, W. (2006). The conviction of delusional beliefs scale: Reliability and validity. *Schizophrenia Research, 86*, 80–88.

Administration time: 10–15 minutes
Rating instructions: Self-report or interview with a clinician or experienced rater
Population groups: Psychiatric populations

DESCRIPTION:

This scale assesses the contents of delusions, and the conviction with which the beliefs are held. It contains nine items, which are summed to represent the strength of conviction about delusion beliefs. Validation was conducted in 50 clinical participants with delusions. Internal consistency was good (Chronbach's $\alpha = 0.80$) and high test–retest reliability correlation coefficient was 0.81.

CORRESPONDENCE:

Dr. D. Combs, University of Tulsa, Department of Psychology, Lorton Hall, Tulsa, OK 74104, USA. dennis-combs@utulsa.edu

Source: In the original publication

SOCRATES ASSESSMENT OF PERCEPTUAL ABNORMALITIES AND UNUSUAL THOUGHT CONTENT

Reference:

Kelleher, I. & Cannon, M. (2014). SOCRATES assessment of Perceptual Abnormalities and Unusual Thought Content.

Administration time: 5–10 minutes per symptom assessed
Rating instructions: Semi-structured interview followed by a structured assessment. Some clinical experience or training is recommended.
Population groups: Children and adults

DESCRIPTION:

This scale starts with a semi-structured interview to assess for the presence of psychotic experiences, and is follow by a structured assessment to define the characteristics and features of these experiences along multiple dimensions (e.g.

frequency, attribution, associated distress, etc.). There are two sections asking about perceptual abnormalities and unusual thought content. The scale was developed not only to determine the presence of psychotic experiences, but also to systematically characterize these experiences in order to determine whether certain features contribute to a poor prognosis. The SOCRATES assessment may be used alone or in combination with other interview instruments. The psychometric properties of this new scale are currently being evaluated.

CORRESPONDENCE:

Dr. Ian Kelleher, Karolinska Institutet, National Centre for Suicide Research & Prevention of Mental Ill-Health, World Health Organization Collaborating Centre, Granits vag 4, 17177 Stockholm, Sweden. Email: Ian.Kelleher@gmail.com

Source: Available by contacting the corresponding author

DELIRIUM INDEX (DI)

Reference:

McCusker, J., Cole, M., Bellavance, F., & Primeau, F. (1988). The reliability and validity of a new measure of severity of delirium. *International Psychogeriatrics, 10*(4), 421–433.

Administration time: 10 minutes
Rating instructions: Semi-structured interview by a clinician or experienced rater
Population group: Delirium

DESCRIPTION:

This seven-item scale was designed to provide a severity rating of delirium, and was based on the DSM-III-R criteria for delirium. It is used in conjunction with the Mini-Mental State Examination (MMSE) and is based solely on observation. Each item is scored on a four-point scale (total score = 21). The perceptual disturbance items refer to illusions and hallucinations. Validation was conducted in a sample of inpatients with delirium. Interrater correlation coefficient was 0.78–0.88. There was convergent validity with the Delirium Rating Scale (DRS).

CORRESPONDENCE:

Dr. Jane McCusker, Department of Clinical Epidemiology and Community Studies, St. Mary's Hospital Center, Room 2508, 3830 Lacombe Avenue, Montreal, Quebec H3T 1M5, Canada. Email: jane.mccusker@mcgill.ca

Source: Available by contacting the corresponding author

DELIRIUM RATING SCALE (DRS) AND DELIRIUM RATING SCALE REVISED–98 (DRS-R-98)

References:

Trzepacz, P.T., Baker, R.W., & Greenhouse, J. (1988). A symptom rating scale for delirium. *Psychiatry Research, 23*(1), 89–97.

Trzepacz, P.T., Mittal, D., Torres, R., Kanary, K. Norton, J., &Jimerson, M. (2001). Validation of the Delirium Rating Scale Revised–98: Comparison with the Delirium Rating Scale and the Cognitive Test for Delirium. *The Journal of Neuropsychiatry and Clinical Neurosciences, 13*, 229–242.

Administration time: 10 minutes
Rating instructions: Clinician interview assisted by investigations and collateral from nursing staff/relatives
Population group: Delirium

DESCRIPTION:

The original 1988 scale consists of 10 items based on the DSM-III diagnostic criteria for delirium, with the timeframe of enquiry in the preceding a 24-hour period. Psychotic symptoms are assessed across three items: perceptual disturbance (e.g., illusions), hallucinations, and delusions, with severity scores ranging from 0 to 4. The scale was subsequently revised (DRS-R-98) to a 16-item scale, which was validated in 68 patients. Internal consistency was good (Chronbach's $\alpha = 0.88$). The DRS-R-98 was also effective in distinguishing delirium from the other dementia and psychiatric groups, with sensitivity 91% and specificity 100%.

CORRESPONDENCE:

Dr. Paula T. Trzepacz, Lilly Research Laboratories, Lilly Corporate Center, Indianapolis, IN 46285. Email: ptt@lilly.com

Source: Available from Trzepacz, P. et al (2001) or by contacting the corresponding author.

DELIRIUM SYMPTOM INTERVIEW (DSI)

Reference:

Albert, M. S., Levkoff, S. E., Reilly, C., Liptzin, B., Pilgrim, D., Cleary, P. D., et al. (1992). The delirium symptom interview: an interview for the detection of delirium symptoms in hospitalized patients. *Journal of Geriatric Psychiatry and Neurology, 5*(1), 14–21.

Administration time: 10–15 minutes
Rating instructions: Structured interview by lay or experienced raters
Population group: Delirium

DESCRIPTION:

This interview was developed as a structured tool to make a diagnosis of delirium that could be administered by non-clinicians. The DSI assesses seven symptom domains through a series of questions addressed directly to the patient or through observations. Delirium is diagnosed if one of the following is present: disorientation, disturbance of consciousness or perceptual disturbance. Validation was conducted in 50 patients where the DSI was compared to a diagnostic interview by a neurologist and a psychiatrist. The sensitivity and specificity of the DSI was 90% and 80% when compared to the clinician's judgment.

CORRESPONDENCE:

Dr. Marilyn S. Albert, Department of Psychiatry and Neurology, Massachusetts General Hospital, Boston, MA 02114. Email: malbert9@jhmi.edu

Source: Documentation and scoring manual available by contacting Dr. Sue Levkoff, Department of Social Medicine, Harvard Medical School. Email: Sue_Levkoff@hms.harvard.edu

---

DELUSION ASSESSMENT SCALE (DAS)

Reference:

Meyers, B.S., English, J., Gabriele, M., Peasley-Miklus, C., Heo, M., Flint, A.J., et al. (2006). A delusion assessment scale for psychotic major depression: Reliability, validity, and utility. *Biological Psychiatry, 60*(12), 1336–1342.

Administration time: 30–60+ minutes, depending on information gathering needed
Rating instructions: Semi-structured interview by a clinician or experienced rater
Population group: Psychiatric populations

DESCRIPTION:

The scale assesses delusions associated with psychotic depression. Five domains are evaluated: Conviction, Impact, Disorganization, Implausibility, Bizarreness and Extension. There are 14 items in total, rated from 1 to 3. Clear definitions are provided for each score. Items also include observations made during the interview (e.g. Acting irrationally; distrustful during the interview. Internal consistency was adequate (Chronbach's α = 0.72). Interrater correlation coefficient was 0.72, except for the Disorganization domain (correlation coefficient = 0.37).

CORRESPONDENCE:

Dr. Barnett S. Meyers, MD, Weill Medical College of Cornell University, 21 Bloomingdale Road, White Plains, NY 10605. Email: bmeyers@med.cornell.edu

Source: Available by contacting the corresponding author.

DIAGNOSTIC INTERVIEW FOR PSYCHOSIS–FULL VERSION (DIP)

Reference:

Castle, D.J., Jablensky, A., McGrath, J., Carr, V., Morgan, V., Waterreus, A., et al. (2006). The Diagnostic Interview for Psychoses (DIP): Development, reliability and applications. *Psychological Medicine, 1*, 69–80.

Administration time: Several hours
Rating instructions: Semi-structured interviews by a trained rater
Population groups: Psychotic disorders

DESCRIPTION:

This semi-structured interview is used in epidemiological and clinical studies of psychosis. It is designed to provide a diagnosis, as well as to assess symptom profiles (present state, past year and lifetime), social functioning, disablement, service utilization and need. The DIP was developed specifically for the Low Prevalence (Psychotic) Disorders Study (LPDS) 1997–1998 and greatly expanded for the Survey of High Impact Psychosis (SHIP) 2010. A Diagnostic Module (DIPpc-DM 1.0), described separately, is central to the DIP. The revised (SHIP) version includes modules on social demographics; education; employment; housing; finances; activities of daily living; child care; caring; socializing; self harm; victimization and offending; satisfaction with life; inpatient treatment; emergency/casualty treatment; outpatient treatment; public community mental health; community rehabilitation and day therapy; general practice service; non-government agencies; medication use; mental health care & unmet need; other psychopathology and cognition; drug and alcohol use and smoking and physical health.

CORRESPONDENCE:

Winthrop Professor Assen Jablensky, Level 3 Medical Research Foundation Building, 50 Murray Street, Pert WA 6000 Australia. Email: assen.jablensky@uwa.edu.au

Source: Available by contacting the corresponding author.

DIAGNOSTIC INTERVIEW FOR PSYCHOSIS–DIAGNOSTIC MODULE (DIPPC-DM 1.0)

Reference:

Castle, D.J., Jablensky, A., McGrath, J., Carr, V., Morgan, V., Waterreus, A., et al. (2006). The Diagnostic Interview for Psychoses (DIP): Development, reliability and applications. *Psychological Medicine, 1*, 69–80.

Administration time: 60–90 minutes
Rating instructions: Semi-structured interviews by a trained rater
Population group: Psychotic disorders

DESCRIPTION:

This semi-structured interview consists of the 97 items of the Operational Criteria For Psychosis (OPCRIT). The DIP–DM uses probes and differential definitions derived and adapted from the WHO Schedules for Clinical Assessment in Neuropsychiatry (SCAN). A computer algorithm has been written to generate diagnoses using the underlying Operational Criteria For Psychosis (OPCRIT) algorithm. Level of agreement between the DIP and SCAN-generated interview was excellent at 90%. Diagnostic agreement with ICD-10 was high (coefficient = 0.73) but moderate for DSM-III-R (= 0.49). Interrater correlation coefficients ranged 0.60–1.0, and test–retest reliability from 0.8 to 1.00 for most items. The DIP-DM is translated in nine languages. A self-executing PC version of the software was developed and distributed in 2013.

CORRESPONDENCE:

Winthrop Professor Assen Jablensky, Level 3 Medical Research Foundation Building, 50 Murray Street, Pert WA 6000 Australia. Email: assen.jablensky@uwa.edu.au

Source: Available by contacting the corresponding author.

DIAGNOSTIC INTERVIEW SCHEDULE FOR CHILDREN (DISC)–US NATIONAL INSTITUTE OF MENTAL HEALTH

Reference:

Shaffer, D., Fisher, P., Lucas, C.P., Dulcan, M.K., & Schwab-Stone, M.E. (2000). NIMH Diagnostic Interview Schedule for Children Version IV (NIMH DISC-IV): Description, differences from previous versions, and reliability of some common diagnoses. *Journal of the American Academy of Child and Adolescent Psychiatry, 39*(1), 28–38.

Administration time: 1–2 hours (depending on the number of symptoms present)
Rating instructions: Structured interview, no clinical experience necessary but some training is necessary for lay interviewers
Population group: Children only

DESCRIPTION:

This structured diagnostic interview assesses for the most prevalent Axis-1 psychiatric disorders in children and adolescents, including schizophrenia. Paper and computerized versions are available. The schizophrenia section asks about hallucinations and delusions. Symptoms are rated 0 (*not present*), 1 (*sometimes*), and 2 (*present*). Subsequent versions have been made, with the latest Version IV (NIMH DISC-IV), developed in 82 children and 84 parents. The latest version has unknown psychometric properties, but early versions show acceptable reliability and acceptability.

CORRESPONDENCE:

Professor Prudence Fisher, Division of Child and Adolescent Psychiatry, Columbia University/New York State Psychiatric Institute, 1051 Riverside Drive, Unit 78, New York, NY 10032. Email: fisherp@nyspi.columbia.edu

Source: Available by contacting the corresponding author.

DYSFUNCTIONAL BEHAVIOUR RATING INSTRUMENT (DBRI)

Reference:

Molloy, D.W., McIlroy, W.E., Guyatt, G.H., & Lever, J.A. (1991). Validity and reliability of the Dysfunctional Behaviour Rating Instrument. *Acta Psychiatrica Scandinavica, 84*(1), 103–106.

Administration time: 10–15 minutes
Rating instructions: Caregiver ratings
Population groups: Cognitively impaired older adults

DESCRIPTION:

The scale measures behavioral symptoms in cognitively impaired older adults. The questionnaire is completed by the caregivers and assesses frequency and severity of symptoms. There are 25 questions with yes/no answers. If a yes answer is recorded, respondents are prompted to provide ratings from 0 to 5 on symptom frequency (*never* to *>5 times a day*) and severity (*no problem–great deal of a problem*). The DBRI covers a broad range of domains including suspiciousness, persecutory delusions, misidentification syndromes and hallucinations. The psychosis items have been expanded to allow for ratings of delusions (different subtypes) and hallucinations (different modalities). There was convergent validity with the Behavior Problem Checklist and intraclass reliability correlation coefficient was 0.75.

CORRESPONDENCE:

Dr. D W Molloy, St Peter's Centre for Studies on Aging, Hamilton, Ontario L8V 1C3, Canada. Email: molloy@hhsc.ca

Source: Available by contacting the corresponding author.

EXAMINATION OF ANOMALOUS SELF-EXPERIENCES (EASE)

Reference:

Parnas, J., Møller, P., Kircher, T. Thalbitzer, J., Jansson, L., Handest, P., & Zahavi, D. (2005). EASE: Examination of Anomalous Self-Experiences. *Psychopathology, 38*, 236–258.

Administration time: approximately 90 minutes
Rating instructions: Semi-structured interview administered by trained interviewers (it is strongly recommended that the interviewer attends the 3-day EASE training course)
Population groups: Adult populations (preclinical, residual and proneness to psychosis)

DESCRIPTION:

This interview allows for a comprehensive phenomenological exploration of experiential anomalies that reflect a disorder of the basic sense of self, in a symptom checklist format. The EASE scale comprises 57 major items, sometimes subdivided into subtypes. Each item is briefly defined and then illustrated by prototypical examples of complaints. The items are aggregated into five domains: (1) Cognition and stream of consciousness; (2) Self-awareness and presence; (3) Bodily experiences;(4) Demarcation/transitivism; (5) Existential reorientation/solipsism. The EASE scale has excellent internal consistency (Chronbach's α = 0.90) and a mono-factorial structure (Raballo & Parnas, 2012). It also has high interrater reliability in interviewers with detailed knowledge of psychopathology and extensive training in administration of the EASE.

CORRESPONDENCE:

Professor Josef Parnas, Psychiatric Center Hvidovre and Center for Subjectivity Research, University of Copenhagen, Denmark. Email: jpa@hum.ku.dk

Source: Details about the EASE, upcoming courses, contact information, and literature about the EASE scale; see www.easenet.dk for information.

Additional Reference:

Raballo, A., & Parnas, J. (2012). Examination of Anomalous Self-Experience: Initial study of the structure of self-disorders in schizophrenia spectrum. *Journal of Nervous and Mental Disease, 200*, 577–583.

FORMAL THOUGHT DISORDER SCALE (FTDS)

Reference:

Barrera, A., McKenna, P., & Berrios, G. (2008). Two new scales of formal thought disorder in schizophrenia. *Psychiatry Research, 157*, 225–234.

Administration time: 40 minutes–1 hour
Rating instructions: Interview by a clinician or experienced rater
Population groups: Schizophrenia

DESCRIPTION:

The scale was developed to better understand the multidimensional features of formal thought disorder in schizophrenia, including pragmatics, cognition, paralinguistic and non-verbal aspects of communication. It has two scales, one for individuals with schizophrenia (FTD-patient) and one for their relative/carer (FTD-carer). In the former, individuals assess their own verbal communication, and in the latter, their relative/carer makes an independent assessment along similar dimensions. Validation was conducted in 90 individuals with schizophrenia and 25 carers. The FTD-patient and FTD-carer scales had excellent internal validity (Chronbach's α = 0.93 and 0.95), but correlations for FTD-patient scores were low against the clinician's assessment of formal thought disorder.

CORRESPONDENCE:

Dr. Barrera, Department of Psychiatry, University of Cambridge, UK. Email: alvaro.barrera@psych.ox.ac.uk

Source: In the original publication.

GERIATRIC MENTAL STATE SCHEDULE (GMSS)

Reference:

Copeland, J.R.M., Kelleher, M.J., Kellett, J.M., Gourlay, A.J., Gurland, B.J., Fleiss, J.L., & Sharpe, L. (1976). A semi-structured clinical interview for the assessment of diagnosis and mental state in the elderly: The Geriatric Mental State Schedule. I. Development and reliability. *Psychological Medicine, 6*(3), 439–449.

Administration time: 30–40 minutes
Rating instructions: Semi-structured interview by a clinician or experienced rater
Population groups: Older adults

DESCRIPTION:

This semi-structured interview captures a wide range of psychopathology in older people, with the timeframe of enquiring in the previous month. It can be used in a variety of settings but is most useful in community surveys. It is based on the Present State Examination and Psychiatric Status Schedule and has an associated computerized algorithm (AGECAT) for diagnostic purposes. It can be administered electronically and has been translated into a variety of languages. It produces 21 factors (symptom profiles), which include the assessment of paranoid delusions, disordered thoughts, visual and auditory hallucinations. Validation was conducted in a variety of settings, with one community study reporting 90% agreement between GMSS scores and evaluation by a panel of three experienced psychiatrists (Collighan et al., 1993).

CORRESPONDENCE:

Dr. John Copeland, Department of Psychiatry, University of Liverpool, UK. Email: jrmcop@btinternet.com

Source: Available by contacting the corresponding author.

Further Reference:

Collighan, G., Macdonald, A., Herzberg, J., Philpot, M., & Lindesay, J. (1993). An evaluation of the multidisciplinary approach to psychiatric diagnosis in elderly people. *British Medical Journal, 306*(6881), 821–824.

GREEN ET AL. PARANOID THOUGHT SCALES (GPTS)

Reference:

Green, C.E., Freeman, D., Kuipers, E., Bebbington, P., Fowler, D., Dunn, G., & Garety, P.A. (2008). Measuring ideas of persecution and social reference: The Green et al. Paranoid Thought Scales (GPTS). *Psychological Medicine, 38*(1), 101–111.

Administration time: 5–10 minutes
Population groups: General and psychiatric populations
Rating instructions: Self-report

DESCRIPTION:

The scale contains 32 items assessing paranoid thinking over the past month. Each item is rated on a 4-point scale, ranging from 1 (*not at all*) to 5 (*totally*). Part A (16 items) assesses beliefs about social distrust and reference (e.g., It was hard to stop thinking that people were talking about me behind my back), and Part B (16 items) assesses beliefs about other people wanting to cause the respondent harm (e.g., I was convinced there was a conspiracy about me). The items incorporate dimensions of conviction, distress and preoccupation. Some studies have used only the second section to measure clinical paranoia. Validation was conducted in a large cohort of psychiatric patients and non-clinical individuals. Internal consistency was excellent for both scales (Chronbach's α from 0.90 and 0.95), and test–retest correlation coefficients after two weeks were 0.81 to 0.87. There was convergent validity with the Paranoid Scale and Peters et al. Delusion Inventory (PDI).

CORRESPONDENCE:

Professor Philippa Garety, King's College London, WC2R 2LS UK, Email: philippa.garety@kcl.ac.uk

Source: In the original publication.

HALLUCINATIONS CHANGE SCALE (HCS) (ALSO KNOWN AS AUDITORY HALLUCINATIONS RATING SCALE; AHRS)

Reference:

Hoffman, R.E., Hawkins, K.A., Gueorguieva, R., Boutros, N.N., Rachid, F., Carroll, K., et al. (2003). Transcranial magnetic stimulation of left temporoparietal cortex and medication resistant auditory hallucinations. *Archives of General Psychiatry, 60*(1), 49–56.

Administration time: 10–20 minutes
Rating instructions: Structured interview by a clinician or experienced rater
Population groups: Psychiatric populations

DESCRIPTION:

This brief structured interview was originally developed to assess clinical change after repetitive transcranial magnetic stimulation (rTMS). At baseline, patients provide a detailed description of their auditory hallucinations in the 24 hour time period preceding the clinical trial. An overall "change" score is then assessed at different points in time during the clinical trial corresponding to the degree of change, with 0 (*no hallucinations*), 10 (*same as baseline assessment*) and 20 (*twice as bad*). Hallucinations are then rated across several dimensions: frequency

(0 = *stopped* to 10 = *relatively uninterrupted*), subjective reality of voices (0 = *indistinguishable from own thoughts* to 5 = *very real*), loudness of the predominant voice (0 = *faint* to 5 = *screaming/yelling*), content of the predominant voice (1 = single word to 4 = *multiple sentences*), interference (1 = *not at all* to 7 = *only pay attention to my voices*), and distress (1 = *no distress* to 5 = *significant fear and anxiety*). Validation was conducted in 50 psychiatric patients reporting five or more hallucinations per day. Internal consistency was acceptable (Chronbach's $\alpha = 0.60$). The test–retest correlation coefficient for all items was 0.70, except for realness and length = 0.51 and 0.57 respectively. Interrater reliability ranged from 0.80 to 0.98.

CORRESPONDENCE:

Professor Ralph Hoffman, Yale-New Haven Psychiatric Hospital, 184 Liberty Street, New Haven, CT 06518. Email: ralph.hoffman@yale.edu

Source: In the original publications.

Additional Reference:

Hoffman, R.E., Gueorguieva, R., Hawkins, K.A., Varanko, M., Boutros, N.N., Wu, Y.-t., et al. (2005). Temporoparietal transcranial magnetic stimulation for auditory hallucinations: Safety, efficacy and moderators in a fifty patient sample. *Biological Psychiatry, 58*(2), 97–104.

INSIGHT AND TREATMENT ATTITUDE QUESTIONNAIRE (ITAQ)

Reference:

McEvoy, J.P., Apperson, L.J., Appelbaum, P.S., Ortlip, P., Brecosky, J., Hammill, K., et al. (1989). Insight in schizophrenia. Its relationship to acute psychopathology. *The Journal of Nervous and Mental Disease, 177*(1), 43–47.

Administration time: 15–20 minutes, including rating time
Rating instructions: Structured interview by a clinician or experienced rater
Population groups: Psychiatric populations

DESCRIPTION:

The scale assesses patients' insight into their illness, need for hospital admission, and need for treatment. The 11 items are presented as open-ended questions. Clear instructions are provided for item scores, which range from 0 (*no insight*) to 2 (*good insight*), with total score = 22. The ITAQ test–retest reliability correlation coefficient at 1-year follow-up was 0.70 (McEvoy, Freter, Merritt &

Apperson, 1993; n = 20). The ITAQ total score was also highly and significantly correlated with an expert psychiatrist assessment of insight (coefficient = 0.85). Finally, the ITAQ total score was inversely correlated with medication compliance at the initial evaluation (coefficient = -0.35) and at 14 days follow-up (-0.36).

CORRESPONDENCE:

Dr. Joseph P. McEvoy, John Umstead Hospital, 1003 12th Street, Butner, NC 27509. Email: jpmcevoy@duke.edu

Source: The rating scale and scoring instructions are available from the corresponding author.

Additional Reference:

McEvoy, J.P., Freter, S., Merritt, M., & Apperson, L.J. (1993). Insight about psychosis among outpatients with schizophrenia. *Hospital & Community Psychiatry*, 44(9), 883–884.

INSIGHT SCALE–BIRCHWOOD (IS-B)

Reference:

Birchwood, M., Smith, J., Drury, V., Healy, J., Macmillan, F., & Slade, M. (1994). A self-report insight scale for psychosis: Reliability, validity and sensitivity to change. *Acta Psychiatrica Scandinavica, 89*, 62–67.

Administration time: 5 minutes
Rating instructions: Self-report
Population groups: Psychiatric populations

DESCRIPTION:

This brief eight-item scale assesses three different aspects of insight: attribution (relabeling) of symptoms (two items), awareness of illness (two items), and recognition of the need for treatment (four items), each scored as yes, no or unsure. The total score showed good internal consistency (Chronbach's a = 0.75, N = 46 individuals with psychosis). The IS-B total score test–retest reliability correlation coefficient at one week was 0.90; n = 20). With regard to concurrent validity, IS-B scores differentiated between PSE item 104-defined good-insight vs. poor-insight patients. Face validity was shown with significant difference in scores between clinically improved patients compared to non-improved patients.

CONTACT:

Professor Max Birchwood, Academic Department of Psychology, University of Birmingham, All Saints Hospital, Birmingham, B 18 5SD, UK. Email: m.j.birchwood.20@bham.ac.uk

Source: Available by contacting the corresponding author.

INSIGHT SCALE–MARKOVÁ AND BERRIOS (IS-MB)

References:

Marková, I.S., & Berrios, G.E. (1992). The assessment of insight in clinical psychiatry: A new scale. *Acta Psychiatrica Scandinavica, 86*(2), 159–164.

Marková, I.S., Roberts, K.H., Gallagher, C., Boos, H., McKenna, P.J., & Berrios, G.E. (2003). Assessment of insight in psychosis: A re-standardization of a new scale. *Psychiatry Research, 119*(1/2), 81–88.

Administration time: 15–20 minutes
Rating instructions: Self-report
Population groups: Psychiatric populations

DESCRIPTION:

The original 1992 version was a 32-items scale with a categorical scoring system (yes/no/I don't know). The re-standardized IS-MB-2003 revision excludes some of the original items that were thought not to reflect directly the concept of insight (i.e., compliance with treatment). Some other items were added, or rephrased. The revised version includes 30 items with a dichotomous scoring of 0 (*insight absent*) or 1 (*insight present*). Examples include: "I am having difficulties in thinking," "I know that my thoughts are strange but I cannot help it" and "My main problem is my physical health." Validation was conducted in 64 individuals with psychiatric illness recruited from a variety of settings (inpatient, outpatient, rehabilitation wards). The IS-MB-2003 internal consistency was good (Chronbach's α = 0.88). Test–retest reliability correlation coefficient was 0.65, and intraclass correlation coefficient 0.79. The IS-MB-2003 total insight score showed significant correlations with the PSE-defined insight item, but there was no significant correlation with severity of patients' disability, the number of prior hospitalizations or duration of illness.

CORRESPONDENCE:

Dr. Ivana Marková, Centre for Health and Population Sciences, Hull York Medical School, York, UK. Email: ismarkova@psych.hi-net.co.uk

Source: Available by contacting the corresponding author.

INSTITUTE OF PSYCHIATRY VISUAL HALLUCINATIONS INTERVIEW (IP-VHI)

Reference:

Santhouse, A. M., Howard, R. J., & ffytche, D. H. (2000). Visual hallucinatory syndromes and the anatomy of the visual brain. *Brain, 123*, 2055–2064.

Administration time: 20–30 minutes
Rating instructions: Structured interview by a clinician or experienced rater
Population group: Visual hallucinations in eye disease

DESCRIPTION:

This structured interview assesses the detailed characteristics of visual hallucinations and asks about possible etiological causes (acuity, ophthalmic diagnosis, medical history). The "General Characteristics" section has 25 questions assessing the frequency, duration and emotional salience of hallucinatory experience (e.g., Which of the following best describes how the experience feels: pleasant, neutral, unpleasant?), location in space, and perceptual qualities (Are the visions in color? Have you ever tried to talk to your visions, reached out to touch your visions or tried to brush away your visions?). The last section, "Phenomenology," has 18 questions assessing for the presence/absence of specific hallucinations (have you ever seen a face without a body? Have you ever seen words, letters, musical notes or numbers?). Responses to these questions are recorded in the respondent's own words. While the interview was originally used in individuals with Charles Bonnet syndrome, it has also been used in populations with Parkinson's disease and dementia with Lewy bodies. The instrument showed high specificity and positive predictive validity, but other psychometric attributes are unknown.

CORRESPONDENCE:

Professor Dominic ffytche, Center for Neuroimaging Sciences, Institute of Psychiatry, King's College London, UK. Email: d.ffytch@iop.kcl.ac.uk

Source: Available by contacting the corresponding author.

Additional Reference:

Mosimann, U.P., Rowan, E.N., & Partington, C.E. (2006). Characteristics of visual hallucinations in Parkinson disease dementia and dementia with Lewy Bodies. *American Journal of Geriatric Psychiatry, 14*(2) 153–160.

KRAWIECKA, GOLDBERG & VAUGHN (KGV) PSYCHOSIS SCALE

Reference:

Krawiecka M., Goldberg D., & Vaughan M. (1977).A standardised psychiatric assessment scale for rating chronic psychotic patients. *Acta Psychiatrica Scandinavica* , *55*, 299–330.

Administration time: 30–40 minutes
Rating instructions: Structured interview by a trained and experienced rater
Population group: Psychiatric populations

DESCRIPTION:

This interview assesses the severity of psychiatric symptoms most commonly reported by people with psychotic illnesses. The KGV was modified by Stuart Lancashire, King's College London (2004) and now includes 14 items, with scores ranging from absent (0) to severe (4). Items one to six are mandatory questions about the presence of particular symptoms, followed by supplementary questions about the frequency, duration, subjective severity and level of control of the symptoms. Questions refer to hallucinations (auditory, verbal, olfactory, somatic, gustatory, changed perceptions), delusions (persecution, interference, grandiose, religious) and passivity symptoms (thought interference and replaced will), anxiety, mood, affect, psychomotor retardation and abnormal movements, activity, speech.The timeframe for the assessment of symptoms is the month prior to the interview. Ratings for items seven to 13 are based on observation of the person's behaviour during the interview. Item 14 is an index of the accuracy and completeness of the assessment and not a psychiatric symptom. Psychometric properties are not known.

Source: In the public domain on the Internet.

CORRESPONDENCE:

Mr. Stuart Lancashire, Institute of psychiatry, De Crespigny Park, London United Kingdom, SE5 8AF, UK. Email: stuart.lancashire@kcl.ac.uk

LAUNAY-SLADE HALLUCINATION SCALE (LSHS)

Reference:

Launay, G., & Slade, P. (1981). The measurement of hallucinatory predisposition in male and female prisoners. *Personality and Individual Differences, 2*, 221–234.

Administration time: 5–10 minutes
Rating instructions: Self-report
Population group: General population

DESCRIPTION:

This scale assesses hallucinatory predisposition in non-clinical people with 12 items (true–false). Approximately half of the items are concerned with "vivid" or "intrusive thoughts," and "vivid daydreams," which would appear to represent sub-clinical forms of hallucinatory pathology (e.g., The sounds I hear in my day-dreams are generally clear and distinct). The remaining items are concerned with overt "auditory hallucinations" (e.g., In the past I have had the experience of hearing a person's voice and then found that there was no one there) and visual hallucinations in varying degrees of severity. The LSHS was revised by Bentall and Slade (1985) who changed the true–false response format to a 5-point rating scale ranging from *certainly does not apply to me* to *certainly applies to me*. See other versions RLSHS and LSHS-E.

CORRESPONDENCE: N/A

Source: In the original publication

LAUNAY-SLADE HALLUCINATION SCALE–EXTENDED VERSION (LSHS-E)

Reference:

Larøi, F., & Van der Linden, M. (2005). Normal subjects' reports of hallucinatory experiences. *Canadian Journal of Behavioural Science, 37*, 33–43.

Administration time: 10 minutes
Rating instructions: Self-report
Population group: General population

DESCRIPTION:

This version of the LSHS contains 16 items rated on a 5-point scale ranging from 1 (*certainly does not apply to me*) to 5 (*certainly applies to me*). Other modifications to the original LSHS are the inclusion of items assessing tactile and olfactory hallucinations, presence hallucinations and hypnagogic and hypnopompic hallucinations. In addition, items that posed problems in previous research (very low variation rates) were removed from the original scale (I have heard the voice of the devil; In the past I have heard the voice of God speaking to me). Finally, participants are explicitly asked not to report experiences that occurred when under the influence of alcohol or a narcotic substance.

CORRESPONDENCE:

Dr. Frank Larøi, University of Liège, Department of Psychology: Cognition and Behavior, Belgium. Email: flaroi@ulg.ac.be

Source: In the original publication or available by contacting the corresponding author.

LAUNAY SLADE HALLUCINATION SCALE–REVISED (RLSHS)

Reference:

Morrison, A. P., Wells, A., & Northard, S. (2000). Cognitive factors in predisposition to auditory and visual hallucinations. *British Journal of Clinical Psychology, 29*, 67–78.

Administration time: 10 minutes
Rating instructions: Self-report
Population group: General population

DESCRIPTION:

The original 12-item questionnaire by Launay and Slade (1981) underwent a revision by Morrison and colleagues (2000) to include the assessment of both pathological and non-pathological experiences of visual and auditory hallucinations. The response format was also changed to a frequency scale (1 = *never* to 4 = *almost always*).

CORRESPONDENCE:

Professor Tony Morrison, School of Psychological Sciences, The University of Manchester, Oxford Rd., Manchester M13 9PL, UK. Email: anthony.p.morrison@manchester.ac.uk

Source: In the original publication.

MAASTRICHT ASSESSMENT OF COPING STRATEGIES (MACS-I)

Reference:

Bak, M., van der Spil, F., Gunther, N., Radstake, S., Delespaul, P., & van Os, J. (2001). Maastricht Assessment of Coping Strategies (MACS-I): A brief instrument to assess coping with psychotic symptoms. *Acta Psychiatrica Scandinavica, 103*(6), 453–459.

Administration time: 10–15 minutes
Rating instructions: Semi-structured interview administered by a clinician or experienced rater
Population groups: Psychiatric populations

DESCRIPTION:

This interview assesses coping, distress and control regarding psychotic symptoms. Thirteen symptoms are defined (e.g., "Sometimes we notice that we become easily irritated, agitated or angry. We might have trouble cooperating with other people"), and then a series of questions are asked about levels of distress, and amount of control over the symptom (rated between 1 = *not present* to 7 = *maximum*). Finally, the patient is asked about coping strategies that have been used to influence or change these experiences. The manual provides a listing for 14 different types of strategies, across five domains (behavioral, social, cognitive, care and symptomatic). Validation was conducted using 23 individuals with schizophrenia on two occasions. There was good internal consistency (Chronbach's α = 0.86–0.62 for control and distress domains) and test–retest reliability correlation coefficients ranged between 0.75 and 0.80. Interclass reliability between raters was high (correlation coefficients = 0.90–0.97) although reliability with case managers was low.

CORRESPONDENCE:

Professor Jim van Os, Department of Psychiatry and Psychology, South Limburg Mental Health Research and Teaching Network, EURON, Maastricht University Medical Center, Maastricht, Netherlands. Email: j.vanos@sp.unimaas.nl

Source: A copy of the MACS may be obtained from the following website: www.macsinfo.homestead.com/index.html

---

MAGICAL IDEATION SCALE (MIS)

Reference:

Eckblad, M., & Chapman, L. J. (1983). Magical ideation as an indicator of schizotypy. *Journal of Consulting and Clinical Psychology, 51*, 215–225.

Administration time: 5–10 minutes
Rating instructions: Self-report
Population group: General population

DESCRIPTION:

The scale assesses beliefs based on superstition and magical thinking (e.g., "I have occasionally had the silly feeling that a TV or radio broadcaster knew I was listening to him.") and the capacity of thought reading or thought broadcasting ("I have sometimes felt that strangers were reading my mind"). It comprises 30 items rated true or false. Validation was conducted in 1,512 university students. Internal consistency was good (Chronbach's α = 0.83). Test–retest reliability of items ranged from 0.41 to 0.84. There was convergent validity on other measures of perceptual aberration and psychoticism.

Contact: n/a

Source: The MIS (and norms) may be obtained by contacting Thomas Kwapil. Email: t_kwapil@uncg.edu

Further References:

Chapman, J. P., Chapman, L. J., & Kwapil, T. R. (1995). Scales for the measurement of schizotypy. In A. Raine, T. Lencz, & S. A. Mednick (Eds.), *Schizotypal personality* (pp. 79–106). New York, NY: Cambridge University Press.

Kwapil, T. R., Barrantes Vidal, N., & Silvia, P. J. (2008). The dimensional structure of the Wisconsin schizotypy scales: Factor identification and construct validity. *Schizophrenia Bulletin, 34*, 444–457.

MANCHESTER AND OXFORD UNIVERSITIES SCALE FOR THE PSYCHOPATHOLOGICAL ASSESSMENT OF DEMENTIA (MOUSEPAD)

Reference:

Allen, N.H., Gordon, S., Hope, T., & Burns, A. (1996). The Manchester and Oxford Universities Scale for the psychopathological assessment of dementia (MOUSEPAD). *British Journal of Psychiatry, 169*(3), 293–307.

Administration time: 20–30 minutes
Rating instructions: Clinician interview with carer
Population group: Dementia

DESCRIPTION:

The interview was adapted from the Present Behavioural Examination (PBE) to offer a comprehensive assessment of behavioral and psychiatric symptoms of dementia in a more user-friendly and concise format. The questioning style is similar to the PBE with a yes/no answer followed by a frequency and severity rating. There are 59 questions in total and the rating covers the time period from illness onset with a supplementary question about presence in the past month. The MOUSEPAD covers a range of delusions and hallucinations. Questions about delusions are followed by a question about the strength of conviction—"Could the patient be persuaded that their belief was not true?" Test–retest reliability varied amongst items (correlation coefficients = 0.43–0.81) and interrater reliability ranged from 0.56 to 1.

CORRESPONDENCE:

Dr. N H Allen, Consultant Old Age Psychiatrist, York House, Manchester Royal Infirmary, Manchester M13 9WL. Email: harry.allen@mhsc.nhs.uk

Source: Available by contacting the corresponding author.

MATSUZAWA ASSESSMENT SCHEDULE FOR AUDITORY HALLUCINATIONS (MASAH)

Reference:

Hayashi, N., Igarashi, Y., Suda, K., & Nakagawa, S. (2004). Phenomenological features of auditory hallucinations and their symptomatological relevance. *Psychiatry and Clinical Neuroscience, 58*(6), 651–659.

Administration time: 10–15 minutes
Rating instructions: Structured interview by a mental health clinician
Population groups: Psychiatric populations

DESCRIPTION:

The interview has 23 questions enquiring about a limited set of phenomenological variables relating to auditory hallucinations. Items enquire about the content, negative response, affect, content and control of voices. The questions also enquire about the presence of associated delusions and beliefs about voices. Responses are rated on a continuous scale each with different definitions. Validation was conducted in a group of 141 individuals with schizophrenia and auditory hallucinations. Test–retest reliability was 0.40, (n = 20) and interrater reliability 0.82. There were significant correlations between MASAH score and Negative Syndrome Scale (PANSS) thought disturbances, paranoia and depression scale scores.

CORRESPONDENCE:

Naoki Hayashi, Department of Psychiatry, Tokyo Metropolitan Matsuzawa Hospital, 2–1-1 Kamikitazawa, Setagaya-ku, Tokyo 156–0057, Japan. Email: nhayashi55@nifty.com

Source: In the original publication.

MAUDSLEY ASSESSMENT OF DELUSIONS SCHEDULE (MADS)

References:

Buchanan, A., Reed, A., Wessely, S., Garety, P., Taylor, P., Grubin, D., et al. (1993). Acting on delusions: II. The phenomenological correlates of acting on delusions. *British Journal of Psychiatry, 163*, 77–81.

Wessely, S., Buchanan, A., Reed, A., Cutting, J., Everitt, B., Garety, P., et al. (1993). Acting on delusions: 1. Prevalence. *British Journal of Psychiatry, 163*, 69–76

Administration time: 30+ minutes in full; individual items/sections (5–10 minutes) can be used

Rating instructions: A semi-structured interview by a clinician or experienced rater

Population groups: Psychiatric populations

DESCRIPTION:

This interview covers eight aspects of delusional phenomenology and actions related to abnormal beliefs in depth. Domains include conviction, belief maintenance factors, affect related to beliefs, action due to beliefs (e.g., self-harm, move, etc.), preoccupation, systematization and insight. On belief maintenance factors, the MADS also differentiates between internal experiences (e.g., mood, anomalous experience) and external events (e.g., the actions of others). It is a lengthy interview, but particular sections can be used in isolation. For example, a subset of items has been frequently used in psychological studies on belief flexibility: "possibility of being mistaken." "Reaction to hypothetical contradiction" and "accommodation" assess potential or actual impact of information incompatible with the person's delusion. Correlations between self-reported and observer accounts of violent behaviors provide face validity. Interrater reliability correlation coefficient was 0.82, test–retest reliability 0.60. There was also convergent validity with the SUMD Awareness of Delusion item.

CORRESPONDENCE:

Professor Simon C. Wessely, King's College London, Denmark Hill, SE5 9RJ UK. Email: simon.wessely@kcl.ac.uk

Source: In the original publication.

Further Reference:

Garety, P.A., Freeman, D., Jolley, S., Dunn, G., Bebbington, P.E., Fowler, D.G., et al. (2005). Reasoning, emotions, and delusional conviction in psychosis. *Journal of Abnormal Psychology, 114*, 373–384.

MEMORIAL DELIRIUM ASSESSMENT SCALE (MDAS)

Reference:

Breitbart, W., Rosenfeld, B., Roth, A., Smith, M.J., Cohen, K., & Passik, S. (1997). The Memorial Delirium Assessment Scale. *Journal of Pain and Symptom Management, 13*(3), 128–137.

Administration time: 10 minutes (plus time spent gathering collateral information)
Rating instructions: Clinician interview assisted by investigations and collateral from nursing staff/relatives
Population group: Delirium

DESCRIPTION:

This interview quantifies the severity of delirium symptoms for use in clinical trials. It was intended to be especially sensitive to symptom change, and to allow for multiple repeated measurements. It is a 10-item scale, each with ratings of 0 to 3. The ratings are based on a clinician interview, with collateral information (family, nursing staff) preceding the interview. Items included in the MDAS reflect the DSM-IV criteria. Internal consistency was high (Chronbach's $\alpha = 0.91$). Interrater reliability correlation coefficient was 0.92. There was convergent validity with the Delirium Rating Scale (DRS).

CORRESPONDENCE:

Dr. William Breitbart, Department of Psychiatry, Memorial Sloan-Kettering Cancer Center, 1275 York Avenue, New York, NY 10021. Email: breitbaw@mskcc.org

Source: Commercially available from the publishers: www4.parinc.com/Products/Product.aspx?ProductID = MFAST

MENTAL HEALTH RESEARCH INSTITUTE UNUSUAL PERCEPTIONS SCHEDULE (MUPS)

Reference:

Carter, D.M., Mackinnon, A., Howard, S., Zeegers, T., & Copolov, D.L. (1995). The development and reliability of the Mental Health Research Institute Unusual Perceptions Schedule (MUPS): An instrument to record auditory hallucinatory experience. *Schizophrenia Research, 16,* 157–165.

Administration time: Variable depending on illness severity, 3 hours average
Rating instructions: Semi-structured interview by a trained interviewer
Population groups: Psychiatric populations

DESCRIPTION:

This interview includes a very comprehensive evaluation of the phenomenology of auditory hallucinations. Its 365 questions cover a range of phenomenological variables including physical characteristics, personal characteristics, relationship/emotion, form and content, cognitive processes, perceptions of experience and psychosocial issues. The scale is administered in a semi-structured interview format with follow-up questions. For respondents with poverty of thought, the MUPS also includes cards to assist in response selection. The MUPS provides both categorical and continuous scales measurements depending on the phenomenological variable being assessed. The authors report high section dependent interrater reliability (correlation coefficient = 0.81–0.89), and face validity based on the successful administration of the scale in 100 patients with auditory hallucinations. Although lengthy, Carter and colleagues report that the administration of the MUPS scale is well tolerated by participants. Different modules of this scale may also be selected depending on the interest of the professional.

CORRESPONDENCE:

Professor David Copolov, Monash University, Wellington Road, Clayton Victoria 3800, Australia. Email: david.copolov@monash.edu

Source: Available by contacting the corresponding author.

MILLER FORENSIC ASSESSMENT OF SYMPTOMS TEST™ (M-FAST™)

Reference:

Miller, H.A. (2005). The Miller-Forensic Assessment of Symptoms Test (M-FAST): Test generalizability and utility across race, literacy, and clinical opinion. *Criminal Justice & Behavior, 32*(6), 591–611.

Administration time: 5–10 minutes
Rating instructions: Structured interview by a clinician or experienced rater
Population groups: Adults in forensic settings

DESCRIPTION:

The structured interview is a screening tool to assess for malingering or possible feigning with 25 items. There are seven subscales: Reported/observed symptoms, Extreme symptomatology, Rare combinations, Unusual hallucinations, Unusual symptom course, Negative Image and Suggestibility. The M-FAST manual also assists in identifying response styles and interview strategies that may identify individuals feigning psychopathology.

CORRESPONDENCE:

Holly A. Miller, PhD, Associate Professor, College of Criminal Justice, Sam Houston State University, Huntsville, TX. Email: hmiller@shsu.edu

Source: The kit, manual and interview booklets are available for purchase from the publishers: www4.parinc.com/Products/Product.aspx?ProductID=MFAST

MINI INTERNATIONAL NEUROPSYCHIATRIC INTERVIEW (M.I.N.I.)

Reference:

Sheehan, D., Lecrubier, Y., Sheehan, K., Amorim, P., Janavs, J., Weiller, E., et al. (1998). The Mini-International Neuropsychiatric Interview (MINI): The development and validation of a structured diagnostic psychiatric interview for DSM-IV and ICD-10. *Journal of Clinical Psychiatry, 59*(Suppl. 20), 22–33.

Administration time: M.I.N.I.: 15 minutes. M.I.N.I. Plus: 30 minutes.
Rating instructions: Structured interview by mental health professionals after a relatively brief training. Non-clinical raters need more extensive training.
Population groups: Psychiatric populations

DESCRIPTION:

This highly structured interview assesses for Axis I diagnoses consistent with DSM-IV and ICD-10 criteria. It is designed for epidemiological surveys as well as clinical studies. The instrument is divided into modules, each corresponding to a diagnostic category. Each module starts with screenings questions. There are different versions available: the M.I.N.I. (17 diagnostic modules); the M.I.N.I. Plus (26 diagnostic modules); the M.I.N.I. Schizophrenia and Psychotic Disorders Studies; and the M.I.N.I. Kid (Sheehan et al., 1997). Importantly, when the standard M.I.N.I. is used, only a more general diagnosis of "psychotic illness" can be determined. In cases where a more specific classification of psychotic disorder is needed, the use of the decision tree from the M.I.N.I. Plus is required (Diagnostic Algorithms for psychotic disorders). It has been validated against the SCID-III-R (n = 370): Concordance for psychotic disorder diagnoses is good to very good (correlation coefficient = 0.53–0.76). Interrater reliability correlation coefficient was >0.75 and test–retest reliability >0.75.

CORRESPONDENCE:

Professor Emeritus, David V. Sheehan, University Health University of South Florida College of Medicine. Email: dsheehan@health.usf.edu

Source: Available by contacting the corresponding author.

Further Reference:

Sheehan, D., Lecrubier, Y., Harnett-Sheehan, K., Janavs, J., Weiller, E., Bonara, L., et al. (1997). Reliability and Validity of the M.I.N.I. International Neuropsychiatric Interview (MINI): According to the SCID-P. *European Psychiatry, 12*, 232–241.

MULTISENSORY HALLUCINATIONS SCALE FOR CHILDREN (MHASC)

Reference:

Jardri, R., Demeulemeester, M., Fligans, B., Tabet, A., & Thomas, P. (under construction). *Multisensory Hallucinations Scale for Children* (MHASC). Lille, France.

Administration time: 10–30 minutes.
Rating instructions: Self-report (with avatar support) and interview
Population group: Child (age 7–11) and adolescent (age 12–18) psychiatry

DESCRIPTION:

The scale is a touch-screen app developed to explore early-onset hallucinations. The child is first asked to customize his or her own avatar, which will accompany him/her during the entire session by providing help when necessary. In this regard, the MHASC can be viewed as a game and as a highly structured test (a "serious game") that enables children to freely communicate their own view with regard to early-onset hallucinations. The MHASC assesses multiple modalities of hallucinatory experiences rated on a continuum of severity across different domains (frequency, intensity, conviction, insight, degree of control, discomfort in daily life, distress, emotional valence, coping strategy). The scale also assesses a range of other cognitive functions (theory of mind, mental imagery) that may help in the clinical decision process. MHASC is currently under validation in French and will soon be translated into multilanguage versions with the support of the International Consortium of Hallucination Research (ICHR).

CORRESPONDENCE:

Dr. Renaud Jardri, MCU-PH de pédopsychiatrie, HDR, Centre Universitaire de Recherche et d'Exploration (CURE) Hôpital Fontan, Centre Hospitalier Universitaire de Lille CS 70001, F-59037 Lille cedex, France. Email: renaud.jardri@chru-lille.fr

Source: App for tablet devices and manual available on the website: https://www.mhasc.fr or mhasc.eu and soon: mhasc.app.

NEUROPSYCHIATRIC INVENTORY (NPI)

Reference:

Cummings, J.L., Mega, M., Gray, K., Rosenberg-Thompson, S., Carusi, D.A., & Gornbein J. (1994). The Neuropsychiatric Inventory: Comprehensive assessment of psychopathology in dementia. *Neurology, 44*, 2308–2314.

Administration time: 10–15 minutes
Rating: Clinician interview with carer
Population groups: Alzheimer's disease and other neurodegenerative disorders

DESCRIPTION:

This scale is used to characterize the neuropsychiatric profile of individuals with Alzheimer's disease (AD) and other neurodegenerative disorders. It is sensitive to change, making it a popular rating instrument in clinical trials. The NPI is a relatively brief instrument assessing 10 behavioral (including delusions and hallucinations) and two neurovegetative areas. The questions relate to changes in the person's behavior since illness onset or the preceding four weeks. Each item starts with a screening question and the rater is prompted to ask further questions if the answer to the question is positive. Frequency (1–4) and severity (1–3) are rated separately and a total domain score for each item is calculated as the "frequency x severity" (maximum score of 144). A caregiver distress scale (0–5) for each item is also included. The NPI is available in over 40 languages; in addition, outpatient, residential and brief clinical versions are available. Interrater reliability correlation coefficient ranged from 0.93–1.00, and test–retest reliability was 0.79. Content validity was established with an independent expert panel.

CORRESPONDENCE:

Dr. J. L. Cummings, UCLA School of Medicine, 10911 Weyburn Avenue, Los Angeles, CA 90095–7226. Email: jcummings@mednet.ucla.edu

Source: the NPIA is made available at no charge for noncommercial research and clinical purposes. Please contact the corresponding author for further information.

NORTH-EAST VISUAL HALLUCINATIONS INTERVIEW (NEVHI)

Reference:

Mosimann, U., Collerton, D., Dudley, R., Meyer, T., Graham, G., Dean, J., et al. (2008). A semi-structured interview to assess visual hallucinations in older people. *International Journal of Geriatric Psychiatry, 23*(7) 712–718.

Administration time: 5–15 minutes
Rating instructions: Semi-structured interview by a clinician or experienced rater
Population groups: Older adults with eye disease and visual hallucinations

DESCRIPTION:

This interview is designed to characterize visual hallucinations in elderly patients with eye disease and cognitive impairment. The instrument comprises 17 questions in three sections. Section one has four screening questions to identify the presence of visual hallucinations (e.g., Do you feel like your eyes ever play tricks on you? Have you ever seen something or things that other people could not see?) as well as instructions for clinicians to rate these experiences as simple or complex hallucinations. Section two assesses the time course, and frequency, of hallucinations. Section three evaluates the emotional content and response (e.g., How often were your hallucinations pleasant?) as well as perceived control (e.g., How often could you control the content of your hallucinations?). Validation was conducted in 80 older people with visual and/or cognitive impairments. The internal consistency of screening questions was high (Chronbach's $\alpha = 0.71$) and the interrater agreement for simple and complex hallucinations was 0.72 and 0.83, respectively.

CORRESPONDENCE:

Professor U. P. Mosimann, Department of Old Age Psychiatry, University of Bern, Murtenstrasse 21, 3011 Bern, Switzerland. Email: urs.mosimann@gef.be.ch

Source: Available by contacting the corresponding author.

OLFACTORY HALLUCINATIONS PHENOMENOLOGICAL SURVEY

Reference:

Stevenson, R.J., Langdon, R., & McGuire, J. (2011). Olfactory hallucinations in schizophrenia and schizoaffective disorder: A phenomenological survey. *Psychiatry Research, 185*, 321–327.

Administration time: 5–10 minutes
Rating instructions: Structured interview by a clinician or experienced rater
Population groups: Psychiatric populations

DESCRIPTION:

The interview assesses the characteristic features of olfactory hallucinations. The first five questions examine the frequency, valence and cause of olfactory hallucinations. The remaining questions focus on the specific phenomenological characteristics of the person's most bothersome and most frequently occurring olfactory hallucinations. This includes, for example, a description of the smell, a rating of its vividness, behavioral reactions to the hallucination and its emotional impact. Its psychometric properties are unknown.

CORRESPONDENCE:

Professor Richard Stevenson, Faculty of Human Sciences, Department of Psychology, Macquarie University, NSW 2109, Australia. Email: dick.stevenson@mq.edu.au

Source: Available by contacting the corresponding author.

OXFORD-LIVERPOOL INVENTORY OF FEELINGS AND EXPERIENCES (O-LIFE)

Reference:

Mason, O., Claridge, G., & Jackson, M. (1995). New scales for the assessment of schizotypy. *Personality and Individual Differences, 18*, 7–13.

Administration time: 10–15 minutes
Rating instructions: Self-report
Population group: General population

DESCRIPTION:

The questionnaire contains 104 items, each rated as yes or no. The O-LIFE has four scales: the Unusual Experiences scale, which contains 30 items describing perceptual aberrations, magical thinking, and hallucinations. This scale is phenomenologically related to the positive symptoms of psychosis and measures a trait often termed positive schizotypy. The Cognitive Disorganization scale contains 24 items that tap aspects of poor attention and concentration, as well as poor decision making and social anxiety. It is thought to reflect thought disorder and other disorganized aspects of psychosis. The Introvertive Anhedonia scale contains 27 items that describe a lack of enjoyment from social and physical sources of pleasure, as well as avoidance of intimacy. It can be seen to reflect weakened forms of negative symptoms, so-called negative schizotypy or alternatively the schizoid temperament. Finally, the Impulsive Nonconformity scale contains 23 items describing impulsive, anti-social, and eccentric forms of behavior, often suggesting a lack of self-control.

CORRESPONDENCE:

Professor Oliver Mason, University College London, Department of Clinical, Educational and Health Psychology, UK. Email: o.mason@ucl.ac.uk

Source: Available with extended norms in Mason & Claridge (2006) and in Mason, Linney & Claridge (2005).

Further References:

Mason, O., & Claridge, G. (2006). The Oxford-Liverpool Inventory of Feelings and Experiences (O-LIFE): Further description and extended norms. *Schizophrenia Research, 82*, 203–211. (Extensive norms presented by age and gender.)

Mason, O., Linney, Y., & Claridge, G. (2005). Short scales for measuring schizotypy. *Schizophrenia Research, 78*, 293–296.

PARANOIA CHECKLIST

Reference:

Freeman, D., Garety, P.A., Bebbington, P. E., Smith, B., Rollinson, R., Fowler, D., et al. (2005). Psychological investigation of the structure of paranoia in a non-clinical population. *British Journal of Psychiatry, 186*, 427–435.

Administration time: 5–10 minutes
Rating instructions: Self-report
Population groups: General and psychiatric populations

DESCRIPTION:

This questionnaire was designed to provide a multidimensional assessment of paranoid ideation. The Paranoia Checklist assesses paranoid thoughts of a more clinical nature than those in the Paranoia Scale. The Paranoid Checklist has 18 items such as "I need to be on my guard against others," "Strangers and friends look at me critically." Each question requires a rating on distress (ranging from 0 = *not distressing* to 4 = *very distressing*), frequency (0 = *rarely* to 5 = *weekly*), and conviction (0 = *I do not believe it* to 5 = *somewhat or greater*). The frequency dimension makes it a useful scale to assess fluctuations over time. Validation was conducted in 1,202 individuals using the Internet. There was excellent internal reliability (Chronbach's $\alpha > 0.9$ for the three dimensions) and there was convergent validity with Paranoia Scale ($n = 1{,}016$).

CORRESPONDENCE:

Professor Daniel Freeman, University College, Oxford, UK. Email: Daniel.freeman@psych.ox.ac.uk

Source: In the initial academic publication.

PARANOIA SCALE

Reference:

Fenigstein, A., & Vanable, P. (1992). Paranoia and self-consciousness. *Journal of Personality and Social Psychology, 62*, 129–138.

Administration time: 5–10 minutes
Rating instructions: Self-report
Population group: General population

DESCRIPTION:

The questionnaire investigates normal paranoid tendencies in everyday life with 20 items. Questions include: "Someone has it in for me"; "I am sure I have been talked about behind my back"; "People often disappoint me." Items are rated on a 5-point scale ranging from 1 (*not at all applicable*) to 5 (*extremely applicable*). Total scores can range from 20 to 100. The questionnaire was validated using 581 university students. There was high internal consistency (Chronbach's $\alpha = 0.84$), and adequate item-total correlation (correlation coefficient = 0.42). Gumley & Gillan (2011) modified it to include an additional measure of distress for each item, measured on a 1–5 rating scale. Internal consistency including the distress scale was good ($\alpha = 0.91$).

CORRESPONDENCE:

Professor Allan Fenigstein, Kenyon College, Samuel Mather 304, Gambier, OH. Email: fenigstein@kenyon.edu

Source: In the original academic publication.

Additional Reference:

Gumley, A. I., Gillan, K., Morrison, A. P., & Schwannauer, M. (2011). The development and validation of the Beliefs about Paranoia Scale (Short Form). *Behavioural and Cognitive Psychotherapy, 39*(1), 35–53.

PARKINSON'S PSYCHOSIS QUESTIONNAIRE (PPQ)

Reference:

Brandstaedter, D., Spieker, S., Ulm, G., Siebert, U., Eichhorn, T.E., Krieg, J.C., et al. (2005). Development and evaluation of the Parkinson Psychosis Questionnaire: A screening-instrument for the early diagnosis of drug-induced psychosis in Parkinson's disease. *Journal of Neurology, 252*, 1060–1066.

Administration time: 5–10 minutes
Rating instructions: Interview by a clinician or experienced rater
Rating: 15 minutes

DESCRIPTION:

This 14-item screening instrument was developed to detect the early signs of psychosis in Parkinson's disease (PD). The scale includes probe questions followed by detailed questions in four clinical categories: sleep disturbance, hallucinations/illusions (4 items), delusions (5 items), and spatiotemporal orientation. Positive answers are followed by questions regarding frequency and severity of symptoms. Validation was conducted using 50 individuals with PD. Internal consistency was good (Cronbach's $\alpha = 0.68$). There was convergent validity with the BPRS and excellent agreement with the SCID.

CORRESPONDENCE:

Wolfgang H. Oertel, MD, K. Eggert Department of Neurology, Philipps-University, Marburg, Rudolf-Bultmann-Straße 8, 35039 Marburg, Germany. E-Mail: oertelw@med.uni-marburg.de

Source: In the initial academic publication.

PASSIVITY SYMPTOMS INTERVIEW (PSI)

Reference:

Waters, F., Badcock, J., Dragovic, M., & Jablensky, A. (2009). Neuropsychological functioning in schizophrenia patients with first-rank (passivity) symptoms. *Psychopathology, 42*, 47–58.

Administration time: 10–15 minutes
Rating instructions: Structured interview by a clinician or experienced rater
Population groups: Psychiatric populations with passivity symptoms

DESCRIPTION:

This structured interview comprises selected items from the Schedules for Clinical Assessment in Neuropsychiatry (SCAN). Scoring now includes a 4-point scale ranging from 0 (*absent*) to 3 (*present and frequent*). The PSI assesses passivity symptoms (experience of alien control), with a total of 13 items. There are three sections: Thought Interference (5 questions), Replacement of will (6 questions), and Auditory Hallucinations (2 questions). This interview is typically administered in conjunction with a full psychiatric interview to assess the presence and severity of other psychiatric symptoms. Items include: "Do your thoughts seem so loud in your head, almost as though someone standing near could hear them?", "Does there seem to be thoughts in your mind which are not your own, which seem to come from elsewhere?", "Do you feel that your will or intention has been replaced by that of some force or power outside of yourself?" Responses are recorded in the informant's own words. Interview ratings may be summed to produce a total score. The PSI comes with a glossary with symptom definitions.

CORRESPONDENCE:

A/Professor Flavie Waters, School of Psychiatry and Clinical Neurosciences, The University of Western Australia, 35 Stirling Highway, Crawley 6019, Perth, Australia. Email: flavie.waters@health.wa.gov.au

Source: The interview and glossary are available by contacting the corresponding author.

PERCEPTUAL ABERRATION SCALE (PAS)

Reference:

Chapman, L.J., Chapman, J.P., & Raulin, M.L. (1978). Body-image aberration in schizophrenia. *Journal of Abnormal Psychology, 87*, 399–407.

Administration time: 5–10 minutes
Rating instructions: Self-report
Population group: General population

DESCRIPTION:

The questionnaire assesses perceptual aberrations in the general population with 35 items rated as true or false. Instructions to the respondents are as follows: "We want you to describe yourself as you have been during most of your adult life." Items assess a range of experiences including: perceptual changes ("Ordinary colors sometimes seem too bright to me"; "Now and then when I look in the mirror my face seems different than usual"), bodily discontinuities (e.g., "I have felt that something outside my body was a part of my body"; "I sometimes have had the feeling that my body is abnormal") and other unusual experiences. Its internal consistency was high (Chronbach's α = .84) and the test–retest reliability correlation coefficient was 0.43–0.84 (Chapman et al, 1995)

CORRESPONDENCE:

Professor Thomas Kwapil, Department of Psychology. UNC-Greensboro. P.O. Box 26170. Greensboro, NC. Email: t_kwapil@uncg.edu; or Professor Mike Raulin, Youngstown State University, Youngstown, OH 44555. Email: mlraulin@ysu.edu

Source: The PAS and PAS norms may be obtained from the following websites: www.uncg.edu/psy/people/faculty/Kwapil/ppscales.html or http://mikeraulin.com/reprints/default.html

Further Reference:

Chapman, J.P., Chapman, L.J., & Kwapil, T.R. (1995). Scales for the measurement of schizotypy. In A. Raine, T. Lencz, & S. A. Mednick (Eds.), *Schizotypal personality* (pp. 79–106). New York, NY: Cambridge University Press.

PERSECUTORY IDEATION QUESTIONNAIRE (PIQ)

Reference:

McKay, R., Langdon, R., & Coltheart, M. (2006) The persecutory ideation questionnaire. *Journal of Nervous and Mental Disease, 194*(8), 628–631.

Administration time: 5 minutes
Rating instructions: Self-report
Population group: General population

DESCRIPTION:

The questionnaire assesses paranoid thinking with 10 items rated on a 5-point scale ranging from 0 (*very untrue*) to 4 (*very true*). The items assess paranoia experiences related to social distrust and conspiracy rather than overt harm. Questions include: "I sometimes feel as if there is a conspiracy against me"; "I often feel that others have it in for me"; "Some people try to steal my ideas and take credit for me." The scale was evaluated with 98 university students and 20 clinical patients with persecutory delusions. The internal consistency was excellent (Chronbach's $\alpha = 0.90$) and criterion validity was demonstrated in the clinical sample with correlations with severity of persecutory delusions on the SAPS.

CORRESPONDENCE:

Dr. Ryan McKay, Department of Psychology, Royal Holloway, University of London.
Email: ryantmckay@mac.com; ryan.mckay@rhul.ac.uk

Source: In the original publication.

PETERS ET AL. DELUSIONS INVENTORY (PDI)

References:

Peters, E.R., Joseph, S.A., Garety, P.A. (1999). Measurement of delusional ideation in the normal population: Introducing the PDI (Peters et al. Delusions Inventory). *Schizophrenia Bulletin, 25*(3), 553–576. (40-item version; PDI-40)

Peters, E. R, Joseph, S.S., Day, S. & Garety, P.A. (2004). Measuring delusional ideation: The 21-item Peters et al. Delusions Inventory (PDI). *Schizophrenia Bulletin, 30*(4), 1005–1022. (21-item version; PDI-21)

Administration time: 10–15 minutes
Rating instructions: Self-report
Population groups: General and psychiatric populations

DESCRIPTION:

This scale asks about a range of delusion-like beliefs or experiences. It first requires respondents to rate them as present or absent. If respondents rate the item as present, they are asked to provide a rating ranging from 1 to 5 on dimensions of distress, preoccupation and conviction. Items are summed to provide a total score and three subscale scores. A 40-item version (Peters et al., 1999) and a more recent and more widely used 21-item version (Peters et al., 2004) are available. On the questionnaire, respondents are asked not to report experiences that may have occurred "under the influence of drugs." Validation was conducted in 44 healthy individuals and 33 psychiatric individuals with delusions. There was high internal consistency (Cronbach's α = 0.82), and test–retest reliability correlation coefficient ranged between 0.78 and 0.81. There was convergent validity with similar delusion scales.

CORRESPONDENCE:

Dr. Emmanuelle Peters, Department of Psychology, Institute of Psychiatry, King's College London. Email: Emmanuelle.Peters@kcl.ac.uk

Source: In the original academic publications.

POSITIVE AND NEGATIVE SYNDROME SCALE (PANSS)

Reference:

Kay, S.R., Opler, L.A., & Fiszbein, A. (2000). *The Positive and Negative Syndrome Scale (PANSS) manual.* Toronto, ON: Multi-Health Systems.

Administration time: 30–60 minutes, depending on familiarity with patient
Rating instructions: Semi-structured interview by a clinician or experienced rater, complemented by information from case notes and other informants
Population groups: Psychiatric populations

DESCRIPTION:

This interview was developed to evaluate symptom severity in schizophrenia, but also in depressive or bipolar disorder and substance related disorders. This 30-item rating instrument has three subscales: Positive symptoms (7 items), Negative symptoms (7 items) and General psychopathology (16 items). Item is scored on a 7-point severity scale (1 = *absent*; 7 = *extreme*) and clear anchor points and descriptions are provided for each score. The PANSS is completed via a structured interview (SCI-PANSS). The rater is allowed to cross-probe until confidence with regards to presence/absence of symptoms has been satisfactorily established. A number of items require information from collateral sources. A 5-factor model has been included in the PANSS user manual. Internal consistency assessments (n = 101) were high (Chronbach's α = 0.73–0.83). The interrater reliability increased when using the SCI-PANSS compared to the PANSS (correlation coefficients 0.95–0.98).

CORRESPONDENCE/SOURCE:

The PANSS Institute (www.panss.org) which provides training and certification. Email: info@panss.org. The PANSS and SCI-PANSS can be obtained from the publishers Multi-Health Systems Inc., PO Box 950, North Tonawanda, NY 14120-0950. Website: www.mhs.com, Email: customerservice@mhs.com

Further Reference:

Kay, S., Fiszbein, A., & Opler, L. (1987). The Positive and Negative Syndrome Scale (PANSS) for schizophrenia. *Schizophrenia Bulletin, 13*(2), 261–276.

PRESENT BEHAVIOURAL EXAMINATION (PBE)

Reference:

Hope, T., & Fairburn, C. G. (1992). The Present Behavioural Examination (PBE): The development of an interview to measure current behavioural abnormalities. *Psychological Medicine, 22*(1), 223–230.

Administration time: Up to 1 hour
Rating instructions: Trained interviewer with carer
Population groups: Dementia and other neuropsychiatric disorders

DESCRIPTION:

This detailed instrument was designed for the comprehensive assessment of behavior in dementia and other neuropsychiatric disorders. It covers a number of areas including mental health (including psychotic symptoms), mobility, eating, diurnal rhythm, aggression, sexual behavior, continence and other behaviors. There are 121 probe questions, with another 66 secondary questions if the initial response is positive. The scale consists of a mixture of frequency and severity ratings with 115 of the questions rated on a discontinuous scale (varying from a 2- to 7-point rating) rated on an unlimited integer scale. Items for assessing psychosis include Hallucinations, Suspiciousness, Inaccurate Insight and Unusual Thought Content. The interview covers the 4 weeks preceding the interview. Interrater reliability and test–retest reliability varies amongst domains (correlation coefficients = 0.65–1 and 0.16–0.70, respectively).

CORRESPONDENCE:

Dr. Tony Hope, Professor of Medical Ethics, Oxford University, Oxford OX3 7JK, UK. Email: admin@ethox.ox.ac.uk

Source: Available by contacting the corresponding author.

PRESENT STATE EXAMINATION SCHEDULE (PSE)

Reference:

Wing, J.K., Cooper, J.E., & Sartorius, N. (1974). *The measurement and classification of psychiatric symptoms*. New York, NY: Cambridge University Press.

Administration time: 60–90 minutes
Rating instructions: Structured interview by a clinician or experienced rater
Population groups: Psychiatric populations

DESCRIPTION:

This interview is designed to provide a clinically meaningful profile of psychopathological features of psychotic disorders. It contains 140 items and a glossary of definitions that provide a comprehensive coverage of mental symptoms. Following the 10th edition, PSE can be administered separately or as part of the more comprehensive Schedules for Clinical Assessment in Neuropsychiatry (SCAN). The PSE has been widely used in a number of large international epidemiological studies. Its main advantage is that it allows for a focused assessment of symptoms within the broader context of the patient's psychopathology.

CORRESPONDENCE:

Professor N. Sartorius, 14, Chemin Colladon, 1209 Geneva, Switzerland. Email: Sartorius@normansartorius.com

Source: Please contact the corresponding author.

Further Reference:

Luria, R.E., & McHugh, P.R. (1974). Reliability and clinical utility of the Wing Present State Examination. *Archives of General Psychiatry, 182*(6), 866–671.

PSYCHOTIC-LIKE EXPERIENCES QUESTIONNAIRE FOR CHILDREN (PLEQ-C)

Reference:

Laurens, K., Hobbs, M., Sunderland, M., Green, M., & Mould, G. (2012). Psychotic-like experiences in a community sample of 8,000 children aged 9 to 11 years: an item response theory analysis. *Psychological Medicine, 42*(7), 1495–1506.

Administration time: 5 minutes
Rating instructions: Self-reports
Population groups: Children and adolescents

DESCRIPTION:

The scale has nine items designed to assess psychotic-like experiences in children and adolescents. Each questions is rated 0 (*no, never*), 0.5 (*maybe*) or 1 (*yes, definitely*). Global rating is the sum of scores on the individual items.

1. Some people believe that their thoughts can be read. Have other people ever read your thoughts?
2. Have you ever believed that you were being sent special messages through the television?
3. Have you ever thought that you were being followed or spied upon?
4. Have you ever heard voices that other people could not hear?
5. Have you ever felt as though your body had been changed in some way that you could not understand?
6. Have you ever felt that you were under the control of some special power?
7. Have you ever known what another person was thinking even though that person wasn't speaking?
8. Do you have any special powers that other people don't have?
9. Have you ever seen something or someone that other people could not see?

CORRESPONDENCE:

Dr. Kristin Laurens, School of Psychiatry, University of New South Wales, Australia; or Department of Forensic and Neurodevelopmental Sciences (Box P023), Institute of Psychiatry, King's College London, De Crespigny Park, London, SE5 8AF, UK. Email: K.Laurens@iop.kcl.ac.uk

PSYCHOSIS SCREEN (PS)

Reference:

Jablensky, A., McGrath, J., Herrman, H., Castle, D., Gureje, O., Evans, M., et al. (2000). Psychotic disorders in urban areas: An overview of the study on low prevalence disorders. *Australian and New Zealand Journal of Psychiatry, 34*, 221–236.

Administration time: 5–10 minutes
Rating instructions: Self-report
Population group: General population

DESCRIPTION:

The scale was developed to screen individuals with psychotic disorders. It includes six questions targeting specific psychotic symptoms (current or at any time in the past), and one question asking whether the person had been told they may have psychosis. Questions are as follows:

1. Have there been times when you felt that something strange and unexplainable was going on, things that other people would find very hard to believe?
2. Have you ever felt that you had special powers or talents that other people lack, and that are not shared by any group of people?
3. Have you ever felt that people were too interested in you, singling you out, or deliberately trying to harm you?
4. Have you ever felt that things were arranged, or happened, or were said in a way so as to have a special meaning or message just for you?
5. Have you ever felt that your thoughts were being directly interfered with or controlled by another person in a way that people would find hard to believe, for instance, through telepathy?
6. Have there been times when you heard voices or noises when there was no-one around and no ordinary explanation seemed possible? OR: Have you ever seen visions or things that other people could not?
7. Have you ever been told that you might have schizophrenia, schizoaffective disorder, bipolar disorder, or manic depression?

Each item is rated yes or no. Using a sample of 116 patients, of whom one-third had psychosis, the authors selected a cut-off at two or more positive screen items (out of the first six) as a threshold for psychosis. There was good sensitivity and specificity with a positive predictive value (PPV) at 0.70 and the negative predictive value (NPV) 0.80.

CORRESPONDENCE:

Winthrop Professor Assen Jablensky, Level 3 Medical Research Foundation Building, 50 Murray Street, Pert WA 6000 Australia. Email: assen.jablensky@uwa.edu.au

---

PSYCHOSIS SCREENING QUESTIONNAIRE (PSQ)

Reference:

Bebbington, P.E., & Nayani, T. (1995). The Psychosis Screening Questionnaire. *International Journal of Methods in Psychiatric Research, 5*, 11–19.

Administration time: 5–10 minutes
Rating instructions: Self-report
Population groups: General and psychiatric populations

DESCRIPTION:

The scale was developed to screen for the presence of psychotic symptoms in the past year. It has five probe questions asking about hypomania, thought insertion, paranoia, strange experiences, and hallucinations. If the respondent's response is affirmative, a follow-up question is asked in each section. Questions are as follows:

Hypomania probe: Over the past year, have there been times when you felt very happy indeed without a break for days on end? If yes, (a) Was there an obvious reason for this? (b) Did your relatives or friends think it was strange or complain about it?

Thought insertion: Over the past year, have you ever felt that your thoughts were directly interfered with or controlled by some outside force or person? If yes, did this come about in a way that many people would find hard to believe, for instance, through telepathy?

Paranoia Probe: Over the past year, have there been times when you felt that people were against you? If yes, have there been times when you felt that people were deliberately acting to harm you or your interests? Have there been times when you felt that a group of people were plotting to cause you serious harm or injury?

Strange experiences: Over the past year, have there been times when you felt that something strange was going on? If yes, did you feel it was so strange that other people would find it very hard to believe?

Hallucinations: Over the past year, have there been times when you heard or saw things that other people couldn't? If yes, did you at any time hear voices saying quite a few words or sentences when there was no one around that might account for it?

CORRESPONDENCE:

Professor Paul Bebbington, University College London, Mental Health Sciences Unit, Charles Bell House, 67–73 Riding House Street, London. Email: p.bebbington@ucl.ac.uk

---

PSYCHOTIC SYMPTOM RATING SCALES (PSYRATS)

Reference:

Haddock, G., McCarron, J., Tarrier, N., & Faragher, E.B. (1999). Scales to measure dimensions of hallucinations and delusions: The psychotic symptom rating scales (PSYRATS). *Psychological Medicine, 29*, 879–889.

Administration time: 20–30 minutes
Rating instructions: Semi-structured interview by a clinician or experienced rater
Population groups: Psychiatric populations

DESCRIPTION:

The scale was developed to quantify the multidimensional features of hallucinations and delusions in psychosis. It has been used as an outcome measure in clinical trials, and in empirical studies. The PSYRATS has 17 items and two subscales: the auditory hallucination subscale (AHS) comprising 11 dimensions: Frequency (How often do you experience voices?); Duration (How long do they last?); Location (Where do they sound like they are coming from?); Loudness; Conviction in beliefs about origin; Amount of negative content; Degree of negative content; Amount and Intensity of distress; and Disruption and Controllability. The Delusion subscale (DS) has six items: Amount of preoccupation; Duration of preoccupation; Conviction; Amount of distress; Intensity of distress; and Disruption to life caused by beliefs. A series of questions are provided to help the clinician in eliciting symptoms. A revised edition of the PSYRATS is being prepared at the time of writing. Validation in 257 individuals with first-episode psychosis showed convergent validity with the PANSS and SAPS hallucination item, interrater reliability correlation coefficients between .79 to 1, and test–retest reliability of 0.70 after one week (n = 103).

CORRESPONDENCE:

Professor Gillian Haddock, Section for Clinical and Health Psychology, University of Manchester, UK. Email: gillian.haddock@manchester.ac.uk

Source: Available by contacting the corresponding author.

Further Reference:

Drake, R., Haddock, G., Tarrier, N., Bentall, R., & Lewis, S. (2007). The Psychotic Symptom Rating Scales (PSYRATS): Their usefulness and properties in first episode psychosis. *Schizophrenia Research, 89*(1/3), 119–122.

QUEEN SQUARE VISUAL HALLUCINATIONS INVENTORY (QSVHI)

Reference:

Williams, D.R., Warren, J.D., & Lees, A.J. (2008). Using the presence of visual hallucinations to differentiate Parkinson's disease from atypical parkinsonism. *Journal of Neurology, Neurosurgery and Psychiatry, 79*, 652–655.

Administration time: 5–10 minutes
Rating instructions: Screening interview by a clinician or experienced rater
Population groups: Parkinson's disease

DESCRIPTION:

The interview is a rapid screen for establishing the presence or absence of minor/benign hallucinations as well as formed visual hallucinations in Parkinson's disease in the past 3 months. It comprises 10 questions. The first one is a screening question. The following three questions ask about the presence of minor hallucinations/illusions (Have you experienced a brief vision of movement past you, or perhaps an animal or person, when in fact there was nothing there?) and two questions about formed visual hallucinations (Have you had visions of people, animals or objects that were in fact not there?). Finally, there is one question about auditory hallucinations, and circumstances surrounding hallucinations. The sensitivity and predictive value was calculated using responses from 115 patients with PD and others not fitting this clinical diagnosis. The QSVHI identified 75% of those with PD correctly. The specificity of hallucinations identified for PD was 91%, sensitivity was 62%.

CORRESPONDENCE:

A/Professor David Williams, Faculty of Medicine, Research Office 7, West Alfred Hospital, Melbourne, Victoria, 3004, Australia. Email: david.williams@med.monash.edu.au

Source: Available by contacting the author.

RESPONSES TO AUDITORY HALLUCINATION QUESTIONNAIRE (RAHQ)

Reference:

Mann, B., & Pakenham, K. (2006). Development of a measure to assess coping for auditory hallucinations. *Australian Journal of Psychology, 58*(2), 93–100.

Administration time: 10 minutes
Rating instructions: Self-report
Population group: Psychiatric populations

DESCRIPTION:

This questionnaire assesses responses to, and coping with, the experience of auditory hallucinations. There are 18 items and three subscales: active coping (measuring volitional activities and distraction), withdrawal coping (escape and avoidance), and suppression coping (efforts to suppress or block voices). Items are rated on a 4-point scale, ranging from 1 (*never*) to 4 (*almost always*). Internal consistency was good (Chronbach's $\alpha = 0.69–0.76$, $n = 125$), and test–retest reliability over two to nine months was adequate for withdrawal coping but not for the other two subscales.

CORRESPONDENCE:

Dr. K. Pakenham, School of Psychology, University of Queensland, Brisbane, QLD 4072, Australia. Email: K.Pakenham@psy.uq.edu.au

Source: Available by contacting the corresponding author.

RUSH HALLUCINATION INVENTORY

Reference:

Goetz, C.G., Leurgans, S., Pappert, E.J., Raman, R., & Stemer, A.B. (2001). Prospective longitudinal assessment of hallucinations in Parkinson's disease. *Neurology, 57*, 2078–2082.

Administration time: 20 minutes
Rating instructions: Self-report
Population group: Parkinson's disease

DESCRIPTION:

This scale assesses hallucinations in individuals with Parkinson's disease. It has 53 structured questions that ask about the frequency, modality and content of hallucinations. The timeframe covers the past month. The first set of questions addresses sleep and sleep disorders. The second section is devoted to visual illusions and hallucinations (7 questions). The third section relates to auditory illusions. The fourth section asks about the frequency of, and emotional response to, visual hallucinations. This section also asks about the duration of hallucinations, time of day and environmental context, and whether they are frightening. Similar questions are then asked about auditory hallucinations. There is a question about presence hallucinations ("During the past month, have you had the experience of feeling something or someone out of nowhere … that is, have you had a sensation when nothing was there?"). The last section asks about olfactory hallucinations.

CORRESPONDENCE:

Dr. Christopher Goetz, Department of Neurological Sciences, Rush University Medical Center, Chicago, IL., Email: cgoetz@rush.edu

Source: Available by contacting the authors.

SCALE FOR OLFACTORY HALLUCINATIONS

Reference:

Kwapil, T.R., Chapman, J.P., Chapman, L.J., & Miller, M.B. (1996). Deviant olfactory experiences as indicators of risk for psychosis. *Schizophrenia Bulletin, 22*, 371–380.

Administration time: 10 minutes
Rating instructions: Semi-structured interview by a clinician or experienced interviewer
Population group: Psychiatric populations

DESCRIPTION:

This scale assesses the relative "deviancy" of olfactory hallucinations. Deviancy is defined in terms of how implausible or bizarre the experience. Level of detail, duration, and level of preoccupation are also assessed. Olfactory hallucinations are rated across three sections (1. The participant hallucinated odors while resting, meditating or in the context of sleep; 2. The participant hallucinated odors outside of the context of resting, meditating or sleep; 3. The participant mis-smelled odors). Each item is rated on an 11-point scale, scored 0 to 10. A score of 0 indicates experiences that are not deviant—these include experiences shared by others, hallucinations that occur during migraine or epilepsy, and odors of smoke or leaking gas, which the authors consider to be quite common. Scores between 6 and 10 indicate olfactory hallucinations of the severity typically seen in psychotic patients.

CORRESPONDENCE:

Professor Thomas R. Kwapil, Department of Psychology, The University of North Carolina, PO Box 26170, Greensboro, NC. Email: tkwapil@uncg.edu

Source: Available by contacting the authors.

SCALE FOR THE ASSESSMENT OF PASSIVITY PHENOMENA (SAPP)

Reference:

Spence, S.A., Brooks, D.J., Hirsch, S.R., Liddle, P.F., Meehan, J., & Grasby, P. M. (1997). A PET study of voluntary movement in schizophrenia patients experiencing passivity symptoms (delusions of alien control). *Brain, 120*(11), 1997–2011.

Administration time: 15 minutes
Rating instructions: Structured interview by a clinician or trained interviewer
Population groups: Psychiatric populations

DESCRIPTION:

The scale assesses the severity of passivity symptoms. The authors developed the scale in consideration of the variability in the expression of passivity phenomena. A distinction is made between alien influences on the body and replacement of will by alien forces. The distinction is made by placing different weights to answers, with replacement items scoring higher than influences items. The scale has items referring to the following domains: Thought, Impulses to act, Actions, Emotions and Bodily integrity. The participant's score is summed out of a possible 14, providing an index of the severity of passivity symptoms.

CORRESPONDENCE:

Professor Peter F Liddle, Institute of Mental Health, University of Nottingham, Triumph Rd., Nottingham, NG7 2TU, UK. Email: Peter.Liddle@nottingham.ac.uk

Source: In the original publication.

SCALE FOR THE ASSESSMENT OF POSITIVE SYMPTOMS (SAPS)

Reference:

Andreasen, N. C. (1984). *Scale for the Assessment of Positive Symptoms* (SAPS). Iowa City: University of Iowa.

Administration time: 30–60 minutes, depending on familiarity with patient
Rating instructions: Semi-structured interview by a clinician or experienced rater complemented by information from case notes
Population groups: Psychiatric populations

DESCRIPTION:

This is the most commonly used clinician-rated scale to assess for the presence and severity of positive symptoms. It consists of 34 items across four subscales that assess hallucinations, delusions, bizarre behavior and formal thought disorder. The SAPS was developed together with the Scale for the Assessment of Negative Symptoms (SANS) to provide quantification of both positive and negative symptoms of schizophrenia. In 1992 both scales were merged to create the Positive and Negative Syndrome Scale (PANSS). The timeframe covers the past month, but this scale can be used for weekly ratings. Each item is scored on a 5-point severity scale, and clear descriptions are provided for each score. Its internal consistency for the global scores is moderate (Chronbach's α = .58) but better for the total score (.86). Interrater and test–retest reliability correlation coefficient were 0.83–0.92 and = 0.40–0.50, respectively.

CORRESPONDENCE:

Professor Nancy C. Andreasen, c/o MH-CRC Administrator, Department of Psychiatry. Mental Health Clinical Research Center, University of Iowa Hospitals & Clinics, 200 Hawkins Drive, 2911 JPP, Iowa City, IA 52242–1057.

Source: Available by contacting the corresponding author.

Further References:

Andreasen, N.C., Arndt, S., Alliger, R., Miller, D., & Flaum, M. (1995). Symptoms of schizophrenia: Methods, meanings, and mechanisms. *Archives of General Psychiatry, 52*(5), 341–351.

Andreasen, N.C., & Grove, W.M. (1986). Evaluation of positive and negative symptoms in schizophrenia. *Psychiatry and Psychobiology, 1*, 108–121.

SCALE FOR THE ASSESSMENT OF POSITIVE'S SYMPTOMS-PARKINSONS DISEASE (SAPS-PD)

Reference:

Voss, T., Bahr, D., Cummings, J., Mills, R., Ravina, B., & Williams, H. (2013). Performance of a shortened Scale for Assessment of Positive Symptoms for Parkinson's disease psychosis. *Parkinsonism Related Disorders, 19*, 295–299.

Administration time: About 5 minutes
Rating instructions: Clinician rated

DESCRIPTION:

This scale is a shortened form of the Scale for the Assessment of Positive Symptoms (SAPS). Specifically, the authors selected nine items assessing visual and auditory hallucinations that were frequent in Parkinson's disease and which were considered to have face validity. The SAPS-PD has good sensitivity to change. Other psychometric properties are currently under study.

CORRESPONDENCE:

Tiffini Voss, MD, University of Virginia, Department of Neurology, PO Box 800394, Charlottesville, VA. Email: Tv4e@virginia.edu

Source: Please contact the corresponding author.

SCALE FOR THE EVALUATION OF NEUROPSYCHIATRIC DISORDERS IN PARKINSON'S DISEASE (SEND-PD)

Reference:

Martinez-Martin, P., Frades-Payo, B., Aguera-Oretiz, L., & Ayuga-Martinez, A. (2012). A short scale for evaluation of neuropsychiatric disorders in Parkinson's disease: First psychometric approach. *Journal of Neurology, 259*, 2299–2308.

Administration time: About 10 minutes
Rating instructions: Clinician administered

DESCRIPTION:

This scale consists of 12 items assessing neuropsychiatric symptoms in Parkinson's disease. Each item assesses frequency (from 0 to 4) and severity (0 to 4) of psychosis (irritability, delusions and hallucinations), mood, anxiety, obsessive/compulsive behaviors and impulse control. Internal consistency was good (Chronbach's α = 0.7), and there was convergent validity with measures such as the SCOPA-PC; and discriminant validity with categories such as patient age, severity of illness and type of treatment.

CORRESPONDENCE:

Pablo Martinez-Maring MD, PhD, Alzheimer Disease Research Unit, CIEN Foundation, Carlos III Institute of Health, Alzheimer Center Reina Sofia Foundation, C/O Valderrebollo, 5, 28031 Madrid, Spain. Email: pmartinez@fundacioncien.es

---

SCALE OF PRODROMAL SYMPTOMS (SOPS)

Reference:

McGlashan, T., Miller, T., Woods, S., Hoffman, R., & Davison, L. (2001). Instrument for the assessment of prodromal symptoms and states. In T. Miller et al. (Eds.), *Early intervention in psychotic disorders* (pp. 135–149). Netherlands: Kluwer Academic Publishers.

Administration time: 30 minutes
Rating instructions: Semi-structured interview by a trained rater
Population groups: Adolescents and adults (pre-clinical)

DESCRIPTION:

The SOPS is embedded within the SIPS structured interview, and is used to determine the severity of the prodromal state once it has been diagnosed. It rates 19 symptoms on a 6-point scale within four domains: Positive (Unusual thought content, Suspicion, Grandiosity, Perceptual Abnormalities, Disorganized communication), Negative (including: Social anhendonia/withdrawal, Apathy, Decreased expression of emotions), Disorganized (including: Odd appearance and behavior, Bizarre thinking) and General Symptoms (including: Sleep disorders, Dysphoric mood). Rater agreement was good after training workshop (correlation coefficient = 0.85) but poor without it (0.31) pointing to the need for adequate training. The authors reported positive predictive value (PPV) for schizophrenia psychosis at 50% at 12 months (n = 14). Sensitivity and specificity were 1 and 0.71, respectively, at 6 months.

CORRESPONDENCE:

Thomas McGlashan, Yale Psychiatric Institute, 184 Liberty Street, PO Box 208038, New Haven, CT 06520. Email: Thomas.mcGlashan@yale.edu

Source: Available by contacting the corresponding author.

Further Reference:

Miller, T.J., McGlashan, T.H., Rosen, J.L., Cadenhead, K., Cannon, T., Ventura, J., et al. (2003). Prodromal assessment with the structured interview for prodromal syndromes and the scale of prodromal symptoms: predictive validity, interrater reliability, and training to reliability. *Schizophrenia Bulletin, 29*(4), 703–715.

SCALE TO ASSESS UNAWARENESS OF MENTAL DISORDER (SUMD)

References:

Amador, X.F., Flaum, M., & Andreasen, N.C. (1994). Awareness of illness in schizophrenia and schizoaffective and mood disorders. *Archives of General Psychiatry, 51*(10), 826–836.

Amador, X.F., Strauss, D.H., Yale, S.A., Flaum, M.M., Endicott, J., & Gorman, J.M. (1993). Assessment of insight in psychosis. *The American Journal of Psychiatry, 150*(6), 873–879.

Administration time: 15–20 minutes for SUMD-9
Rating instructions: Semi-structured interview by a trained rater aided by a casenote review
Population groups: Psychiatric populations

DESCRIPTION:

The original 1993 version comprised four subscales with 17 items each assessing different domains of insight. The revised and abridged version has nine items (SUMD-9) rated on a 4-point scale ranging from 0 (*not applicable*) to 3 (*severely unaware*). Three items evaluate awareness of mental disorder, effect of medications, and the social consequences of having the illness, and six items assess for awareness of specific signs and symptoms of the illness. Examples include: "What is the subject's belief regarding the reason(s) he/she has been unemployed, evicted, hospitalized?", "In the most general terms, does the subject believe that he/she has a mental disorder?" Internal consistency for the SUMD-9 is high (Chronbach's $\alpha = 0.79–0.90$, $n = 531$), and reliability correlation coefficients ranged between .76-.83. Convergent validity was shown with the PANSS G12 item (lack of judgment and awareness).

CORRESPONDENCE:

Dr. Xavier Amador, Dept. of Clinical Psychobiology Box 2, New York State Psychiatric Institute, 722West 168th St, New York, NY 10032.

Source: In the original publication.

Additional Reference:

Michel, P., Baumstarck, K., Auquier, P., Amador, X., Dumas, R., Fernandez, J., et al. (2013). Psychometric properties of the abbreviated version of the Scale to Assess Unawareness in Mental Disorder in schizophrenia. *BMC Psychiatry, 13*, 229.

SCALES FOR RATING PSYCHOTIC AND PSYCHOTIC-LIKE EXPERIENCES AS CONTINUA

Reference:

Chapman, L.J., & Chapman, J.P. (1980). Scales for rating psychotic and psychotic-like experiences as continua. *Schizophrenia Bulletin, 6*, 476–489.

Administration time: 10 minutes
Rating instructions: Interview
Population groups: General population; adolescents and adults (pre-clinical)

DESCRIPTION:

The scale assesses psychotic symptoms across a continuum of "deviancy" in order to identify individuals believed to be at high risk for future development of clinical psychosis. Eighty types of experiences are classed into six categories: Transmission of one's own thoughts, Passivity experiences, Thought withdrawal, Voice and other auditory experiences, Aberrant beliefs and Visual experiences. Experiences are rated on a 12-point scale: 1 (*normal*), 2–5 (*psychotic-like to slightly "deviant"*), and 6–11 (*psychotic in increasing order of severity*); 11 (*as deviant as that of the most deeply disturbed psychotic patient*); 12 (*very psychotic*).

CORRESPONDENCE:

Professor Mike Raulin, Youngstown State University, Youngstown, OH 44555. Email: mlraulin@ysu.edu

Source: In the public domain and can be obtained from the following website: http://mikeraulin.com/reprints/default.html

---

SCALES IN OUTCOMES IN PARKINSONS DISEASE-PSYCHIATRIC COMPLICATIONS (SCOPA-PC)

Reference:

Visser, M., Verbaan, D., Van Rooden, S.M., Stiggelbout, A. M., Marinus, J., & Van Hilten, J. J. (2007). Assessment of psychiatric complications in Parkinson's disease: The SCOPA-PC. *Movement Disorders, 22*, 2221–2228.

Administration time: 5–10 minutes
Rating instructions: Clinician administered
Population group: Parkinson's disease

DESCRIPTION:

This scale assesses hallucinations, illusions, paranoid ideation, altered dream phenomena, confusion, sexual preoccupation and compulsive behavior in Parkinson 's disease. Item scores range from 0 (*no symptoms*) to 3 (*severe symptoms*), with a total of 21. Internal consistency was adequate (Chronbach's $\alpha = 0.68$) and test–retest and interrater reliability correlation coefficients were 0.91 and 0.95, respectively. There was convergent validity with the Neuropsychiatric Inventory scale (NPI).

CORRESPONDENCE:

Martine Visser, PhD. Department of Neurology, K5 Q 92, Leiden University Medical Center, P.O. Box 9600, NL-2300 RC Leiden, The Netherlands. E-mail: m.visser@lumc.nl

Source: Available by contacting the author.

SCHEDULE FOR AFFECTIVE DISORDERS AND SCHIZOPHRENIA FOR SCHOOL-AGED CHILDREN (KIDDIE-SADS; K-SADS)

Reference:

Kaufman, J., Birmaher, B., Brent, D., Rao, U., & Ryan, N. (1996). *The schedule for affective disorders and schizophrenia for school aged children: Present and lifetime version*. Pittsburgh, PA: University of Pittsburgh, Western Psychiatric Institute and Clinic.

Administration time: 1–2 hours (depending on the number of symptoms present)
Rating instructions: Semi-structured interview with parents and child by a clinician or experienced rater
Population group: Children and adolescents only

DESCRIPTION:

The interview is a research diagnostic instrument for the assessment of axis-1 disorders in children and adolescents (ages 6–18). The psychotic disorders section is divided into two parts: Hallucinations and Delusions. Symptoms are rated 1 (*not present*), 2 (*subthreshold*) or 3 (*definitely present*). A score of 3 requires the interviewer to complete a psychosis supplement, enquiring about a broad range of psychotic experiences. Both parents and the child are interviewed, and summary ratings include all sources of information. A psychometric study in 204 children (aged 2 to 5) showed high discriminant validity between diagnoses. Interrater reliability was also high (correlation coefficients = .80–.90). Validity two years after intake interview showed that 74% of those with lifetime disorder at intake had definite psychiatric disorder at time two (17/23), compared to 37% who did not have a lifetime disorder at intake, but had at time two. There was also good convergent agreement with other diagnostic instruments.

CORRESPONDENCE:

Dr. Joan Kaufman, Yale University School of Medicine, Congress Place, 301 Cedar Street, Rm. 221, PO Box 208098, New Haven, CT 06520. E-Mail: joan.kaufman@yale.edu

Source: Available by contacting the author.

Additional Reference:

Birmaher B., Ehmann, M., Axelson, D., Goldstein, B., Monk, K., Kalas, C., et al. (2009). Schedule for Affective Disorders and Schizophrenia for School-Age Children (K-SADS-PL) for the Assessment of Preschool Children—A Preliminary Psychometric Study. *Journal of Psychiatric Research, 43*(7), 680–686.

SCHEDULE FOR ASSESSING THE COMPONENTS OF INSIGHT (SACI)

References:

David, A., Buchanan, A., Reed, A., & Almeida, O. (1992). The assessment of insight in psychosis. *The British Journal of Psychiatry, 161*, 599–602.

David, A.S. (1990). Insight and psychosis. *The British Journal of Psychiatry, 156*(6), 798–808.

Administration time: 10–15 minutes
Rating instructions: Self-report
Population groups: Psychiatric populations

DESCRIPTION:

The 7-item scale assesses three different domains of insight: Recognition of the need for treatment (2 items), Awareness of illness (3 items), and Attribution of symptoms (e.g., labeling hallucinations as pathological) (2 items). Items are scored on a 3-point scale ranging from 0 (*zero insight*) to 2 (*full insight*). The scale also provides a supplementary question probing hypothetical contradiction (i.e., "How do you feel when people don't believe you when you talk about ... *delusion or hallucinatory experience*?"). The question is rated on a 4-point scale from 0 ("*People are lying*") to 4 ("*That is when I know I am sick*"), with intermediate ratings reflective of partial levels of insight. Interrater reliability correlation coefficient was 0.72, $n = 8$. There was convergent validity with PSE item 104 and total score.

CONTACT:

Professor Anthony David; PO Box 68, Institute of Psychiatry, King's College, London, SE5 8AF, UK. Email: anthony.david@kcl.ac.uk

Source: Available by contacting the author.

SCHEDULES FOR CLINICAL ASSESSMENT IN NEUROPSYCHIATRY (SCAN)

Reference:

Wing, J.K., Babor, T., Brugha T., Burke, J. Cooper, J.E. Giel, R., et al. (1990). SCAN: Schedules for Clinical Assessment in Neuropsychiatry. *Archives of General Psychiatry, 47*(6), 589–593.

Administration time: 60–90 minutes (varies according to the number of sections applied)
Rating instructions: Semi-structured interview by a clinician or experienced rater, after extensive training
Population groups: Psychiatric disorders

DESCRIPTION:

The SCAN is a highly detailed diagnostic interview, suitable to yield research diagnoses according to both the DSM-IV or ICD-10 systems. The entire interview consists of 1,872 items. The items are rated on a 0–2 or 0–3 point scale. The SCAN consists of four components: PSE-10 (the 10th edition of the Present State Examination), the Item Group Checklist; information from secondary sources, the Clinical History Schedule; an optional section that relates to items such as social disability, personality traits and childhood disorders, and a Glossary of Definitions. The PSE-10 is the core schedule of the interview, consisting of 25 sections. Orienting questions are used at the beginning of each section to determine if the section is relevant, or can be skipped. Patients' current state, the most representative episode, or "lifetime ever" psychiatric status can be determined. There is an electronic/computer assisted version and a paper version available. The test–retest reliability for diagnostic caseness was good (0.64) (*n* = 92; Rijnders et al., 2000), and interrater reliability was also good (0.67). Broad diagnostic agreement was demonstrated with other psychiatric interviews.

CORRESPONDENCE:

WHO SCAN Experts Advisory Committee, Prof. Dr. Terry Brugha, Professor of Psychiatry, Department of Health Sciences, University of Leicester. Email: tsb@le.ac.uk

Source: Available by contacting WHO SCAN Experts Advisory Committee.

Further References:

Andrews, G., Peters, L., Guzman, A., & Bird, K. (1995). A comparison of two structured diagnostic interviews: CIDI and SCAN. *Australian and New Zealand Journal of Psychiatry, 29*(1), 124–132.

Rijnders, C., van den Berg, J., Hodiamont P., Nienhuis F., Furer J., Mulder J., et al. (2000). Psychometric properties of the schedules for clinical assessment in neuropsychiatry (SCAN-2.1). *Social Psychiatry & Psychiatric Epidemiology, 35*(8), 348.

SCHIZOPHRENIA COMMUNICATION DISORDER SCALES (SCD)

Reference:

Bazin, N., Sarfati, Y., Lefrere, F., Passerieux, C., & Hardy-Bayle, M. C. (2005). Scale for the evaluation of communication disorders in patients with schizophrenia: A validation study. *Schizophrenia Research, 77,* 75–84.

Administration time: 30 minutes
Rating instructions: Clinician-rated based on conversations during an interview
Population group: Schizophrenia

DESCRIPTION:

This scale was developed to assess language and communication disorders in schizophrenia and includes processing deficits and problems in the attribution of mental states. There are seven items rated from 0 to 3. The items assess the ability to: Clarify speech, Summarise speech, Process an ambiguity, Attribute one own's intention, Describe clinician's intention, Attribute to an intention to one's own speech, and Attribute a false belief. There was strong convergent validity with the Thought, Language and Communication interview (TLC) scores. Change of score was also associated with improved clinical status.

CORRESPONDENCE:

Dr. Nadine Bazin, Hospital Richaud, SHU de Psychiatrie, 1 rue Richaud, 78000 Versailles, France.

Source: In the original publication or available by contacting the authors.

SCHIZOPHRENIA PRONENESS INSTRUMENT–ADULT (SPI-A)

Reference:

Schultze-Lutter, F., et al. (2007). *The Schizophrenia Proneness Instrument, Adult Version (SPI-A).* Rome, Italy: Giovanni Fioriti Editore.

Administration time: 30 minutes–2 hours
Rating instructions: Clinician-rated on the basis of observations and interview
Population groups: Psychiatric populations (pre-clinical)

DESCRIPTION:

The scale reflects the ongoing refinement of the Bonn Scale for the Assessment of Basic Symptoms (BSABS). The SPI-A has 35 items assessing experiences in self-perception, rated on a 7-point severity scale. There are six subscales: Affective-dynamic disturbances, Cognitive-attentional impediments, Cognitive disturbances, Disturbances in experiencing self and surroundings, Body perception disturbances, and Perception disturbances. It identifies two major domains of risk, Cognitive-Perceptive and Cognitive Disturbances. While these domains are thought to differ in symptom severity, they do not necessarily confer different risk of conversion to psychosis. The SPI-A and the Schizophrenia Proneness Instrument for Children and Youth (SPI-CY) can both be combined with the Structured Interview for Prodromal Symptoms (SIPS) to add a basic symptom assessment if desired.

CORRESPONDENCE:

Dr. Frauke Schultze-Lutter, University Hospital of Child and Adolescent Psychiatry and Psychotherapy, University of Bern, Bolligenstr. 111, Haus A, 3000 Bern 60, Switzerland. Email: frauke.schultze-lutter@kjp.unibe.ch

Source: www.fioriti.it or by contacting the corresponding author.

Further Reference:

Schultze-Lutter, F., Ruhrmann, S., Fusar-Poli, P., Bechdolf, A., Schimmelmann, B.G., & Klosterkötter, J. (2012). Basic symptoms and the prediction of first-episode psychosis. *Current Pharmacological Design, 18*(4), 351–357.

SCHIZOPHRENIA PRONENESS INSTRUMENT–CHILDREN AND YOUTH (SPI-CY)

Reference:

Schultze-Lutter, F., et al. (2012). *The Schizophrenia Proneness Instrument, Children and Youth (SPI-CY)*. Rome, Italy: Giovanni Fioriti Editore.

Administration time: 30 minutes–2 hours
Rating instructions: Clinician rated based on observation and interview.
Population groups: Children and adolescents, aged 8 and older

DESCRIPTION:

The SPI-CY reflects the refinement of the SPI-A for children, to reflect different development of expected symptoms and metacognitive processes associated with schizophrenia. Some elements can be gathered from parent interviews, although an interview with the child is paramount as the core feature of basic symptoms is the subjective experience. Separate work validating the scale has been published (Fux, Walger, Schimmelmann, & Schultze-Lutter, 2013). The Schizophrenia Proneness Instrument for Adults (SPI-A) and the SPI-CY can both be combined with the Structured Interview for Prodromal Symptoms (SIPS) to add a basic symptom assessment if desired.

Further Reference:

Fux, L., Walger, P., Schimmelmann, B.G., & Schultze-Lutter, F. (2013). The Schizophrenia Proneness Instrument, Child and Youth version (SPI-CY): Practicability and discriminative validity. *Schizophrenia Research, 146*(1–3), 69–78.

CORRESPONDENCE:

Dr. Frauke Schultze-Lutter, University Hospital of Child and Adolescent Psychiatry and Psychotherapy, University of Bern, Bolligenstr. 111, Haus A, 3000 Bern 60, Switzerland. Email: frauke.schultze-lutter@kjp.unibe.ch

Source: www.fioriti.it or by contacting the authors (Fux et al., 2013).

SCHIZOTYPAL PERSONALITY QUESTIONNAIRE (SPQ), AND SCHIZOTYPAL PERSONALITY QUESTIONNAIRE-BRIEF (SPQ-B)

Reference:

Raine, A. (1991). The SPQ: A scale for the assessment of schizotypal personality based on DSM-II-R criteria. *Schizophrenia Bulletin, 17*, 555–564.

Administration time: 5–10 minutes
Rating instructions: Self-report
Population groups: General and psychiatric populations

DESCRIPTION:

The questionnaire was modelled on *Diagnostic Statistical Manual–Third Edition* (DSM-III-R) criteria for schizotypal personality disorder, and contains subscales for all nine schizotypal traits. There are a total of 74 items rated yes or no. The nine subscales include: Ideas of Reference, Social Anxiety, Odd Beliefs/Magical Thinking, Unusual Perceptual Experiences, Eccentric/Odd Behavior, No Close Friends, Odd Speech, Constricted Affect, Suspiciousness. Three factors can be calculated: Cognitive-Perceptual, Interpersonal, Disorganization. In 1995, Raine and Benishay developed a shorter screening version of the SPQ (the Schizotypal Personality Questionnaire-Brief; SPQ-B), containing 22 items and scales for the three factors. A version for children (SPQ-C; Raine et al., 2010) is also available.

CORRESPONDENCE:

Dr. Adrian Raine, 3718 Locust Walk, University of Pennsylvania, Philadelphia, PA; Email: araine@sas.upenn.edu

Source: In the original publication.

Further Reference:

Raine, A., & Benishay, D. (1995). The SPQB: A brief screening instrument for schizotypal personality disorder. *Journal of Personality Disorders, 9*, 346–355.

SELF-APPRAISAL OF ILLNESS QUESTIONNAIRE (SAIQ)

Reference:

Marks, K.A., Fastenau, P.S., Lysaker, P.H., & Bond, G.R. (2000). Self-Appraisal of Illness Questionnaire (SAIQ): Relationship to researcher-rated insight and neuropsychological function in schizophrenia. *Schizophrenia Research, 45*(3), 203–211.

Administration time: 15–25 minutes
Rating instructions: Self-report
Population groups: Psychiatric populations

DESCRIPTION:

This questionnaire assesses insight on a number of related concepts, such as awareness of illness, beliefs about the outcome of the illness, worry about the illness, worry about related issues, and recognition of the need for treatment. Items are rated on a 4-point scale, ranging from *strongly agree* to *strongly disagree*. Based on factor analysis, the 17-item scores can be organized along the dimensions of Presence/Outcome of Disease, Worry, and Need for Treatment. The items are presented as statements or questions. Examples of items include: "When someone first recommended the present treatment, how did you feel about this person's recommendation for treatment?"; "There's no doubt in my mind that I'll be better someday"; "I have symptoms of mental illness." Internal reliability was good (Chronbach's α = .83). Reliability of the three domains ranged 0.77 to 0.86. There was convergent with the total SAMD score (Amador et al., 1993) as well as with the PANSS G12 insight item.

CORRESPONDENCE:

Dr. K.A. Marks: Indiana University, Purdue University Indianapolis (IUPUI) 402 N. Blackford Street, LD124, Indianapolis, IN 46202.

Source: In the initial publication.

SELF-RATED VISUAL HALLUCINATION QUESTIONNAIRE FOR PARKINSON'S DISEASE (VHQ-PD)

Reference:

Barnes, J., & David, A. S. (2001). Visual hallucinations in Parkinson's Disease: A review and phenomenological survey. *Journal of Neurology, Neurosurgery & Psychiatry, 70*, 727–733.

Administration time: 15–30 minutes
Rating instructions: Self-report
Population group: Parkinson's disease

DESCRIPTION:

This questionnaire assesses for visual hallucinations in Parkinson's disease in the past 3 months. It assesses hallucinations across four dimensions: temporal aspects (frequency, duration, onset), content and form (quantity, color clarity, movement), subjective factors (affect, arousal, perceived control), and external factors (triggers, eyes open or close).

CORRESPONDENCE:

Professor Jim Barnes, Department of Psychology, University of Bedfordshire, Park Square Luton, Bedfordshire, LU1 3JU. Email: James.Barnes@beds.ac.uk

Source: Available by contacting the corresponding author.

Additional Reference:

Barnes, J., & Boubert, L. (2011). Visual memory errors in Parkinson disease patients with visual hallucinations. *International Journal of Neuroscience, 121*, 159–164.

SEMI-STRUCTURED INTERVIEW ABOUT VISIONS IN PSYCHIATRIC PATIENTS

Reference:

Gauntlett-Gilbert, J., & Kuipers, E. (2005). Visual hallucinations in psychiatric conditions: Appraisals and their relationship to distress. *British Journal of Clinical Psychology, 44*(1), 77–87.

Administration time: 30 minutes–1 hour
Rating instructions: Semi-structured interview by a clinician or experienced rater
Population groups: Psychiatric populations

DESCRIPTION:

This interview asks detailed questions about the phenomenology of visual hallucinations, and the person's subjective response to them. Participants are required to make quantitative ratings on each item. Responses to the questions are recorded in the participant's own words, and then coded into response categories. Questions ask about content and qualitative features of the experience. The role of mood and distress is also explored, as well as control/coping strategies, and appraisals. For two questions, participants were required to sort 17 cards describing common stressors, and 24 cards with emotion adjectives into yes and no piles. Their perceived reality of the vision, at the time and in hindsight, are rated on a 5-point Likert scale.

CORRESPONDENCE:

Professor Elizabeth Kuipers, Department of Psychology, PO Box 77, Institute of Psychiatry, King's College London, London SE5 8AF, UK. Email: E.Kuipers@iop.kcl.ac.uk

Source: Available by contacting the corresponding author.

SEMI-STRUCTURED INTERVIEW ON COMPLEX VISUAL HALLUCINATIONS FOR CHARLES BONNET'S SYNDROME

Reference:

Teunisse, R., Cruysberg, J., Hoefnagel, W., Verbeek, A., & Zitman, F. (1996). Visual hallucinations in psychologically normal people: Charles Bonnet's syndrome. *The Lancet, 247*, 794–796.

Administration time: 10 minutes
Rating instructions: Semi-structured interview by a clinician or experienced rater
Population group: Eye disease and visual hallucinations

DESCRIPTION:

This interview assesses the characteristics of complex visual hallucinations in individuals with eye disease. Domains include temporal aspects (frequency, duration), content, perceptual dimensions (colors, movement, clarity), and whether hallucinations are repetitive and stereotyped. A second section asks about the situational circumstances in which hallucinations occur, such as time of day, light intensity, being alone and at home, other circumstances (e.g., fatigue, stress). Finally, the interview asks about behavioral acts initiated to stop hallucinations.

CORRESPONDENCE:

Dr. R. Teunisse, Department of Geriatric Psychiatry, Dimence, Deventer, The Netherlands. Email: r.teunisse@dimence.nl

Source: Available by contacting the corresponding author.

SPECIFIC PSYCHOTIC EXPERIENCES QUESTIONNAIRE (SPEQ)

References:

Ronald, A., Sieradzka, D., Cardno, A., Haworth, C., McGuire, P., & Freeman, D. (2013). Characterization of Psychotic Experiences in Adolescence Using the Specific Psychotic Experiences Questionnaire: Findings From a study of 5000 16-year-old twins. *Schizophrenia Bulletin, 40*(4), 868–877.

Administration time: 30 minutes
Rating instructions: Self-report
Population group: Adolescents

DESCRIPTION:

The questionnaire assesses the most common experiences traditionally associated with psychosis in adolescents. It was developed by selecting items from existing scales, and was devised using 5,000 16-year-old twin adolescents and their parents. A principal component analysis identified a six-component solution: paranoia (15 items), hallucinations (9 items), cognitive disorganization (11 items), grandiosity (10 items), anhedonia (10 items), and parent-rated negative symptoms (8 items). Internal consistency was good (Chronbach's α = 0.77–0.93), and test–retest reliability across 9 months was 0.65–0.74. Correlations between SPEQ subscales were also good.

CORRESPONDENCE:

Angelica Ronald, Centre for Brain and Cognitive Development, Birkbeck, Malet Street, London WC1E 7HX, UK. E-mail: a.ronald@bbk.ac.uk

Source: In the original academic publication.

STATE SOCIAL PARANOIA SCALE (SSPS)

Reference:

Freeman, D., Pugh, K., Green, C., Valmaggia, L., Dunn, G. & Garety, P. A. (2007). A measure of state persecutory ideation for experimental studies. *Journal of Nervous & Mental Disease, 195*, 781–784.

Administration time: 5–10 minutes
Rating instructions: Self-report
Population group: General population

DESCRIPTION:

The scale assesses state paranoia, specifically capturing paranoid thinking in social situations. The items conform to definitions of persecutory thinking that comprise both feared harm and perpetrator intent. The 20 items are rated on a 5-point rating scale. The authors suggest the SSPS is useful in experimental studies wanting to investigate moment-by-moment variations in paranoia. The scale was tested in 164 non-clinical participants and 24 individuals at risk of psychosis, and was found to have high internal reliability (Chronbach's $\alpha = 0.91$). Test–retest reliability correlation coefficient was 0.78. Convergent validity as assessed using structured interviews.

CORRESPONDENCE:

Professor Daniel Freeman, University College, Oxford, UK. Email: Daniel.freeman@psych.ox.ac.uk

Source: In the original academic publication.

STRUCTURED CLINICAL INTERVIEW FOR DSM AXIS 1 DISORDERS (SCID-I)

Reference:

Spitzer, R., Williams, J., Gibbon, M., & First, M. (1992). The Structured Clinical Interview for DSM-III-R (SCID): I. History, rationale, and description. *Archives of General Psychiatry, 49*(8), 624–629.

Administration time: 60–120 minutes
Rating instructions: Semi-structured interview by a clinician or experienced rater; training is 1or 2 days
Population groups: Psychiatric populations

DESCRIPTION:

The interview provides diagnoses according to DSM criteria with a broad coverage of axis I diagnoses. The SCID is organized in modules that begin with screening questions and answers which are rated on a 3-point scale. The module for psychotic (and mood disorders) of the SCID consists of two parts. There is one section on psychotic symptoms. Another separate section is used for differentiation, and is essentially a psychosis decision-tree for making the final diagnosis. The remainder of the SCID is organized in sections that combine symptom and diagnosis. Several versions are available. The SCID-CV (Clinician Version), the SCID-I-RV (Research Version, which contains additional disorders and subtypes), the SCID-I/P (Patient Edition, for use in psychiatric populations), the SCID-I/NP (Non-patient Edition, for community surveys or family studies), and the SCID-CT (Clinical Trials). The validity and reliability of the scale has been established.

CORRESPONDENCE:

Michael First, MD, Biometrics Research Department, Columbia University at NYSPI, Columbia University, 1051 Riverside Drive, Unit 60, New York, NY 10032. Email: scid4@columbia.edu

Source: Score sheets and manual available commercially through APA American Psychiatric Publishing: www.appi.org

---

STRUCTURED INTERVIEW FOR ASSESSING PERCEPTUAL ANOMALIES (SIAPA)

Reference:

Bunney, W.E. Jr., Hetrick, W.P., Bunney, B.G., Patterson, J.V., Jin, Y., Potkin, S.G., et al. (1999). Structured interview for assessing perceptual anomalies (SIAPA). *Schizophrenia Bulletin, 25*, 577–592.

Administration time: 30 minutes
Rating instructions: Structured interview by a clinician or experienced rater
Population group: General and psychiatric populations

DESCRIPTION:

This interview measures perceptual anomalies as distinct from hallucinations. It also assesses their frequency across different sensory modalities. The interview includes 15 items assessing sensory perception and attention, rated on a 5-point scale (0 = *absent* to 4 = *pervasive*). The following three domains are explored: Hypersensitivity to stimuli (e.g., "Have you ever had the feeling or sensation that sounds were particularly loud? Or louder than usual?"); The feeling of inundation or flooding by external sensory stimuli (e.g., "Have you ever had the experience or felt like you were being flooded or inundated by sounds? Or that you couldn't block out sounds?"); and Difficulty with selective attention to external sensory stimuli (e.g., "Have you ever had the experience or felt like you couldn't pay attention to one sound, or a conversation, because of interference from other sounds like background noise?"). The authors report good interrater agreement, face validity, and good discriminant validity.

CORRESPONDENCE:

Distinguished Professor William Bunney MD, Psychiatry & Human Behavior, University of California, Irvine D438 Medical Sciences 1 Mail Code: 1675 Irvine, CA. Email: webunney@uci.edu

Source: Available by contacting the corresponding author.

STRUCTURED INTERVIEW FOR PRODROMAL SYMPTOMS (SIPS)

Reference:

McGlashan, T., Miller, T., Woods, S., Hoffman, R., & Davison, L. (2001). Instrument for the assession of prodromal symptoms and states. In T. Miller et al. (Eds.), *Early intervention in psychotic disorders* (pp. 135–149). Netherlands: Kluwer Academic Publishers.

Administration time: 2–3 hours
Rating instructions: Structured interview by a clinician or experienced rater
Population groups: Adolescents and adults (pre-clinical)

DESCRIPTION:

The SIPS is a diagnostic interview closely modeled on the CA-ARMS. The SIPS was developed to define the presence/absence of psychosis and prodromal states (Brief Intermittent Psychotic Symptom Syndrome, Attenuated Positive Symptom Syndrome, and Genetic Risk and Deterioration Syndrome). The SIPS contains the Scale of Prodromal Symptoms (SOPS). Prodrome classification was reported to yield acceptable interrater reliability (kappa = 0.81) (Miller et al., 2003). The predictive value of the SIPS was examined in a sample of prodromal patients over 6 and 12 months follow-up. The results show a positive predictive value of 43% at 6 months, and 50% at 12 months. Sensitivity and specificity were 100% and 71% at 6 months, and 100% and 74% at 12 months (Miller et al., 2003).

CORRESPONDENCE:

Professor Thomas McGlashan, Yale Psychiatric Institute, 184 Liberty Street, PO Box 208038, New Haven, CT 06520. Email: Thomas.mcGlashan@yale.edu

Source: Available by contacting the corresponding author.

Further Reference:

Miller, T.J., McGlashan, T.H., Rosen, J.L., Cadenhead, K., Cannon, T., Ventura, J., et al. (2003). Prodromal assessment with the structured interview for prodromal syndromes and the scale of prodromal symptoms: predictive validity, interrater reliability, and training to reliability. *Schizophrenia Bulletin, 29*(4), 703–715.

STRUCTURED INTERVIEW OF REPORTED SYMPTOMS–SECOND EDITION (SIRS-2)

Reference:

Rogers, R., Sewell, K.W., & Gillard, N.D. (2010). *Structured interview of reported symptoms* (2nd ed.). Denton: University of North Texas.

Administration time: 30–40 minutes; Scoring Time: 20 minutes
Rating instructions: Structured interview for experienced clinicians who have been specifically trained in administration of the instrument
Population groups: Adults in forensic settings

DESCRIPTION:

This structured interview assesses deliberate distortions in the reports of psychiatric symptoms. The manual provides information regarding how individuals may distort or fabricate their symptoms. The primary focus of the SIRS-2 is on the evaluation of feigning, and the manner in which it is likely to occur—for example, exaggeration of symptom severity versus fabrication of symptomatology.

CORRESPONDENCE:

Dr. Rogers, Professor, University of North Texas. Email: Richard.rogers@unt.edu

Source: Introductory kit, manual and interview booklets available commercially from ACER (www.shop.acer.edu.au) or PAR publishers (www4.parinc.com).

SURVEY PSYCHIATRIC ASSESSMENT SCHEDULE (SPAS)

Reference:

Bond, J., Brooks, P., Carstairs, V., & Giles, L. (1980). The reliability of a survey psychiatric assessment schedule for the elderly. *British Journal of Psychiatry, 37*, 148–162.

Administration time: 20–30 minutes
Rating instructions: Semi-structured interview by a clinician or experienced interviewer
Population group: Older psychiatric adults

DESCRIPTION:

This interview was adapted from the Geriatric Mental State Schedule (GMSS). It is a structured tool to be used by experienced clinicians to detect a wide range of psychiatric symptoms in older adults. It consists of 51 items divided into three sections. The sections assess for cognitive organic dysfunctions, affective disorders and schizophrenia/paranoid disorders. The third section contains 10 yes/no questions covering a range of psychotic experiences (e.g., "Do you feel that people are controlling your mind against your will? If yes, in what way?"; "Do you ever think you hear a voice when there is nobody there? If yes, where does the voice come from, what does it say?"). Validation was conducted in 246 older adults from hospital, clinic and community populations with the GMSS and the SPAS. Agreement was reasonable for the diagnosis of organic disorders but less so for psychotic disorders.

The psychiatrist identified 10 cases of schizophrenia or paranoid disorder and seven of these were correctly identified with the SPAS. There were however 42 false positives.

CORRESPONDENCE:

Dr. John Bond, Baddiley-Clark Building, Institute of Health and Society, Richardson Road, Newcastle University NE2 4AX. Email: john.bond@ncl.ac.uk

Source: In the original publication.

THOUGHT AND LANGUAGE INDEX (TLI)

Reference:

Liddle, P. F, Elton, T.C. N, Caissie, S. L, Anderson, C. M, Bates, D. J, Quested, D. J, et al. (2002). Thought and Language Index: An instrument for assessing thought and language in schizophrenia. *British Journal of Psychiatry, 181*, 326–330.

Administration time: <30 minutes
Rating instructions: Assessment based on informant responses, rated by a clinician or experienced interviewer
Population: Psychosis

DESCRIPTION:

This brief instrument assesses formal thought disorder. The assessment is based on responses elicited by standard stimuli from the Thematic Apperception Test (TAT; Murray, 1943) or similar. Eight pictures from the TAT are presented sequentially for one minute each, and the participant is asked to talk about each picture.

After the one-minute presentation, the interviewer asks the informant to explain any odd or unusual speech made during the minute. The entire procedure lasts approximately 15 minutes. The interview is videotaped and subsequently transcribed. The speech samples are assessed for the presence of poverty of speech and weakening of goal (impoverishment of thought and speech), looseness, peculiar word use, peculiar sentence construction and peculiar logic (i.e., disorganization of thought and language; disorganization phenomenon) and perseveration and distractibility. A score of 0.25, 0.50, 0.75 or 1.0 is assigned based on an increasing severity of individual instances of thought or language disorder using a manual. Interrater reliability for individual items ranged between 0.60–0.93. Convergent validity was established with the Assessment of Positive Symptoms (SAPS) thought disorder global score.

CORRESPONDENCE:

Peter F. Liddle, Professor of Psychiatry, faculty of Medicine and Health Sciences, Room B25 Institute of Mental Health, Innovation Park Triumph Road Nottingham NG7 2TU UK. Email: peter.liddle@nottingham.ac.uk

Source: The manual and instrument are available by contacting the corresponding author.

THOUGHT DISORDER INDEX (TDI)

Reference:

Johnston, M. H., & Holzman, P.S. (1979). *Assessing schizophrenic thinking: A clinical and research instrument for measuring thought disorder.* San Francisco, CA: Jossey-Bass.

Administration time: Several hours
Rating instructions: Clinical interview by an experienced rater
Population: Psychosis

DESCRIPTION:

This interview is a comprehensive scale designed to assess, classify, and measure instances of disordered thought. The TDI is usually derived from verbatim responses to the Rorschach test (Rorschach, 1943) or from the verbal subscales of the Wechsler Adult Intelligence Scale (WAIS; Wechsler, 1958). The scale provides different scoring levels assigned to specific items. The sum of each instance of thought disorder provides a total TDI score, which is then weighted for severity level. For example, 0.25 level is designated for inappropriate distance, flippant response, vagueness, peculiar verbalizations and responses, clangs, perseveration and incongruous combinations; 0.50 level is used for relationship verbalization, autistic logic, idiosyncratic symbolism, queer responses, confusion, looseness, fabulized combinations, playful confabulations and fragmentation; 0.75 level is assigned to fluidity, absurd responses, confabulations, autistic logic; and finally 1.0 level is scored for neologism, contamination and incoherence. Thus, the score assigned best captures the process evident in the response. This instrument has shown high interrater reliability (Coleman et al., 1993). In addition, correlations for the same variables for all possible pairings of the teams were also significant. The internal and predictive validity of TDI has also been supported.

CORRESPONDENCE:

Dr. Mary Hollis Johnston. 4820 S Greenwood Ave; Chicago IL 60615.

Source: The scale and scoring manuals are available in the book (Johnston & Holzman, 1979) and from Solovay et al. (1986).

Additional References:

Coleman, M. J., Carpenter, J. T., Waternaux, C., Levy, D.L., Shenton, M.E., Perry, J., et al. (1993). The thought disorder index: A reliability study. *Psychological Assessment: A Journal of Consulting and Clinical Psychology, 3*(3), 336–342.

Solovay, M., Shenton, M., Gasperetti, C., Coleman, M., Kestnbaum, E., Carpenter, J., & Holzman, P. (1986). Scoring manual for the Thought Disorder Index. *Schizophrenia Bulletin, 12*(3), 483–496.

THOUGHT DISORDER QUESTIONNAIRE (TDQ)

Reference:

Waring, E., Neufeld, R., & Schaefer, B. (2003). The Thought Disorder Questionnaire. *Canadian Journal of Psychiatry, 48*, 45–51.

Administration time: 20–30 minutes
Rating instructions: Self-report
Population: Psychosis

DESCRIPTION:

This questionnaire assesses for the presence and severity of thought disorder. The scale contains six subscales: Content of thought, Control of thought, Orientation, Perception, Fantasy, and Symptoms, each with 10 items. Each question is assessed on a 5-point rating scale from 0 (never) to 4 (always). Adequate internal consistency was reported (Chronbach's alpha = 0.78). Significant differences between healthy controls (n = 30) and individuals with schizophrenia (n = 102) were also demonstrated.

CORRESPONDENCE:

Dr. Edward Waring, Surrey Memorial Hospital, 13750 96th Avenue, Surrey BC Canada. Email: ted.waring@fvhr.hnet.bc.ca

Source: Available by contacting the corresponding author.

THOUGHT, LANGUAGE AND COMMUNICATION (TLC) SCALE

Reference:

Andreasen, N.C. (1979). Thought, Language, and Communication Disorders II: Diagnostic significance. *Archives of General Psychiatry, 36*(12), 1325–1330.

Administration time: 30 minutes–1 hour (depending on severity of thought disorder and rater's experience)
Rating instructions: Clinical interview by an experienced rater
Population: Psychosis

DESCRIPTION:

The interview assesses formal thought disorder through verbal output. The scale provides substantial autonomy to the patient in determining the content of the verbal output. This is because TLC does not make assumptions about the nature of thought disorder and simply describes abnormalities in speech based on a standardized psychiatric interview. This scale captures various deficits in thought disorder and language processing such as poverty of speech, tangentiality, derailment, neologism, clanging, circumstantiality, loss of goal, and phonemic and semantic paraphasias. Each item is defined through the use of clinical examples and is rated from 0 to 4 (i.e., 0 = *absent*; 1 = *slight*; 2 = *medium*; 3 = *severe*; 4 = *extreme*). The scale has been shown to provide diagnostic specificity within and across psychotic disorders. Discriminant validity was assessed in 100 psychiatric patients and 94 healthy controls. Fluency and productivity were the most helpful in distinguishing affective psychosis from schizophrenia. Reliability was found to be good as established using recorded and live interviews.

CORRESPONDENCE:

Professor Nancy C. Andreasen, c/o MH-CRC Administrator. Department of Psychiatry. Mental Health Clinical Research Center. University of Iowa Hospitals & Clinics. 200 Hawkins Drive, 2911 JPP, Iowa City, IA 52242–1057.

Source: Please contact the author.

Additional Reference:

Andreasen, N. C. (1979). Thought, language, and communication disorder: Clinical assessment, definition of terms and evaluation of their reliability. *Archives of General Psychiatry, 36*(12), 1315–1321.

TOTTORI UNIVERSITY HALLUCINATIONS RATING SCALE (TUHRAS)

Reference:

Wada-Isoe, K., Ohta, K., Imamura, K., Kitayama, M., Nomura, T., Yasui, K., et al. (2008). Assessment of hallucinations in Parkinson's disease using a novel scale. *Acta Neurologica Scandinavica, 117*(1), 35–40.

Administration time: 20 minutes
Rating instructions: Semi-structured interview by clinician or experienced interview
Population group: Parkinson's disease

DESCRIPTION:

This scale assesses hallucinations in Parkinson's disease on seven items, rated 0 to 5. Item 1 asks about the presence of visual, auditory, olfactory, tactile and cenesthetic hallucinations. Items 2 and 3 ask about frequency and severity. Item 4 asks the caregiver about burden imposed by the patient's hallucinations. Items 5, 6 and 7 ask about presence of hallucinations at night, vivid hallucinations and vivid dreams. Validation was conducted in 41 individuals. Internal consistency was good (Chronbach's α = 0.88). Convergent validity as demonstrated against the Parkinson Psychosis Questionnaire.

CORRESPONDENCE:

Kenji Wada-Isoe, Department of Neurology, Faculty of Medicine, Institute of Neurological Sciences, Tottori University, 36–1 Nishi-cho, Yonago 683–8504, Japan. E-mail: Kewada@grape.med.tottori-u.ac.jp

Source: Available in the original publication.

UNIVERSITY OF MIAMI PARKINSON'S DISEASE HALLUCINATIONS QUESTIONNAIRE (UM-PDHQ)

Reference:

Papapetropoulos, S., Katzen, H., Schrag, A., Singer, C., Scanlon, B., Nation, D., et al. (2008). A questionnaire-based (UM-PDHQ) study of hallucinations in Parkinson's disease. *BMC Neurology, 8*, 21.

Administration time: 5–15 minutes
Rating instructions: Semi-structured interview by a clinician or experienced rater
Population group: Parkinson's disease

DESCRIPTION:

This 20-item interview is used as a screening instrument to assess hallucinations in Parkinson's disease. It rates the severity and quality of hallucinations in different modalities (visual, auditory, somatic/cutaneous, gustatory, olfactory). There are two main sections. Section one has six items that assess the frequency, duration, and emotional salience of hallucinatory experiences (e.g., How often do you experience hallucinations? Do you think what you are seeing/experiencing is real? How severe/emotionally distressing do you find these images/sensations or visions?). Scoring on each item can be summed to provide a total score of the severity of hallucinations. Section 2 has 14 items assessing general qualitative features of hallucinations, such as the content, size, change, and multimodal hallucinations. This instrument is yet to be validated, and main psychometric attributes are unknown.

CORRESPONDENCE:

Dr. Spiridon Papapetropoulos, Divisions of Movement Disorders Department of Neurology, University of Miami, Miller School of Medicine, Miami, FL. Email: spapapetropoulos@med.miami.edu

Source: Available by contacting the corresponding author.

Additional Reference:

Gallagher, D., Parkkinen, L., O'Sullivan, S. et al. (2011). Testing an aetiological model of visual hallucinations in Parkinson's disease. *Brain, 134*, 3299–3309.

US NATIONAL INSTITUTE OF MENTAL HEALTH DIAGNOSTIC INTERVIEW SCHEDULE FOR CHILDREN (DISC)

Reference:

Shaffer, D., Fisher, P., Lucas, C.P., Dulcan, M.K., & Schwab-Stone, M.E. (2000). NIMH Diagnostic Interview Schedule for Children, Version IV (NIMH DISC-IV): Description, differences from previous versions, and reliability of some common diagnoses. *Journal of the American Academy of Child and Adolescent Psychiatry, 39*(1), 28–38.

Administration time: 1–2 hours (depending on the number of symptoms present)
Rating instructions: Structured interview; no clinical experience necessary but some training is necessary for lay interviewers
Population group: Children and adolescents only

DESCRIPTION:

This structured diagnostic interview assesses for the most prevalent axis-1 psychiatric disorders in children and adolescents, including schizophrenia. Paper and computerized versions are available. The schizophrenia section asks about a range of hallucinations and delusions. Symptoms are rated 0 = *not present*, 1 = *sometimes/somewhat present* and 2 = *yes, present*. Adequate diagnostic agreement was demonstrated against Symptom Check List Revised (SCL-90-R) in an adolescent population.

CORRESPONDENCE:

Dr. Prudence Fisher, Division of Child and Adolescent Psychiatry, Columbia University/New York State Psychiatric Institute, 1051 Riverside Drive, Unit 78, New York, NY 10032. Email: Fisherp@nyspi.columbia.edu

Source: Available by contacting the authors.

Additional Reference:

Roberts, N., Parker, K., & Dagnone, M. (2005). Comparison of Clinical Diagnoses, NIMH-DISC-IV Diagnoses and SCL-90-R Ratings in an adolescent psychiatric inpatient unit: A brief report. *Canadian Child and Adolescent Psychiatric Review, 14*(4), 103–105.

VALIDITY INDICATOR PROFILE (VIP)

Reference:

Frederick, R.I., & Crosby, R.D. (2000). Development and validation of the Validity Indicator Profile. *Law and Human Behavior, 24(1).*

Administration time: Verbal subtest: 20 minutes; nonverbal subtest: 30 minutes
Rating instructions: Self-report administered by a mental health professional who has received training in the administration and scoring of this scale
Population groups: Adults in forensic settings

DESCRIPTION:

The forced-choice procedure was developed to identify occasions when the results of neuropsychological testing may be invalid because of malingering or other clinical response styles. The test comprises 100 nonverbal abstraction capacity items and 78 word-definition problems. The VIP attempts to establish whether an individual's performance is representative of his or her true overall capacities. Validation was conducted in 944 nonclinical participants (104 undergoing neuropsychological evaluation), and samples of brain-injured adults, individuals considered to be at risk for malingering. The non-verbal subtest of the VIP demonstrated an overall classification rate of 79.8%, with 73.5% sensitivity and 85.7% specificity, and the verbal subtest of the VIP demonstrated classification rate of 75.5%, with 67.3% sensitivity and 83.1% specificity.

CORRESPONDENCE:

Dr. Richard Frederick, 1244 E Walnut St, Springfield, MO 65802. Email: richardfrederick@yahoo.com

Source: Available from Pearson's Clinical Assessment publishers (www.pearsonsclinical.com).

VOICES ACCEPTANCE AND ACTION SCALE (VAAS)

Reference:

Shawyer, F., Ratcliff, K., Mackinnon, A., Farhall, J., Hayes, S. C., & Copolov, D. (2007). The Voices Acceptance and Action Scale (VAAS): Pilot data. *Journal of Clinical Psychology, 63*, 583–606.

Administration time: 5–10 minutes
Rating instructions: Self-report
Population groups: Psychiatric populations

DESCRIPTION:

This scale is typically used in treatment settings where the goal is to accept auditory verbal hallucinations ("voices") rather than modify beliefs about them. In this type of therapy, individuals are encouraged to develop the capacity to act independently from voices. The VAAS consists of 31 questions including: acceptance (16 items) and action (15 items) of hallucinations in general (section A) and of command hallucinations (section B). The authors report high internal consistency for the whole rating scale (Chronbach's α = .90), and for the subscales (.76-.85). Test–retest reliability over a 4 month period ranged between 0.73 and 0.82 (n = 17).

CORRESPONDENCE:

Dr. Frances Shawyer, Southern Synergy, Administration, Research & Training (ART) Building, Dandenong Hospital, 126-128 Cleeland St, Dandenong VIC 3175. Email: frances.shawyer@monash.edu

Source: In the original publication.

VOICE AND YOU (VAY)

Reference:

Hayward, M., Denney, J., Vaughan, S., & Fowler, D. (2008). The voice and you: Development and psychometric evaluation of a measure of relationships with voices. *Clinical Psychology and Psychotherapy, 15*(1), 45–52.

Administration time: 15–20 minutes
Rating instructions: Self-rated
Population groups: Psychiatric populations

DESCRIPTION:

The questionnaire assesses the relationship between a person and his/her auditory verbal hallucinations ("voices"), particularly in relation to their predominant voice. There are 29 items, rated on a 4-point rating scale (*nearly always true, quite often true, sometimes true, rarely true*). There are four domains being assessed: Voice dominance (7 items), Voice intrusiveness (5 items), Hearer dependence (9 items), and Hearer distance (7 items).

Questions include: Item 1. My voice wants things done his/her way; Item 2. My voice helps me make up my mind; Item 3. I prefer to keep my voice at a safe distance; Item 5. My voice does not let me have time to myself. The scale is reported to have good internal consistency (Chronbach's α = 0. 78–0.92, n = 30), and good stability over time measured over a 3-week period (0.72 and 0.91, n = 17). Convergent validity was shown with the Belief About Voices Questionnaire (BAVQ-R) and the Psychotic Symptoms Rating Scale (PSYRATS).

CORRESPONDENCE:

Dr. Mark Hayward, Psychology Department, University of Surrey, Guildford GU2 7XH, UK. Email: m.hayward@surrey.ac.uk

Source: In the original publication.

WEST AUSTRALIAN MISPERCEPTION AND HALLUCINATION INVENTORY (WAMHI)

Reference:

Mitchell, C., Russell-Smith, S., Maybery, M., Collerton, D., & Waters, F. (2014). The Western Australian Misperception and Hallucination Inventory (WAMHI). Perth, Australia.

Rating instructions: Self-report
Population group: General population

DESCRIPTION:

This questionnaire is being developed by PhD student Claire Mitchell to assess for the presence and severity of a range of misperceptions and hallucination-like experiences in non-clinical populations. Five sensory modalities are assessed (Auditory, Visual, Olfactory, Gustatory, Somatic experiences). The questionnaire also assesses hypnogogic and hypnopompic hallucinations, intrusive thoughts and levels of cognitive control. Items are rated on a 5-point rating scale (0 = *never happen*, 4 = *frequently, at least monthly*). In each section, additional items enquire about the context in which these experiences occurred (e.g., drug taking, sleep, migraine, etc.). The scale is currently under development and psychometric properties of this new questionnaire are being examined.

CORRESPONDENCE:

A/Professor Flavie Waters, School of Psychiatry and Clinical Neurosciences, the University of Western Australia, 35 Stirling Highway, Perth 6010. Email: Flavie.waters@health.wa.gov.au

YOUTH SELF REPORT (YSR)

Reference:

Achenbach, T. (1991). *Manual for the Youth Self-Report and Profile*. Burlington: University of Vermont, Department of Psychiatry.

Administration time: 10 minutes
Rating instructions: Self-report
Population groups: Children and adolescents (11–18 years of age)

DESCRIPTION:

This questionnaire assesses a wide variety of principally non-psychotic symptoms of psychopathology. It is typically used to screen for behavioral and emotional problems in children and adolescents. The 2001 revised YSR comprises 112 items on a 3-point rating scale (absent-frequent), and the timeframe of enquiry the past 6-months. There are eight syndrome scales: withdrawn, somatic complaints, anxiety and depression, social problems, thought problems, attention problems, aggressive behavior, and delinquent behaviors. Two items (numbers 40 and 70) assess for hallucinations:

1. I hear sounds or voices that other people think aren't there
2. I see things that other people think aren't there

Internal consistency ranged between Chronbach's α 0.68 and 0.89 (n = 215).

CORRESPONDENCE:

Dr. Thomas Achenbach, Department of Psychiatry, University of Vermont, 1 So. Prospect St., Burlington, VT 05401-3456. E-mail: Thomas.achenbach@uvm.edu

Source: The YSR is part of the Achenbach System of Empirically Based Assessment (ASEBA) and can be purchased on www.aseba.org. Enquiries to: mail@aseba.org

APPENDIX 2

Index of Acronyms and Initialisms of Rating Scales

Abbreviation	Rating scale name
AHRS	Auditory Hallucinations Rating Scale (also known as Hallucinations Change Scale)
APSS	Adolescent Psychotic Symptom Screener
AVHRS	Auditory Vocal Hallucinations Rating Scale
BABS	Brown Assessment of Beliefs Scale
BACS	Brief Assessment of Cognition in Schizophrenia
BaPS	Beliefs About Paranoia Scale
BAVQ-R	Beliefs About Voices Questionnaire
BCIS	Beck Cognitive Insight Scale
BEHAVE-AD	Behavioral Symptoms in Alzheimer's Disease
BPRS	Brief Psychiatric Rating Scale
BSABS	Bonn Scale for the Assessment of Basic Symptoms
CA-ARMS	Comprehensive Assessment of the At-Risk Mental State
CAM	Confusion Assessment Method
CAMDEX	Cambridge Mental Disorders of the Elderly Examination
CAPA	Child and Adolescent Psychiatric Assessment
CAPE	Community Assessment of Psychic Experiences
CAPS	Cardiff Anomalous Perceptions Scale
CASH	Comprehensive Assessment of Symptoms and History
cbSASH	Computerized Binary Scale of Auditory Speech Hallucinations
CCAH	Clinical Characteristics of Auditory Hallucinations
CDBS	Conviction of Delusion Beliefs Scale
CERAD-BRS	Consortium to Establish a Registry for Alzheimer's Disease–Behavioral Rating Scale
CPRS	Comprehensive Psychopathological Rating Scale

(Continued)

Abbreviation	Rating scale name
CUSPAD	Columbia University Scale for Psychopathology in Alzheimer's Disease
DAS	Delusion Assessment Scale
DBRI	Dysfunctional Behaviour Rating Instrument
DI	Delirium Index
DIP	Diagnostic Interview for Psychose–Full Version
DIPpc-DM 1.0	Diagnostic Interview for Psychose–Diagnostic Module
DISC	Diagnostic Interview Schedule for Children–US National Institute of Mental Health
DISC	US National Institute of Mental Health Diagnostic Interview Schedule for Children
DRS	Delirium Rating Scale (DRS) and Delirium Rating Scale Revised–98
DSI	Delirium Symptom Interview
EASE	Examination of Anomalous Self-Experiences
FTDS	Formal Thought Disorder Scale
GMSS	Geriatric Mental State Schedule
GPTS	Green et al. Paranoid Thought Scales
HCS	Hallucinations Change Scale (also known as Auditory Hallucinations Rating Scale)
IP-VHI	Institute of Psychiatry Visual Hallucinations Interview
IS-B	Insight Scale–Birchwood
IS-MB	Insight Scale–Marková and Berrios
ITAQ	Insight and Treatment Attitudes Questionnaire
KGV	Krawiecka, Goldberg & Vaughn Psychosis Scale
K-SADS	Schedule for Affective Disorders and Schizophrenia for School-Aged Children (Kiddie–SADS)
LSHS	Launay-Slade Hallucination Scale
LSHS-E	Launay-Slade Hallucination Scale–Extended Version
MACS-I	Maastricht Assessment of Coping Strategies
MADS	Maudsley Assessment of Delusions Schedule
MASAH	Matsuzawa Assessment Schedule for Auditory Hallucinations
MDAS	Memorial Delirium Assessment Scale
M-FAST™	Miller Forensic Assessment of Symptoms Test™
MHASC	Multisensory Hallucinations Scale for Children
M.I.N.I.	Mini International Neuropsychiatric Interview
MIS	Magical Ideation Scale
MOUSEPAD	Manchester and Oxford Universities Scale for the Psychopathological Assessment of Dementia
MUPS	Mental Health Research Institute Unusual Perceptions Schedule
NEVHI	North-East Visual Hallucinations Interview
NPI	Neuropsychiatric Inventory
OHPS	Olfactory Hallucinations Phenomenological Survey
O-LIFE	Oxford-Liverpool Inventory of Feelings and Experiences
PANSS	Positive and Negative Syndrome Scale
PAS	Perceptual Aberration Scale

(Continued)

Abbreviation	Rating scale name
PBE	Present Behavioural Examination
PC	Paranoia Checklist
PDI	Peters et al. Delusions Inventory
PIQ	Persecutory Ideation Questionnaire
PLEQ-C	Psychotic-Like Experiences Questionnaire for Children
PPQ	Parkinson's Psychosis Questionnaire
PS	Paranoia Scale
PS	Psychosis Screen
PSE	Present State Examination Schedule
PSI	Passivity Symptoms Interview
PSQ	Psychosis Screening Questionnaire
PSYRATS	Psychotic Symptom Rating Scales
QSVHI	Queen Square Visual Hallucinations Inventory
RAHQ	Responses to Auditory Hallucination Questionnaire
RHI	Rush Hallucination Inventory
RLSHS	Launay Slade Hallucination Scale–Revised
SACI	Schedule for Assessing the Components of Insight
SAIQ	Self-Appraisal of Illness Questionnaire
SAPP	Scale for the Assessment of Passivity Phenomena
SAPS	Scale for the Assessment of Positive Symptoms
SAPS-PD	Scale for the Assessment of Positive Symptoms–Parkinson's Disease
SCAN	Schedules for Clinical Assessment in Neuropsychiatry
SCD	Schizophrenia Communication Disorder Scales
SCID-I	Structured Clinical Interview for DSM Axis 1 Disorders
SCOPA-PC	Scales in Outcomes in Parkinson's Disease–Psychiatric Complications
SEND-PD	Scale for the Evaluation of Neuropsychiatric Disorders in PD
SIAPA	Structured Interview for Assessing Perceptual Anomalies
SIPS	Structured Interview for Prodromal Symptoms
SIRS-2	Structured Interview of Reported Symptoms–Second Edition
SOH	Scale for Olfactory Hallucinations
SOPS	Scale of Prodromal Symptoms
SPAD	Clinical Rating Scale for Symptoms of Psychosis in Alzheimer's Disease
SPAS	Survey Psychiatric Assessment Schedule
SOCRATES	SOCRATES Assessment of Perceptual Abnormalities and Unusual Thought Content
SPEQ	Specific Psychotic Experiences Questionnaire
SPI-A	Schizophrenia Proneness Instrument–Adult
SPI-CY	Schizophrenia Proneness Instrument–Children and Youth
SPQ	Schizotypal Personality Questionnaire
SSPS	State Social Paranoia Scale
SUMD	Scale to Assess Unawareness of Mental Disorder
TDI	Thought Disorder Index
TDQ	Thought Disorder Questionnaire

(*Continued*)

Abbreviation	Rating scale name
TLC	Thought, Language and Communication Scale
TLI	Thought and Language Index
TUHRAS	Tottori University Hallucinations Rating Scale
UM-PDHQ	University of Miami Parkinson's Disease Hallucinations Questionnaire
VAAS	Voices Acceptance and Action Scale
VAY	Voice and You
VHQ-PD	Self-Rated Visual Hallucination Questionnaire for Parkinson's Disease
VIP	Validity Indicator Profile
WAMHI	West Australian Misperception and Hallucination Inventory
YSR	Youth Self Report

APPENDIX 3

Hallucination-Specific Rating Scales (Auditory, Visual, Olfactory, Gustatory, Somatic)

Rating scale name	Acronym	Hallucination modality
Hallucination-specific scales		
Auditory Hallucinations Rating Scale	AHRS	A
Auditory Vocal Hallucinations Rating Scale	AVHRS	A
Beliefs About Voices Questionnaire	BAVQ-R	A
Clinical Characteristics of Auditory Hallucinations	CCAH	A
Computerized Binary Scale of Auditory Hallucinations	cbSASH	A
Hallucination Change Scale (HCS; also known as Auditory Hallucinations Rating Scale; AHRS)	HCSAHRS	A
Institute of Psychiatry Visual Hallucination Interview	IP-VHI	V
Launay-Slade Hallucination Scale	LSHS	A,V
Launay-Slade Hallucination Scale–Extended version	LSHS-E	A,V,O,S
Launay-Slade Hallucination Scale–Revised	RLSHS	A,V
Maastricht Assessment of Coping Strategies	MACS-I	A
Matsuzawa Assessment Schedule for Auditory Hallucinations	MASAH	A
Mental Health Research Institute Unusual Perceptions Schedule	MUPS	A
Multisensory Hallucinations Scale for Children	MHASC	A,V,O,G,S
North-East Visual Hallucination Interview	NEVHI	V

(Continued)

Rating scale name	Acronym	Hallucination modality
Olfactory Hallucinations Phenomenological Survey	OHPS	O
Psychotic Symptoms Rating Scales	PSYRATS	A
Queen Square Visual Hallucinations Inventory	SQVHI	V
Responses to Auditory Hallucination Questionnaire	RAHQ	A
Rush Hallucination Inventory	RHI	A, V, O, S
Scale for Olfactory Hallucinations	SOH	O
Scale for the Assessment of Positive Symptoms of Parkinson's Disease	SAPS-PD	A, V
Self-Rated Visual Hallucination Questionnaire for Parkinson's Disease	VHQ-PD	V
Semi-Structured Interview About Visions in Psychiatric Patients		V
Semi-Structured Interview on Complex Visual Hallucinations for Charles Bonnet Syndrome		V
Tottori University Hallucination Rating Scale	TUHRAS	A, V, O, S
University of Miami Parkinson's Disease Hallucination Questionnaire	UM-PDHQ	A, V, O, G, S
Voices Acceptance and Action Scale	VAAS	A
Voices and You	VAY	A
West Australian Misperception and Hallucination Inventory	WAMHI	A, V, O, G, S

Hallucination modality code:
A = Auditory hallucinations
V = Visual hallucinations
O = Olfactory hallucinations
G = Gustatory hallucinations
S = Somatic hallucinations

APPENDIX 4

Delusion and Delusional Ideation Rating Scales

Rating scale name	Acronym
Beliefs About Paranoia Scale	BaPS
Brown Assessment of Beliefs Scale	BABS
Conviction of Delusion Beliefs Scale	CDBS
Delusion Assessment Scale	DAS
Green et al. Paranoid Thought Scales	GPTS
Magical Ideation Scale	MIS
Maudsley Assessment of Delusions Schedule	MADS
Paranoia Checklist	PC
Paranoia Scale	PS
Persecutory Ideation Questionnaire	PIQ
Peters et al. Delusions Inventory	PDI
Psychotic Symptoms Rating Scale	PSYRATS
State Social Paranoia Scale	SSPS

APPENDIX 5

Language (Formal Thought Disorder) Rating Scales

Rating scale name	Acronym
Formal Thought Disorder Scale	FTDS
Schizophrenia Communication Disorder Scales	SCD
Thought and Language Index	TLI
Thought Disorder Index	TDI
Thought Disorder Questionnaire	TDQ
Thought Language and Communication	TLC

APPENDIX 6

Insight-Specific Rating Scales

Rating scale name	Acronym	Rating instructions	Administration time
Beck Cognitive Insight Scale	BCIS	Self-report	15–20 minutes
Insight and Treatment Attitudes Questionnaire	ITAQ	Interview	15–20 minutes
Insight Scale–Birchwood	IS-B	Self-report	5 minutes
Insight Scale–Marková and Berrios	IS-MB	Self-report	15–20 minutes
Scale to Assess Unawareness of Mental Disorder	SUMD	Interview	20–40 minutes
Schedule for Assessing the Components of Insight	SACI	Self-report	10–15 minutes
Self-Appraisal of Illness Questionnaire	SAIQ	Self-report	15–25 minutes

APPENDIX 7

Self-Disturbances, Body Perception Disturbances and Passivity Symptoms Rating Scales

Rating scale name	Acronym	Rating instructions	Administration time
Bonn Scale for the Assessment of Basic Symptoms	BSABS	Interview	2–3 hours
Comprehensive Psychopathological Rating Scale	CPRS	Interview	Up to 60 minutes
Examination of Anomalous Self-Experiences	EASE	Interview	90 minutes
Passivity Symptoms Interview	PSI	Interview	10–15 minutes
Scale for the Assessment of Passivity Phenomena	SAPP	Interview	15 minutes
Schedules for Clinical Assessment in Neuropsychiatry (selected items)	SCAN	Interview	60–90 minutes
Schizophrenia Proneness Instrument	SPI	Interview	30 minutes–2 hours (patient interview time varies)

INDEX